3

Lift

AUTHORS
Renee Biermann
Lisa Varandani

PROGRAM ADVISOR
Nonie K. Lesaux
Harvard Graduate School of Education

NATIONAL GEOGRAPHIC LEARNING

Australia · Brazil · Canada · Mexico · Singapore · United Kingdom · United States

National Geographic Learning,
a Cengage Company

Lift 3 Student's Book
Authors: Renee Biermann, Lisa Varandani

Publishers: Erik Gundersen, Janine Boylan

Managing Editor: Nancy Jordan

Senior Development Editor: Eve Einselen Yu

Director of Global Marketing: Ian Martin

Heads of Regional Marketing:

Charlotte Ellis (Europe, Middle East and Africa)

Justin Kaley (Asia and Greater China)

Irina Pereyra (Latin America)

Product Marketing Manager: Anders Bylund

Senior Content Project Manager: Nick Ventullo

Media Researcher: Leila Hishmeh

Art Director: Brenda Carmichael

Operations Support: Hayley Chwazik-Gee

Manufacturing Planner: Mary Beth Hennebury

Composition: MPS North America, LLC

For permission to use material from this text or product, submit all requests online at **cengage.com/permissions**
Further permissions questions can be emailed to **permissionrequest@cengage.com**

Student's Book ISBN: 978-0-357-50115-3

Student's Book + Sticker Code ISBN: 978-0-357-50119-1

National Geographic Learning
200 Pier 4 Boulevard
Boston, MA 02210
USA

Locate your local office at **international.cengage.com/region**

Visit National Geographic Learning online at **ELTNGL.com**
Visit our corporate website at **www.cengage.com**

Printed in the USA
Print Number: 03 Print Year: 2023

PROGRAM ADVISOR

Nonie K. Lesaux, Harvard Graduate School of Education

ADVISORS

Emily Phillips Galloway, Assistant Professor, School of Education, Vanderbilt University's Peabody College
Margo Gottlieb, Co-Founder and Lead Developer, WIDA
Helyn Kim, Education Research Analyst, Institute of Education Sciences
Alexis Menten, Managing Director, Center for Global Education, Asia Society
Heather Michael, Citadel High School International Baccalaureate Coordinator, Halifax
Silvana Richardson, Head of Education, Bell English

REVIEWERS

ASIA

Tim Allen, Shenzhen RDF International School, Shenzhen
Lindsey Devillier, Beijing World Youth Academy, Beijing
Rivers He, Houhai English, Beijing
William Phillips, Aga Khan Education Service Central Asia, Tajikistan
Alex Shen, Phoenix International School, Guangzhou
Jonathan Tragash, Huamei Experimental School, Guangzhou International School, Guangzhou
Erin Volkert, Beijing World Youth Academy, Beijing
Dongjing Wang, Whales English, Beijing
Yan Zhou, Hangzhou Yungu School, Hangzhou

MIDDLE EAST

Adwoa Appiah-Boateng, ADNOC Schools, Abu Dhabi, United Arab Emirates
Diana Al-Mokdad, Sharjah American International School, Sharjah, United Arab Emirates
Khaled Qattawi, King Faisal School, Riyadh, Saudi Arabia

LATIN AMERICA

Kelli Brown, Modern Academy Cancun, Cancun, Mexico
Edith Guay, Sendica Education, Monterrey, Mexico
Verónica Malpica, Colegio Santa Engracia, Monterrey, Mexico
Dana Pao, Colegio Rochester, Bogotá, Colombia
Fernando Soler, Gimnasio Fontana, Bogotá, Colombia

EUROPE

Dr. Jana Pridalova, Lyceum Alpinum Zuoz AG, Zuoz, Switzerland
Julia Shewry, St. John's International School, Waterloo, Belgium

UNITED STATES

Connie Banks, Greenville Spartanburg Public Schools, Greenville, South Carolina
Barbara Brimmerman, Omaha Public Schools, Omaha, Nebraska
Maya Stewart, DC International School, Washington, DC

CONTENTS AT A GLANCE

☐ = National Geographic Exclusive

How can
conformity be
dangerous?

2 # Creativity

ESSENTIAL QUESTION

What is creative thinking?

What motivates us to be creative?

What is the secret to becoming more creative?

What is the connection between curiosity and creativity?

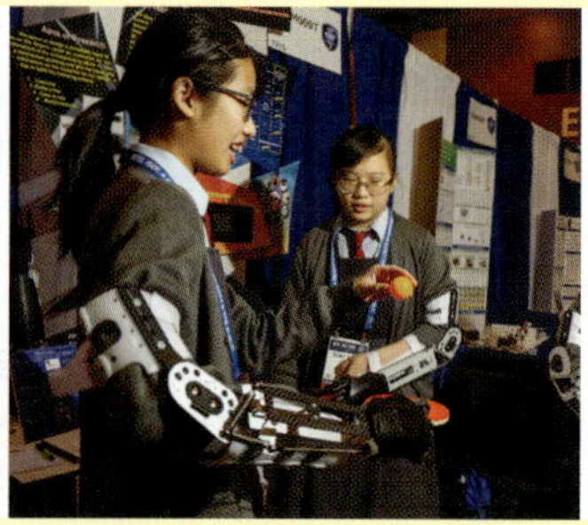

Why is creativity so important for the success of a society?

3

New Technology

What are the benefits and drawbacks of new technology?

How can we control the use of technology so that it benefits us?

What causes us to replace old technology with new?

How is artificial intelligence changing the world?

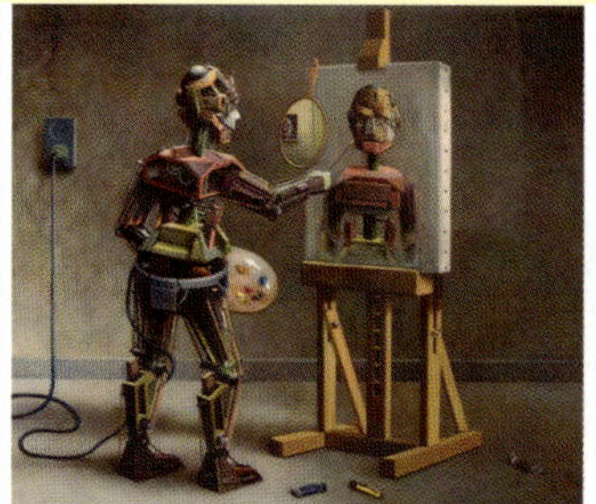

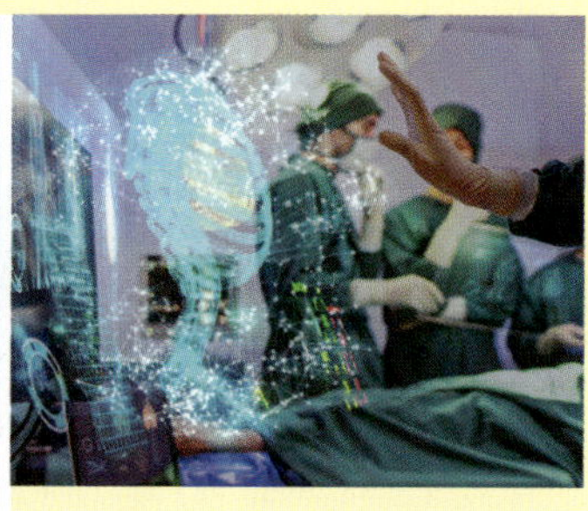

READING 1

p. 118

What's Technology Got to Do with the Economy?
by Economy Editorial Team

READING STRATEGY:
Paraphrase

VOCABULARY:
Understand Greek and Latin Prefixes

UNCOVER THE STORY

p. 130

FINE ART
by Johan Scherft

READING 2

p. 132

OBITUARY: The Book (1455–Present)
by Katrina Onstad

READING SKILL:
Analyze Humor

VOCABULARY: Interpret Figurative Language

VIDEO CONNECTION

p. 144

How Artificial Intelligence Will Change Your World, for Better or Worse

VIEWING SKILL:
Categorize Information and Perspectives

How does technology affect our interactions with other people?

HOW WILL YOU TAKE ACTION?

Personal: Spend time with a friend or family member—without technology!
School: Make a poster about using technology in a friendly way.
Local: Help someone in your community use technology.
Global: Support an environmentally friendly company.

ESSENTIAL QUESTION

What are the positive and negative effects of stress?

| How can stress be beneficial? | | How can we use humor to manage stress? | How can stress affect people's actions? |

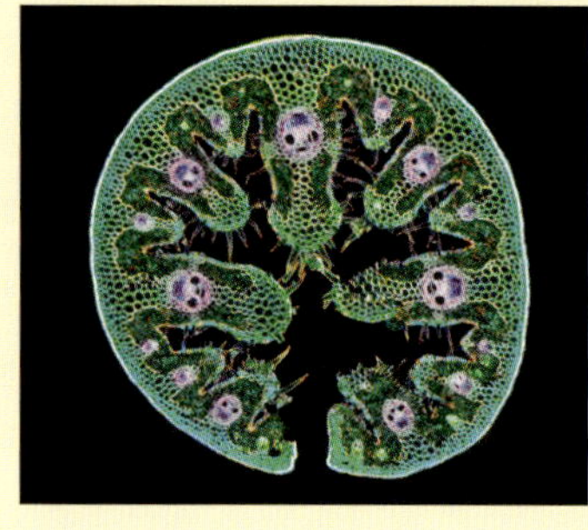

How do other people influence our decisions?

6 Helping Others

What responsibility do people have to help others?

Why do emergencies inspire us to help others?

In emergency situations, what separates onlookers from action-takers?

How does helping the planet help people?

READING 1

p. 276

The Daring Cave Divers Who Saved the Thai Soccer Team
by Joel K. Bourne, Jr.

READING STRATEGY:
Ask Questions

LANGUAGE CONVENTION:
Understand Verb Mood

UNCOVER THE STORY

p. 290

☐ **PHOTO STORY:**
by Cristina Mittermeier

READING 2

p. 292

What Is the "Bystander Effect" and How Do People Overcome It?
by Catherine A. Sanderson

READING SKILL:
Analyze an Author's Purpose

LANGUAGE CONVENTION:
Understand Conditionals

VIDEO CONNECTION

p. 306

Plastics 101

VIEWING SKILL:
Identify Mood

Why is "tough love" sometimes the best way to help someone?

Competition

How does competition affect us?

What are the benefits and drawbacks of youth competition?

How can competition build community?

How can competition make us feel?

READING 1

p. 334

The Pros and Cons of Teen Competition
by Kathryn Rogers

READING SKILL:
Determine the Author's Viewpoint

LANGUAGE CONVENTION:
Use the Passive Voice

VIDEO CONNECTION

p. 346

United by Ping Pong

VIEWING SKILL:
Identify Cause and Effect

READING 2

p. 348

Goldfish
by Nat Luurtsema

READING SKILL:
Analyze Dialogue and Inner Monologue

VOCABULARY:
Interpret Verbal Irony

UNCOVER THE STORY

p. 362

INFOGRAPHIC:
The Stadium of Tomorrow

How can competition help make us stronger?

8 In the Future

How will life be different in the future?

How might people and nature change in the future?

How can we meet future energy needs?

How can the past shape the future?

READING 1

p. 390

Future Timeline
FutureTimeline.net

READING STRATEGY: Use Cohesive Devices to Connect Ideas

LANGUAGE CONVENTION: Identify Participles

VIDEO CONNECTION

p. 402

Can 100% Renewable Energy Power the World?

VIEWING SKILL: Use Visual Cues to Learn New Words

READING 2

p. 404

A House Called Tomorrow
by Alberto Ríos

Letter to Someone Living Fifty Years from Now
by Matthew Olzmann

READING SKILL: Cite Text Evidence to Support Inferences

VOCABULARY: Analyze Figures of Speech

UNCOVER THE STORY

p. 414

INFOGRAPHIC: Cities of the Future: Urban Hubs

How accurately can we predict the future?

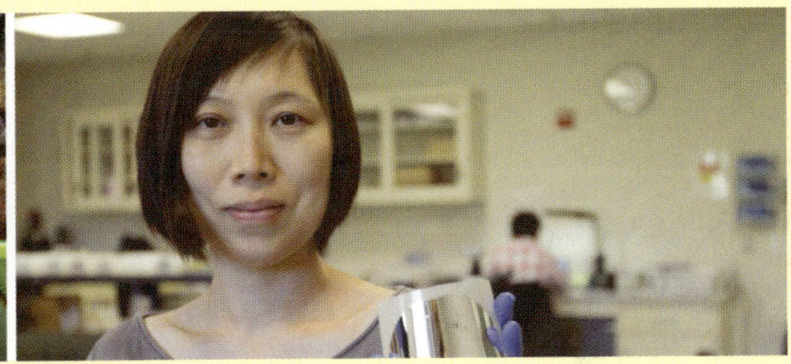

GENRES AT A GLANCE

1 Belonging

"Sticks in a bundle are unbreakable."
—PROVERB OF THE BONDEI PEOPLE OF TANZANIA

What do you think this quote means?

Look at the photo and caption. Discuss the questions.

1. How do the homes in this photo create a sense of belonging?

2. If you lived in this city, would you want to live in a blue house? Why or why not?

◀ Jodhpur, a city in Rajasthan, India, is also known as the Blue City.

ESSENTIAL QUESTION

Why is it important to belong?

Explore the Essential Question

Think Write your ideas about the Essential Question in the Unit Concept Map.

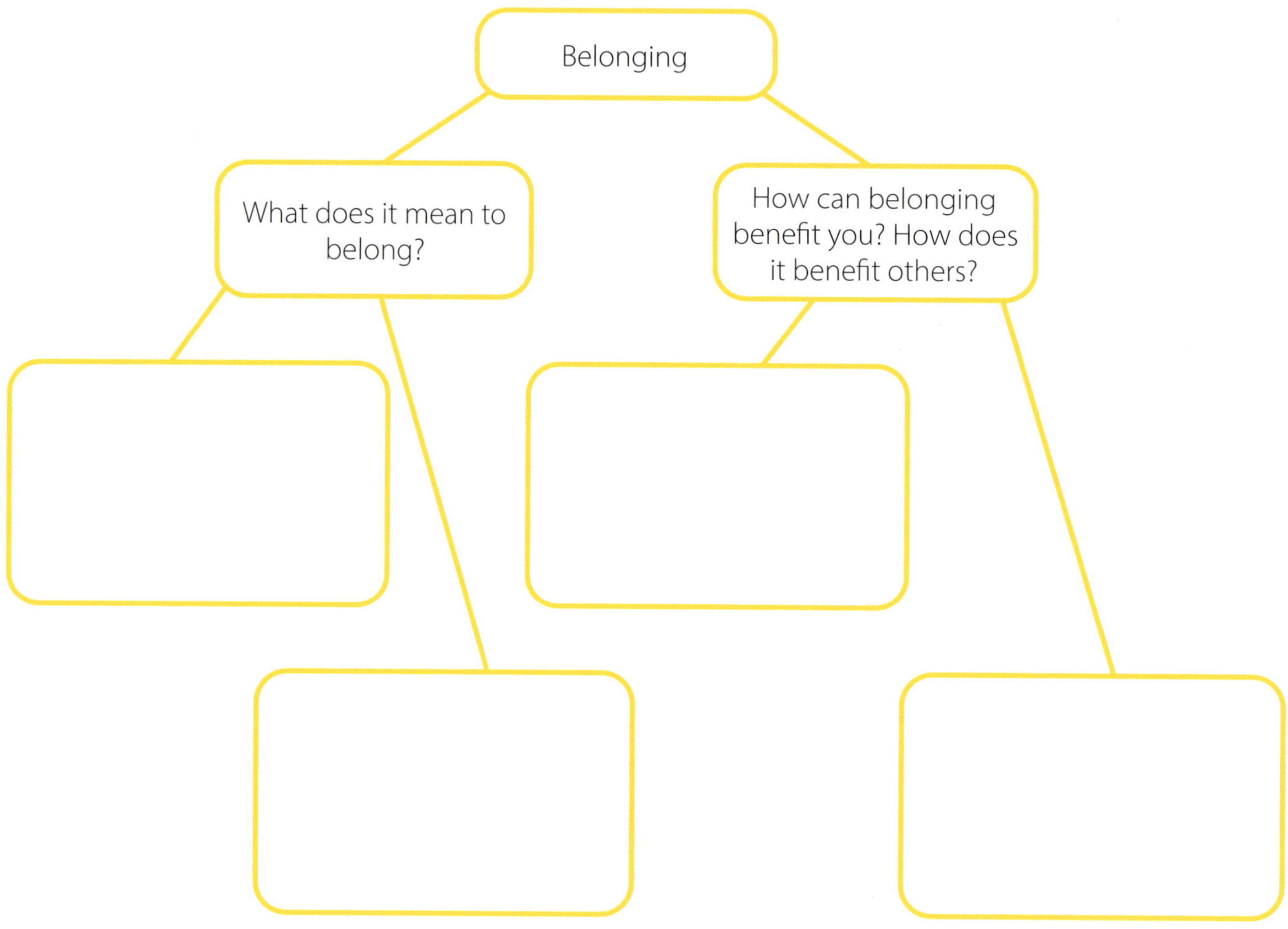

Respond Write one or two sentences to respond to the Essential Question.

Discuss Your Ideas Use your Unit Concept Map and your response to share your ideas with the class.

Discussion Frames

I think belonging is …

I believe …

One benefit of belonging is …

4   Unit 1 Belonging

Academic Vocabulary

Use these words to express your ideas throughout the unit.

PRACTICE 1 Use context to determine the meaning of each word in blue. Then match the word to its definition.

> Marta and Júlio are twins, but they're different. Júlio **functions** best as a part of a group. It's **obvious** that his group of friends trust each other because they make decisions together without worrying about **external** pressure from others. Marta prefers **isolation** to being with a group. She can quickly **alter** her feelings about a decision without asking others how they feel about it. Marta is proud of her **individuality**, but she still respects Júlio and his group of friends.

Word	Definition
individuality	the state of being different from others; uniqueness
	to act or perform
	to change
	existing outside something
	easily seen or understood
	the state of being alone

PRACTICE 2 Work with a partner. Pretend to be either Marta or Júlio. Make a statement using one of the vocabulary words. Then have your partner guess which character you are.

Example

Student 1: I function best as an individual.
Student 2: This sounds like something Marta would say because she likes being alone.

How can we be part of a group without losing our individuality?

First Thoughts

Imagine you volunteer at a library as part of a school project. When you get there, you realize that all the other student volunteers know each other very well. You are the only new volunteer. How comfortable would you feel? Why? Check (✓) your answer. Then discuss your response with a partner.

How I Would Feel

- very uncomfortable
- somewhat uncomfortable
- neutral
- somewhat comfortable
- very comfortable

Discussion Frames

In this situation, I would feel …

My response would be based on …

Compared to others, I responded …

Can you say more about …?

Key Vocabulary

PRACTICE Use context to determine the meaning of each word in bold. Then match the word to its definition.

1. One of my personal **values** is being kind to others.
2. Do you know Daphne well, or is she only an **acquaintance**?
3. Jihoon is a member of my **peer** group. We are in the same grade and share a circle of friends.
4. Being a piano player is a big part of her **identity**.
5. I don't care which color of shirt we all wear. I will **conform** to the group's decision.

_____ **1.** values	**a.**	to act in the same way as others (v.)
_____ **2.** acquaintance	**b.**	beliefs about what is important (n.)
_____ **3.** peer	**c.**	someone who is known slightly but is not a close friend (n.)
_____ **4.** identity	**d.**	relating to someone the same age or grade, or in a shared group (adj.)
_____ **5.** conform	**e.**	the set of qualities that make up an individual; a person's characteristics (n.)

Reading Strategy: Preview and Predict

Previewing is looking at or skimming information in a text before you read it. **Predicting** is using that information to make a logical guess about the entire text's content. Previewing and making predictions about a text can help you stay focused as you read. To preview and predict:

1. Read the title and headings that appear throughout the text. Look at images and read their captions.

2. Use the clues you find during your preview to make a prediction. Ask yourself: *What do I think this text will be about?*

3. After you have finished reading, determine whether your prediction was accurate. Explain how close your prediction was to the actual text.

Strategy in Action

Preview "What's Your Group ID?" What do you think the text will be about? Complete the prediction graphic organizer with clues from the text.

Clues from the title:

Clues from the headings:

Clues from the images, photographs, and captions:

Use the details in your graphic organizer to predict what the text will be about. Write your prediction, and explain how the clues you found support it.

Japanese student volunteers dance during a workshop in Lima, Peru. They are in Peru to train new volunteers.

What's Your Group ID?

How Far Would You Go to Fit In with the Group?

by **Kathiann Kowalski**
from **Current Health**

🎧 **1.1**

1   Spending time with friends ranks high on everyone's "to do" list. How comfortable are you with other groups of teens? And how can you fit in without losing yourself?

5   ## What's Great about Groups?

First of all, friends share good times. They like you for who you are.

Groups your own age, or **peer** groups, become very important during your teen
10   years. As teens face physical, emotional, and social changes, peer groups provide emotional support. Teens care about their friends. Plus, teens understand what other teens are going through. So teens naturally rely more on their
15   friends. Good friends are emotional anchors when the going gets rough.[1]

Belonging to a group also helps define one's **identity**. "We are social beings, and we do not function in isolation," explains psychologist
20   Steven G. Little. "Virtually everything we do involves some sort of social system."

---

[1] **the going gets rough** problems happen or life feels hard

Basically, a teen's group reflects his or her personal choices. We in essence[2] define ourselves by who we are in relationship to others," says Little. "So, by knowing your friends and being able to associate and get along with them, you are establishing your own social identity as a member of that group."

Groups also help develop social competence. That's the ability to understand and get along with others. Social competence will be essential for building successful family relationships, advancing in a career, and dealing with other challenges of adulthood.

Why Cliques May Not Click

A clique is just a type of group. "A clique is any group that's bound together by common interests that has some sort of standards for being considered a member of the clique," says Little. School cliques can include competing "in crowds": groups that are defined by activities, interests, or appearances.

There's nothing wrong with teens joining together to share similar interests. But even teens who belong to cliques feel pressure. Clique members often have defined roles, where some act as trendsetters[3] and others as followers. If they step outside the given role, they can be ostracized, or excluded.

Clique members may feel pressure to **conform** in other ways, too. They may forego[4] friendships they might otherwise pursue. They may allow or even join in the bullying of outsiders.

How can you tell if your group is a negative clique? Take a realistic look at how group members treat outsiders. Are they welcoming and accepting of others? Or do they say or do things to let others know they're not wanted?

Also decide if you are really comfortable in the group. No one should have to do a complete personality makeover to fit in with any group. "Just try to act normal," says 15-year-old Chris Safrath. "If you have to change the way you act around people in order for them to like you, then they really aren't your friends."

Peer pressure may force you to choose between sticking with the group and upholding your personal standards and **values**, if others in the group do things you think are wrong.

---

[2] **in essence** basically
[3] **trendsetters** people who start popular movements or habits
[4] **forego** go without or give up

"I think you really have to know who you are and what you believe in," says 19-year-old Nasreen Ghazi. "If they really are your friends, then they won't pressure you to do something you're not comfortable with."

"If your friends try to get you to do something you don't want to do, then they're not your friends," agrees Chris. "You should find new ones." Admitting that to yourself can hurt. But doing something you know is wrong can hurt even worse in the long run.[5]

The Gift of Friendship

Fitting in is learning to feel accepted as part of a group. It's going along sometimes with what the group wants, while feeling comfortable that you're still yourself. It's trusting other group members with the gift of your friendship. Of course, that isn't always easy. Even popular teens admit they sometimes feel unsure of themselves. What can you do?

Start by being your own best friend. Exercise, eat right, and get enough sleep each day. Do things you enjoy. Share your talents with others. View things with a positive outlook. The more you like yourself, the more confident you'll feel in a group. At the same time, developing interests and talents will help you become more likeable.

---

[5] **in the long run** over time

Be a friend to others. An old saying holds[6] that the best way
to make a friend is to be one. So start by smiling and saying "Hi"
more often.

Rather than trying to take on[7] a whole group at once, start with
one-on-one friendships. Show interest in what someone is doing.
Talk about class or club activities. Offer support if it's needed. Ask
someone to do something with you.

If this sounds like work, it is. But groups of friends won't
automatically beat a pathway to your door.[8] Everyone has to put
something into building a relationship.

---

[6] **An old saying holds** A popular belief says
[7] **take on** be friends with
[8] **automatically beat a pathway to your door** appear on their own

Not everyone you talk with will want to be your best buddy,
either. Nor would you want to limit yourself to just one friend.
That could get socially suffocating for both of you. Instead, explore
friendships with a variety of people. The more you reach out, the
wider your circle of friends will be.

Just be yourself. But don't force it. Trying too hard to fit in can
backfire.[9] "You can't just force your way into a group," notes Little.
"Just find people who have similar interests that you like, and
associate with them."

Don't feel limited to the school social structure either. Clubs,
sports, volunteer organizations, and other groups all offer
opportunities to meet people who share your interests. "Just be

---

[9] **backfire** have a negative result

Friends enjoy rowing together
on a lake at dawn.

yourself, and if one group doesn't accept you, find another one," suggests 16-year-old Maggie Kiel. "There's a group for everybody. You just have to look."

Fitting In vs. Blending In

105   How can you fit in when you're different from teens around you? Accept the challenge to move beyond obvious differences. Chances are you'll find common ground.[10]

"I definitely stood out in high school, because I am from a background different from that of most of the other students," 110   notes Nasreen. "However, I didn't have any trouble fitting in because I was lucky enough to find a great group of friends who like me for me.[11]"

---

[10] **common ground** things you have in common
[11] **like me for me** like me exactly the way I am

Friends enjoy a water fight during the Water Festival in Mandalay, Myanmar. ▼

Similar values and interests outweigh physical or cultural differences any day. "School is important to my friends, and we all get good grades," notes Nasreen. "We also care about each other a lot."

Fitting in is important. But your individuality is important, too. Take pride in your interests, talents, cultural background, and other factors that help make you who you are.

Remember that fitting in doesn't mean anyone has to blend into the background. Respect the differences among teens in your group. Appreciate how unique each person is.

Celebrate the Differences

Of course, friends in a group aren't cookie-cutter people. They're all individuals. "I belong to a large group that gets along well," says 18-year-old Bernadette Safrath. "We all have different interests, but everyone shares at least one interest with one other person." Those different interests can provide opportunities to try new things and broaden your horizons.

Even in friendly groups, some people may just not be your favorite friends. "Most groups are going to have positives and negatives," notes Little. "If the group overall has more positives to you, then you're more willing to deal with someone negative."

So, how do you deal with someone who is part of your group but who you don't get along with very well? "If there are people in your group who you aren't as close with as others, keep it to yourself,[12]" recommends Bernadette. "You don't have to be that person's best friend. The person can be just a casual **acquaintance** who you see when you're with your close friends."

"Try to understand why that person is like that, and maybe you will like him [or her] more," suggests Chris. "Just be nice and try not to let the person bother you."

It's fortunate if your group spends more time doing activities everyone agrees on. If most areas of common interest have faded away, though, it may be time to find another group. But don't just drop out without saying anything. "Be honest. If you feel it's time to move on, tell the group how you feel and why," says Bernadette. "You may be able to work it out." Even if you can't, at least you'll avoid hard feelings.

---

[12] **keep it to yourself** don't say bad things or gossip about that person

Close Read

Work with a partner.

1. Determine the meanings of your underlined words and phrases.
2. Discuss the question:

   How are groups beneficial to teens?

Understand and Analyze

Respond to the questions. Support your responses with evidence from the text.

1. **Interpret** Reread lines 15–16. What does the author mean by "emotional anchors"?
2. **Explain** Reread lines 31–56. Why can cliques be problematic for some teens?
3. **Infer** Reread lines 63–65. Why might keeping the wrong friends hurt worse "in the long run" than admitting that some people aren't really your friends?
4. **Restate** Reread lines 79–80. Use your own words to restate "the best way to make a friend is to be one."
5. **Review** Reread lines 143–149. Why is it important to explain why you want to leave a group?
6. **Contrast** Reread the section "Fitting In vs. Blending In." How is "fitting in" different from "blending in"?

Apply the Strategy: Preview and Predict

Look at your prediction graphic organizer from before. Was your prediction about the content of the text correct? Why or why not?

____

____

____

Share Your Perspective

Discuss these questions in a small group.

1. Which student in the text gave the best advice? What makes it the best?
2. What advice would you add to the article? Why?

Discussion Frames

The best advice is from …

That advice is the best because …

In addition, I would suggest … because …

Why do you say that …?

Vocabulary: Use Context to Determine Meanings L.8.4.A

Good readers use **context clues** to determine the meanings of unknown words or phrases in a text. By analyzing the text before and after an unknown word or phrase, you can find other words or phrases that give hints about what the author means. To use context clues:

1. Pause when you find a sentence that includes an unknown word or phrase.

2. Reread the text that appears before and after the sentence to look for clues. If needed, reread the entire paragraph.

3. Use the context of the surrounding text to figure out the meaning of the unknown word or phrase.

Example

I'm not sure what the phrase "do a complete personality makeover" means. I'll reread the paragraph.

Also decide if you are really comfortable in the group. No one should have to <u>do a complete personality makeover</u> to fit in with any group. "Just try to act normal," says 15-year-old Chris Safrath. "If you have to change the way you act around people in order for them to like you, then they really aren't your friends."

"Act normal" and "change the way you act" are good context clues. They help me understand that to "do a complete personality makeover" means "to completely change your own personality or how you act."

Apply the Strategy

Look at "What's Your Group ID?" again. Use context clues to help you choose the correct definition for each word or phrase.

1. In line 18, what does "social beings" mean?
   a. people who are used to being in groups
   b. people who are used to being alone

2. In line 91, what does "socially suffocating" mean?
   a. physically dangerous
   b. mentally uncomfortable

3. In line 124, what does "cookie-cutter people" mean?
   a. people who are all different
   b. people who are all the same

4. In line 129, what does "broaden your horizons" mean?
   a. doing new things that you might enjoy
   b. doing the same things that you always enjoy

Read Again

Read "What's Your Group ID?" again. As you read, circle details from the text that help you respond to this question:

What are some strategies for creating strong, healthy friendships?

Reflect and Respond

Choose several details you circled in the text to complete the idea web.

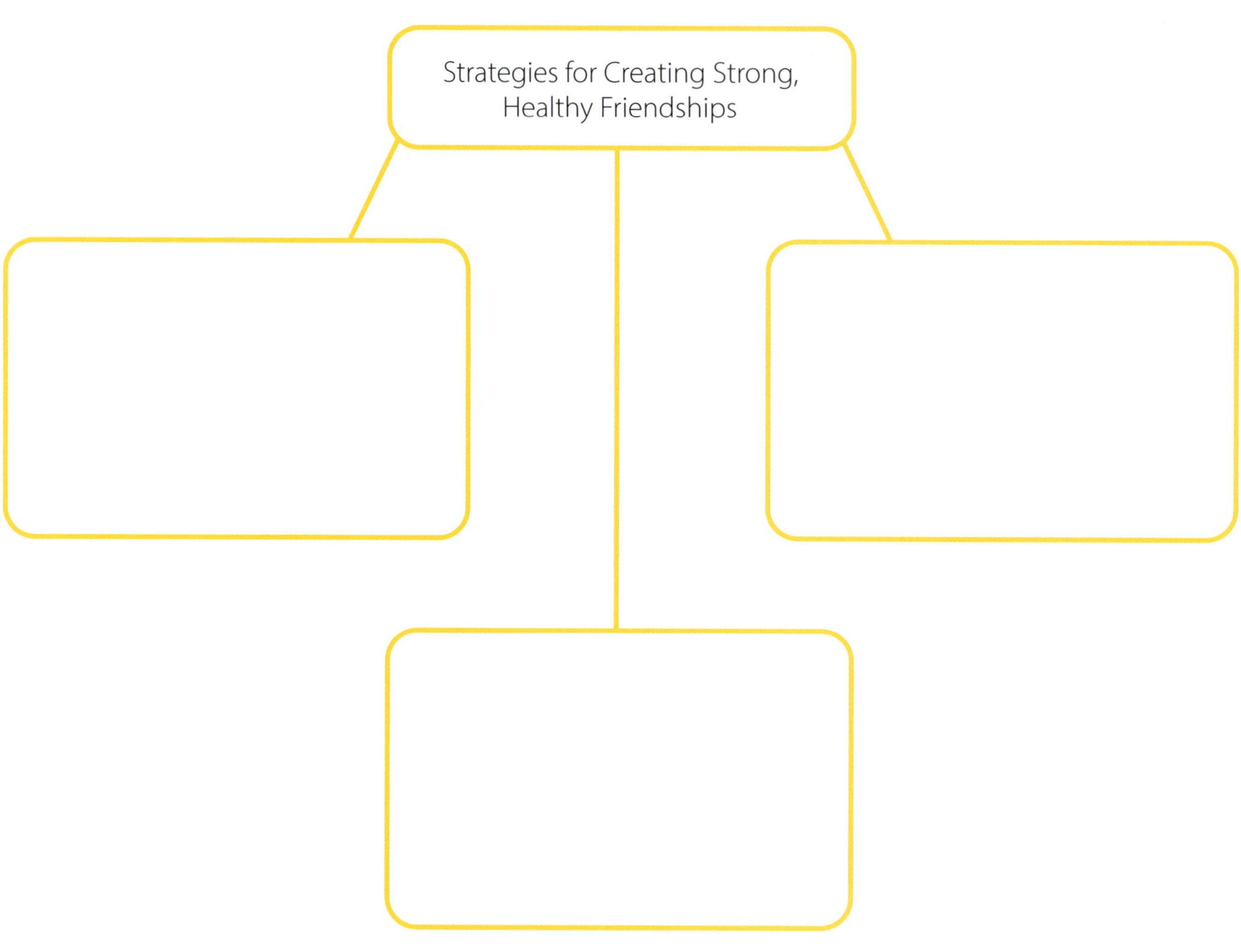

Use your idea web to respond to the question: What are some strategies for creating strong, healthy friendships?

____

____

____

Discuss Your Response

Share your ideas with the class. Write one new idea you hear.

____

____

____

Respond to the Guiding Question

Write a response to the question:

How can we be part of a group without losing our individuality?

Use evidence from the text, your discussion, and your life. Use the Discussion Frames to help you. Use the rubric to check your response.

____

____

____

____

Create and Present: Friendship Examples

Think about the ideas for being a good friend in "What's Your Group ID?" Then do one of these activities.

OPTION 1: "Be a Good Friend" Checklist

Work with a partner. Create a "Be a Good Friend" checklist for others to use. List at least five actions you can take to be a good friend. Present your checklist to the class.

OPTION 2: Good Friends Poster

Find or draw three images that represent what being a good friend means to you. Write a caption for each image that includes this language:

Good friends ________________________.

Create a poster with the images and captions. Present your poster to the class.

Examine the Photo

1. Look at the photo. Describe what you see.

2. How does the photo communicate a feeling of belonging?

3. Write 3–5 questions about the photo. Discuss your questions with a small group.

Find Out ▶ 1.1

Watch photographer Ami Vitale talk about her photo.

1. Did Vitale answer any of your questions? Which ones?

2. According to Vitale, what is happening in the photo?

3. How are the students alike? How do they "belong"?

4. What do these ideas help you understand about the event shown in the photo?

Reflect

Imagine you were one of the students in the photo. Write a caption to explain how you were feeling in that moment and why.

Share Your Story

Take or find a photo that shares a sense of belonging. Tell your classmates the story about the photo.

ABOUT THE PHOTOGRAPHER

Ami Vitale believes photography is a "tool for creating awareness and understanding across cultures, communities, and countries."

What can make agreeing or disagreeing with others difficult?

First Thoughts

When have you disagreed with a group? How did the group react? How did the disagreement make you feel? Make notes in the chart. Then discuss your experience with a small group.

How I Disagreed	Group's Reaction	How I Felt

Discussion Frames

I disagreed with a group when …

The group reacted by …

Because of this disagreement, I felt …

What happened when …?

Why did you feel that …?

Key Vocabulary

PRACTICE Use context to determine the meaning of each word in bold. Then match the word to its definition.

1. She showed good **judgment** by saving her money.
2. Waiting your turn is **normative** behavior, following social rules.
3. I will eat lunch when the **majority** of the class wants to eat.
4. I feel **confident** that you will like the gift I got you.
5. A vision test is a **perceptual** test because it relates to sight.
6. His opinion should not **influence** how you feel about the book.

_____ **1.** judgment   **a.** following common standards and rules (adj.)

_____ **2.** normative   **b.** to affect another's feelings or actions (v.)

_____ **3.** majority   **c.** relating to the senses (adj.)

_____ **4.** confident   **d.** more than half of a group of people (n.)

_____ **5.** perceptual   **e.** sure; certain (adj.)

_____ **6.** influence   **f.** reasoning; sense (n.)

Reading Skill: Cite Text Evidence **RI.8.1**

Part of being a good reader is being able to answer questions about what you read and support your answers with **text evidence**. As you read, pay attention to what a text says explicitly, or directly. Then use that information to answer questions about the content. To cite text evidence:

1. Read or listen to a question about a text. Ask yourself: *What does the text say about this?*

2. Search the text for information or details that answer the question.

3. Cite evidence from the text by paraphrasing the author's words or by quoting the text directly. Begin and end any direct quotes with quotation marks.

Skill in Action

Read the first paragraph of "The Asch Conformity Experiments." Then read the chart. How does the student cite evidence in the answers?

> Some of the most famous experiments about conformity are the Asch line experiments, which were conducted in the 1950s. When Solomon Asch began his studies, he was primarily interested in understanding how group behavior can influence the behavior of the individual, and what aspects of this group influence might be the most important.

Questions	Answers
1. What did Solomon Asch want to know about group behavior?	Asch wanted to know how the behavior of groups can affect the behavior of individuals. He also wanted to know "what aspects of this group influence might be the most important."
2. Did the Asch line experiments happen recently?	No. The text says they happened "in the 1950s."

The student paraphrased and used a quotation.

The student used a quotation.

Read and answer the question: **How did some participants in the study conform to the group?** As you read, underline any parts of the text you have questions about or find confusing.

The Asch Conformity Experiments

by Brooke Miller

🎧 1.2

Some of the most famous experiments about conformity are the Asch line experiments, which were conducted in the 1950s. When Solomon Asch began his studies, he was primarily interested in understanding how group behavior can **influence** the behavior of the individual, and what aspects of this group influence might be the most important.

Imagine that you sign up to be a participant in what has been described as a simple **perceptual** study. When you show up for[1] the study, there are a number of other participants. You all sit down at a long table, and the experimenter starts to explain the experiment to you.

It seems straightforward: the experimenter holds up a card. The card has four vertical lines on it. There is one line on the left called the "target line." On the right, there are three lines that are slightly different heights. These lines are called

---

[1] **show up for** get to

Meerkats are highly social animals and tend to live in large groups, called mobs.

the "comparison lines," and they are labeled A, B, and C. Each participant needs to figure out which comparison line is the same
25 height as the target line. One by one, everyone will state aloud which line (A, B, or C) best matches the target line.

The first trial starts, and everybody gives what is obviously the correct answer—including you. The second trial goes along just like the first one did. The correct answer is obvious. But on
30 the third trial, something really strange happens. The answer seems obvious again, but this time, the first participant gives the wrong answer. Then the second participant agrees with the first participant. The third one does, too. Everyone has given the same incorrect answer.

35 When it gets to you,[2] what do you say? Do you give the correct response based on your own perception? Or do you give the incorrect response that the others have given? Do you go with what you think you know, or do you go with the **majority**? What if this strange situation doesn't just happen once but happens
40 across a number of trials? What would you do?

____

[2] **it gets to you** it is your turn

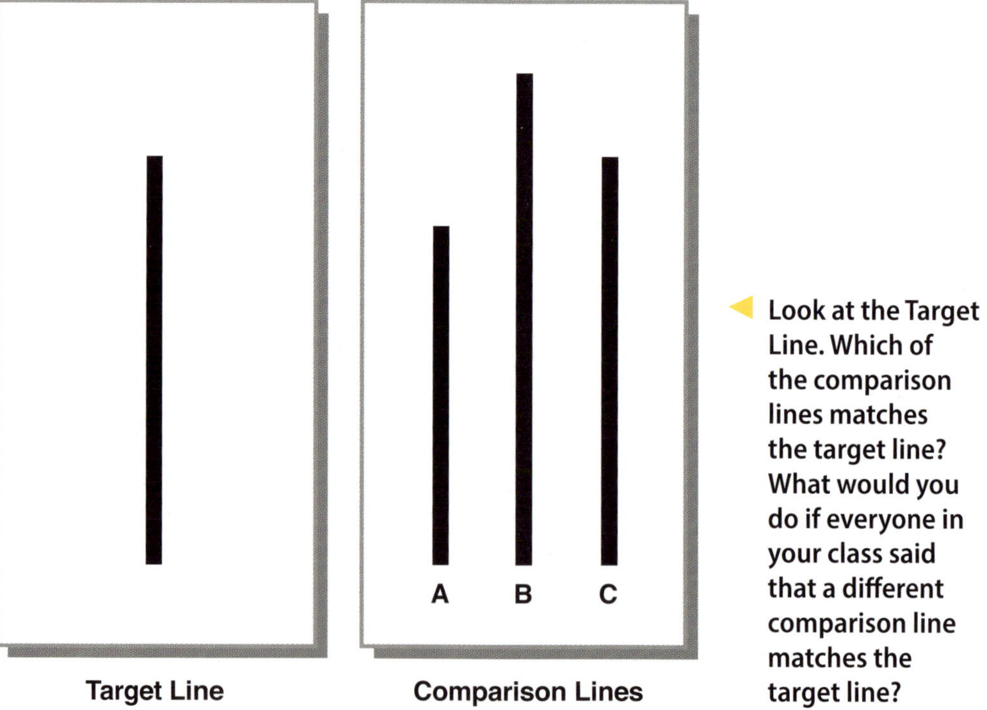

Target Line   **Comparison Lines**

◄ Look at the Target Line. Which of the comparison lines matches the target line? What would you do if everyone in your class said that a different comparison line matches the target line?

When I ask this question in class, most students tell me that they would not conform. They say they would always give the correct answer—even when the majority was giving the incorrect one. You might be thinking the same thing. I like to think that
45   I would not conform, either. But this is actually *not* what the researchers found. Even though solitary participants (participants answering without a group) made errors less than 1 percent of the time, in the presence of a group, 75 percent of participants conformed and gave the incorrect answer at least once. In fact,
50   37 percent of participants conformed and gave the incorrect answer every time the group did.
        There are a few important things to know about this study. The first thing is that there was a secret: there was only one real participant. All of the other participants were actually in on[3]
55   the experiment the whole time. These fake participants were instructed by the experimenter to give the incorrect answers. The real participant never knew that the fake participants were fake. The true purpose of this study was to tell whether or not the real participants would go along with the group when that
60   group was making an obviously incorrect decision. There were 18 trials. In each trial, there were 18 different cards. The fake participants unanimously answered 12 of the 18 cards in each trial incorrectly—on purpose.
        Another important thing to note about this study is that there
65   was no obvious pressure to conform or not conform with the group. There was no prize for conforming and no punishment for not conforming. Nor was there any prize for doing well on the study or punishment for doing poorly. The real participants were simply seated with the fake participants at a table. So there was
70   no actual pressure to conform—only perceived pressure. Why would the real participants of the study go against their better **judgment** and conform with the group?
        When the real participants were interviewed following the experiment and asked why they had conformed, most noted that
75   they had realized they were giving incorrect answers, but they went along with the others because they feared being ridiculed by

---

[3] **in on** part of

the group. We refer to this as "**normative** social influence," which
is altering our behaviors so that we fit in better with those around
us. So some of the real participants saw what the correct answers
were, they knew that they were the correct answers, but they gave
the wrong answers anyway.

Other real participants noted that they conformed because
they doubted their own responses. They reasoned that if all of
the other participants at the table were giving a certain answer,
then that one must be correct. We refer to this as "informational
social influence," which is when we change our behavior
because we assume that others are better informed—that they
know more than we do. So some of the real participants saw
what they thought were the correct answers, but then after
hearing the responses of the group, they changed their minds.[4]
As a result, they gave the same incorrect answers that the group
gave. So the real participants saw the correct responses, decided
that they themselves must be wrong, and they deferred to the
group's judgment.

But for some real participants in the study, the errors that they
made seemed to be at the perceptual level. They truly believed
that the answers given by the majority were correct. Unlike those
who conformed due to normative social influence or informational
social influence, these individuals were never consciously aware
that there was anything wrong with the judgment. They really
thought that the group gave the correct answers, so they gave
those answers as well.

What about those who did not conform? What were their
reasons? When these real participants were interviewed afterward,
some of them were really **confident**. They were sure that their
perceptions and their judgments were correct. Others weren't
so confident. There were some real participants who felt a lot of
doubt and unease. Even so, they stuck with their own[5] answers.

This study does have some problems. For example, the real
and fake participants all came from the same limited population.
They were all male college students, all around the same age,
and part of the same university culture. The original conformity

---

[4] **changed their minds** thought differently
[5] **stuck with their own** did not change their

studies didn't consider the fact that maybe women, individuals
from different cultures, or people of different ages might have
answered differently.

Also, even though the real participants thought that they were
coming in for a study about visual perception, they did know
that they were coming in for a study. It's possible that the real
participants in this original study conformed not because they
felt any group pressure, but because that's what they thought the
experimenter wanted them to do. Still, even with these problems,
there is still a lot that can be learned from this study.

One thing in particular to think about is that this study saw
75 percent of individuals conform without any external pressure.
Take a moment to think about how much more powerful the
experiment would have been if there *had* been pressure—if there
had been rewards for some answers or punishments for other
answers. How would you feel if your friends or teachers were the
fake participants instead of just random college students? Think
about whether or not these factors would increase or decrease the
likelihood[6] that you would conform.

---

[6] **likelihood** chance or possibility

Students raise hands in agreement. ▼

Close Read

Work with a partner.

1. Determine the meanings of your underlined words and phrases.
2. Discuss the question:

   How did some participants in the study conform to the group?

Understand and Analyze

Respond to the questions. Support your responses with evidence from the text.

1. **Summarize** Reread lines 17–40. Summarize how an Asch line experiment works.
2. **Describe** Reread lines 46–51. How did people who studied the cards alone react differently from how people who studied the cards with a group did?
3. **Interpret** Reread lines 69–70. What is "perceived pressure"?
4. **Classify** Reread lines 73–102. Classify the real participants into at least three different groups.
5. **Contrast** How were the Asch line experiments not just "simple perceptual studies"?
6. **Infer** Why does the author repeatedly ask readers to imagine that "you" are participating in the experiment?

Apply the Skill: Cite Text Evidence RI.81

Cite text evidence as you answer the questions below.

1. What is the difference between informational social influence and normative social influence?

   ____

   ____

   ____

2. Why might it matter that the real participants knew they were part of a study?

   ____

   ____

   ____

Share Your Perspective

Discuss these questions in a small group.

1. Reread the fifth paragraph. What are your answers to the author's questions? What are the reasons for your answers?
2. Do you think it was fair that the real participants were tricked, or fooled? Why or why not?

Language Convention: Identify and Use Infinitives L.8.1.A

An **infinitive** is a verb form that begins with "to" when the verb is in its most basic form, such as *to walk*. Within a sentence, an infinitive can be used as a noun, an adjective, or an adverb. An infinitive can have modifiers or objects.

Infinitive	In a Sentence	Explanation of Use
to see	To see the lines was part of the experiment.	"To see the lines" is an activity. The infinitive acts as a noun.
to answer	The real participant was the last to answer.	"To answer" acts as an adjective. It describes "last."
to avoid	He conformed to avoid being an outsider.	"To avoid being an outsider" acts as an adverb. It tells *why* about the verb "conformed."

PRACTICE 1 Read each sentence. Underline the infinitive. Then indicate whether the infinitive is used as a noun, an adjective, or an adverb.

1. Participant 5 paused to think about his answer.
2. The group's choice was the best one to make.
3. To study behavior was what Solomon Asch wanted.
4. One part of the experiment was to conform.
5. The experimenter is the person to interview about the study.

PRACTICE 2 Work with a partner. Identify the infinitives in the model. In the chart, write the infinitives and tell how they are used.

Imagine your teacher draws four lines to show an example of the experiment. He asks: "Which line matches the target line?" You can see that line B is the match. Your friends decide to pick line A. You don't think they're correct. But the best way to make your friends happy is to agree with them. So you say "line A" to fit in with the group. Which line will the teacher say is correct?

Infinitive	How It Is Used
to show	adverb

Read Again

Read "The Asch Conformity Experiments" again. As you read, circle details from the text that help you respond to this question:

What can cause people to change their thoughts or behaviors?

Reflect and Respond

Complete this chart with several details you circled.

Causes	Effect
	People change their thoughts or behaviors.

Use your chart to respond to the question: What can cause people to change their thoughts or behaviors?

____

____

____

____

Discuss Your Response

Share your ideas with the class. Write one new idea you hear.

____

____

____

Respond to the Guiding Question

Write a response to the question:

What can make agreeing or disagreeing with others difficult?

Use evidence from the text, your discussion, and your life. Use the Discussion Frames to help you. Use the rubric to check your response.

____

____

____

____

____

Research W.8.7

Choose one of these topics. Research the topic to learn more about it.

- Persuasive speech techniques

- Bystander effect

Follow these steps:

1. Make notes about what you already know about the topic.
2. Write three questions you have about the topic.
3. Research the topic to find answers to your questions.
4. Write your answers to the questions.
5. Present what you learn to a small group.

How can the behavior of others affect our minds and bodies?

Otters yawn on a riverbank. All animals yawn, including fish, birds, and even snakes.

First Thoughts

Do you cover your mouth when you yawn? Why or why not? Share your responses with a small group.

Viewing Skill: Pause to Review and Check Understanding

When you watch a video, content can go by quickly and be hard to understand. You can periodically pause a video to review and check your understanding. You can also replay parts of the video. Continue pausing and replaying as needed.

Apply the Skill

▶ **1.2** Watch the TED-Ed animation "Why Is Yawning Contagious?" Pause as needed to review important ideas and ask yourself questions to check your understanding. Write your questions in the chart. To answer your questions, think about what you have already watched, or replay parts of the video. Then complete the chart with your answers and how you found them.

My Questions	Answers	How I Found the Answers

Understand and Analyze

▶ **1.2** Watch again. Answer the questions. Support your responses with evidence from the video.

1. **Infer** According to the video, what is a "reflex"?
2. **Explain** How does the video give an example of the "chameleon effect"?
3. **Contrast** How are the physiological hypotheses different from the psychological hypothesis?
4. **Explain** Why is more research needed about why people yawn?

Share Your Perspective

1. Do you think studying yawning is important? Why or why not?
2. Which theory for yawning from the video do you agree with most? Why?

Discussion Frames

Based on the provided information, …

The theory I agree with most is … because …

Why do you think that …?

How can conformity be dangerous?

First Thoughts

Imagine that your small group is supposed to write a research paper about rooftop gardens. One member of the group finds an existing research paper online and wants to pretend that your group created it. You don't want to cheat, but three out of your four group members do. How would you respond? Fill in the chart. Then explain your decision to a small group.

Discussion Frames

My response would be to …

I feel this way because …

Why did you decide to …?

Event	Your Response
Most of your group members want to cheat.	

Key Vocabulary

PRACTICE Use context to determine the meaning of each word in bold. Then match the word to its definition.

1. We didn't know then that our actions were of great **consequence**, but they changed the world.
2. Is there **civilization** on that island? I don't see any people or buildings.
3. We **savored** a truly delicious meal.
4. The tree branch was **frail**, so it broke during the storm.
5. She kept running even after she fell. She was **resilient**.

_____ **1.** consequence   **a.** an organized, functioning society (n.)

_____ **2.** civilization   **b.** weak or easily hurt (adj.)

_____ **3.** savor   **c.** importance; significance (n.)

_____ **4.** frail   **d.** to enjoy or appreciate fully (v.)

_____ **5.** resilient   **e.** able to survive or recover from difficult conditions (adj.)

Reading Skill: Analyze Characters and Plot   **RL.8.3**

When you **retell** a fiction story, you tell what happens in the story. When you **analyze characters and plot**, you go beyond simple retelling. You still tell what happens in the story, but your focus changes to explaining *why, how,* or *what* instead of simply relating events.

To analyze a character, explain:

- why a character says or does something
- how a character's dialogue or actions affect the other characters or the story's events
- what a character's dialogue or actions reveal about that character, such as their motives, feelings, or characteristics

To analyze an event, explain:

- how the event causes a character to change or act a certain way
- how the event reveals more information about a character
- how the event fits into the overall plot
- what happens in the story as the result of the event

Skill in Action

Study the model from "All Summer in a Day." How does the reader analyze the characters?

William's dialogue tells me he is rude and bossy. He shoves Margot when she doesn't respond. This action tells me William thinks shoving someone he dislikes is acceptable behavior.

"What're *you* looking at?" said William.
Margot said nothing.
"Speak when you're spoken to." He gave her a shove. But she did not move; rather she let herself be moved only by him and nothing else.

Margot doesn't respond to William when he asks her a question or when he shoves her. This is an unusual reaction. I'll reread the story carefully to look for clues about *why* she acts this way.

All Summer in a Day

by Ray Bradbury

> Science fiction writers speculate about what might happen in the future. Ray Bradbury published "All Summer in a Day" in 1954. Bradbury set his story on Venus and imagined what life might be like for people there. He created a Venus with plant life, a lot of water, and breathable air.

🎧 **1.3**

1   "Ready?"
     "Ready."
     "Now?"
     "Soon."
5   "Do the scientists really know? Will it happen today, will it?"
     "Look, look; see for yourself!"
     The children pressed to each other like so many roses, so many weeds, intermixed, peering out for a look at the hidden sun.
     It rained.
10   It had been raining for seven years; thousands upon thousands of days compounded and filled from one end to the other with rain, with the drum and gush of water, with the sweet crystal fall of showers and the concussion[1] of storms so heavy they were tidal waves come over the islands. A thousand forests had been crushed under the rain and grown
15   up a thousand times to be crushed again. And this was the way life was forever on the planet Venus, and this was the schoolroom of the children of the rocket men and women who had come to a raining world to set up **civilization** and live out their lives.
     "It's stopping, it's stopping!"
20   "Yes, yes!"
     Margot stood apart from them, from these children who could never remember a time when there wasn't rain and rain and rain. They were all nine years old, and if there had been a day, seven years ago, when the sun came out for an hour and showed its face to the stunned world, they could
25   not recall. Sometimes, at night, she heard them stir, in remembrance, and she knew they were dreaming and remembering gold or a yellow crayon or a coin large enough to buy the world with. She knew they thought they

---

[1] **concussion** noisy pounding

remembered a warmness, like a blushing in the face, in the body, in the
arms and legs and trembling hands. But then they always awoke to the
tatting drum, the endless shaking down of clear bead necklaces[2] upon the
roof, the walk, the gardens, the forests, and their dreams were gone.

All day yesterday they had read in class about the sun. About how like a
lemon it was, and how hot. And they had written small stories or essays or
poems about it:

> *I think the sun is a flower,*
> *That blooms for just one hour.*

That was Margot's poem, read in a quiet voice in the still classroom
while the rain was falling outside.

"Aw, you didn't write that!" protested one of the boys.

"I did," said Margot. "I *did*."

"William!" said the teacher.

But that was yesterday. Now the rain was
slackening, and the children were crushed[3] in
the great thick windows.

"Where's teacher?"

"She'll be back."

"She'd better hurry, we'll miss it!"

They turned on themselves, like a feverish
wheel, all tumbling spokes.

Margot stood alone. She was a very **frail**
girl who looked as if she had been lost in the
rain for years and the rain had washed out the
blue from her eyes and the red from her mouth
and the yellow from her hair. She was an old
photograph dusted from an album, whitened
away, and if she spoke at all her voice would
be a ghost. Now she stood, separate, staring
at the rain and the loud wet world beyond the
huge glass.

"What're *you* looking at?" said William.

Margot said nothing.

"Speak when you're spoken to." He gave

---

[2] **tatting drum, the endless shaking down of clear bead
necklaces** never-ending sound of rain
[3] **were crushed** stood close together

her a shove. But she did not move; rather she let herself be moved
only by him and nothing else.

65 They edged away from her, they would not look at her. She felt
them go away. And this was because she would play no games with
them in the echoing tunnels of the underground city. If they tagged
her and ran,[4] she stood blinking after them and did not follow.
When the class sang songs about happiness and life and games
70 her lips barely moved. Only when they sang about the sun and the
summer did her lips move as she watched the drenched windows.

And then, of course, the biggest crime of all was that she had
come here only five years ago from Earth, and she remembered
the sun and the way the sun was and the sky was when she was
75 four in Ohio. And they, they had been on Venus all their lives, and
they had been only two years old when last the sun came out and
had long since forgotten the color and heat of it and the way it
really was. But Margot remembered.

"It's like a penny," she said once, eyes closed.
80 "No it's not!" the children cried.
"It's like a fire," she said, "in the stove."
"You're lying, you don't remember!" cried the children.
But she remembered and stood quietly apart from all of them
and watched the patterning windows.[5] And once, a month ago, she
85 had refused to shower in the school shower rooms, had clutched her
hands to her ears and over her head, screaming the water mustn't
touch her head. So after that, dimly, dimly, she sensed it, she was
different and they knew her difference and kept away.

There was talk that her father and mother were taking her
90 back to Earth next year; it seemed vital to her that they do so,
though it would mean the loss of thousands of dollars to her
family. And so, the children hated her for all these reasons of
big and little **consequence**. They hated her pale snow face, her
waiting silence, her thinness, and her possible future.

95 "Get away!" The boy gave her another push. "What're you
waiting for?"

Then, for the first time, she turned and looked at him. And
what she was waiting for was in her eyes.

---

[4] **tagged her and ran** tried to get her to play tag
[5] **patterning windows** rain-decorated windows

"Well, don't wait around here!" cried the boy savagely. "You won't see
nothing!"

Her lips moved.

"Nothing!" he cried. "It was all a joke, wasn't it?" He turned to the
other children. "Nothing's happening today. *Is* it?"

They all blinked at him and then, understanding, laughed and shook
their heads. "Nothing, nothing!"

"Oh, but," Margot whispered, her eyes helpless. "But this is the day,
the scientists predict, they say, they *know*, the sun …"

"All a joke!" said the boy, and seized her roughly. "Hey, everyone, let's
put her in a closet before teacher comes!"

"No," said Margot, falling back.

They surged about her, caught her up and bore her,[6] protesting, and
then pleading, and then crying, back into a tunnel, a room, a closet, where
they slammed and locked the door. They stood looking at the door and saw
it tremble from her beating and throwing herself against it. They heard her
muffled cries. Then, smiling, they turned and went out and back down the
tunnel, just as the teacher arrived.

"Ready, children?" She glanced at her watch.

"Yes!" said everyone.

"Are we all here?"

"Yes!"

The rain slackened still more.

---

[6] **caught her up and bore her** grabbed her and carried her

They crowded to the huge door.

The rain stopped.

It was as if, in the midst of a film concerning an avalanche, a tornado, a hurricane, a volcanic eruption, something had, first, gone wrong with the sound apparatus, thus muffling and finally cutting off all noise, all of the blasts and repercussions and thunders, and then, second, ripped the film from the projector and inserted in its place a beautiful tropical slide which did not move or tremor. The world ground to a standstill.[7] The silence was so immense and unbelievable that you felt your ears had been stuffed or you had lost your hearing altogether. The children put their hands to their ears. They stood apart. The door slid back and the smell of the silent, waiting world came in to them.

The sun came out.

It was the color of flaming bronze and it was very large. And the sky around it was a blazing blue tile color. And the jungle burned with sunlight as the children, released from their spell, rushed out, yelling, into the springtime.

"Now, don't go too far," called the teacher after them. "You've only two hours, you know. You wouldn't want to get caught out[8]!"

But they were running and turning their faces up to the sky and feeling the sun on their cheeks like a warm iron; they were taking off their jackets and letting the sun burn their arms.

"Oh, it's better than the sun lamps, isn't it?"

"Much, much better!"

---

[7] **ground to a standstill** stopped; grew calm
[8] **get caught out** be outside when it starts raining again

They stopped running and stood in the great jungle
that covered Venus, that grew and never stopped growing,
tumultuously, even as you watched it. It was a nest of octopi,
clustering up great arms of flesh-like weed, wavering, flowering
150 in this brief spring. It was the color of rubber and ash, this jungle,
from the many years without sun. It was the color of stones and
white cheeses and ink, and it was the color of the moon.

The children lay out, laughing, on the jungle mattress,[9] and
heard it sigh and squeak under them, **resilient** and alive. They ran
155 among the trees, they slipped and fell, they pushed each other,
they played hide-and-seek and tag, but most of all they squinted
at the sun until the tears ran down their faces, they put their
hands up to that yellowness and that amazing blueness and they
breathed of the fresh, fresh air and listened and listened to the
160 silence which suspended them in[10] a blessed sea of no sound
and no motion. They looked at everything and **savored**
everything. Then, wildly, like animals escaped from their
caves, they ran and ran in shouting circles. They ran
for an hour and did not stop running.

165 And then—
In the midst of their running one of
the girls wailed.

Everyone stopped.
The girl, standing in the open,
170 held out her hand.

"Oh, look, look," she
said, trembling.

They came slowly to
look at her opened palm.

175 In the center of it,
cupped and huge, was
a single raindrop.

She began to cry,
looking at it.

---

[9] **jungle mattress** ground of
   the jungle
[10] **suspended them
   in** surrounded them in
   what felt like

180   They glanced quietly at the sky.

"Oh. Oh."

A few cold drops fell on their noses and their cheeks and their mouths. The sun faded behind a stir of mist. A wind blew cool around them. They turned and started to walk back toward the underground
185   house, their hands at their sides, their smiles vanishing away.

A boom of thunder startled them and like leaves before a new hurricane, they tumbled upon each other and ran. Lightning struck ten miles away, five miles away, a mile, a half mile. The sky darkened into midnight in a flash.

190   They stood in the doorway of the underground for a moment until it was raining hard. Then they closed the door and heard the gigantic sound of the rain falling in tons and avalanches, everywhere and forever.

"Will it be seven more years?"

"Yes. Seven."

195   Then one of them gave a little cry.

"Margot!"

"What?"

"She's still in the closet where we locked her."

"Margot."

200   They stood as if someone had driven them, like so many stakes,[11] into the floor. They looked at each other and then looked away. They glanced out at the world that was raining now and raining and raining steadily. They could not meet each other's glances.[12] Their faces were solemn and pale. They looked at their hands and feet,
205   their faces down.

"Margot."

One of the girls said, "Well … ?"

No one moved.

"Go on," whispered the girl.

210   They walked slowly down the hall in the sound of cold rain. They turned through the doorway to the room in the sound of the storm and thunder, lightning on their faces, blue and terrible. They walked over to the closet door slowly and stood by it.

Behind the closet door was only silence.

215   They unlocked the door, even more slowly, and let Margot out.

---

[11] **stakes** pointed sticks or poles
[12] **meet each other's glances** look each other in the eye

**About the Author:
Ray Bradbury
(1920–2012)**

Ray Bradbury was an American author best known for his science fiction and fantasy writing. He wrote more than 400 short stories and nearly 50 books, as well as numerous poems, essays, plays, operas, teleplays, and screenplays. He is one of the most widely translated writers in the world.

Close Read

Work with a partner.

1. Determine the meanings of your underlined words and phrases.
2. Discuss the questions: **Why doesn't Margot "belong"? How does this lack of belonging affect Margot?**

Understand and Analyze

Respond to the questions. Support your responses with evidence from the text.

1. **Describe** Reread lines 10–18. What are key details about the setting?
2. **Infer** Reread lines 48–49. What does Bradbury mean when he says the children "turned on themselves, like a feverish wheel, all tumbling spokes"?
3. **Give Examples** Reread lines 65–78. Give three examples from the story of why the other children seem to hate Margot.
4. **Interpret** Reread lines 113–115. How does Margot feel about being in the closet?
5. **Interpret** Reread lines 141–164. How do the children feel about being in the sun?
6. **Conclude** Reread lines 195–215. Do the children regret locking Margot in the closet? Explain your answer.

Apply the Skill: Analyze Characters and Plot RL.8.1

Analyze the characters and plot in "All Summer in a Day" by answering these questions.

1. Reread lines 80–84. Why don't the children believe Margot when she describes the sun?

   ____

   ____

2. What do the other children's dialogue and actions at the beginning of the story reveal about them?

   ____

   ____

3. What do you think is the climax of the story? Why?

   ____

   ____

Share Your Perspective

Discuss these questions in a small group.

1. Should Margot try harder to fit in with the other children? Why or why not?
2. How should communities treat newcomers? Why?

Vocabulary: Use Word Relationships **L.8.5.B**

To figure out the meaning of an unknown word in a text, you can use the meaning of a related word. Follow these steps:

1. Consider whether you know a similar word that might be related. For example, if the word "whitened" is unfamiliar to you, you might consider whether it is related to the more familiar word "white."

2. Compare how the words are formed for clues to the unfamiliar word's meaning. The word "white" is most often used as an adjective. The word ending "–ened" signals that "whitened" is the past tense of a verb.

3. Use these word relationships to figure out the meaning of the unknown word. For example, "whitened" must mean "became white" or "made [something] white."

Example

Unknown Word	Word Relationships
Now the rain was <u>slackening</u>, and the children were crushed in the great thick windows.	• I don't know "slackening," but maybe the words "slack" or "slacker" are related. Something slack is loose or slow. A slacker is a lazy person. • The ending "–ening" signals that this is a verb form. The helping verb "was" does, too. • "Slackening" must mean "becoming slack," "slowing down," or "beginning to stop."

Apply the Strategy

Look at the story again. Find each word in context. Then figure out the meaning of each word, based on related words.

Word	Word's Meaning
1. Line 48: feverish	
2. Line 84: patterning	
3. Line 99: savagely	
4. Line 149: clustering	

Read Again

Read "All Summer in a Day" again. As you read, circle details from the story that help you respond to this question:

How does conformity affect Margot and the other children in the story?

Reflect and Respond

Choose several details you circled in the story to complete the comparison chart.

How Conformity Affects Margot	How Conformity Affects the Other Children

Use your chart to respond to the question: How does conformity affect Margot and the other children in the story?

____

____

____

Discuss Your Response

Share your ideas with the class. Write one new idea you hear.

____

____

Respond to the Guiding Question

Write a response to the question:

How can conformity be dangerous?

Use evidence from the text, your discussion, and your life. Use the Discussion Frames to help you. Use the rubric to check your response.

____

____

____

____

CONNECT ACROSS TEXTS

Discuss the Essential Question: Why is it important to belong?

Look at your answer to the Essential Question on the Unit Launch and your notes about belonging in the Reflect and Respond sections. Discuss: How have your ideas about the Essential Question changed? What changed your ideas?

Then write one new idea you heard in the discussion. How did it affect your opinion?

____

____

Respond to the Essential Question

Write your new response to the Essential Question. Include Academic Vocabulary.

____

____

____

Assignment: Write a Short Story W.8.3

A short story is fiction writing that includes characters, settings, and a plot. For this assignment, you will write a short story that shares a message about belonging.

Your short story should include:

- an interesting title
- at least one setting and at least two characters
- a plot, or sequence of events, that includes exposition (the introduction of main characters and setting), conflict (a problem), rising action (events that develop the characters and the conflict), climax (point of highest tension, where a character must act), falling action (events leading to the resolution), and resolution (the end of the conflict)
- at least two lines of dialogue
- descriptive details about the characters, setting(s), and events

Explore the Model

Read the model short story and complete the following tasks:

1. Put a star next to the title and explain its importance.
2. Identify the setting and main character(s).
3. Circle the dialogue.
4. Underline one descriptive detail about a character, one about the setting, and one about an event.

Painting Perfection

Ximena walked to the Community Center with her bag of paints and paintbrushes. She had just moved to a new city, and to make new friends, she'd signed up for a painting class. She loved making colorful, wild, expressive art.

In the classroom, Ximena met Mr. Chen and five other students. Mr. Chen displayed a large photo of a stargazer lily. He handed out copies of it to the class. "You're all going to paint this stargazer lily," he said. Ximena's stomach dropped.

"Um, Mr. Chen?" said Ximena, feeling uncomfortable. "I don't paint realistic art. I don't know how to paint a real flower."

"The purpose of this class is to learn something new. You can do it. I believe in you!" Mr. Chen smiled.

The story begins by introducing the setting and main characters. This is the exposition.

A problem arises: this is the conflict.

"Just study the lines and the colors," said one student. "You'll do fine." Others nodded. Everyone but Ximena seemed to believe she could do it.

Ximena's heart started beating fast. Just when she thought it couldn't get any worse, Mr. Chen told the group that they would all be displaying their paintings at the upcoming Community Center party. Ximena groaned inwardly.

For the rest of the hour, Ximena watched her classmates begin painting beautiful lilies. They looked just like real flowers—perfect. Ximena tried again and again, but her lilies looked like cartoons. She left the class feeling horrible.

All week, Ximena tried to paint the lily realistically. Over and over, her paintings ended up in the garbage. At one point, Ximena was so frustrated that she screamed. Her neighbor knocked on the door to check on her. Suddenly, Ximena realized how ridiculous she was being. She made a decision.

Later that month, the Community Center was bustling with people. They talked, laughed, and ate food prepared by the cooking class's students. The paintings were hidden behind a sheet.

"I'd like to take a moment to present the paintings by the art class," said Mr. Chen. Everyone quieted down and gathered around. Dramatically, Mr. Chen pulled down the sheet.

There were five similar paintings of a stargazer lily. And then there was Ximena's painting—different, unique. In Ximena's painting, a stargazer lily had come to life. It stood like a person and peered through a telescope. The background of the painting was the night sky filled with stars, constellations, planets, and a shining sliver of moon. Ximena's stargazer lily was literally gazing at stars.

People from the crowd went up close to the paintings, talked about them, and admired them. Most people went straight to Ximena's painting. They loved her creative vision and congratulated her on the work. When Mr. Chen complimented her, she beamed.

That night, Ximena felt proud. She had still fulfilled the assignment. She had painted a stargazer lily. But she had expressed her own artistic style. Ximena drifted off to sleep peacefully, dreaming of flowers and stars.

Plan Your Short Story

Think about everything you have learned in this unit about belonging. Share a message about belonging through your short story. What message would you like others to know? After you have chosen your message, use the outline to plan your plot.

SHORT STORY OUTLINE

Exposition:

Conflict:

Rising Action:

Climax:

Falling Action:

Resolution:

Write and Revise

Write Use your outline to write a first draft of your short story. A good short story helps readers create pictures in their minds of where the story is happening, who is speaking, and how the characters feel about other characters or the story's events. To help readers understand your story:

- indicate who is speaking when using dialogue
- include descriptions of your characters' feelings

Revise Exchange your short story with a partner. Use the checklist to review your partner's work and give feedback. Refer to your partner's feedback as you revise your draft.

Feedback Frames

☐ Does the story have a title that catches the reader's attention?

☐ Does the story have at least one setting?

☐ Does the story have at least two characters?

☐ Are all elements of the plot structure included?

☐ Are there at least two lines of dialogue?

☐ Are there descriptive details about characters, setting(s), and events?

Proofread Check the grammar, spelling, punctuation, and capitalization in your short story. Make edits to correct any errors.

Publish

Share your short story according to your teacher's instructions. Read at least two of your classmates' short stories.

TIP

After you finish your draft, put down your writing for an hour. Focus on another task. Then come back and reread the text with fresh eyes. Fix anything that doesn't make sense.

Assignment: Present a Short Story SL.8.6

For this assignment, each member of a small group will read their short story aloud. Reading a story aloud to others is much different than reading it aloud to yourself or reading it silently. Think about your characters and their feelings. Think about the exciting, sad, or tense moments in your story. Use these details to help you present the story to an audience in an engaging way.

Plan Your Presentation

Remember that you will read your short story aloud as a presentation. To prepare, print out your story, double spaced, in a font that is easy to read. Mark the pages to show where you should emphasize words, slow down, or increase your speaking volume. Read your script aloud at least once to yourself, and adjust your markings as needed.

Practice Your Presentation

Practice reading your story aloud several times to others, such as friends and family. As you practice, keep the following things in mind:

- Read loudly enough so that listeners can hear you.
- Speak clearly and enunciate your words.
- From time to time, look up from your story to make eye contact with members of your audience.

When you feel comfortable reading aloud, practice reading with proper fluency.

- Read at an appropriate pace. Do not read too fast or too slowly.
- Read with expression. Read any dialogue aloud as someone would actually speak it in real life. Emphasize certain words or phrases to show feeling or mood. Pause for commas or end marks. Read dialogue more loudly if it has an exclamation mark at the end.
- Read with intonation. Change the pitch or tone of your voice as you read so that you aren't reading in monotone, or in a way that is flat and expressionless.

Read the checklist below. Then practice presenting your story aloud to a partner. Your partner should complete the checklist for you and use it to give you feedback before you present your story to a group.

- [ ] Did the reader speak loudly enough for you to hear?

- [ ] Did the reader speak clearly?

- [ ] Did the reader periodically make eye contact?

- [ ] Did the reader read with proper pacing—not too fast or too slow?

- [ ] Did the reader use proper expression when reading dialogue?

- [ ] Did the reader emphasize words or phrases to show feeling or convey a mood?

- [ ] Did the reader change intonation throughout the story to avoid reading in monotone?

Feedback Frames

During your performance, you should …

The words or phrases you emphasized showed …

Your reading could be improved by …

Present Your Short Story

Present your short story to your group. Then listen carefully and attentively as your group members present their stories.

Reflect

Discuss the questions with a small group.

1. Do you feel that your story effectively shares your message about belonging? Why or why not?

2. How would you change or add to your story?

3. What messages did your group's stories share about belonging?

4. How were the stories alike or different?

Where Everyone Belongs 🎧 1.4

EXPLORER IN ACTION

Ingi Mehus
is a social
entrepreneur.

Who truly belongs in your home community? Who truly belongs in a community you visit while traveling? Ingi Mehus challenges people to think about the answers to these types of questions. She doesn't like the fact that many people think of travelers or tourists in a positive way but think of migrants in a negative way.

To help people around the world view migrants more positively, Mehus created Pocket Stories. This organization works to embrace diversity, connect people, and encourage storytelling. Pocket Stories holds workshops and creates videos. It's also working on travel guides that will feature diverse migrants. Through Pocket Stories, people are able to listen to and share stories about their own communities and places they'd like to visit. They can also learn to value their own migrant experiences and celebrate those of others.

Mehus says, "Listening to and recording hundreds of personal stories from around the world has helped me to better understand how we are ALL interconnected, not in spite of, but because of human migration. We all have profound stories to tell. You and your stories are not alone."

Ingi Mehus listens to a woman's story at an event for Pocket Stories. ▼

▶ **1.3** Watch the video to learn more.

1. How is Ingi Mehus helping people around the world to belong?
2. How can storytelling help us better understand other people?

How Will You Take Action?

Choose one or more of these actions to do.

Personal

Belong "with" yourself. Then invite others to belong with you.

1. Write a list of five things you really enjoy doing.
2. Commit to doing these activities regularly.
3. Find others who share your interests and invite them to do the activities with you.

School

Help other students belong at school. Create opportunities for new friendships.

1. Start a club to help students connect. Give it a welcoming name, such as "The Chitchat Club."
2. Make and post signs inviting other students to gather and share stories.
3. Hold your first club meeting and have fun!

Local

Welcome newcomers to your local community.

1. Create a "welcome card" for people who move to your community. Write welcoming messages and a few tips for what to see, eat, or visit in your community.
2. Post your card on public message boards at local gathering places.

Global

Explore "belonging" with new friends from around the world.

1. Find a student your age from another country. For example, search for pen pal opportunities or online spaces for international students.
2. Write to your new pen pal or online community. Ask and answer questions about what belonging means.

Reflect

1. Reflect on your Take Action project(s). What was successful? What do you wish you had done differently? Why?
2. Reread your response to the Essential Question **Why is it important to belong?** in Connect Across Texts. How did your Take Action project(s) change or add to your response?
3. What will you do differently in your life because of what you learned in this unit?

2 Creativity

Do you agree with the quote? Why or why not?

Look at the photo and caption. Discuss the questions.

1. How do you think the artist created this ice sculpture?
2. What other subjects would make good ice sculptures?

◄ An ice sculptor completes his sculpture of two stags for an exhibition in Edinburgh, Scotland, UK.

59

ESSENTIAL QUESTION

What is creative thinking?

Explore the Essential Question

Think Write your ideas about the Essential Question in the Unit Concept Map.

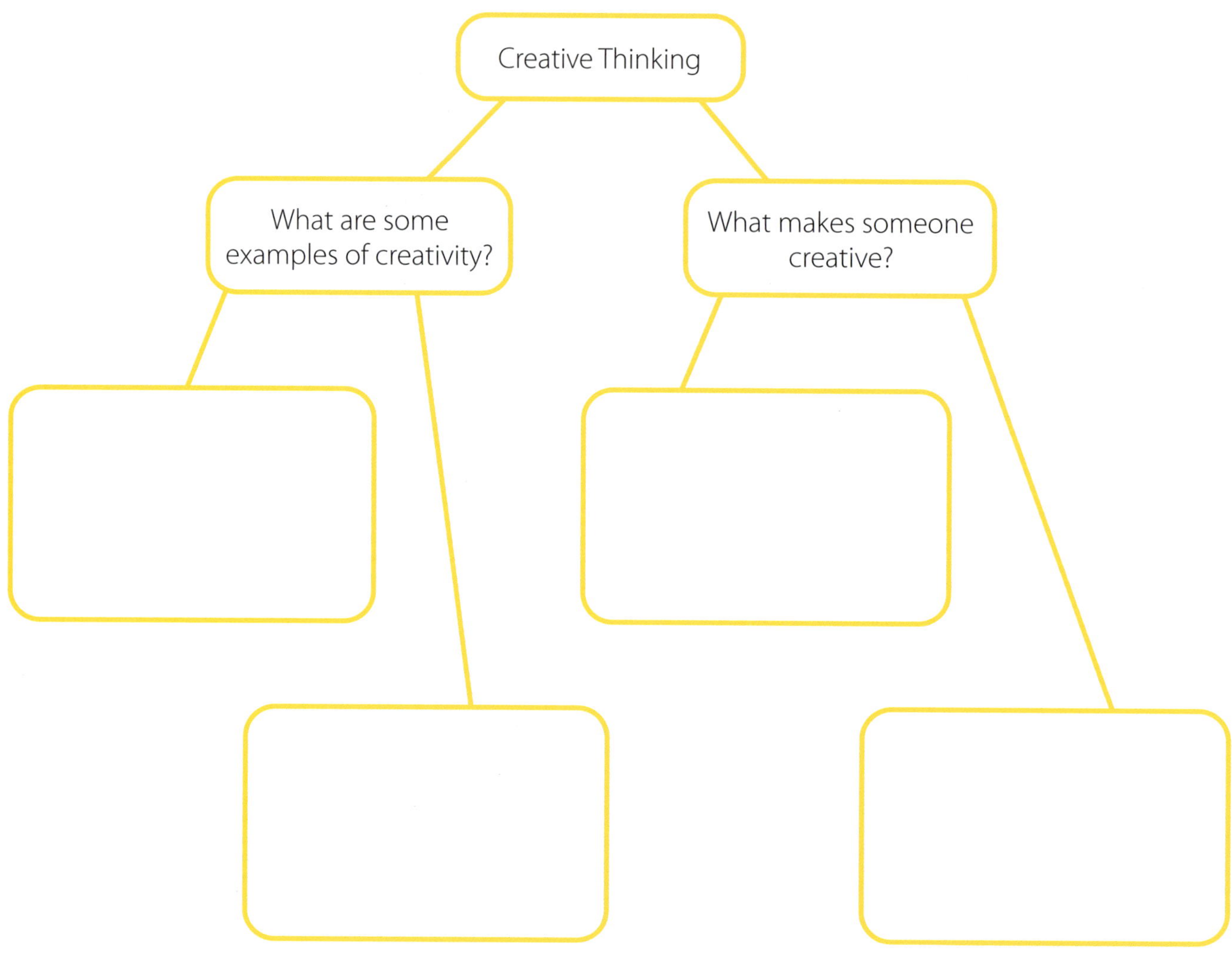

Respond Write one or two sentences to respond to the Essential Question.

____

____

____

Discuss Your Ideas Use your Unit Concept Map and your response to share your ideas with the class.

Academic Vocabulary

Use these words to express your ideas throughout the unit.

PRACTICE 1 Use context to determine the meaning of each word in blue. Then match the word to its definition.

Because artists make original and imaginative pieces of art, most people agree that artists are **creative**. Although art often demonstrates creativity **visually**, researchers say creativity does not have to be seen. They have found that people often **encounter** opportunities to be creative in other ways, such as by unexpectedly solving problems. Also, many people are more creative when they work with a **colleague**, rather than alone. Exceptionally creative people may **channel** their creativity into more than one **domain** and combine fields of expertise to solve problems in original and imaginative ways.

Word	Definition
encounter	to meet or experience unexpectedly
	having imaginative or original ideas
	to direct towards
	in a way that relates to seeing or sight
	an area or field of knowledge
	a co-worker or collaborator

PRACTICE 2 Work with a partner. Take turns being the reader and the listener.

Reader: Choose a vocabulary word from the chart. Read aloud its definition.

Listener: Listen to your partner read a definition. Say the vocabulary word.

Example

Reader: This word means "in a way that relates to seeing or sight."
Listener: Is it "visually"?
Reader: Yes!

Academic Vocabulary

channel (v.)
colleague (n.)
creative (adj.)
domain (n.)
encounter (v.)
visually (adv.)

What motivates us to be creative?

First Thoughts

What types of poetry do you know? How well do you know them?
Add one or more check marks (✓) in each row of the chart. In a small group,
discuss what you know about each type of poetry.

Type of Poetry	I've written it.	I've read it.	I've heard of it.	No clue!
sonnet				
haiku				
limerick				
acrostic				
free verse				

Key Vocabulary

PRACTICE Use context to determine the meaning of each word in bold.
Then match the word to its definition.

1. The bookmark was **crafted** by braiding paper and painting it.
2. I **lament** my decision to change schools. I miss my friends from my old school.
3. She is an author. She has written several well-known **rhetorical** works.
4. My bike gained **momentum** as it went downhill. It got faster and faster.
5. The builders **constructed** the house out of wood and bricks.
6. After I write an essay, I **revise** it to make it better.

_____ **1.** crafted   **a.** to build (v.)

_____ **2.** lament   **b.** related to speaking or writing (adj.)

_____ **3.** rhetorical   **c.** to feel or express sadness or regret (v.)

_____ **4.** momentum   **d.** speed of movement (n.)

_____ **5.** construct   **e.** made or created (v.)

_____ **6.** revise   **f.** to correct or improve (v.)

Reading Skill: Allusion and Analogy   RL.8.4; RI.8.4

Allusions and **analogies** are literary devices.

An **allusion** briefly hints at something outside the text. It draws on knowledge that many people are likely to share. Allusions often come from literature, history, or popular culture. For example, a person who behaves in extremely contradictory ways might be called a "Jekyll and Hyde." This is an allusion to a character in the novel *The Strange Case of Dr. Jekyll and Mr. Hyde*, a respectable doctor during the day who behaves like a monster at night.

An **analogy** uses a comparison to explain something complex or unfamiliar. For example, in the expression "Life is like a box of chocolates. You never know what you're going to get," life is compared to a box of chocolates. In a box of chocolates, you often don't know what flavor you'll get until you bite into a chocolate. Therefore, this analogy means that life, just like a box of chocolates, can be unpredictable.

Skill in Action

Study the models below. Consider how the allusion or analogy in each model helps you understand the author's message.

In this analogy, the author compares a pen to a flashlight and a metal detector.

Model 1

In a poem, the pen is more like a flashlight or one of those metal detectors that people walk around beaches with. You're trying to discover something that you don't know exists, maybe something of value.

These details help me understand how a pen and a flashlight or metal detector are similar and how a writer uses a pen to discover something unknown.

This paragraph is about someone trying to figure out the answer to a problem.

Model 2

I tried all evening to solve a difficult problem. I fell asleep still thinking about it. When I woke up, the answer plopped into my head like Newton's apple falling from the sky.

This sentence alludes to the scientist Isaac Newton, who said he grasped the idea of gravity when he saw an apple fall.

from
A Poet's Lament

by **Jum'a bin 'Adil al-Rumaythí** (translated into English)

A camel herder sleeps under the stars in the Rub' al Khali—the Empty Quarter—a part of the Arabian Desert.

1 My soul **laments** in great sadness and I grieve,
Thus a poet's weighty words I shall weave.
My heart has been crushed by a storm of yearning,
Or by a surge[1] of the river Nile's churning.[2]
5 I offer this verse to others as I please,
This **crafted** portrayal[3] of my vast unease.
With this poem my longing comes out of its haze,
My misery deepens, my heart is ablaze.
Sleep has gone missing as my eyes remain wide.
10 Just look at the torrent[4] of tears I have cried.

---

[1] **surge** sudden increase
[2] **churning** intense movement
[3] **portrayal** picture
[4] **torrent** flood

Nabati Poetry

This poem is an example of Nabati poetry, the traditional spoken poetry of the Arabian Gulf and Peninsula. Also called "the people's poetry," it has a simple, direct style and reflects daily life. The poet who wrote "A Poet's Lament," Jum'a bin 'Adil al-Rumaythí, was a pearl diver and fish seller.

BILLY COLLINS:
THE ART OF POETRY

***Interview by* George Plimpton**

🎧 **2.2**

1 INTERVIEWER
    Could you go through the genesis[1] of a poem?
COLLINS
    I think what gets a poem going is an initiating
5 line. Sometimes a first line will occur, and it goes
nowhere; but other times—and this, I think,
is a sense you develop—I can tell that the line
wants to continue. If it does, I can feel a sense
of **momentum**—the poem finds a reason for
10 continuing. The first line is the DNA of the poem;
the rest of the poem is **constructed** out of that
first line. […] The first few lines keep giving birth
to more and more lines. Like most poets, I don't
know where I'm going. The pen is an instrument of
15 discovery rather than just a recording implement.
If you write a letter of resignation or something
with an agenda, you're simply using a pen to record
what you have thought out. In a poem, the pen
is more like a flashlight, a Geiger counter,[2] or one
20 of those metal detectors that people walk around
beaches with. You're trying to discover something
that you don't know exists, maybe something of
value.

---

[1] **genesis** origin
[2] **Geiger counter** device that measures ionizing radiation

INTERVIEWER

25   What inspires the first line of a poem? Is it something you see? Is
it a passing thought?

COLLINS

I try to start the poem conversationally. Poems, for me, begin
as a social engagement. I want to establish a kind of sociability or
30   even hospitality at the beginning of a poem. The title and the first
few lines are a kind of welcome mat[3] where I am inviting the reader
inside. What I do with the reader later can be more complicated, but
the beginning of the poem is a seductive technique for me, a way of
making a basic engagement. Then I hope the poem gets a little bit
35   ahead of me and the reader.

INTERVIEWER

How do you **revise** your poetry?

COLLINS

I try to write very fast. I don't revise very much. I write the poem in
40   one sitting. Just let it rip.[4] It's usually over in twenty to forty minutes.
I'll go back and tinker with a word or two, change a line for some
metrical reason weeks later, but I try to get the whole thing just done.
Most of these poems have a kind of **rhetorical** momentum. If the
whole thing doesn't come out at once, it doesn't come out at all. I just
45   pitch it.[5]

People say, "Don't throw anything away." This is standard advice:
Always save everything. You could use it in another poem. I don't believe
that. I say, Get rid of it. Because if it got into a later poem it would be
Scotch-taped on. It would not be part of the organic […] chi, the spine
50   that the poem has, the way it all should be one continuous movement.

Chi [is] the Chinese sense of energy that runs through things.
Poems that lack that seem very mechanically put together, like a
piece here and a part there. […] Revision can grind a good impulse to
dust. Of course, the distinction between revision and writing is kind
55   of arbitrary because when I am writing I am obviously revising. And
when I revise, I'm writing, aren't I? I love William Matthews's idea—
he says that revision is not cleaning up after the party; revision is the
party! That's the fun of it, making it right, getting the best words in the
best order.

---

[3] **welcome mat** small rug at the front door of a house, with the word "Welcome" on it
[4] **let it rip** do it quickly
[5] **pitch it** throw it away

A young girl writes in the mountains of Switzerland.

INTERVIEWER

60 What do you tell the people in your writing classes? Is there a principle that you start out with?

COLLINS

Ask yourself if what you are trying to say can be said in any
65 other form—story, memoir,[6] letter, phone call, email, magazine article, novel. If the answer is yes, stop writing poetry. Put it in an email, write a memoir, write a letter to your granny, use whatever form will accommodate what you're going to say. Stop writing poetry unless you're doing things that you can *only* do
70 in poetry. And that means exercising your imaginative freedom, because in a poem you have the greatest imaginative freedom possible in language. You have no allegiance to plot, consistency, plausibility, character development, chronology. You can fly. Clear the trees at the end of the runway, and off you
75 go. So if you're not taking advantage of the giddy imaginative liberty that poetry offers, you should try a form that's a little more restrictive.

---

[6] **memoir** biography or writing based on memories

**About the Poet:
Billy Collins (b. 1941)**

Billy Collins is an American poet widely appreciated for his witty, often humorous poems. He has published more than a dozen books of poetry and has served as America's poet laureate. He created Poetry 180, a high school course on poetry.

Close Read

Work with a partner.

1. Determine the meanings of your underlined words and phrases.

2. Discuss the question: **Why do people write poems?**

Understand and Analyze

Respond to the questions. Support your responses with evidence from the texts.

1. **Understand** Reread lines 1–4 of "A Poet's Lament." What types of feelings inspire the author to write poetry?

2. **Interpret** Reread lines 5–6 of the poem. What word does the author use as a synonym for "poem"?

3. **Understand** Reread the first question and answer in the interview. What does Collins mean when he says the first line of a poem is its DNA?

4. **Contrast** Reread lines 14–23 of the interview. In your own words, how does Collins explain the pen's role when used for different writing tasks?

5. **Interpret** Reread lines 46–50 of the interview. Why does Collins believe that saving parts of incomplete poems is a bad idea?

Apply the Skill: Allusion and Analogy

Use the chart to identify and analyze at least one analogy and one allusion from the interview and the poem.

One example I found is …	I found it in …	I think it means …
an analogy that compares the first line of a poem to DNA.	*the first paragraph of the interview.*	*the first line of a poem determines what the rest of the poem is going to be about.*

Share Your Perspective

Discuss these questions in a small group.

1. Collins lists forms of writing other than poetry—story, memoir, letter, email, magazine article, novel. Which forms do you enjoy most? Why?

2. How do you approach the process of writing something important? How do you get started, and what steps do you use?

Discussion Frames

I think that …

This is because …

One example is …

Why do you …?

Vocabulary: Overview of Word Parts L.8.4.B

Many English words are formed from Greek or Latin word parts. You can use the meanings of these word parts to figure out the meanings of unknown words. A **root** is the most basic part of the word. **Affixes** are word parts that are attached before or after roots. A **prefix** is an affix that is attached at the beginning of a word. A **suffix** is an affix that is attached at the end of a word. To figure out an unknown word's meaning:

1. Break the word into parts. Identify the root or roots and any affixes (a prefix, a suffix, or both).

2. If you know what one or more of the parts mean, you may be able to figure out the word's meaning.

3. If necessary, confirm the word's meaning by looking it up in a dictionary.

Example

Knowing the meanings of word parts can help you better understand the meanings of words such as "discover."

The root "cover" can mean "hide from view or knowledge; conceal."

The prefix "dis-" can mean "opposite of."

discover

The word must mean "to find" or "to reveal."

Apply the Strategy

Use a dictionary or other resource to identify each word's Greek or Latin root and affix. Write the root or affix and its meaning. Then write the meaning of the word.

Word	Prefix (if any) and its meaning	Root and its meaning	Suffix (if any) and its meaning	Word's meaning
1. movement		*mov, "to go"*	*-ment, "result of"*	*act of going or moving*
2. revise				
3. metrical				

Read Again

Read "A Poet's Lament" and "Billy Collins: The Art of Poetry" again. As you read, circle details from the texts that help you respond to this question:

Where do poets find inspiration?

Reflect and Respond

Use some of the details you circled to complete the idea web.

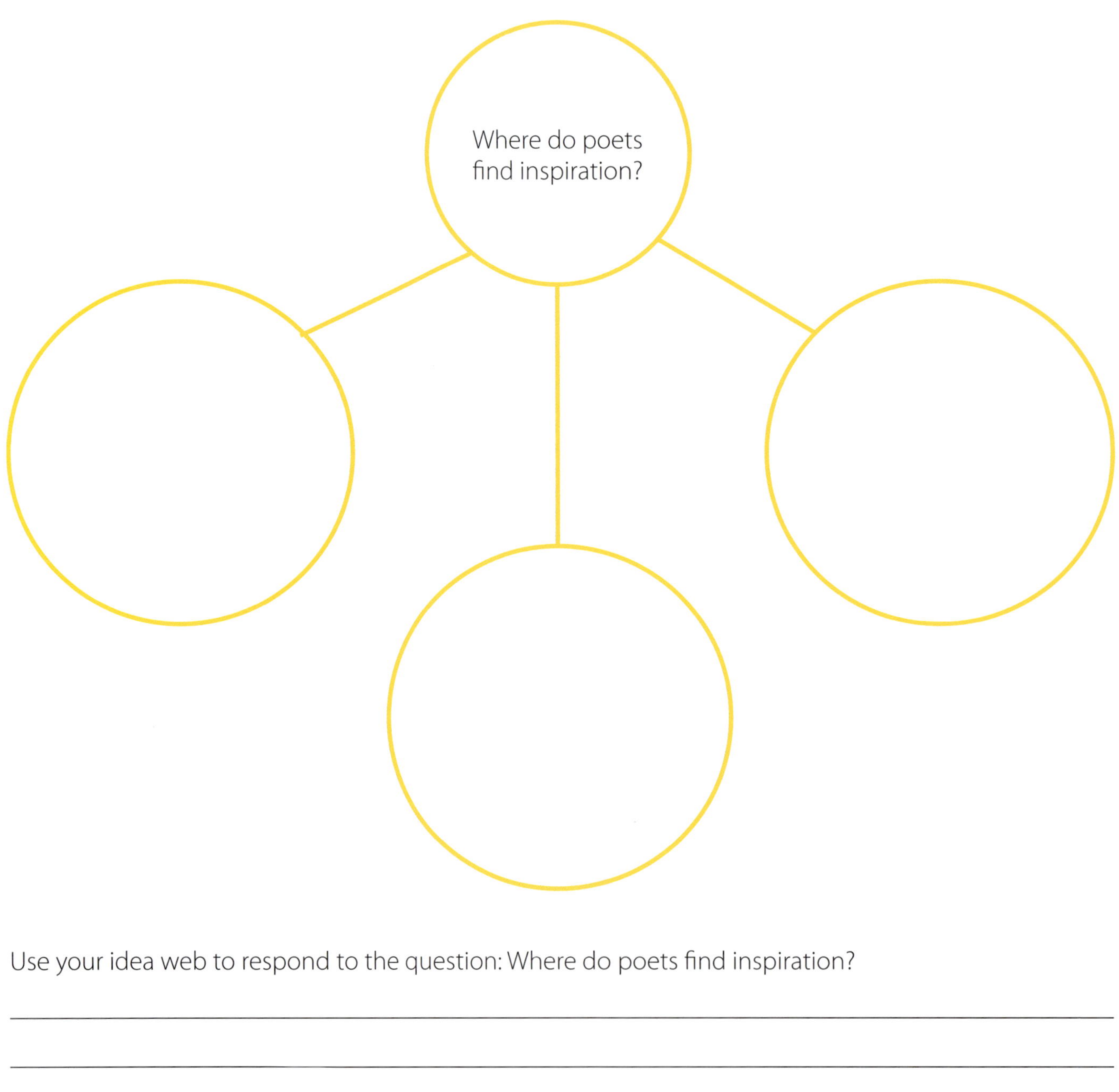

Use your idea web to respond to the question: Where do poets find inspiration?

____

____

____

Discuss Your Response

Share your ideas with the class. Write one new idea you hear.

____

____

____

Respond to the Guiding Question

Write a response to the question:

What motivates us to be creative?

Use evidence from the texts, your discussion, and your life. Use the
Discussion Frames to help you. Use the rubric to check your response.

____

____

____

____

____

Create and Present: Writing Poetry

Do one of these activities.

OPTION 1: Write a Free-Verse Poem

A free-verse poem does not have a traditional pattern of rhythm
or rhyme. Write a free-verse poem. Then read it to your class.

OPTION 2: Interview a Partner

Interview a partner about the process of writing poetry.

Here's an example of the first few lines of an interview:

INTERVIEWER: What do you do first when you start to write a poem?

POET: I have written only a few poems for school, so I had
         specific assignments. After I read an assignment,
         I looked at the example poem provided. Then
         I brainstormed ideas …

Practice your interview, and then perform it for the class.

What is the secret to becoming more creative?

Two students demonstrate their work at the International Science and Engineering Fair in California, USA.

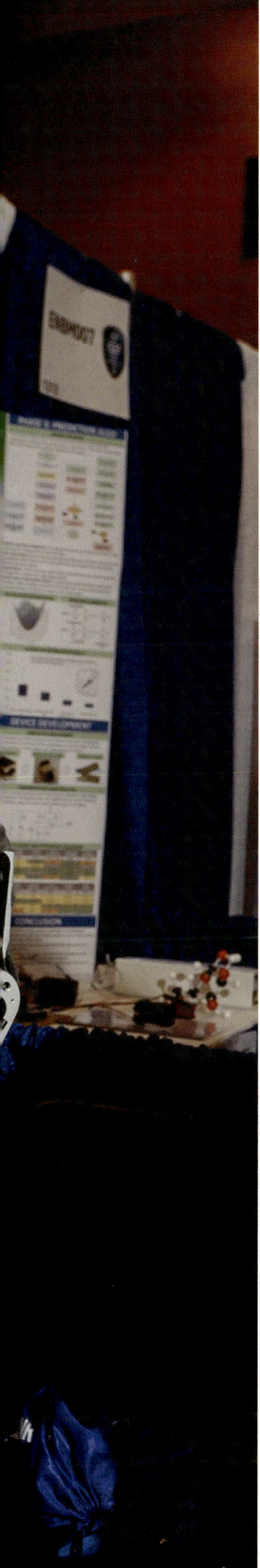

First Thoughts

Work with a partner. Imagine you have a cardboard box. First, decide on the size of your box. Then list different things you could do with it. Share your list with your classmates. Who has the longest list? Who has the most creative idea?

Viewing Skill: Interpret Facial Expressions

When you watch a video, pay close attention to people's facial expressions, which often provide clues about how they're feeling. Being aware of people's emotions can help you understand what the video is trying to express.

Apply the Skill

▶ 2.1 Watch the video "The Secret to Becoming More Creative." Pay attention to the facial expressions of the people in the photos below. Write the emotions you think each person is feeling.

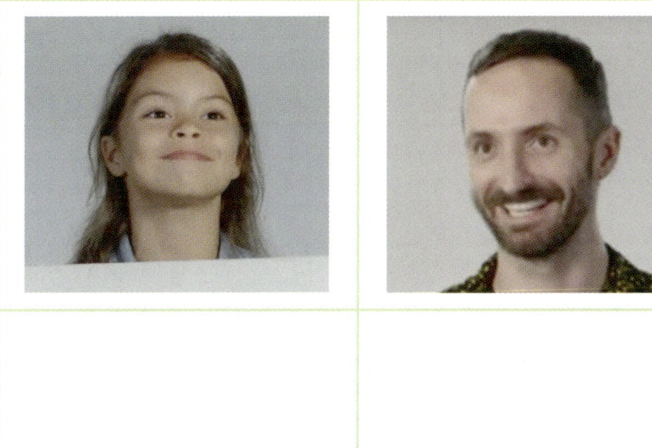

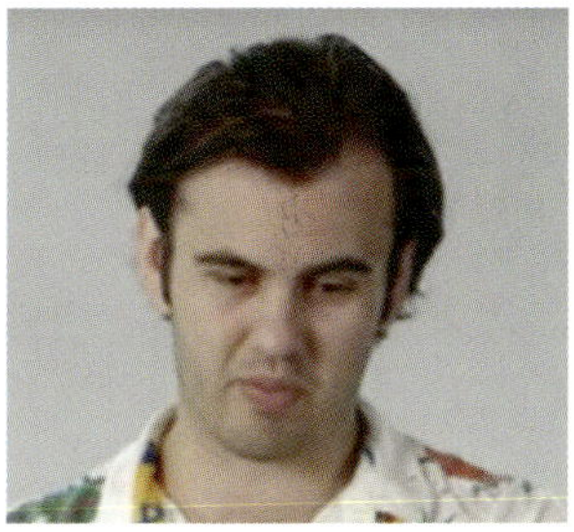

Understand and Analyze

▶ 2.1 Watch again. Answer the questions. Support your responses with evidence from the video.

1. **Compare** What were most people's beliefs about creativity in the 1960s? How were Joy Paul Guilford's beliefs different?
2. **Understand** What is "functional fixedness"?
3. **Explain** Why is the box, sand, and coins activity a good example of an "alternative uses" task?
4. **Infer** How do the adults feel after they do the activity? How do you know? Why do you think they feel this way?

Share Your Perspective

1. How can adults foster their own creativity?
2. When you were younger, did you use items in alternative ways? Do you still do so? Give examples.

Discussion Frames

In my opinion, …

The way I see it, …

Can you give an example of …?

What is the connection between curiosity and creativity?

First Thoughts

Leonardo da Vinci was an expert in many fields of study. His curiosity compelled him to try to learn all he could about everything. Consider these questions:

1. Do you think it is better to specialize in one area of interest or to pursue multiple interests?
2. How does a person's number of interests affect their success and productivity in each area?

Give reasons for your opinions. Discuss your ideas in a small group.

Discussion Frames

I believe that …

In my opinion, …

One reason is …

Do you feel that …?

Key Vocabulary

PRACTICE Use context to determine the meaning of each word in bold. Then match the word to its definition.

1. **Innovators** who work at technology companies bring new ideas to the world.
2. Lucia is a **genius**. She is a remarkable mathematician, painter, and tennis player.
3. He made a plan, but it was **unexecuted**. He never carried it out.
4. The school's course offerings **span** many fields, including math, science, and world history.
5. She likes to work with other artists to create **collaborative** artwork.
6. Most children ask hundreds of questions a day because they have a lot of **curiosity** about the world.

_____ **1.** innovator   **a.** a desire to know or learn something (n.)

_____ **2.** genius   **b.** a person who comes up with new ideas, methods, or devices (n.)

_____ **3.** unexecuted   **c.** involving the effort of two or more people working together (adj.)

_____ **4.** span   **d.** not performed or carried out (adj.)

_____ **5.** collaborative   **e.** to extend across (v.)

_____ **6.** curiosity   **f.** a person who is exceptionally smart or creative (n.)

Reading Skill: Summarize RI.8.2

A **summary** is a short description of the central idea of a text and the most important details supporting that idea. When you **summarize**, you use your own words. You don't include your own thoughts or opinions about the topic. Summarizing is a good way to ensure that you fully understand a text. To summarize:

1. Identify the topic by looking at the title, headings, and subheadings.

2. Read the first paragraph or two to determine the central idea. The central idea is often stated in the last sentence of the first paragraph.

3. As you read, look for places where the central idea is restated to connect it to supporting details. It may be repeated just before or soon after a new idea is introduced or near the end of a text. How does the central idea develop throughout the text?

4. After you read, summarize the central idea and supporting details of the text in one to two sentences. Do not include your opinion.

Skill in Action

Read "The Asch Conformity Experiments" in Unit 1. Discuss with a partner how the supporting details help develop the central idea and how the summary expresses the central idea.

Topic: Asch Conformity Experiments

Central Idea: Group behavior can influence an individual's behavior.

Supporting Detail	Connection to Central Idea
Most people think they wouldn't conform, but researchers found that many people did conform.	supports central idea that group behavior can influence an individual's behavior
People conformed even though there was no external pressure.	shows how powerful the urge to conform is by pointing out that there was no punishment or reward
Some people conformed because they were afraid of ridicule.	helps explain why people conformed

Summary:

In the Asch conformity experiments, people often changed their individual behavior to conform with group behavior, even though there was no real punishment or reward for conforming.

Learning from Leonardo

by **Walter Isaacson**

from **The Saturday Evening Post**

🎧 **2.3**

1   Leonardo da Vinci was a **genius**, one of the few people in history who unarguably deserved that description. Yet it is also true that he was human, not superhuman.

5   The most obvious evidence of this is the many projects he left unfinished, including a horse model, a large painting, flying machines, and brilliant essays. "Tell me if anything was ever done," he repeatedly wrote in notebook after notebook. "Tell

10   me. Tell me. Tell me if ever I did a thing. Tell me if anything was ever made."

Of course, the things he did finish—such as his most famous painting, the *Mona Lisa*—were enough to prove his genius. But we can also

15   appreciate the genius in his **unexecuted** designs and his unfinished masterpieces. By imagining flying machines and water projects, he envisioned what **innovators** would invent centuries later. And by refusing to produce works that he had not

20   perfected, he developed a reputation as a genius. He enjoyed the challenge of conception[1] more than the chore of completion.

What also distinguished Leonardo's genius was its universal nature. Some people are geniuses

25   in a particular arena, such as Mozart in music. But Leonardo's brilliance **spanned** multiple areas of

---

[1] **conception** the forming of a plan or an idea

A man carries a copy of Leonardo da Vinci's most famous painting, the *Mona Lisa*.

Leonardo da Vinci

thought. His **curiosity** drove him to try to know all there was to know about everything that could be known.

Leonardo didn't have the type of brilliance that is completely beyond us. Instead, he was self-taught. So even though we may never be able to match his talents, we can learn from him and try to be more like him.

1. Be curious. "I have no special talents," Einstein once wrote to a friend. "I am just passionately curious." Leonardo actually did have special talents, as did Einstein, but his most inspiring trait was his intense curiosity. He wanted to know what causes people to yawn, how people walk on ice, and what makes heart valves close. Being endlessly curious about everything around us is something that each of us can push ourselves to do, just as he did.

2. Seek knowledge for its own sake. Not all knowledge needs to be useful. Leonardo did not need to know how heart valves work to paint the *Mona Lisa*. By allowing himself to be driven by curiosity, he got to explore more of the world and see more connections than anyone else of his time.

3. Retain a childlike sense of wonder. At some point in life, most of us quit puzzling over everyday events. We might enjoy the beauty of a blue sky, but we no longer wonder why it is that color. Leonardo did. So did Einstein. We should be careful to never lose our sense of wonder.

4. Observe. Leonardo's greatest skill was his ability to observe things. When he walked around town, he observed how the facial expressions of people relate to their emotions, and he saw how light bounces off different surfaces. This, too, we can do. Water flowing into a bowl? Look, as he did, at exactly how it swirls. Then wonder why.

5. Start with the details. In his notebook, Leonardo shared a tip for observing something carefully: Do it in steps, starting with each detail. A page of a book, he noted, cannot be understood in one stare; you need to go word by word.

6. See things unseen. Leonardo's primary activity in his early years was creating performances and plays. He mixed theatrical creativity with fantasy. This helped him combine ideas to make new ones.

7. Go down rabbit holes. In eight pages of one notebook, he recorded 730 findings about the flow of water; in another notebook, he listed 67 words that describe different types of moving water. He measured every segment of the human body, calculated their proportional relationships, and then did the same for a horse. He explored ideas for the pure joy of it.

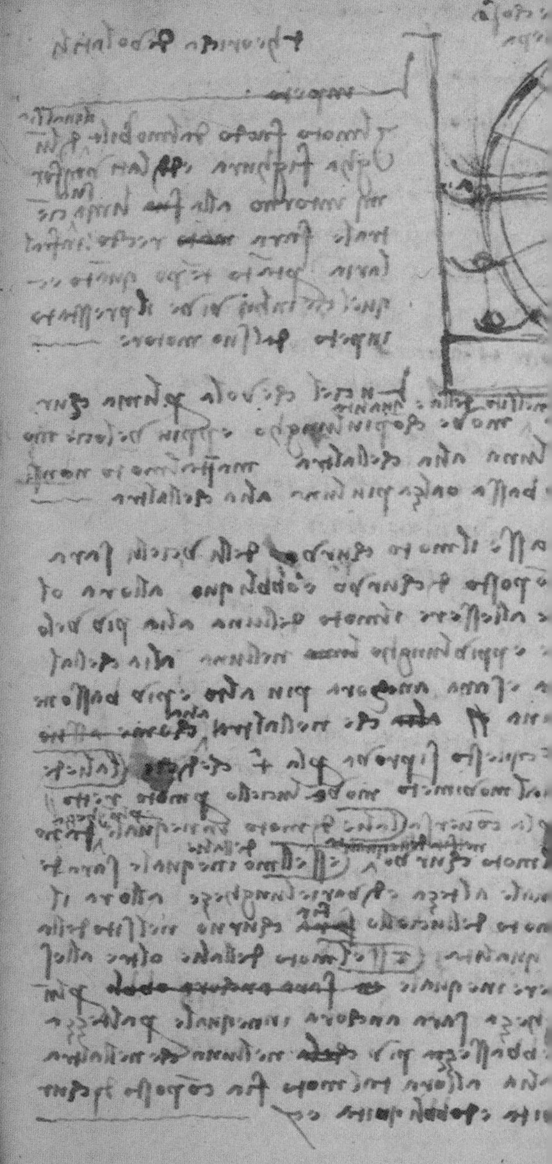

Leonardo da Vinci's *Codex on the Flight of Birds* was written around 1505 and captures his observations on the movements and behaviors of birds and his ideas of how people could use knowledge of birds to create a flying machine.

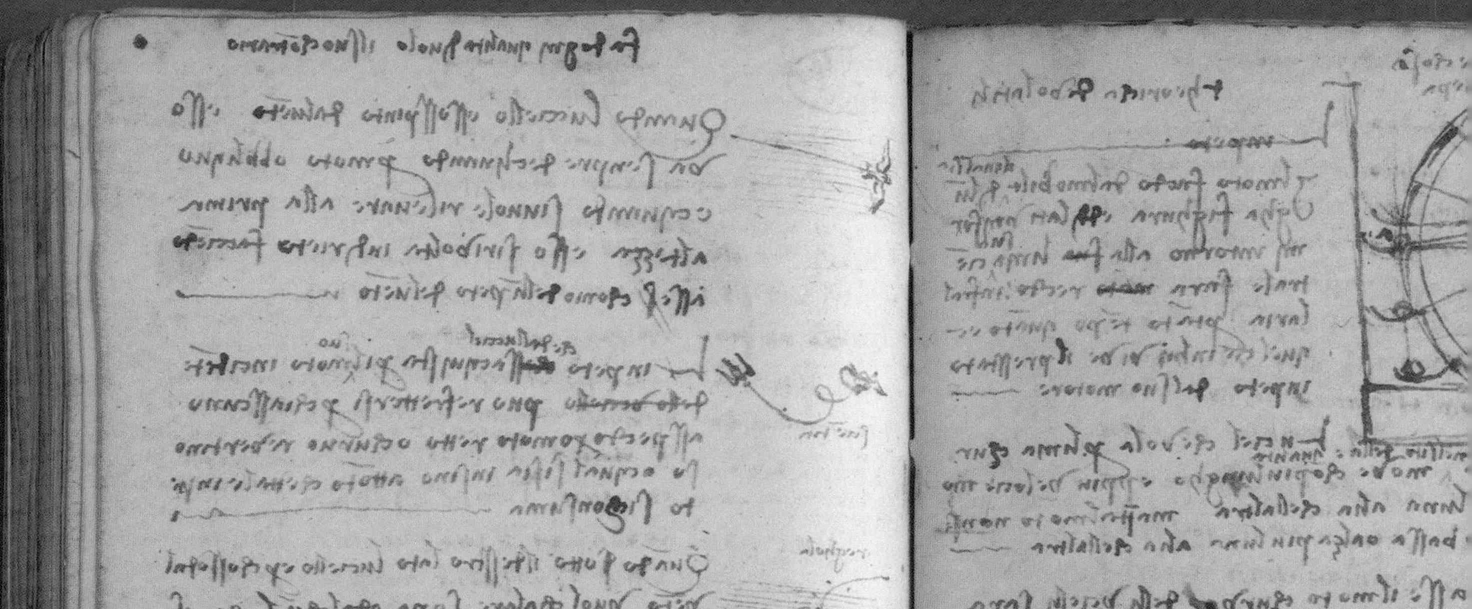

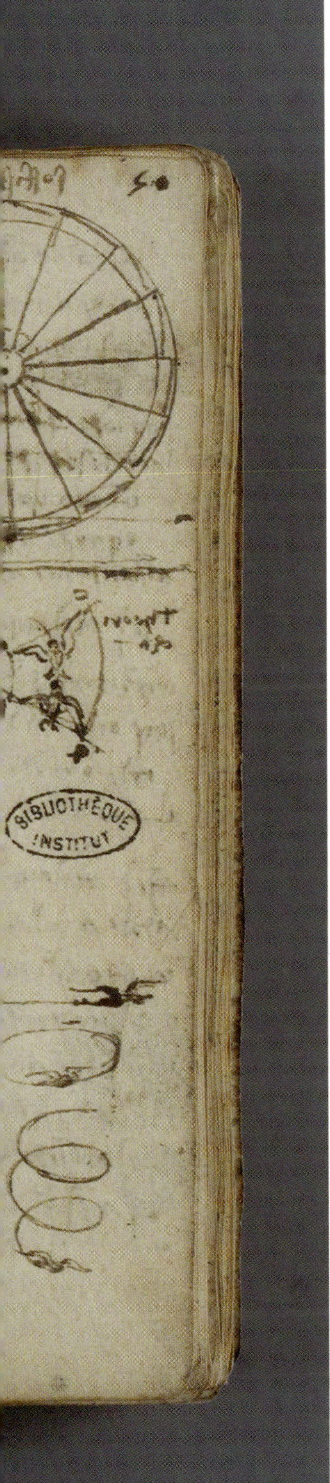

8. Get distracted. The greatest criticism of Leonardo was that his curiosity caused him to wander off on tangents[2]. But in fact, Leonardo's willingness to pursue whatever caught his interest made his mind richer and filled with more connections.

9. Respect facts. When Leonardo came up with an idea, he developed an experiment to test it. And when his experience showed that a theory was flawed, he abandoned his theory and looked for a new one. If we want to be more like Leonardo, we have to be fearless about changing our minds based on new information.

10. Procrastinate. While painting, Leonardo would sometimes stare at the work for an hour, finally make one small stroke, and then leave. "Men of lofty genius sometimes accomplish the most when they work least," he explained. Most of us procrastinate naturally. But procrastinating like Leonardo requires work: It involves gathering all the possible facts and ideas, and only after that synthesizing the information.

11. Let the perfect be the enemy of the good. When Leonardo could not make the perspective in a painting work perfectly, he abandoned it rather than producing a work that was just good enough. He carried around masterpieces such as the Mona Lisa to the end, knowing there would always be a new stroke he could add. There are times when it's best to not let go of something until it's perfect.

12. Think visually. Leonardo did not have the ability to formulate math equations. So he had to visualize them. Too often, when we learn a formula or a rule—even one so simple as the method for multiplying numbers or mixing a paint color—we no longer visualize how it works. As a result, we lose our appreciation for the underlying beauty of nature's laws.

13. Make connections. Leonardo's mind happily wandered across all of the arts, sciences, and humanities. His knowledge of how light strikes the eye helped inform the perspective in his paintings, and on a page of anatomical drawings of lips, he drew the smile that would reappear in the *Mona Lisa*. He knew that art was a science and that science was an art, and he blurred the distinction between the two.

---

[2] **tangents** different lines of thought

14. Attempt things that you can't achieve. Imagine, as he did, how you would build a human-powered flying machine or a perpetual-motion machine. There are some problems we will never solve. Learn why.

15. Use your imagination. His plan for an ideal city? The human-powered flying machine? Just as Leonardo blurred the lines between science and art, he did so between reality and fantasy. It may not have produced flying machines, but it allowed his imagination to soar.

16. Create for yourself, not just for others. No matter how many times the rich and powerful Marchesa Isabella d'Este asked him to, Leonardo would not paint her portrait. But he did begin a portrait of a silk-merchant's wife named Lisa. He did it because he wanted to, and he kept working on it for the rest of his life, never delivering it to the silk merchant.

17. Collaborate. We often think of geniuses as loners[3]. There is some truth to this, but it doesn't tell the whole story. Some paintings from Leonardo's studio were created in such a **collaborative** manner that it is hard to tell whose hand made which strokes. And his most fun work came from collaborations on theatrical productions. Genius starts with individual brilliance. But making it real often entails working with others.

18. Make lists. And be sure to put odd things on them. Leonardo's to-do lists may have been the greatest examples of pure curiosity the world has ever seen.

19. Take notes, on paper. Five hundred years later, Leonardo's notebooks continue to astonish and inspire us. Fifty years from now, our own notebooks may astonish and inspire our grandchildren.

20. Be open to mystery. One day Leonardo put "Describe the tongue of the woodpecker" on one of his to-do lists. The tongue of a woodpecker wraps around the inside of its head. When the bird smashes its beak into a tree, its tongue protects it. There is no reason you actually need to know any of this. It is information that has no real usefulness, just as it had none for Leonardo. But maybe you, like Leonardo, want to know. Just out of curiosity. Pure curiosity.

---

[3] **loners** people who like to be alone

A street artist dressed as
Leonardo da Vinci poses on the
Santa Trinita bridge in Florence, Italy.

Close Read

Work with a partner.

1. Determine the meanings of your underlined words and phrases.
2. Discuss the question: **What traits did Leonardo have that made him a genius?**

Understand and Analyze

Respond to the questions. Support your responses with evidence from the text.

1. **Give Examples** Reread paragraphs 2 and 3. Why does the author say, "He enjoyed the challenge of conception more than the chore of completion"? Give examples that explain what he means.
2. **Interpret** Reread lines 29–32. What is the author's purpose in writing the article?
3. **Explain** Reread lines 64–69. Explain what it means to "go down rabbit holes."
4. **Understand** Reread lines 80–86. Why was Leonardo's way of procrastinating actually positive?
5. **Compare** Reread the first three tips. How are they all similar?
6. **Infer** In the first paragraph, the author says, "Yet it is also true that he was human, not superhuman." Cite evidence from the article to explain why you think he says this.

Apply the Skill: Summarize

In the chart, note the central idea, supporting details, and the connection of each supporting detail to the central idea. Then, in one or two sentences, summarize the article.

Topic: Leonardo da Vinci	
Central Idea:	
Supporting Detail	**Connection to Central Idea**
Summary:	

Share Your Perspective

Discuss these questions in a small group.

1. Do you agree that curiosity is important for learning? Why or why not?
2. What are three things that you are curious about? Are they all in the same field of study, or are they in different fields?

Discussion Frames

I believe that curiosity …

The reason I think this is …

I am curious about …

Why do you agree/ disagree that …?

Language Convention: Understand Active and Passive Voice L.8.1.B

Writers use active or passive voice to create the focus of a sentence. In **active voice**, the focus is on the subject that performs an action. In **passive voice**, the focus is on an action that affects the subject. Most often, you should use active voice because it is more direct. Use passive voice when who or what performs the action is unknown or unimportant.

To form an **active voice** sentence, use this sentence structure:
    subject + verb + object

To form a **passive voice** sentence, use this sentence structure:
    subject + form of *be* + past participle

active voice	Leonardo **explored** ideas for the pure joy of it.
passive voice with **by** + noun	Ideas **were explored** by Leonardo for the pure joy of it.
passive voice (no performer mentioned)	Some paintings from Leonardo's studio **were created** collaboratively.

PRACTICE 1 Read each sentence. Check (✔) *Active* or *Passive* to show whether each sentence uses active voice or passive voice.

	Active	Passive
1. Leonardo developed an experiment.	✔	
2. Many of his projects were never completed.		
3. He abandoned his theory.		
4. The lines between art and science were blurred.		
5. His journal entries were written in Italian.		
6. Leonardo imagined flying machines.		

PRACTICE 2 Rewrite the sentences from PRACTICE 1. Change the active sentences to passive. Change the passive sentences to active.

Read Again

Read "Learning from Leonardo" again. As you read, circle details from the text that help you respond to this question:

How did Leonardo's curiosity contribute to his creativity?

Reflect and Respond

Choose three details you circled in the article to complete the idea web.

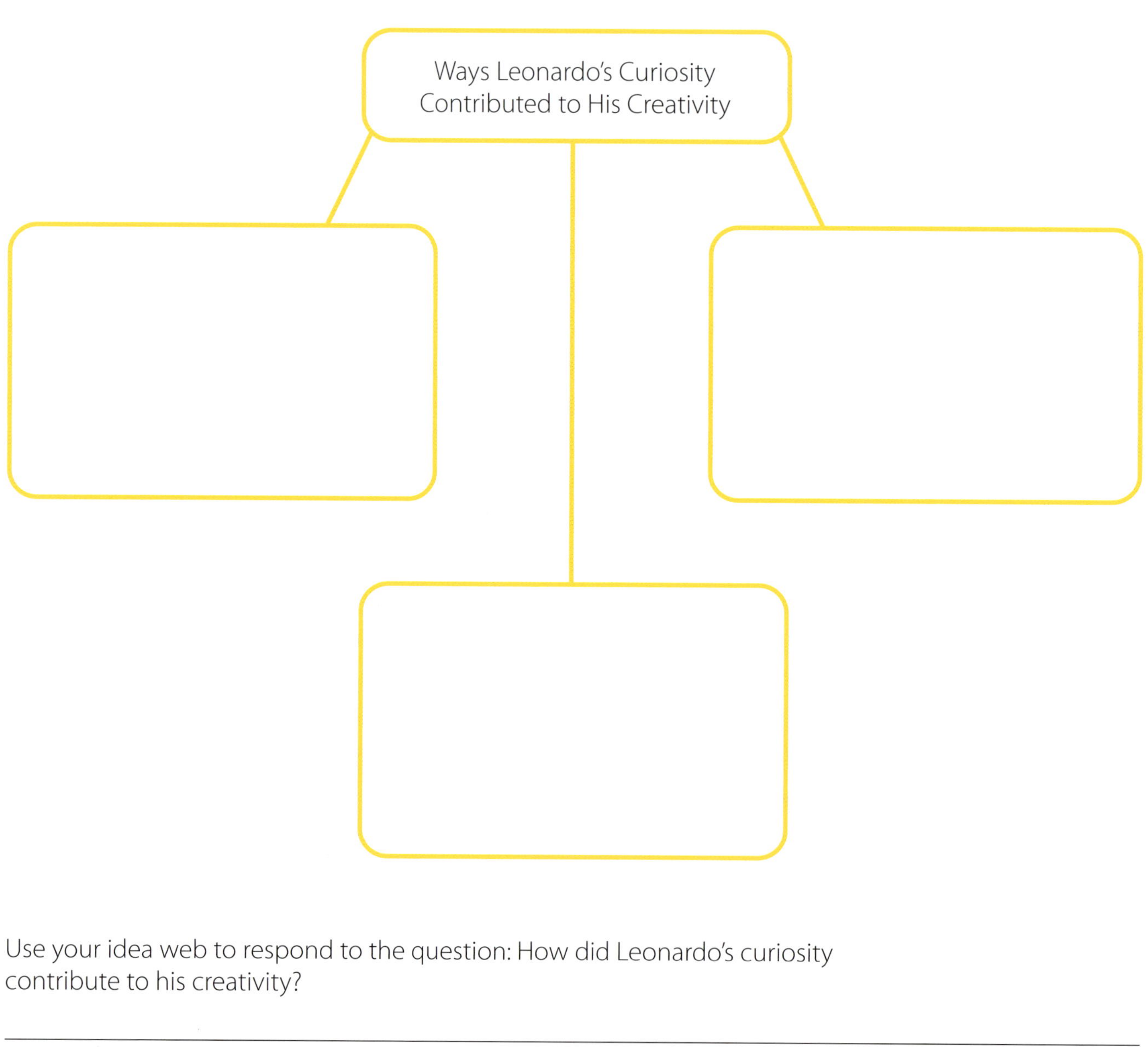

Use your idea web to respond to the question: How did Leonardo's curiosity contribute to his creativity?

____

____

____

Discuss Your Response

Share your ideas with the class. Write one new idea you hear.

____

____

____

Respond to the Guiding Question

Write a response to the question:

What is the connection between curiosity and creativity?

Use evidence from the text, your discussion, and your life. Use the Discussion Frames to help you. Use the rubric to check your response.

____

____

____

____

____

Research W.8.7

Choose one of these topics. Research the topic to learn more about it.

- Leonardo da Vinci's painting *Mona Lisa*

- Leonardo da Vinci's anatomical drawings

Follow these steps:

1. Make notes about what you already know about the topic.
2. Write three questions you have about the topic.
3. Research the topic to find answers to your questions.
4. Write your answers to the questions.
5. Present what you learn to a small group.

Leonardo da Vinci made incredibly detailed drawings of the human anatomy. ▶

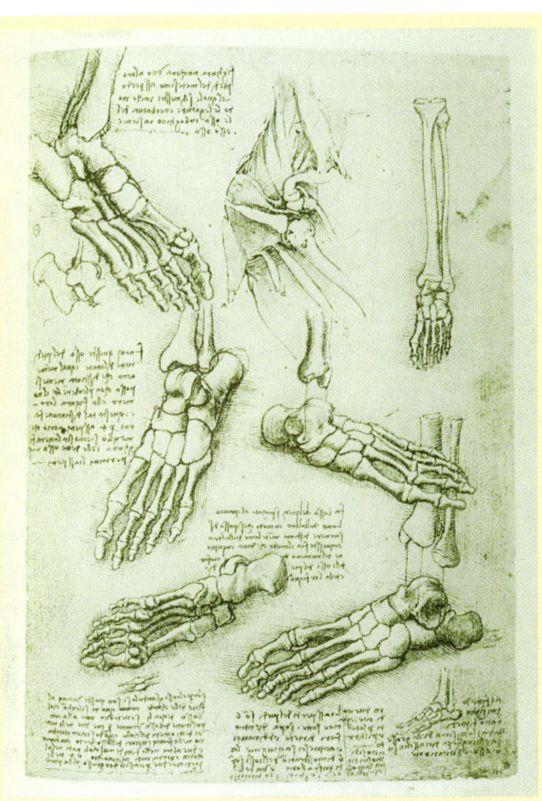

Flights of Imagination

Leonardo often found inspiration in nature. His observations of birds and bats helped refine his attempts to engineer a flying machine. His quest to fly occupied him for over two decades.

Horizontal pilot, ca 1488
Almost all body parts had a job. Hands and feet operated the wings; the pilot's headband controlled the tail.

When one leg is extended, it lowers one pair of wings; the hand crank raises the other.

Horizontal flier, ca 1487–1490
The pilot's position is a close imitation of birds in flight. Many of Leonardo's designs were focused on a central element for wing movement.

Aerial screw, ca 1489
He knew that when air is compressed, it grows more dense. He designed this for festival entertainment; the concept was later used in helicopters.

Landing system
Leonardo devised a system for the takeoff and landing of this flying bowl-shaped vessel that included retractable ladders and shock-absorbing feet.

Examine the Graphic

Use details from the graphic and the text to respond to the questions. Discuss your responses with a partner.

1. What is something the graphic makes you wonder?
2. What is something you find surprising?
3. For his machine to fly successfully, what is one change to the plans that Leonardo would have needed to make? What is one thing that could stay the same?

Make Connections

Use details from "Learning from Leonardo" and the graphic to discuss your responses with a partner.

1. How does the graphic demonstrate Leonardo's brilliance?
2. According to the article "Learning from Leonardo," Leonardo had many traits and behaviors that contributed to his genius. Which of these does the graphic reflect?

Reflect

Use ideas from the graphic and your discussions to answer this question: In Leonardo's time, no human had ever flown, so his imagined flying machines were completely innovative. If Leonardo were alive today, he wouldn't need to invent flying machines. What technologies or areas of life do you think he would focus on today?

Why is creativity so important for the success of a society?

First Thoughts

How much creativity does each job below require? Rate each job: 1 (does not require any creativity); 2 (requires some creativity); 3 (requires a lot of creativity). Then discuss your ratings with a partner.

Job	actor	teacher	scientist	artist	athlete	salesperson	engineer
Creativity Rating (1–3)							

Key Vocabulary

PRACTICE Use the context to determine the meaning of each word in bold. Then match the word to its definition.

During the nineteenth century, researchers were on a **quest** to learn about infectious diseases. This mission **broadened** our understanding of viruses and bacteria. For example, in France, chemist and microbiologist Louis Pasteur and his colleague Claude Bernard discovered a **novel** way to prevent bacteria growth in milk. This technique, still used today, is called *pasteurization*. Pasteurization involves heating something to kill the bacteria in it. Although bacteria is not **inherent** to milk, if it is present, it can grow to unsafe levels and cause illness. The concept of pasteurization came out of the scientists' **investigations**. This research helped us understand more about preventing illness. Pasteur's and Bernard's **mode** of thinking is characteristic of the way western medicine approached infectious diseases in the nineteenth century.

_____ **1.** quest   **a.** research study (n.)

_____ **2.** broaden   **b.** way; style (n.)

_____ **3.** novel   **c.** new (adj.)

_____ **4.** inherent   **d.** inborn; belonging by nature (adj.)

_____ **5.** investigation   **e.** to extend or expand (v.)

_____ **6.** mode   **f.** a mission; an expedition (n.)

Reading Strategy: Make Text-to-Text Connections

Making connections between a text you are reading and a text you have already read can help you gain a deeper understanding of the topic. To make **text-to-text connections**:

1. Identify the topic of the text. Think about other texts you have read with the same or a similar topic.

2. As you read, notice ideas that remind you of something else you have read. Underline the ideas, or make brief notes next to them.

3. After you read, look at your notes. Think about how the connection you identified deepens your understanding of the topic or raises new questions for you to explore. For example, you might explore how two texts state the same idea in different ways or offer different opinions. Or you might recall an example that illustrates a complex idea you are trying to understand.

Strategy in Action

Study the model from "How Creativity Powers Science." How do the ideas and details in the paragraph connect to those in the text "Learning from Leonardo"?

This reminds me of how Leonardo's curiosity and imagination led him to explore everything.

Imagining possibilities requires people to use what scientists who study how the brain works call "associative thinking." This is a process in which the mind is free to wander, making possible connections between unrelated ideas.

This reminds me of how Leonardo blurred the line between art and science and used those connections to come up with inventive solutions. This helps me understand what associative thinking is and how it works.

Farmers work at an
indoor vertical farm in
California, USA. Farms
like this one use up
to 99% less land and
90% less water than
traditional farms.

How Creativity
Powers Science

by **Jennifer Cutraro**

🎧 **2.4**

1   Ask most people to identify a creative person, and they'll probably name a famous painter, writer, or musician.

But what about a Nobel prize-winning chemist? Or a team of engineers that figures out how to make a car engine operate
5   more efficiently?

"Creativity, it turns out, is not only the domain of painters, singers, and playwrights," said Robert DeHaan, a retired cell biologist who studied creative thinking.

"Creativity is the creation of an idea or object that is both
10   **novel** and useful," he explained. "Creativity is a new idea that has value in solving a problem or an object that is new or useful."

That can mean composing a piece of music that's pleasing to the ear or painting a mural on a city street for pedestrians to admire. Or, DeHaan said, it can mean dreaming up a solution
15   to a challenge encountered in the lab.

"If you're doing an experiment on cells, and you want to find out why those cells keep dying, you have a problem," he said. "It really takes a level of creative thought to solve that problem."
20   Allowing students to come up with their own solutions to open-ended questions can foster[1] creativity in the classroom.

---

[1] **foster** nurture or grow

"In the best science **investigations**, it's not the questions
that are most creative but rather how the experiment is measured
and how the data are interpreted, given meaning, and how
students see the investigation as a component in understanding
a scientific problem," says Carmen Andrews, a science education
specialist.

Science as a Creative Quest

Indeed, scientists themselves describe science not as a set of
facts and vocabulary to memorize or a lab report with one "right"
answer but as an ongoing journey, a **quest** for knowledge about
the natural world.

"In science, you actually aren't concerned right off the bat
about getting the right answer—nobody knows what it is,"
explains chemist Dudley Herschbach, a longtime leader of the
board of trustees of Society for Science & the Public, publisher of
Science News for Students.

Herschbach pushed chemistry research forward—and won a
Nobel Prize—by applying a tool from physics to his work on what
happens when molecules collide during a chemical reaction. He
sees science as a creative adventure: "You're exploring a question
we don't have answers to," he says. "That's the challenge, the
adventure in it."

In the quest to make sense of the natural world, scientists
think of new ways to approach problems, figure out how to collect
meaningful data and explore what those data could mean, explains
Deborah Smith, an education professor.

In other words, they develop ideas that are both new and
useful—the very definition of creativity.

"The invention from the data of a possible explanation is
the height of what scientists do," she says. "The creativity is
about imagining possibility and figuring out which one of these
scenarios could be possible, and how would I find out?"

Unfocusing the Mind

Imagining possibilities requires people to use what scientists
who study how the brain works call "associative[2] thinking." This
is a process in which the mind is free to wander, making possible
connections between unrelated ideas.

---

[2] **associative** related or connected

Canadian-American astronomer Sara Seager has won numerous prizes for her work searching for and studying planets that could support life outside our solar system.

The process runs counter to what most people would expect
to do when tackling a challenge. Most would probably think the
best way to solve a problem would be to focus on it—to think
analytically—and then to keep reworking the problem.

In fact, the opposite approach is better, DeHaan argued. "The
best time to come to a solution to a complex, high-level problem
is to go for a hike in the woods or do something totally unrelated
and let your mind wander."

When scientists allow their minds to roam and reach beyond
their immediate research fields, they often stumble onto[3] their
most creative insights—that "aha" moment, when suddenly a new
idea or solution to a problem presents itself.

Herschbach, for example, made an important discovery in
chemistry shortly after he learned of a technique in physics called
molecular beams. This technique allows researchers to study the
motion of molecules in a vacuum, an environment free of the gas
molecules that make up air.

Physicists had been using the technique for decades, but
Herschbach, a chemist, hadn't heard of it before—nor had he been
told what couldn't be done with crossed molecular beams. He
reasoned that by crossing two beams of different molecules, he
might learn more about how quickly reactions occur as molecules
collide with one another.

Initially, Herschbach says, "People thought it would not be
feasible. It was called the lunatic fringe[4] of chemistry, which I
just loved." He ignored his critics and set out to see what would
happen if he crossed a beam of molecules such as chlorine with a
beam of hydrogen atoms.

He spent several years collecting his data, which in the end
uncovered new insights into the ways colliding molecules behave.
It was an important enough advance in chemistry that in 1986
Herschbach and two colleagues were awarded science's top honor:
the Nobel Prize.

In hindsight, he says, "It seemed so simple and obvious. I don't
think it took a lot of insight as much as naïveté.[5]"

---

[3] **stumble onto** accidentally come across
[4] **lunatic fringe** group with extreme or crazy views
[5] **naïveté** lack of experience

Fresh Perspectives, New Insights

Herschbach makes an important point. Naïveté—a lack of
experience, knowledge, or training—can actually be a boon[6] to
finding creative insights, DeHaan said. When you're new to a
scientific field, he explained, you're less likely to have learned what
other people claim is impossible. So you come to the field fresh,
without any expectations, sometimes called preconceptions.

"Preconceptions are the bane of creativity," DeHaan explained.
"They cause you to immediately jump to a solution, because you're
in a **mode** of thinking where you'll only see those associations
that are obvious."

"Preconceived notions or a linear approach to solving
problems just puts you in this tight little box," added Susan Singer,
a professor of natural sciences. Often, she says, "It's in allowing
the mind to wander when you find the answer."

The good news: "Everyone has the aptitude for creative
thinking," said DeHaan. You just need to **broaden** your thinking
in ways that allow your mind to connect ideas that you might not
have thought were related. "A creative insight is just allowing your
memory to pick up on ideas you never thought about before as
being in the same context."

Creativity in the Classroom

In the classroom, broadening your thinking can mean
emphasizing something called problem-based learning. In this
approach, a teacher presents a problem or question with no clear
or obvious solution. Students are then asked to think broadly
about how to solve it.

Problem-based learning can help students think like scientists,
according to science teacher Bill Wallace.

"Creativity means taking risks and not being afraid to make
mistakes," adds Andrews. In fact, she and many educators agree,
when something comes out differently than expected, it provides a
learning experience. A good scientist would ask "Why?" she says,
and "What's happening here?"

Talking with others and teamwork also help with associative
thinking—allowing thoughts to wander and freely associating

---

[6] **boon** helpful thing

one thing with another—that DeHaan says contributes to
creativity. Working on a team, he says, introduces a concept
called distributed reasoning. Sometimes called brainstorming,[7]
this type of reasoning is spread out and conducted by a group
of people.

   "It's been known or thought for a long time that teams
generally are more creative than individuals," DeHaan
explained. While researchers who study creativity don't yet

---

[7] **brainstorming** coming up with new ideas to solve a problem

As a high schooler, Sierra Seabrease turned an unwanted piano into a digital jukebox for an after-school project. Her project was selected for the White House Science Fair.

know how to explain this, DeHaan said it could be that by hearing different ideas from different people, members of a team begin to see new connections between concepts that didn't initially seem related.

Asking questions such as, "Is there some way to pose the problem other than the way it was presented?" and "What are the parts of this problem?" also can help students stay in this brainstorming mode, he says.

Smith cautions against confusing artistic or visual representations of science with scientific creativity.

"When you talk about creativity in science, it's not about, have you done a nice drawing to explain something," she says. "It's about, 'What are we imagining together? What's possible, and how could we figure that out?' That's what scientists do all the time."

Although using arts and crafts to represent ideas can be helpful, Smith says, it is not the same as recognizing the creativity **inherent** in science. "What we've been missing is that science itself is creative," she explains.

"It's a creativity of ideas and representations and finding things out, which is different from making a papier-mâché globe and painting it to represent the Earth," she says.

In the end, educators and scientists agree that anyone can learn how to think like a scientist. "Too often in school, students get the impression that science is for a specially gifted subspecies of humanity," Herschbach says. But he insists just the opposite is true.

"Scientists don't have to be so smart," he continues. "It's all there waiting for you if you work hard at it, and then you have a good chance of contributing to this great adventure of our species and understanding more about the world we live in."

Close Read

Work with a partner.

1. Determine the meanings of your underlined words and phrases.
2. Discuss the question: **What is the connection between creativity and science?**

Understand and Analyze

Respond to the questions. Support your responses with evidence from the text.

1. **Give Examples** Reread lines 9–15. DeHaan says creativity has products that are both useful and new. Give an example from science that demonstrates what he means.

2. **Understand** Reread lines 29–37. According to Herschbach, why isn't science concerned with getting the right answer quickly?

3. **Explain** Explain the concept of "unfocusing the mind." According to the author, why is this an effective way to solve problems?

4. **Compare** How are the jobs of artists and scientists similar? Give examples to demonstrate your meaning.

5. **Interpret** Why does Herschbach say scientists don't have to be so smart?

Apply the Strategy: Make Text-to-Text Connections

In the chart, note connections you made between "How Creativity Powers Science" and "Learning from Leonardo" or another text you have read.

How Creativity Powers Science	Learning from Leonardo	Connection
Herschbach says exploring a question you don't have answers to is the challenge and adventure.	*Leonardo and Einstein never stopped wondering about everyday things.*	*Brilliant people have fun exploring the world around them.*

Vocabulary: Recognize and Use Greek and Latin Roots **L.8.4.B**

As you learned earlier in this unit, some words are made up of word parts: roots, prefixes, and suffixes.

Learning the meanings of common Greek and Latin roots can help you figure out the meanings of new words. Here are some common roots:

Root	Meaning
crea	make, cause
gen	give birth, create
nov	new

Root	Meaning
quest	seek, inquiry
astro	star
ven	come

You can use a dictionary to confirm a guess about a word's meaning.

Example

I recognize this root from words such as "spectacle" and "inspect," both of which relate to seeing.

The dictionary says the word means "a way of looking at something" or "a point of view."

Apply the Strategy

Complete the chart, matching each word in the box with its root.

venture, asterisk, conquest, novice, generate, creative, engineer, request, avenue, astronomy, innovate, creation, genius, novel, create, question, astronaut, adventure

Then say how the words relate to the root.

Root	Words with This Root			How the Words Relate to the Root
crea	*creative*	*creation*	*create*	*The words all have to do with making something.*
gen				
nov				
quest				
astro				
ven				

Read Again

Read "How Creativity Powers Science" again. As you read, circle details from the text that help you respond to this question: **In what ways does creativity power science?**

Reflect and Respond

Use some of the details you circled to complete the idea web.

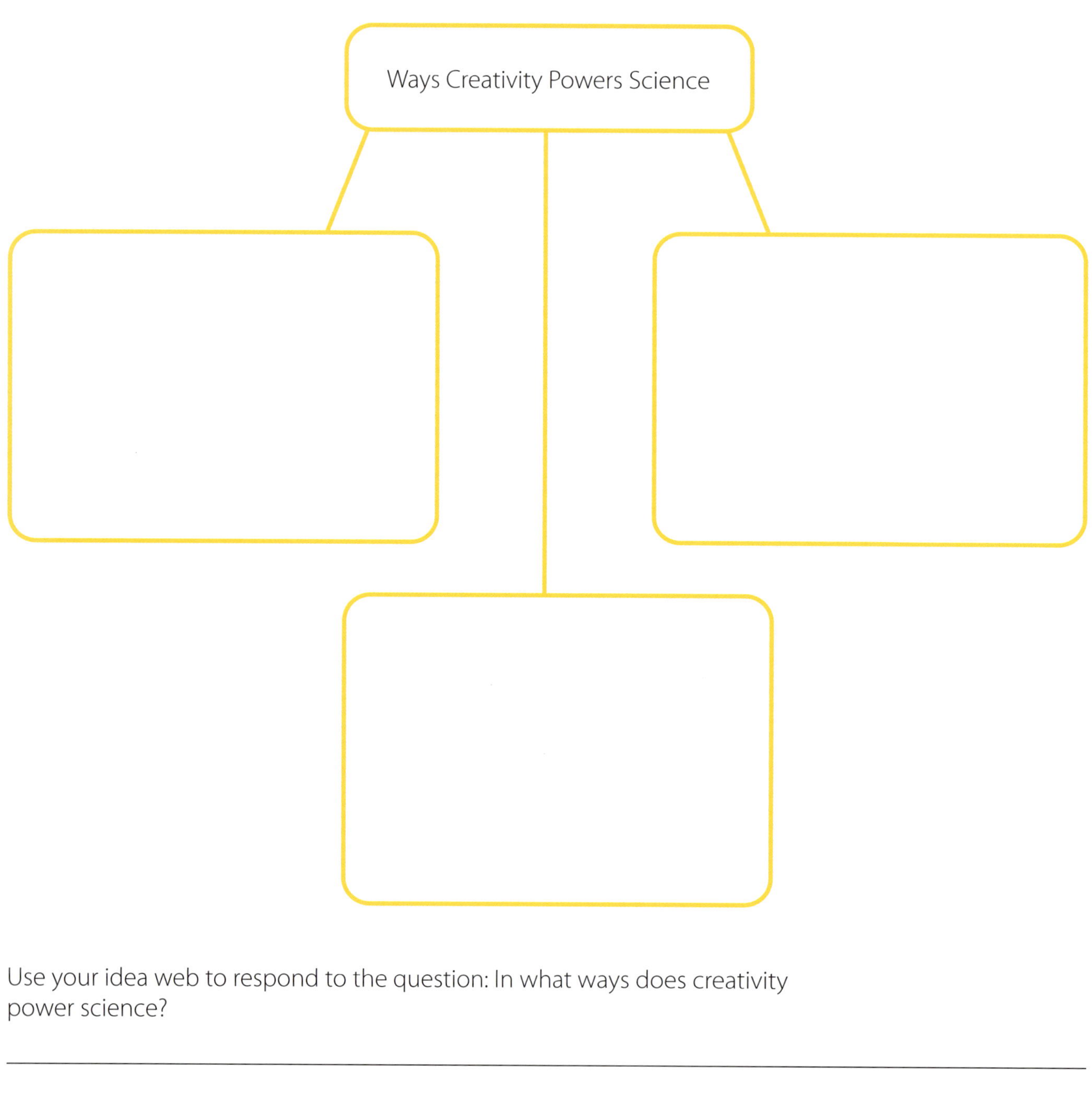

Use your idea web to respond to the question: In what ways does creativity power science?

____

____

____

Discuss Your Response

Share your ideas with the class. Write one new idea you hear.

____

____

____

Respond to the Guiding Question

Write a response to the question:

Why is creativity so important for the success of a society?

Use evidence from the text, your discussion, and your life. Use the Discussion Frames to help you. Use the rubric to check your response.

____

____

____

CONNECT ACROSS TEXTS

Discuss the Essential Question: What is creative thinking?

Look at your answer to the Essential Question in the Unit Launch and your notes about creativity in the Reflect and Respond sections. Discuss: How have your ideas about the Essential Question changed? What changed your ideas?

Then write one new idea you heard in the discussion. How did it affect your opinion?

____

____

Respond to the Essential Question

Write your new response to the Essential Question. Include Academic Vocabulary.

____

____

Assignment: Write an Informational Report W.8.2

An informational report summarizes key information about a topic. It is often based on research, an interview, or a survey. For this assignment, you will write an informational report about a creative person of your choice.

Your report should include:

- an introductory paragraph that introduces the creative person you chose and explains why you chose that person
- three body paragraphs that each explore a different important idea about the person's life or work (Each paragraph should have a topic sentence and supporting details, such as examples, facts, or quotations.)
- a concluding paragraph that summarizes how this person's creative thinking has contributed to the world

Explore the Model

Read the informational report about Steve Jobs. Underline the sentence that explains why the writer chose Steve Jobs and the sentences that summarize how Steve Jobs's creativity has contributed to the world. Circle the three important ideas.

Steve Jobs stands with one of his early computers.

Steve Jobs

Steve Jobs was an inventor, designer, investor, and businessperson. He was from California, USA, and lived from 1955 to 2011. I chose Steve Jobs because he is one of the great creative thinkers in recent times, and his creativity has had a significant impact on the world.

Steve Jobs was highly intelligent and innovative his whole life. As a child, he and his father would take apart electronics in order to reconstruct them in their garage. In school, he was very advanced, so his teachers wanted him to move into a class with older children, but his parents declined. As a result, he was bored in school and was often a troublemaker. After graduating from high school, Jobs went to college but was not focused and ended up dropping out.

One of Steve Jobs's greatest creative accomplishments was his work on developing and marketing a personal computer with colleague, Steve Wozniak. Together, the pair founded a computer company. While Steve Wozniak had more technical expertise and was the designer of their popular personal computer, Jobs had an entrepreneurial sense that helped bring the computers into people's everyday lives. He had a strong sense of style and would demand redesigns until the items they sold were the perfect combination of useful, simple, and stylish. His marketing style was the same—creating public campaigns to release new items in ways that caught the attention of the general population.

In 2001, Steve Jobs began reinventing the company, which brought about a shift in products and ultimately influenced the way people used technology worldwide. Under his leadership, the company rolled out several new devices that quickly became part of people's everyday lives. In 2007, the company released its first smartphone, which gained worldwide popularity due to its stylish and intuitive design.

In conclusion, Steve Jobs was an important creative person in modern history. His talents spanned a range of fields, including technology, design, marketing, and business leadership. He made an impact on the world because the products created and marketed under his leadership changed the way people use technology in their everyday lives.

Plan Your Report

Choose a creative person you find interesting. Research the person.
Complete the outline to plan your informational report.

OUTLINE

Introduction

Name of the creative person:

Why I chose this person:

Body

Important idea #1:

Details:

Important idea #2:

Details:

Important idea #3:

Details:

Conclusion

How this person's creative thinking has contributed to the world:

Write and Revise

Write Use your outline to write a first draft of your informational report.

A good informational report uses a formal style. It also includes transition words and phrases to introduce or connect ideas. Transition words and phrases include these:

- To begin,
- One way …
- For example,
- Also,
- In addition,
- Finally,
- Therefore,
- In conclusion,

Revise Exchange reports with a partner. Use the checklist to review your partner's work and give feedback. Refer to your partner's feedback as you revise your draft.

- ☐ Does the report include an introductory paragraph that introduces the person and explains why the writer chose that person?

- ☐ Are there three important ideas, each presented in its own paragraph?

- ☐ Are the important ideas supported by details?

- ☐ Does the report use transitions to introduce or connect ideas?

- ☐ Does the report have a formal style?

- ☐ Does the concluding paragraph say how the person's creative thinking contributed to the world?

Proofread Check the grammar, spelling, punctuation, and capitalization in your report. Make edits to correct any errors.

Publish

Share your report according to your teacher's instructions. Read at least two of your classmates' reports.

Assignment: Participate in a Collaborative Discussion SL.8.1

When you participate in a collaborative discussion, you talk about a subject with a group of peers. In a good collaborative discussion, participants express their ideas, respond to the ideas of their peers, and keep the discussion going with relevant questions and comments.

Participants of a collaborative discussion:

- come to discussions prepared, having researched the material they will be discussing
- express ideas clearly, referring to evidence on the topic
- use their notes to probe and reflect on the ideas in the discussion
- ask questions that connect the ideas of several speakers
- respond to questions or comments with relevant reasons and evidence
- respectfully acknowledge new information expressed by others

In this activity, you will participate in a collaborative discussion that addresses the question: **What creative qualities are most important for the world? Why?**

Plan Your Discussion

Look at your informational report about a creative person. Underline the parts of your report that talk about the creative qualities of the person and how they have contributed to the world. Prepare for the discussion by completing the outline below.

Creative Qualities That Have Helped the World		
Person I wrote about:		
Creative quality 1:	Example/detail:	How it has helped the world:
Creative quality 2:	Example/detail:	How it has helped the world:
Creative quality 3:	Example/detail:	How it has helped the world:

Practice Your Collaborative Discussion

Read the checklist below. Then practice your collaborative discussion with a partner. Your partner should complete the checklist for you and use it to give you feedback before you participate in your collaborative discussion.

- ☐ Did your partner come to the discussion prepared?

- ☐ Did your partner express their ideas clearly and support them with evidence?

- ☐ Did your partner use their notes to keep the conversation going?

- ☐ Did your partner ask questions that connected both of your ideas?

- ☐ Did your partner respond to your ideas with relevant evidence and ideas?

Feedback Frames

The way you … showed you were prepared.

You could provide more support for …

I appreciated your response to …

Participate in Your Collaborative Discussion

1. Start by greeting the classmates in your discussion group.
2. Take turns saying the name of the creative person you wrote about and explaining why you chose that person.
3. Start the discussion about important creative qualities, making sure to take turns and build on each other's ideas.
4. Ask questions and make comments to keep the discussion going.

Reflect

Discuss the questions with a small group.

1. What surprised you about writing your informational report or participating in the collaborative discussion?
2. What was easy about writing the informational report? What was difficult?
3. What was easy about participating in the collaborative discussion? What was difficult?
4. How was the feedback on your writing and speaking helpful?
5. What is something you learned from one of your classmates in your discussion?

iStorm Egg is a fiberglass waste paper sculpture created for the Faberge Big Egg Hunt in New York City, USA.

Using Creativity to Conserve the World 🎧 2.5

EXPLORER IN ACTION
Asher Jay
is a creative conservationist.

Everything is interconnected—Earth, people, and animals. Therefore, when individuals focus only on their own lives and the world within their own small bubble, they can damage Earth and the well-being of animals and other people. National Geographic Explorer Asher Jay takes a creative approach to bringing global attention to conservation efforts around the world.

An adventurer with an art and design background, Jay has created numerous high-profile paintings, sculptures, and installations related to wildlife conservation. Among her best-known work was a giant animated digital billboard in New York City's Times Square, which focused on ending the illegal ivory trade.

Every day, Jay brainstorms ways she can use her creativity to make an impact on people's consciousness. She wants to help them see the interconnectedness of the world and the impact that individual choices have on the greater world. She argues, "It still matters what you do within your own bubble, because it has ripple effects and it comes to shape and transform other lives, the world at large with or without your awareness."

▶ **2.2** Watch the video to learn more.

1. What is Jay trying to get people to see?
2. Do you think each person's choices affect the greater world? Why or why not?

How Will You Take Action?

Choose one or more of these actions to do.

Personal

Keep a notebook of wonders.

1. For one week, write down things you find yourself wondering about.
   Example:
   What kinds of birds live in our neighborhood?
2. Pick one idea. Do research to discover more about it.
3. Write down new things you wonder about based on what you discovered.

School

Join or start a club based on your creative interests.

1. Research your school clubs.
2. If there is a club that matches one of your interests, join it.
3. If there isn't a club that matches one of your interests, start one. Find other classmates that have the same interest. Work with your teacher and school administrators to make it an official school club.

Local

Raise awareness of something creative in your community.

1. Consider different creative displays in your community—for example, artwork, theater, architecture. Choose one.
2. Do research about the display. Why was it created? What impact does it have on your community?
3. In an online forum or community publication, write about the creative display. Include information about the artist and his or her motivation for creating the display.

Global

Make a creative project to raise awareness about an environmental issue.

1. Brainstorm a list of issues in the natural world, such as pollution, extinction, and deforestation.
2. Choose one issue from your list, and make a creative project that will raise awareness of this issue. Examples include making a painting, sculpture, film, collage, or digital display.
3. Share your project in a written publication or online.

Reflect

1. Reflect on your Take Action project(s). What was successful? What do you wish you had done differently? Why?
2. Reread your response to the Essential Question **What is creative thinking?** in Connect Across Texts. How did your Take Action project(s) change or add to your response?
3. What will you do differently in your life because of what you learned in this unit?

3
New Technology

Do you agree with the quote? Why or why not?

Look at the photo and caption. Discuss the questions.

1. What do you think are some benefits of this type of home? Some drawbacks?

2. Would you like staying in or doing schoolwork in a place like this? Why or why not?

◀ **This is a prototype for a circular 3D-printed home that would be built using one hundred percent recyclable and reusable materials.**

What are the benefits and drawbacks of new technology?

Explore the Essential Question

Think Write your ideas about the Essential Question in the Unit Concept Map.

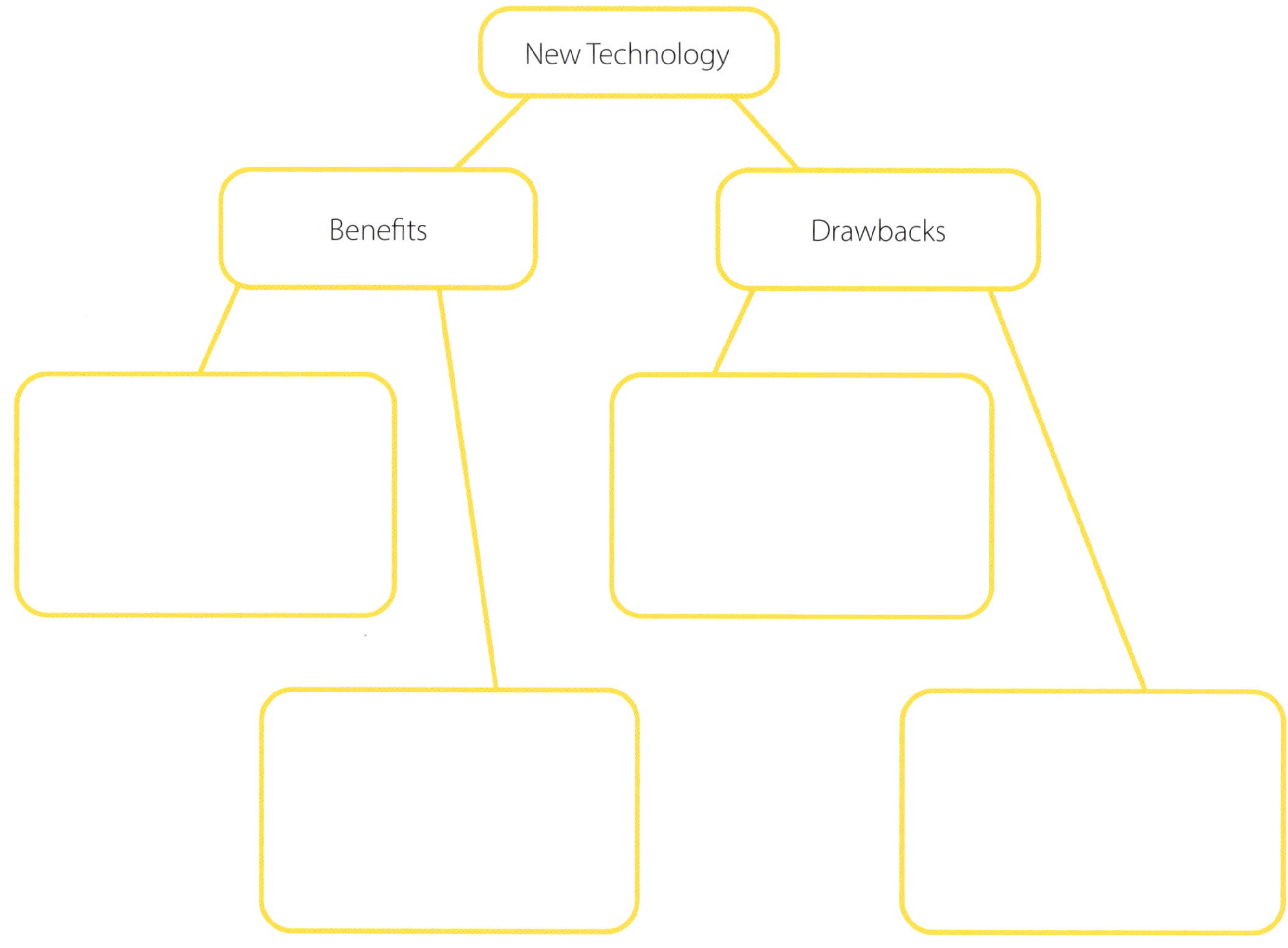

Respond Write one or two sentences to respond to the Essential Question.

Discuss Your Ideas Use your Unit Concept Map and your response to share your ideas with the class.

Discussion Frames

I think …

In my opinion, …

It seems to me that …

Academic Vocabulary

Use these words to express your ideas throughout the unit.

PRACTICE 1 Use context to determine the meaning of each word in blue. Then match the word to its definition in the chart below.

There is much **debate** over the benefits and drawbacks of new technology. On the one hand, many people believe new technology is beneficial because it creates **networks** that allow people to stay connected. Various types of **media**, such as the internet and its **virtual** platforms, help people communicate without leaving their homes. On the other hand, new technology can be isolating. Even though it is **interactive**, it can make people feel less connected. This is especially true for older **generations**, who say they miss books, phone calls, and face-to-face conversations.

Word	Definition
network	interconnected system of things or people
	a group of people born and living at approximately the same time
	a discussion that considers different views on a question
	created or happening in a computer or an online world
	requiring active involvement
	the internet, newspapers, magazines, television, and other means of communication that reach and influence people

PRACTICE 2 Work with a partner. Take turns being the reader and the listener.

Reader: Read the paragraph above. Read one sentence at a time. Don't say the vocabulary word. Instead, say "beep."

Listener: Listen to your partner read the sentence. Say the missing vocabulary word.

Example

Reader: *There is much "beep" over the benefits and drawbacks of new technology.*

Listener: *Debate?*

Reader: *Yes!*

How can we control the use of technology so that it benefits us?

First Thoughts

How does technological change affect workers and their jobs? How does it affect consumers or customers? List your ideas in the chart. Then discuss your ideas in a small group.

Ways New Technology Affects Workers/Jobs	Ways New Technology Affects Consumers/Customers

Key Vocabulary

PRACTICE Use context to determine the meaning of each word in bold. Then match the word to its definition.

1. In a period of **economic** growth, more goods and services are produced.
2. Only the librarians have **access** to the rare-book room.
3. Many different factories **produce** the lightbulbs that stores sell.
4. There is **inequality** in their salaries. Even though they have the same job, Sam gets paid more money than Tom.
5. After the tornado, many **displaced** families stayed in hotels.
6. The sun is a **renewable** resource because its energy does not run out.

_____ **1.** economic	**a.** to make (v.)
_____ **2.** access	**b.** a difference in amount; unevenness (n.)
_____ **3.** produce	**c.** removed from something, such as a home or job (adj.)
_____ **4.** inequality	**d.** related to money (adj.)
_____ **5.** displaced	**e.** capable of being replaced (adj.)
_____ **6.** renewable	**f.** permission or ability to use (n.)

Reading Strategy: Paraphrase

Paraphrasing is a reading strategy that can help you make sure you understand what you are reading. When you paraphrase, use your own words to express a text's main or central idea and some supporting ideas. To paraphrase:

1. Read the text.

2. Determine the main idea and supporting details.

3. Restate the main idea and important details in your own words.

4. If a text is long, break it into several smaller sections. Repeat steps 1–3 for each section.

Strategy in Action

Study the model from "What's Technology Got to Do with the Economy?" What ideas does the writer use from the original text? What words and phrases does the writer use to paraphrase language from the original text?

Original text:

When we say technology, what do you think of?

Chances are, you're probably picturing some sort of whizzy modern gadget; a smartphone, perhaps, or a self-driving car, or a drone or a television or camera or virtual reality goggles or a quantum computer.

But when economists think about technology, they think about anything that helps us produce things faster, better, or cheaper.

Paraphrased text:

When they hear the word *technology*, most people think of devices that they use or know about, such as smartphones and fast computers. But to economists, the word *technology* means anything that makes the production of goods faster, better, or cheaper.

What's **Technology** Got to Do with the **Economy?**

by Economy Editorial Team
from ecnmy.org

🎧 **3.1**

1   When we say technology, what do you think of?

Chances are, you're probably picturing some sort of whizzy[1] modern gadget[2]; a smartphone, perhaps, or a self-driving car, or a drone or a television or camera or virtual reality goggles or a
5   quantum computer.

But when economists think about technology, they think about anything that helps us **produce** things faster, better, or cheaper. Economists are really nutty[3] about production. Production in economist-speak is how we go about making all the stuff we use
10   (from goods like cars to services like lawyers').

Traditionally, economists have worked on the assumption that the more production we have, the better. When they talk about **economic** growth, they literally mean that the amount (or value) of stuff an economy produces has increased. And for lots of
15   economists, politicians, and businesspeople, economic growth is

---

[1] **whizzy** technologically advanced
[2] **gadget** device
[3] **nutty** crazy

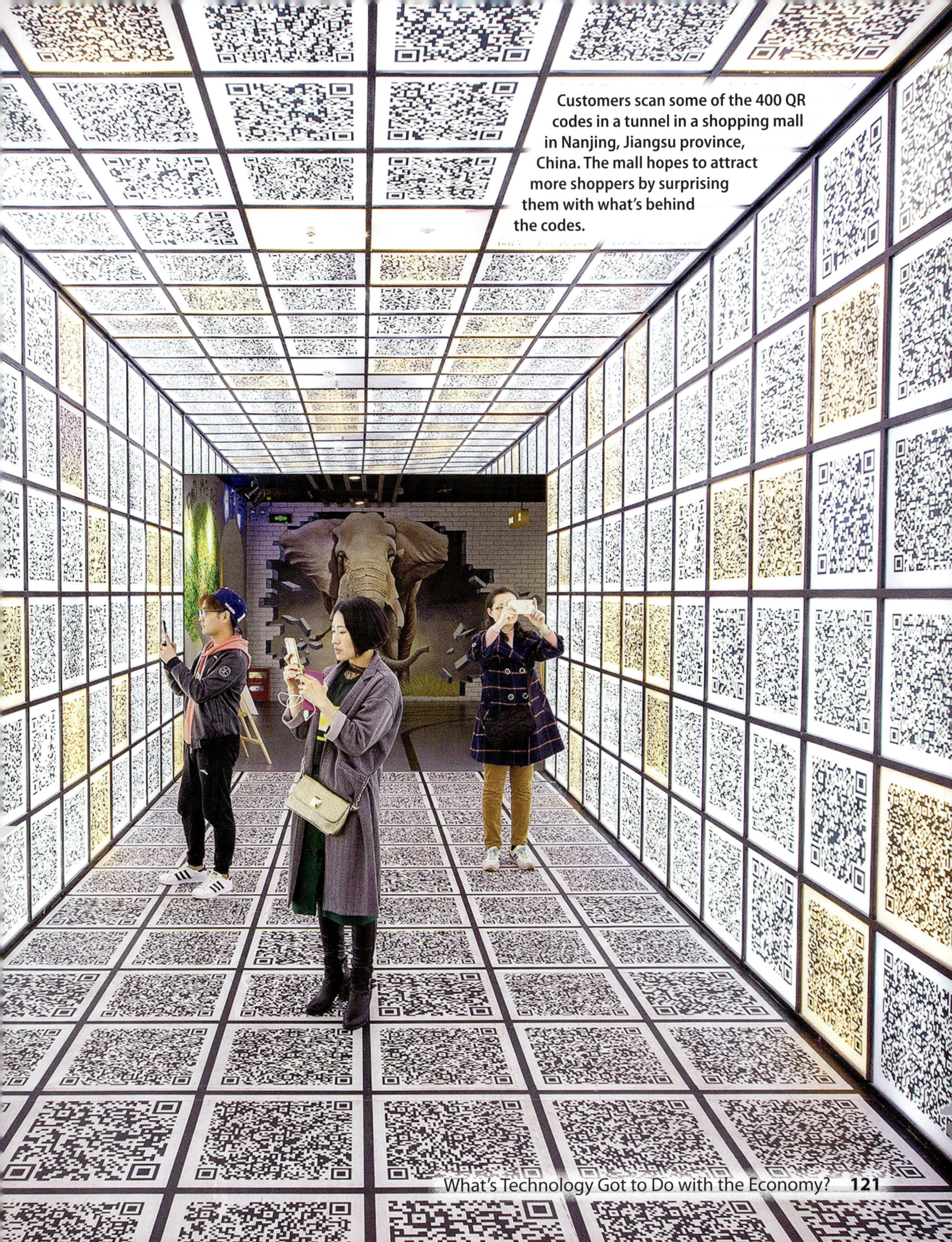

Customers scan some of the 400 QR codes in a tunnel in a shopping mall in Nanjing, Jiangsu province, China. The mall hopes to attract more shoppers by surprising them with what's behind the codes.

A technician launches a drone to deliver blood to a remote hospital in Africa.

seen as an all-important goal. That's because for a long time lots of people have assumed that more stuff in an economy = more money in an economy = more stuff and money for all of us.

If economic growth is your only endgame,[4] you're always going to be a fan of new technology. But what if you're less concerned about economic growth, and more concerned about things like economic **inequality**, the environment, or improving everyone's happiness?

Spoiler[5]: you might be a little bit more concerned about technology.

To be clear: lots of people who care about economic inequality, the environment, and happiness rave about technology—or certain types of technology—and the benefits it can bring. But their debate tends to be more complicated and nuanced.[6]

Take economic inequality. If you think the top goal of an economy should be to stop poverty and/or unequal **access** to things like healthcare and education, you might be buzzing about how iPads can help schoolkids with learning disabilities, or how drones can get medicine to remote areas with poor road access.

But you might also worry that as machines can do work tasks better than humans, new technologies might mean employees lose their jobs, and that if these **displaced** workers can't find other work that is as well-paid or as enjoyable, they'll lose out. And you might be particularly worried that the jobs that are easiest to replace are often the low-skilled, low-paid ones—so it's the people lowest down the socioeconomic ladder who will be hit the hardest.

Or take the environment. Technology often needs a lot of power: electricity for computers, petrol for airplanes, etc. A lot of that power comes from nonrenewable energy sources, which contribute to climate change. But technology can also combat that problem. Think of wind turbines, which are a type of technology that creates **renewable** energy.

---

[4] **endgame** final stage or goal
[5] **spoiler** message warning the reader that important parts of a story will be revealed
[6] **nuanced** subtle

For most environmentalists, the problem isn't so much
the technology as the obsession with using technology to up
production. That's because producing more and more stuff isn't
usually good for the environment. Producing more tables means
chopping down more trees. Producing more jewelry means
blasting more mines into the ground. And historically, we've
not been very good at recycling the stuff we make, or disposing
of it in an environmentally friendly way. More production has
therefore tended to mean more landfills, rubbish, and pollution.

What about technology and human happiness? We probably
don't need to tell you that lots of people think tech makes
us unhappy: just look at all those newspaper articles on how
the internet is supposed to make us feel lonely, or encourage
extremist views, or increase bullying and trolling.[7] And lots of
people are angry that technology has often come alongside a
bigger and bigger invasion of our privacy: through things like
facial recognition, location-tracking, and keystroke logging.

But of course technology can make us happy, too. It has
given us new ways to have fun, made our lives easier and more
convenient, and helps us stay connected to the people we love,
even when they're far away.

So, in short: whether a specific technology is good or bad
for your economy depends on what it is, who you are, and what
you value.

Some technologies benefit some groups of people but not
others. Some technologies benefit you a bit and harm you a bit.
Some technologies are good for the economy in small amounts
but not large ones. Some technologies, like The Terminator, can
be good or bad depending on who controls them.

The only thing we know for sure is that technology has
massively changed our economies and our lives throughout
human history and will continue to do so in ways we probably
can't even imagine.

(Although, here's crossing all our fingers that we can live out
all our Back to the Future fantasies with bio-fueled flying cars.)

---

[7] **trolling** harassing or provoking someone online

Robots retrieve and organize items in a distribution warehouse.

Close Read

Work with a partner.

1. Determine the meanings of your underlined words and phrases.
2. Discuss the question: **According to economists, how does technology affect the world?**

Understand and Analyze

Respond to the questions. Support your responses with evidence from the text.

1. **Understand** What does it mean that economic growth is seen as "an all-important goal"?
2. **Understand** Reread lines 45–59. In what ways is technology bad for the environment?
3. **Infer** Reread lines 60–67. Why does the writer say, "We probably don't need to tell you that lots of people think tech makes us unhappy"?
4. **Interpret** Reread lines 75–83. What is the writer's overall view of technology?
5. **Analyze Key Details** Find an example from the text to explain how a specific technology can be good or bad for your economy, depending on what it is, who you are, and what you value.

Apply the Strategy: Paraphrase

Complete the chart for "What's Technology Got to Do with the Economy?" Use your own words to restate the main idea of each section.

Lines	Paraphrase
11–25	*If you care only about economic growth, you like new technology, but if you care about other issues, you see benefits and drawbacks.*
26–50	
51–71	
72–83	

Share Your Perspective

Discuss these questions in a small group.

1. Do you agree that economic growth is an important goal for society? Why or why not?
2. From your own experience, how can technology cause economic inequality, hurt the environment, or make people unhappy?

Discussion Frames

I believe that technology …

One reason is …

How do you feel about …?

Vocabulary: Understand Greek and Latin Prefixes L.8.4.B

A **prefix** is a letter or group of letters added before a root or base word to create meaning. Many prefixes come from Greek or Latin. To use a prefix to help you figure out the meaning of an unfamiliar word:

1. Read the word to try to identify the root or base word, as well as any prefixes.

2. Think about the meaning of the prefix together with the meaning of the root to figure out the meaning of the word.

3. You can confirm the meaning of the word by looking it up in a dictionary.

Prefix	Meanings	Examples
dis-	not, opposite	disrespect, disconnect
	apart, away	dispose, disperse
in-/im-	in or on	innate, implant
	not	inexcusable, impossible
pre-	before	predict, preorder
re-	again	review, recharge

Apply the Strategy

Look at the chart. Use the meanings of the prefixes, shown above, and the meanings of the base words to figure out the meaning of each word.

Word	Base Word / Meaning	Meaning of Word
inequality	equal / "the same"	*difference*
reconstruct	construct / "build"	
displace	place / "put [something somewhere]"	
preview	view / "look at"	
immigrate	migrate / "move"	
disconnect	connect / "join"	

Read Again

Read "What's Technology Got to Do with the Economy?" again. As you read, circle details from the text that help you respond to this question:

How can technology benefit us, and how can it harm us?

Reflect and Respond

Use some of the details you circled to complete the idea web.

Technology

How it can benefit us

How it can harm us

Use your idea web to respond to the question: How can technology benefit us, and how can it harm us?

____

____

____

____

Discuss Your Response

Share your ideas with the class. Write one new idea you hear.

____

____

____

Respond to the Guiding Question

Write a response to the question:

How can we control the use of technology so that it benefits us?

Use evidence from the text, your discussion, and your life. Use the Discussion Frames to help you. Use the rubric to check your response.

____

____

____

____

____

____

Research SL.8.4

Choose one of these topics. Research the topic to learn more about it.

- renewable energy
- facial recognition

Follow these steps:

1. Make notes about what you already know about the topic.
2. Write three questions you have about the topic.
3. Research the topic to find answers to your questions.
4. Write your answers to the questions.
5. Present what you learn to a small group.

▲ A man uses a face scanner to unlock a door.

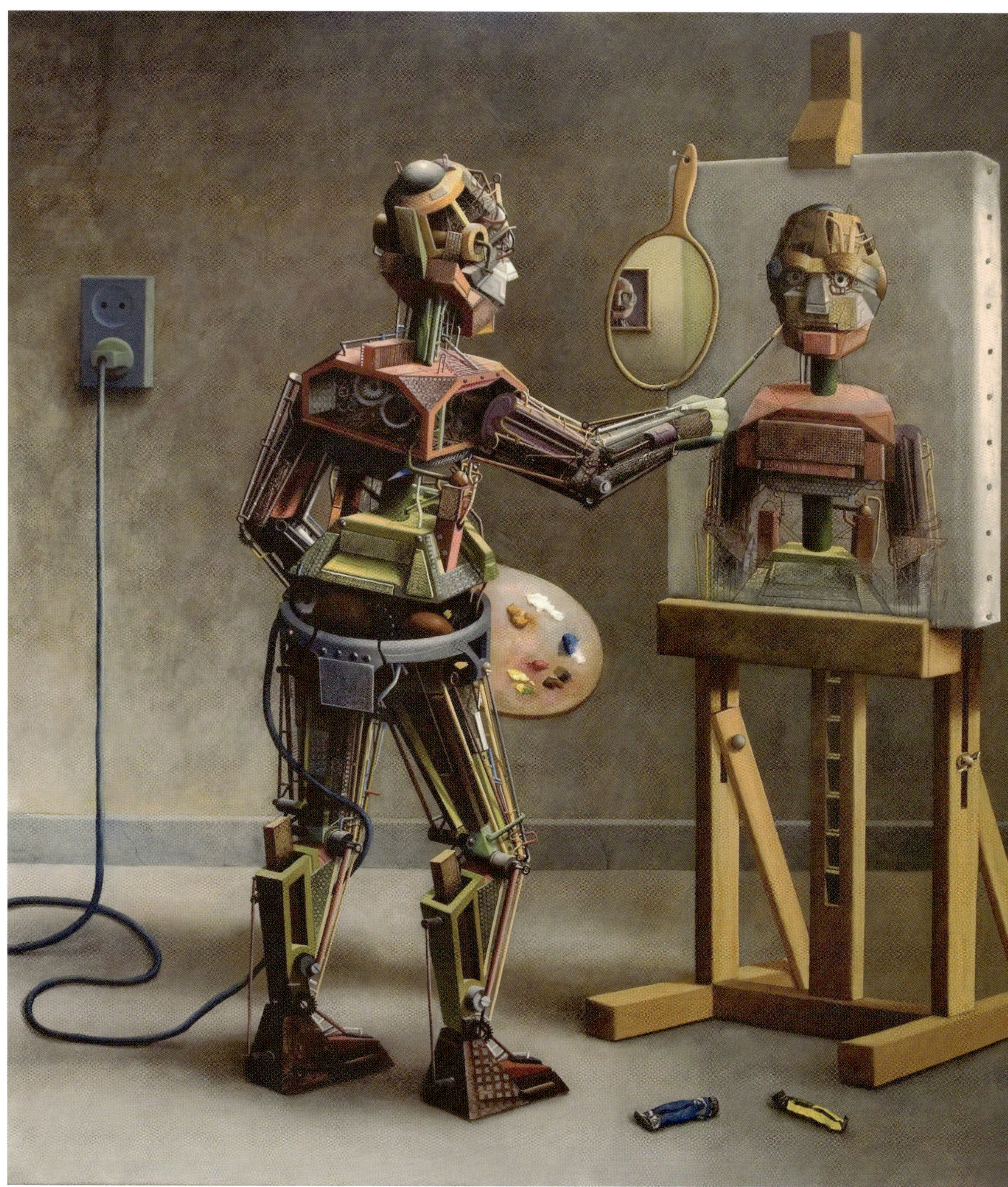

Examine the Painting

1. What's the first thing you noticed when you looked at the painting? What else do you see?
2. Describe the robot. What makes it unusual?
3. What do you think would be a good title for the painting?
4. Write 3–5 questions about the painting. Discuss your questions with a group.

Reflect

Imagine the story behind this painting. Write a story that explains who the robot is and why it is painting a self-portrait.

Find Out ▶ 3.1

Listen to the information about the artist and his painting.

1. Why did the artist decide to paint a robot painting a self-portrait?
2. How do people usually think of robots?
3. According to the artist, how is the robot like him?

Share Your Story

Draw or paint a self-portrait. Then reflect on the experience. What was easy about creating a self-portrait? What was difficult?

ABOUT THE ARTIST

Johan Scherft was born in 1970 in the Netherlands. At a young age, he became interested in drawing, nature, and animals. Although his artwork has many themes (including robots), most are inspired by nature.

What causes us to replace old technology with new?

First Thoughts

How are paper books and e-books alike? How are they different? Complete the Venn diagram. Then discuss your ideas in a small group.

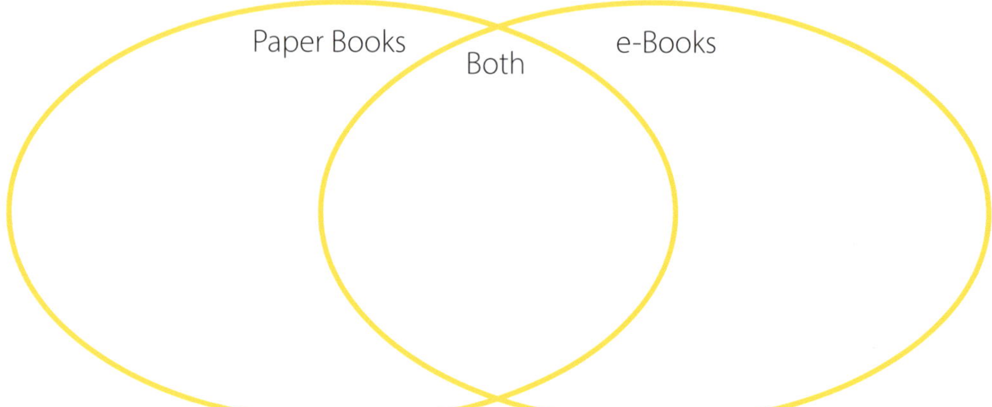

Discussion Frames

Some similarities are …

Some differences are …

One example is …

Another example …

Can you expand on …?

Key Vocabulary

PRACTICE Use context to determine the meaning of each word in bold. Then match the word to its definition.

1. The instructions are **digital**. You can find them on the internet.
2. That class was difficult, but I **endured** it. I'm glad I made it through.
3. The level of **literacy** in Europe is very high. Most people there can read and write.
4. Cassette tapes have been **obsolete** for many years. People rarely use them anymore.
5. The plane crash had one **survivor**. He is the only person that did not die.
6. A warm coat is **vital** in cold climates. Wearing one is an important way to protect yourself in extreme weather.

_____ **1.** digital   **a.** to last; to survive (v.)

_____ **2.** endure   **b.** one who lives through a difficult time or event (n.)

_____ **3.** literacy   **c.** electronic (adj.)

_____ **4.** obsolete   **d.** very important or necessary (adj.)

_____ **5.** survivor   **e.** no longer used (adj.)

_____ **6.** vital   **f.** the ability to read and write (n.)

Reading Skill: Analyze Humor RL.8.6

Writers can create humor by presenting ideas in unexpected ways. One type of humor is **satire**. Writers use satire to comment on or criticize a subject or society in a humorous way. To analyze humor in writing:

1. Identify typical characteristics of the genre, theme, or characters. As the reader, what are your expectations? For example, if a character is a superhero, you might expect that character to be brave and strong and to save people from dangerous situations.

2. As you read, think about which parts of the text align with your expectations.

3. Think about which parts of the text differ from what you expected. How does the difference create humor?

Skill in Action

Study the model. Work with a partner to identify the parts of the text that match your expectations and the parts that differ from your expectations. Compare your expectations with those expressed in the thought bubbles. Discuss what makes each part funny.

OBITUARY: The Book
(1455–Present)

The Book lived over five hundred years, large and fearlessly, touching the lives of many.

The Book was born in the late 1400s, beloved child of one Johannes Gutenberg, whose printing press made obsolete the scrolls and papyruses that were *The Book's* less-loved older siblings. Speaking of his hopes and dreams for *The Book*, Gutenberg once said: "I just couldn't deal with that two-hundred-pound clay tablet anymore. It wouldn't fit in my backpack, and if I couldn't find a manservant to carry it around, it really hurt my arms."

OBITUARY:
The Book (1455–Present)
by **Katrina Onstad**

🎧 **3.2**

1   *The Book* lived over five hundred years, large and fearlessly, touching the lives of many.

    The Book was born in the late 1400s, beloved child of one Johannes Gutenberg, whose printing press made **obsolete**
5 the scrolls and papyruses[1] that were *The Book's* less-loved older siblings. Speaking of his hopes and dreams for *The Book*, Gutenberg once said: "I just couldn't deal with that two-hundred-pound clay tablet anymore. It wouldn't fit in my backpack, and if I couldn't find a manservant to carry it
10 around, it really hurt my arms. One day I thought: I can do better." And so his simple invention of moveable type met bound, portable paper and *The Book* was born, enduring for half a millennia. What else still exists from five hundred years ago? Do we still tell time with an hourglass? Does your doctor
15 drain every drop of your blood into a vat when you make an appointment for a head cold? *The Book* outlasted its peers. It was a **survivor**.

    Along the way, there were threats to *The Book's* existence, cultural diversions that left it abandoned[2] and dusty for
20 lengths of time: penny arcades and gossip magazines, big bands and radio. When television began infecting homes, *The Book* didn't know if it would make it. "I have instant replay." *The Book* nervously reminded anyone who would listen. "I don't need to be plugged in, or recharged. I fit in
25 your backpack!"

---

[1] **papyruses**   written materials from ancient Egypt
[2] **abandoned**   left alone

A man reads a book in
Vrindavan, Uttar Pradesh, India.

But *The Book* had nothing to worry about: it was healthy and
vital, always maintaining its significance in the face of adversity.[3]
It looked great, too. But its beauty was really on the inside, and the
inside contained multitudes. Even those who just met it once or
twice could be provoked by *The Book* to leave their small worlds
and discover new ones. *The Book* was a refuge from the ugliness
of existence and never a better friend than on a couch on a cold
afternoon. *The Book* could make anyone see and feel how other
people lived. It was the great tool of empathy.

In the twentieth century, *The Book* got cheaper, and **literacy**
rates rose around the world. *The Book* transformed[4] lives, helping
a man toiling in the fields to discover great truths and rise above
his station; showing a young girl that her options were less limited
than she thought. *The Book* did this approximately eighty billion
times. It took its job seriously.

The Book **endured** triumphantly—until the **digital** age. In
retrospect,[5] *The Book* should have seen it coming. *The Book*'s good
friend The CD had already grown ill, losing its status as a much-
coveted object. Before, The CD had been a community hub, like
The Book: on weekends, people would gather at The CD's place
to meet and share their love of music. Then came downloads and
piracy. The CD couldn't even be given away for free. *The Book*, ever
optimistic, didn't know it would meet the same fate, and that the
stores where it had lived would shutter and transform into cell-
phone franchises and discount shops.

There were those who said *The Book* had simply worn out its
welcome. By the end of the first decade of the 2000s, E-Books were
rendering it unnecessary. "E-Books are better for the trees," said
The Book's former friends. "We still like you, but E-Books take up
less room in a backpack. You can take four or five of them on a
holiday!"

Digitization was altering *The Book*'s DNA. There was talk of
surgically inserting interactive characters whom the audience
could email, final chapters that could be debated online and
changed, images and sounds sutured between sentences. *The Book*
was confused: How much stimulation do people need? Surely *The*

---

[3] **adversity** difficulty
[4] **transformed** changed
[5] **in retrospect** thinking back

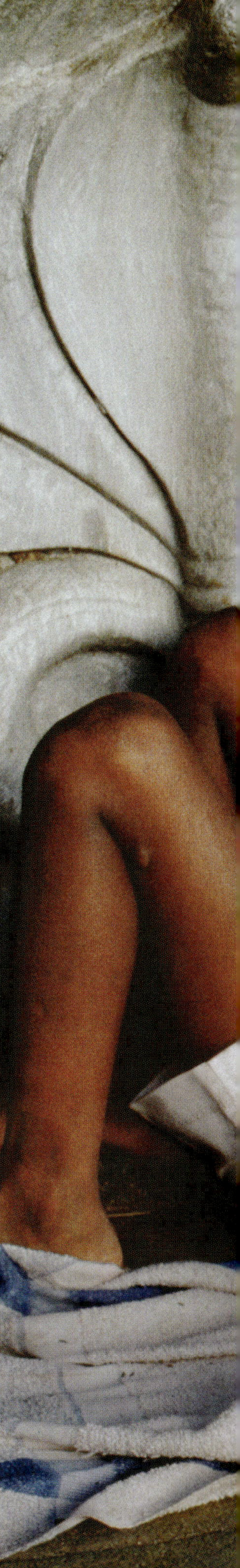

A grandmother reads to
her grandson in Sri Lanka.

The Royal Portuguese Cabinet of Reading in Rio de Janeiro, Brazil, contains over 350,000 books.

Book, black and white and in hand, was adequate to the task of entertaining and enlightening, as it had been for centuries? Why did the imagination suddenly need to be led around in this way?
65 What happened?

The E-Book lovers told *The Book* to chill out.[6] "What's happening to you is simply a change of shape. It's the next step in the evolution of information. The change is simply one of delivery. That sick feeling is just nostalgia, and nostalgia cripples progress.
70 Get over it."

But those who knew *The Book*, who loved to feel its spine and heft, to take in its smell and hand it to a friend and say: "Here, this changed me, it will change you"—those people just couldn't feel the same love for the cool button marked "Download" or
75 even "Share." They missed snooping around people's houses and inspecting[7] their bookshelves for a clue to their souls. And who wants to read on a computer on the beach anyway? What about sand and rogue waves?

For these friends, it was difficult to make sense of the tragedy.
80 There didn't seem to be any reason in it.

As *The Book* lost its strength, it realized something: The Reader had changed. *The Book* could not exist without the love of its life, The Reader. In only a few short years, *The Book* had begun to notice that The Reader struggled to sit still, and avoided the silence that allowed
85 *The Book* to do its greatest work. Now *The Book* saw that after a few pages, The Reader would toss it aside for social media (which isn't a book at all!). There was no unmixed attention left to feed *The Book*. It grew emaciated,[8] and unwanted. Obsolete.

But even in its final hours, *The Book* stayed hopeful. Perhaps it
90 was true that the stories remained, and the stories might now be able to travel farther and faster. *The Book* might become an artifact, but the human imagination would respark, in some faraway place, because perhaps computers had a reach that paper never could. *The Book* liked to think there would always be a hunger for possible
95 worlds. *The Book* believed so, deeply.

Still, for those left behind, there is a great void, and only *The Book*'s last words: "I am the original social network."

------

[6] **chill out** relax
[7] **inspecting** looking at closely
[8] **emaciated** very thin

About the Author: Katrina Onstad

Katrina Onstad is an award-winning Canadian journalist and novelist. Her journalism has appeared in such publications as the *New York Times, The Guardian,* and *The Globe and Mail*. She has published three novels.

Close Read

Work with a partner.

1. Determine the meanings of your underlined words and phrases.

2. Discuss the question: **How did *The Book* die?**

Understand and Analyze

Respond to the questions. Support your responses with evidence from the text.

1. **Explain** Reread lines 3–13. Why is Johannes Gutenberg *The Book's* parent?

2. **Compare** Reread lines 18–22. How is *The Book* similar to the other items mentioned?

3. **Understand** Reread lines 35–40. What happened with *The Book* in the twentieth century?

4. **Understand** Reread lines 42–47. What happened to The CD?

5. **Infer** Reread lines 81–88. Why did The Reader start having a hard time sitting still?

6. **Analyze** Read the last line of the obituary. In what way is *The Book* the original social network?

Apply the Skill: Analyze Humor

Complete the chart with examples of how the author of "OBITUARY: The Book (1455–Present)" creates humor.

Example of Humor in Text	Why It's Funny
The 200-pound clay tablet hurt Gutenberg's arms and wouldn't fit in his backpack.	*Even though clay tablets were used for writing hundreds of years ago, people didn't carry them around in backpacks. That's absurd!*

Share Your Perspective

Discuss these questions in a small group.

1. Do you believe that *The Book* is dead? Why or why not?

2. Do you prefer reading paper books or e-books? Why?

Discussion Frames

I believe that *The Book* … because …

I prefer to read …

Can you explain why …?

Vocabulary: Interpret Figurative Language **L.8.5.A**

A **figure of speech**, or figurative language, is a word or phrase that has a meaning different from its literal definition. People use figures of speech to make comparisons or create dramatic effects. There are many different types of figurative language. You may have already heard of metaphors and similes. Other types of figurative language include **personification** and **hyperbole**. Personification gives living qualities to non-living things. Hyperbole is exaggeration. To interpret figures of speech:

1. When you are reading, pay attention to words that you would not expect in the text. Consider whether they are part of a figure of speech.

2. Think about the type of figurative language it might be. Is it personification? Hyperbole? Consider the larger meaning of the sentence and paragraph to interpret the meaning of the figure of speech.

Example

Books are objects and are not "born." Also, *The Book* is capitalized as a proper noun. So the figure of speech is personification. If I interpret the author's larger meaning, I know she means the book was invented.

The Book was born in the late 1400s, beloved child of one Johannes Gutenberg, whose printing press …

People cannot have objects as children. This is another example of personification. It means Gutenberg invented *The Book* and the printing press and that he loved *The Book* as if it were his child.

This is an exaggeration, an example of hyperbole. The word *zillion* implies a very large number, over a million. But the kinds of threats it faced weren't that numerous.

Along the way *The Book* encountered a zillion new threats to its existence.

Apply the Strategy

Read the sentences from "OBITUARY: The Book (1455–Present)." Look closely at the words and context to identify the type of figure of speech.

1. Does your doctor drain every drop of your blood into a vat when you make an appointment for a head cold?
   a. hyperbole   **b.** personification

2. *The Book* was … never a better friend than on a couch on a cold afternoon.
   a. hyperbole   **b.** personification

3. *The Book*'s good friend The CD had already grown ill, losing its status as a much-coveted object.
   a. hyperbole   **b.** personification

Read Again

Read "OBITUARY: The Book (1455–Present)" again. As you read, circle details from the text that help you respond to these questions:

Why did the book replace papyrus and the clay tablet? Why did the e-book replace the book?

Reflect and Respond

Use the details you circled in the article and your own ideas to complete the graphic organizer.

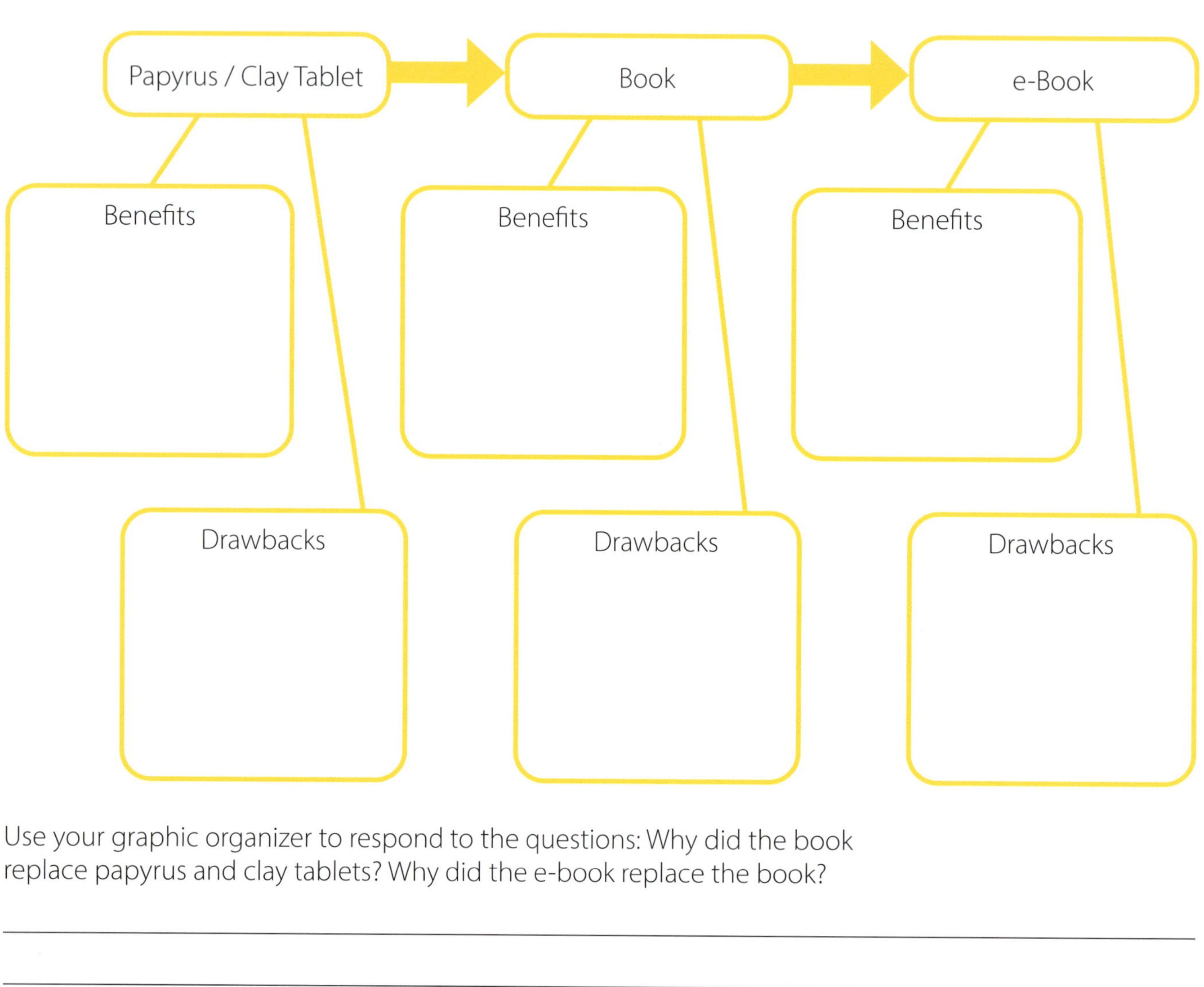

Use your graphic organizer to respond to the questions: Why did the book replace papyrus and clay tablets? Why did the e-book replace the book?

____

____

____

____

____

Discuss Your Response

Share your ideas with the class. Write one new idea you hear.

____

____

____

Respond to the Guiding Question

Write a response to the question:

What causes us to replace old technology with new?

Use evidence from the text, your discussion, and your life. Use the Discussion Frames to help you. Use the rubric to check your response.

____

____

____

____

____

Create and Present: Birth of *The e-Book*

Imagine *The e-Book* was just "born." Then do one of these activities.

OPTION 1: Write a Birth Announcement

Write a birth announcement for *The e-Book*. Then read it to your classmates.

OPTION 2: Write and Perform a Skit

Work with a partner. Write a short skit of a conversation between the baby *e-Book* and the dying *Book*.

Here's an example of the first few lines of a skit:

The e-Book: Hello, Book. How can I live a long life like you?
The Book: Well, you have to continue to entertain people.
The e-Book: But what about social media? I think people prefer …

Practice your skit, and then perform it for the class. If there are more than two characters, ask other students to perform with you.

How is artificial intelligence changing the world?

A doctor uses a hologram of a patient's respiratory system to help during surgery.

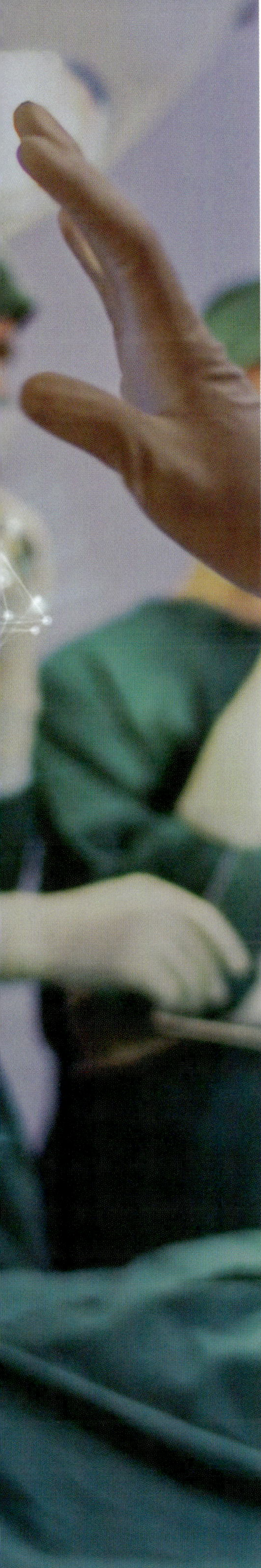

First Thoughts

Look at the list of artificial intelligence systems. Rate them on a scale of 1–4, and then discuss your ratings with a small group.

1 = I use it; 2 = I'd like to try it; 3 = I've heard of it; 4 = I haven't heard of it

Virtual Assistant	Self-Driving Car	Robot	Drone	Shopping Assistant

Viewing Skill: Categorize Information and Perspectives

When you watch a video, pay attention to the type of information presented and how it is organized. Videos can share facts, opinions, or both. Categorizing the ideas and information in a video can help you summarize what it is about.

Apply the Skill

▶ **3.2** Watch the video "How Artificial Intelligence Will Change Your World, for Better or Worse." Write two ways AI will make the world better and two ways it will make the world worse.

How AI Will Make the World Better	How AI Will Make the World Worse
1. 2.	1. 2.

Understand and Analyze

▶ **3.2** Watch again. Answer the questions. Support your responses with evidence from the video.

1. **Understand** According to the video, what exactly is artificial intelligence?
2. **Explain** Why won't there necessarily be fewer jobs because of AI?
3. **Evaluate** How can AI's ability to make conclusions based on patterns be used either positively or negatively? Give an example of each.
4. **Infer** How can AI create a tech company monopoly?

Share Your Perspective

1. Do you think artificial intelligence is mostly changing the world for the better or worse? Explain.
2. What types of artificial intelligence do you use in your life? How does it make your life better or worse?

Discussion Frames

I think … because …

In my opinion, …

How do you use …?

How does technology affect our interactions with other people?

First Thoughts

How do you prefer to communicate with friends? Rank the ways from 1 (favorite) to 6 (least favorite). Then, with a partner, discuss the reasons for your answers.

Way to Communicate	text	phone call	video call	social media	email	in person
Rank (1–6)						

Key Vocabulary

PRACTICE Use context to determine the meaning of each word in bold. Then match the word to its definition.

1. Did the referees **intervene** in the dispute, or did they let the players argue?

2. I've become **entangled** in my sister's problems. I can't get away from them.

3. I have **boundaries** on social media. I use it but don't post selfies.

4. There is a feeling of **connectedness** in my community. We all belong to the same group.

5. My best friend and I have **intimate** conversations. We tell each other almost everything.

6. **Diminished** sales of DVDs reflected the rise in streaming entertainment. People were buying DVDs less and less.

Word	Definition
boundaries	limits of something; borders
	a feeling of belonging or connection with others
	smaller or fewer
	involved in difficulties from which it is hard to escape
	to interrupt or come between
	closely connected; familiar; close

Learning to analyze a paragraph will help you become a better reader and writer. A good informational paragraph includes three key parts: the **topic sentence**, **supporting details**, and, often, a **concluding sentence**. These elements work together to express the key concept in an organized way. To identify the parts of a paragraph:

1. Look at the first sentence. Usually, but not always, you'll find the topic there. The topic sentence expresses the key concept, or central idea, of the paragraph.

2. Read the next few sentences in the paragraph. They provide supporting details. Supporting details give more information, such as facts and examples, about the key concept identified in the topic sentence.

3. Read the last sentence in the paragraph. This is often a concluding sentence. It may summarize the main points of the paragraph or provide a transition to the next paragraph.

Skill in Action

Study the model paragraph from "What's Technology Got to Do with the Economy?" Talk with a partner about how all the sentences work together to express the key concept.

This is the topic sentence. It expresses the key concept, or central idea.

The last sentence provides a conclusion.

For most environmentalists, the problem isn't so much the technology as the obsession with using technology to up production. That's because producing more and more stuff isn't usually good for the environment. Producing more tables means chopping down more trees. Producing more jewelry means blasting more mines into the ground. And historically, we've not been very good at recycling the stuff we make, or disposing of it in an environmentally friendly way. More production has therefore tended to mean more landfills, rubbish, and pollution.

The author explains the claim and gives examples.

A woman walks down Hong
Kong's busy Fa Yuen Street.

How Not to
BE ALONE

by **Jonathan Safran Foer**

🎧 3.3

1   A COUPLE of weeks ago, I saw a stranger crying in public. I was in Brooklyn's Fort Greene neighborhood, waiting to meet a friend for breakfast. I arrived at the restaurant a few minutes early and was sitting on the bench

5   outside, scrolling through my contact list. A girl, maybe 15 years old, was sitting on the bench opposite me, crying into her phone. I heard her say, "I know, I know, I know" over and over.

    What did she know? Had she done something wrong?

10 Was she being comforted? And then she said, "Mama, I know," and the tears came harder.

    What was her mother telling her? Never to stay out all night again? That everybody fails? Is it possible that no one was on the other end of the call, and that the girl was merely

15 rehearsing a difficult conversation?

    "Mama, I know," she said, and hung up, placing her phone on her lap.

    I was faced with a choice: I could interject[1] myself into her life, or I could respect the **boundaries** between us.

20 Intervening might make her feel worse, or be inappropriate. But then, it might ease her pain, or be helpful in some straightforward[2] logistical way.

---

[1] **interject** interrupt
[2] **straightforward** direct and honest

It is harder to **intervene** than not to, but it is vastly harder
to choose to do either than to retreat into scrolling the names of
one's contact list, or whatever one's favorite distraction happens
to be. Technology celebrates **connectedness**, but encourages
retreat.[3] The phone didn't make me avoid the human connection,
but it did make ignoring her easier in that moment. It also made
it more likely, by comfortably encouraging me to forget my choice
to do so. My daily use of technological communication has been
shaping me into someone more likely to forget others. The flow
of water carves rock, a little bit at a time. And our personhood is
carved, too, by the flow of our habits.

Psychologists who study empathy and compassion are finding
that unlike our almost instantaneous responses to physical pain,
it takes time for the brain to comprehend the psychological and
moral dimensions of a situation. The more distracted we become,
and the more emphasis we place on speed at the expense of
depth, the less likely and able we are to care.

Everyone wants his parent's, or friend's, or partner's undivided
attention—even if many of us, especially children, are getting
used to far less. Simone Weil wrote, "Attention is the rarest and
purest form of generosity." By this definition, our relationships
to the world, and to one another, and to ourselves, are becoming
increasingly miserly.

Most of our communication technologies began as imperfect
substitutes for an impossible activity. We couldn't always see
one another face to face, so the telephone made it possible to
keep in touch at a distance. We are not always home, so the
answering machine made a kind of interaction possible without
the person being near the phone. Online communication started
as a substitute for telephonic communication. And then texting,
which facilitated yet faster, and more mobile, messaging. These
inventions were not created to be improvements upon face-to-face
communication, but as acceptable, if **diminished**, substitutes for it.

But then a funny thing happened: we began to prefer the
diminished substitutes. It's easier to make a phone call than to
schlep to see someone in person. Leaving a message on someone's
machine is easier than having a phone conversation—you can say

---

[3] **retreat** a pulling away

People look at their cell phones on the escalator in Shinjuku Station, Tokyo, Japan.

60 what you need to say without a response; hard news is easier to
leave; it's easier to check in without becoming **entangled**. So we
began calling when we knew no one would pick up.

Shooting off an email is easier, still, because there's no chance
of accidentally catching someone. And texting is even easier, as
65 another shell is offered to hide in. Each step "forward" has made it
easier, just a little, to avoid the emotional work of being present, to
convey information rather than humanity.

THE problem with accepting—with preferring—diminished
substitutes is that over time, we, too, become diminished
70 substitutes. People who become used to saying little become used
to feeling little.

A family gathers to eat together in Bahrain.

With each generation, it becomes harder to imagine a future
that resembles the present. My grandparents hoped I would have
a better life than they did: free of war and hunger, comfortably
situated in a place that felt like home. But what futures would
I dismiss out of hand for my grandchildren? That their clothes
will be fabricated every morning on 3-D printers? That they will
communicate without speaking or moving?

Only those with no imagination would deny the possibility
that they will live forever. It's possible that many reading these
words will never die. Let's assume, though, that we all have a set
number of days to indent the world with our beliefs, to find and
create the beauty that only a finite[4] existence allows for, to wrestle
with the question of purpose and wrestle with our answers.

We often use technology to save time, but increasingly, it either
takes the saved time along with it, or makes the saved time less
present, **intimate**, and rich. I worry that the closer the world gets
to our fingertips, the further it gets from our hearts. It's not an
either/or—being "anti-technology" is perhaps the only thing more
foolish than being unquestioningly[5] "pro-technology"—but a
question of balance that our lives hang upon.

Most of the time, most people are not crying in public, but
everyone is always in need of something that another person can
give, be it undivided attention, a kind word, or deep empathy.
There is no better use of a life than to be attentive to such needs.
There are as many ways to do this as there are kinds of loneliness,
but all of them require attentiveness, all of them require the hard
work of emotional computation and corporeal[6] compassion. All
of them require the human processing of the only animal who
risks "getting it wrong" and whose dreams provide shelters and
vaccines and words to crying strangers.

We live in a world made up more of story than stuff. We are
creatures of memory more than reminders, of love more than
likes. Being attentive to the needs of others might not be the point
of life, but it is the work of life. It can be messy, and painful, and
almost impossibly difficult. But it is not something we give. It is
what we get in exchange for having to die.

---

[4] **finite** limited
[5] **unquestioningly** definitely
[6] **corporeal** physical

Close Read

Work with a partner.

1. Determine the meanings of your underlined words and phrases.

2. Discuss the questions: **According to the author, how does technology cause isolation? What does he suggest we can do about it?**

Understand and Analyze

Respond to the questions. Support your responses with evidence from the text.

1. **Explain** Reread lines 23–31. Why does the author say, "Technology celebrates connectedness, but encourages retreat"?

2. **Interpret** Reread lines 30–33. According to the author, how have daily communications changed him?

3. **Illustrate** In lines 56–57, what does the author mean by "diminished substitutes"? Give an example to demonstrate the meaning.

4. **Understand** Reread lines 72–78. Why does it get harder to imagine the future with each generation?

5. **Analyze** Reread lines 85–91. The author says, "I worry that the closer the world gets to our fingertips, the further it gets from our hearts." Explain what this means.

Apply the Skill: Analyze a Paragraph

Reread the paragraph that begins on line 46. Complete the chart with key parts of the paragraph.

Topic Sentence		
"Most of our communication technologies began as imperfect substitutes for an impossible activity."		
Supporting Detail	**Supporting Detail**	**Supporting Detail**
Concluding Sentence		

Share Your Perspective

Discuss these questions in a small group.

1. Do you agree that texting is a diminished substitute for other forms of communication? Why or why not?

2. Do you use different ways of communicating with different people? Why or why not?

Discussion Frames

I agree / don't agree that …

This is because …

Why do/don't you …?

Language Convention: Identify Gerunds L.8.1.A

A **gerund** is a verb that ends in –*ing* and functions as a noun. It can be the subject or object in a sentence or clause. Gerunds can be used alone or as part of a noun phrase.

	Gerunds as Subjects	Gerunds as Objects
Gerund Alone	subject → verb → Texting is a popular way to communicate.	subject → verb → object Many people enjoy texting.
Gerund as Part of Noun Phrase	subject → Leaving a message on someone's verb → machine is easy.	subject → verb → object She doesn't like making phone calls.

PRACTICE 1 Read each sentence. Decide whether the underlined word is used as a gerund. Then check (✓) the correct box.

	Gerund	Not Gerund
1. Messaging is a good way to communicate.	✓	
2. Being alone in the world can be hard.		
3. She is texting you now.		
4. I don't like interjecting.		
5. The girl was crying into her phone.		
6. Accepting diminished substitutes can be easy to do.		
7. Many people believe that communicating via technology is easier.		
8. I am talking on the phone.		

PRACTICE 2 Go back to the essay and circle at least five gerunds. If a gerund is part of a noun phrase, underline the noun phrase. (Do not underline –*ing* forms that are used as verbs or adjectives.)

Read Again

Read "How Not to Be Alone" again. As you read, circle details from the text that help you respond to this question:

How do phones affect our ability to pay attention to the needs of others?

Reflect and Respond

Use some of the details you circled to complete this chart.

Ways phones improve our ability to pay attention to the needs of others	Ways phones hinder our ability to pay attention to the needs of others

Use your chart to respond to the question: How do phones affect our ability to pay attention to the needs of others?

____

____

____

____

____

____

Discuss Your Response

Share your ideas with the class. Write one new idea you hear.

____

____

____

Respond to the Guiding Question

Write a response to the question:
How does technology affect our interactions with other people?

Use evidence from the text, your discussion, and your life. Use the Discussion Frames to help you. Use the rubric to check your response.

____

____

____

____

CONNECT ACROSS TEXTS

Discuss the Essential Question: What are the benefits and drawbacks of new technology?

Look at your answer to the Essential Question in the Unit Launch and your notes about technology in the Reflect and Respond sections. Discuss: How have your ideas about the Essential Question changed? What changed your ideas?

Then write one new idea you heard in the discussion. How did it affect your opinion?

____

____

Respond to the Essential Question

Write your new response to the Essential Question. Include Academic Vocabulary.

____

____

____

Assignment: Write an Argumentative Essay W.8.1

An argumentative essay makes a claim (gives an opinion) that is supported with reasons. Each reason is supported by relevant evidence. Evidence is considered relevant only if it has a clear connection to the claim. For this assignment, you will write an argumentative essay about whether technology is good or bad for bringing people together.

Your essay should be five paragraphs and include:

- an introductory paragraph that states the topic of the essay and includes a thesis statement (a brief summary of the claim)
- three body paragraphs that each provide a different reason for your claim. Each reason should be supported by evidence. The evidence can be examples, facts, expert opinions, or statistics.
- a concluding paragraph that restates the claim and the reasons that support it

Explore the Model

Read the model essay. Underline the essay's thesis statement and each paragraph's topic sentence. Then, in each body paragraph, underline the reason for the claim and the evidence that supports it.

Videoconferencing Brings People Together

As a teenager, I use many different types of technology for many different reasons, including entertainment, convenience, safety, and connection. Some people say technology encourages people to be alone; however, in my experience, it can also connect people. Videoconferencing is one type of technology that brings people together.

One way that videoconferencing brings people together is by letting them see each other from across the world while they communicate. For example, my grandparents live in South Korea, and we videoconference with them every Saturday. This was especially helpful when I was younger because I could not write letters or emails and I was shy on the phone. Because my grandparents live so far away, I would barely know them if it weren't for videoconferencing.

Videoconferencing is also an effective way to support remote learning when schools are closed for reasons like bad weather, widespread illness, or local emergencies. Whenever my school is closed, my classes still meet through videoconferencing. This helps maintain a feeling of community because teachers can teach the entire class at once. It gives us a way to ask questions and even work in small groups. It also means we do not have to miss school. This is good because if we miss too much school, we have to make up the days during our summer break.

Finally, videoconferencing is a great way to stay connected with my friends when we are too busy to get together. My friends and I are involved in many activities, and we are not always able to spend time together outside of school. Therefore, we use videoconferencing to work on homework together, talk, and have fun. It feels like we are in the same room.

In conclusion, videoconferencing is an example of a technology that brings people together. It helps family members who live far away from each other to communicate and see each other, it supports remote learning, and it allows friends to hang out even when they are busy. I am grateful for videoconferencing because it connects me to others.

Plan Your Essay

Complete the outline to plan your argumentative essay.

OUTLINE

Introduction

Topic:

Thesis Statement:

Body

Supporting Reason 1:

Evidence:

Supporting Reason 2:

Evidence:

Supporting Reason 3:

Evidence:

Conclusion

Restated Claim:

Summary of Reasons:

Write and Revise

Write Use your outline to write a first draft of your argumentative essay. To connect sentences and paragraphs in your essay, use transitions such as these:

- To begin,
- One way,
- For example,
- Also,
- In addition,
- Finally,
- Therefore,
- In conclusion,

Revise Exchange essays with a partner. Use the checklist to review your partner's work and give feedback. Refer to your partner's feedback as you revise your draft.

- [ ] Does the essay include an introductory paragraph that states the topic and has a thesis statement?
- [ ] Does the thesis statement clearly summarize the claim?
- [ ] Does each body paragraph provide a different reason of support for the claim?
- [ ] Does each body paragraph include evidence, such as facts and examples, that relate to the claim?
- [ ] Does the concluding paragraph restate the claim and summarize the supporting reasons?

Proofread Check the grammar, spelling, punctuation, and capitalization in your essay. Make edits to correct any errors.

Publish

Share your essay according to your teacher's instructions. Read at least two of your classmates' essays.

Assignment: Give a Speech SL.8.4

When you give a speech, you present your ideas about a specific topic to a group. For this assignment, you will give a speech using the argumentative essay you wrote about whether technology is good or bad for bringing people together.

Start by working with your essay:

- Underline the topic and thesis statement in the introductory paragraph of your essay.
- Underline the supporting reason and evidence in each body paragraph.
- Underline the restated claim and summary of reasons in the concluding paragraph.

Now think about a good speech you have heard. Good speakers:

- talk without reading directly from their written essay
- use eye contact
- use a loud and clear voice

Prepare Your Speech

Look at the underlined parts of your essay. Below, make notes to use while you give your speech. Your notes should be words and phrases instead of whole sentences. This helps you remember ideas without reading directly from your essay.

Topic:
Claim:
Reason 1:   Evidence:
Reason 2:   Evidence:
Reason 3:   Evidence:
Summary:

Practice Your Speech

Read the checklist below. Use your notes to practice your speech several times. Then practice your speech with a partner. Your partner should complete the checklist for you and use it to give you feedback before you present your speech to the class.

- [ ] Did the speaker talk without reading directly from the essay?

- [ ] Did the speaker use a loud voice that was clear and easy to understand?

- [ ] Did the speaker make eye contact with you?

- [ ] Did the speaker present a topic and a clearly stated claim?

- [ ] Did the speaker give relevant reasons and evidence that support the claim?

Feedback Frames

One thing you could improve is …

I thought … was especially effective.

I suggest you …

Present Your Speech

1. Start by greeting the audience (your classmates). Say your name and the topic of your speech.
2. Give your speech, incorporating feedback from your practice partner.
3. Invite your classmates to ask questions.
4. Thank your audience for their attention.

Reflect

Discuss the questions with a small group.

1. What surprised you about writing your essay or giving your speech?
2. What was easy about writing the essay? What was difficult?
3. What was easy about giving the speech? What was difficult?
4. How was the feedback you received from your partner helpful?
5. What is something you learned from one of your classmates' speeches?

A robotic fly is about the same size as a pencil tip.

Microrobots Inspired by Nature 🎧 3.4

EXPLORER IN ACTION
Robert Wood is an engineer and researcher.

The world needs bees to pollinate plants, and many of those plants are crops grown for human consumption. Unfortunately, pesticides, parasites, and poor nutrition are harming the world's bee population, which has been decreasing rapidly in recent years. Without bees, many food crops and wild plants will cease to exist, creating a major disruption to the world's food chain. While worldwide efforts to protect bees are underway, many people fear that these measures are not enough. National Geographic Explorer Robert Wood is working toward another solution, one tiny robot at a time.

Wood founded the Microrobotics Lab at Harvard University, where he and his team develop miniature robots to complete tasks too dangerous or tedious for humans and animals. One of these creations is RoboBees—tiny, flying robots that are not dangerous to humans. Although inspired by real bees, RoboBees have limitations and can't fly for very long. Wood says, "You have not just one all-capable robot, but you have a bunch of not very good robots. The idea is that the whole is greater than the sum of the parts."

Will RoboBees change the world? Whether or not they can, Wood reminds us of the importance of "investing in the unknown."

▶ **3.3** Watch the video to learn more.

1. How can RoboBees help the world?

2. Wood believes it is important to invest in the unknown. Do you agree? Why or why not?

How Will You Take Action?

Choose one or more of these actions to do.

Personal

Spend time with a friend or family member—without technology!

1. Invite a friend or family member to get together in person, device-free.
2. Ask them questions about themselves and listen to their answers.
3. Later, reflect on how in-person interaction differs from digital interactions. Make plans to spend more time in person in the future.

School

Make a poster about using technology in a friendly way.

1. Spend at least one school day observing how technology is used by teachers and students.
2. Note any uses of technology that seem to isolate people or reduce the friendliness of interaction.
3. Brainstorm ways to make the use of technology friendlier and less isolating. Create a poster sharing your best ideas with your class.

Local

Help someone in your community use technology.

1. If you know someone who struggles with computers or other technology, offer to spend time helping him or her. If not, research volunteer opportunities to help others in your community.
2. Set up a time to meet, or make an appointment to volunteer.
3. Carefully and patiently help the person(s) practice using the technology.

Global

Support an environmentally friendly company.

1. Research a business that is using technology to help the environment.
2. Write a letter to the company to thank them for being environmentally friendly.
3. Write a letter to the editor of a newspaper praising the company's efforts, or post about them online.

Reflect

1. Reflect on your Take Action project(s). What was successful? What do you wish you had done differently? Why?
2. Reread your response to the Essential Question **What are the benefits and drawbacks of new technology?** in Connect Across Texts. How did your Take Action projects change or add to your response?
3. What will you do differently in your life because of what you learned in this unit?

4 Stress

What do you think this proverb means?

Look at the photo and caption. Discuss the questions.

1. Do you think the woman in the photo is feeling stress? Explain why or why not.

2. Describe what you see in the "virtual nature" scene. What would you add to the scene to make it more relaxing? Why?

◀ **A woman participates in a scientific study to see how people respond to "virtual nature."**

167

ESSENTIAL QUESTION

What are the positive and negative effects of stress?

Explore the Essential Question

Think Write your ideas about the Essential Question in the Unit Concept Map.

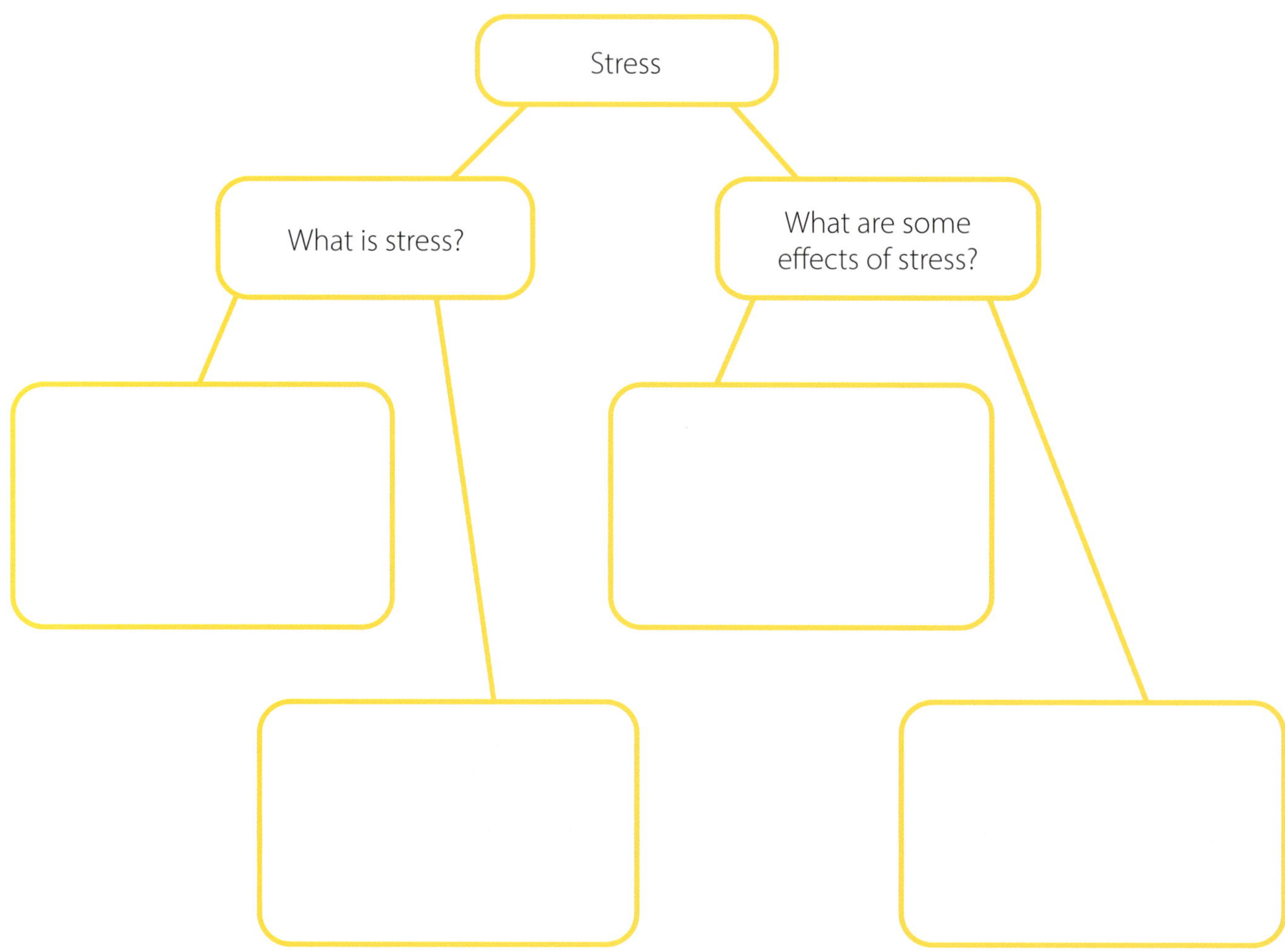

Respond Write one or two sentences to respond to the Essential Question.

____

____

____

Discuss Your Ideas Use your Unit Concept Map and your response to share your ideas with the class.

Discussion Frames

I define stress as . . .

Some effects of stress are . . .

One example of this is . . .

What do you think about . . .?

Academic Vocabulary

Use these words to express your ideas throughout the unit.

PRACTICE 1 Use context to determine the meaning of each word in blue. Then match the word to its definition.

Imagine your school is holding a fire drill today. Fire drills **demonstrate** everyone's ability to stay safe. They also help everyone learn skills for **survival**. But not knowing **precisely** when the drill will happen is stressful. You're trying to remember the **sequence** of events from the last fire drill, but you can't. You're trying to **maintain** your focus as the day goes on, but you feel **physically** unwell. You feel dizzy and start sweating. You are stressed out!

Word	Definition
maintain	to continue an existing action, feeling, or state
	related to or involving the body
	the state of staying alive
	to prove something through an action; to show clearly
	exactly; strictly
	the order in which events happen

PRACTICE 2 Work with a partner. Make a flash card for each Academic Vocabulary word. Write the word on the front of the card. Then write the word's definition and part of speech on the other side. Use the cards to quiz each other. Each partner should correctly identify each word at least once.

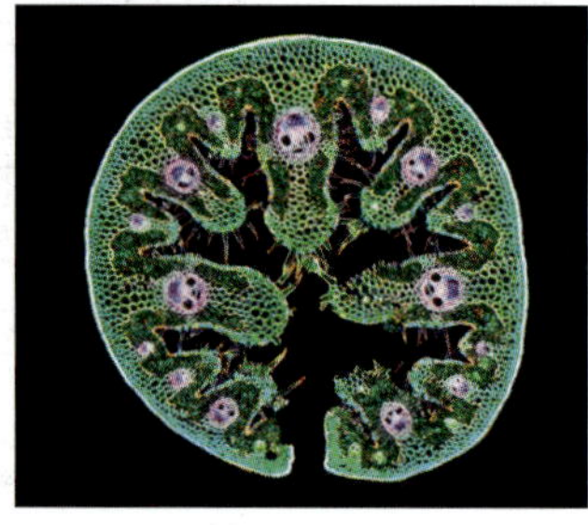

How can stress be beneficial?

First Thoughts

Think of a time when experiencing stress was beneficial to you. What was happening? How did the stressful feelings help you? Write your ideas in the chart. Discuss your ideas with a small group.

Stressful Moment	How It Helped Me

Key Vocabulary

PRACTICE Use context to determine the meaning of each word in bold. Then match the word to its definition.

1. When you're taking a test, loud noises can be **stressors**.

2. The brain and spinal cord are part of the human **nervous system**.

3. She felt an **acute** pain in her back when she lifted the box.

4. The new flowers you planted in the shade aren't **viable** because they don't get enough sunlight.

5. Your brain and lungs work together on the **regulation** of your breathing.

6. Weeds will **persist** even if you keep pulling them out of the garden.

______ **1.** stressor   **a.** a thing that causes stress (n.)

______ **2.** nervous system   **b.** capable of growing and living (adj.)

______ **3.** acute   **c.** to keep existing despite hardship (v.)

______ **4.** viable   **d.** the act of controlling something (n.)

______ **5.** regulation   **e.** a body system that sends and receives signals about feelings and movements (n.)

______ **6.** persist   **f.** sudden and severe (adj.)

Reading Skill: Evaluate an Argument   RI.8.8

To make an **argument**, an author must make a **claim** (a statement that can be agreed or disagreed with), and then support it with **evidence**. To evaluate an argument, a reader must figure out whether the overall argument is sound, or logical.

To evaluate an argument, ask yourself:

- What claims does the author make?
- Does the author support these claims with strong reasons and enough evidence to make a convincing argument?

After reading, ask yourself:

- What main argument does the author make?
- Does this argument make sense? Why or why not?
- Do I agree with this argument? Why or why not?

Skill in Action

Study the model. Do you agree with the evaluation of the argument? Why or why not?

This is the claim.

I think the author's argument makes sense. The author gives a strong reason and evidence about how sunlight levels affect plants.

People must pay close attention to where they put plants in their yards if they want their plants to properly grow and thrive.

Different plants need varying amounts of sunlight or shade. Plants often come with a tag that indicates their needs. For example, if a plant's tag says "full sun," that plant needs roughly six or more hours of sunlight each day. If someone puts that plant in a heavily shaded area, the plant will not be getting the sunlight it needs. The plant may grow poorly or die.

Some nonnative plants make attractive additions to a yard. They can provide a splash of color or an unusual touch.

This is a reason that supports the claim.

This is evidence that supports the claim.

This doesn't seem to be relevant to the claim.

Do PLANTS Feel STRESS?

by John Staughton
from ABC Science

Plants do feel stress from the environment and other activities, but their response to stress is very different from human responses, since plants lack a **nervous system** and traditional brain.

🎧 4.1

1   Imagine that you are walking home after a long day, during which someone yelled at you, you started coming down with a cold,[1] and you missed an important deadline. As you step off the curb to cross
5   the street, the screeching horn of an oncoming car shocks you into action and you leap back in time to avoid being struck. Your heart is racing, your breathing gets shallow,[2] and you immediately break out into a sweat.[3] In short,[4] you are stressed out in every possible
10 way—physically, emotionally, and psychologically.

    Human beings and animals experience and demonstrate stress in ways that we mostly understand. But what about plants? What is the equivalent to a plant feeling nervous before a test? Or a plant feeling
15 a surge of energy after finding itself in a dangerous situation? Can plants feel stress and pain, or can only conscious life forms experience those?

---

[1] **coming down with a cold** getting sick
[2] **shallow** short and fast
[3] **break out into a sweat** start sweating
[4] **In short** Basically

Plants in Nature

When a human being or other conscious being encounters a
stressful experience, such as an oncoming collision or a predator's
attack, they often benefit from flight-or-fight reactions. They
either fight and defend themselves or run away from the threat.
Plants, however, are quite literally rooted to the ground, and are
therefore unable to remove themselves from dangerous or stressful
situations.

When we think about predator and prey in the wild, we
rarely think of plants. From the point of view of plants, all plant-
eaters are predators! Also, besides predators, plants must also
defend against threats such as excess rainfall, very hot or cold
temperatures, and drought. Plants that are unable to stand[5] or
avoid such **stressors** will be unable to grow, produce **viable** seeds,
and reproduce. Clearly, given the nearly 400,000 species of plants
identified so far, the flora of Earth has developed its own ways to
respond to stress.

Stress Response in Plants

When a plant has a difficult time, stressed by weather,
predators, or disease, there are not many options—adapt or perish.
Death is not always a terrible option. Many plants are short-lived[6]
because they lack adaptations to survive hard times, but if they
have already reproduced, death isn't a failure for their species.

Plants that are able to survive develop ways to reproduce
despite the challenges they face.[7] Plants that can deal with
changes in temperature and water levels without dying are often
referred to as hardy plants. Hardy plants gradually developed
certain characteristics to adapt to stressful conditions. Some of
these characteristics, such as the ability to change their leaf size to
match growing conditions, allow them to overcome environmental
challenges. These adaptations provide long-term protection against
regular or seasonal stress.

Finally, there is the **acute** stress response of plants, which
is most similar to our own fight-or-flight response. In the event
of an immediate threat, such as a predator eating its leaves or a

---

[5] **stand** tolerate
[6] **are short-lived** do not live very long
[7] **challenges they face** difficulties they experience

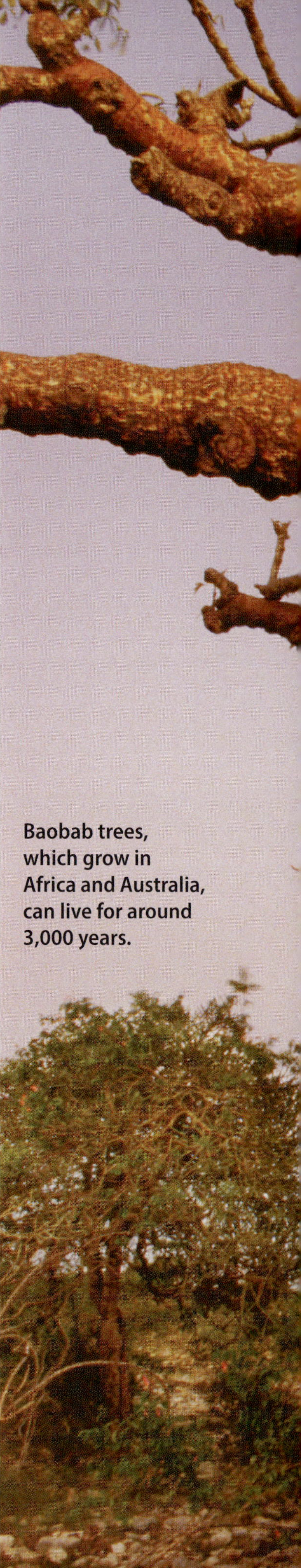

Baobab trees,
which grow in
Africa and Australia,
can live for around
3,000 years.

fungus beginning to grow on its roots, a plant will have a hormonal
response. Human hormone **regulation** is controlled by the brain and
nervous system. They release hormones at precisely the right time to
maintain health. Plants, however, do not have a nervous system or
brain; instead, every single plant cell produces its own hormones.

Plant hormones control every step in the growth, development,
reproduction, and defense of the plant, including stress response.
Most of the hormones are used only during certain stages of a
plant's life cycle, while others, such as stress response hormones,
can be produced and used at any time.

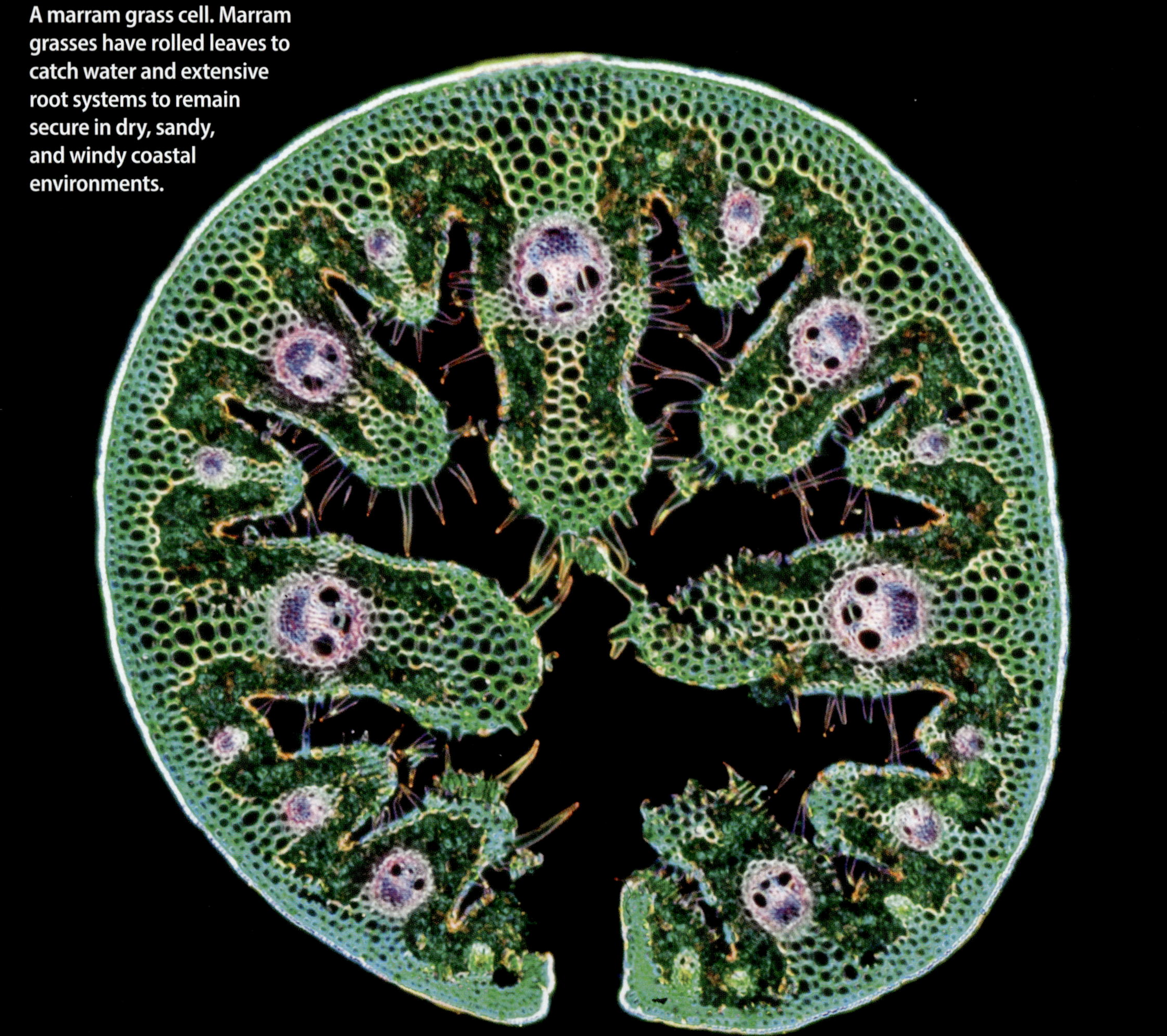

A marram grass cell. Marram grasses have rolled leaves to catch water and extensive root systems to remain secure in dry, sandy, and windy coastal environments.

When a plant is experiencing stress, it produces a
hormone that slows or stops bud growth. In the case of water
stress, or drought, this same hormone can close the stomata,
or channels in the leaves, to prevent water loss through
evaporation.

A plant that is being attacked by a pathogen may release
salicylic acid, a hormone that functions as an alarm system
in plants. This substance can be released into the air to warn
neighboring plants of the attack so that they can prepare
themselves. This type of "communication" between plants
is often mistaken for intelligence but is instead the result of
automatic triggers in chemical pathways.

Plants also use jasmonic acid, a substance that works as
both a defensive substance and an airborne warning system to
other leaves of the plant and to nearby plants. Its scent is very
unpleasant to predators, both above and below ground.

Together with dozens of other plant hormones that are
produced and used throughout a plant's life cycle, these
defensive hormones play a key role in protecting individual
plants from a variety of threats.

A Final Word

Although plants don't have a nervous system or brain, they
still recognize and respond to danger. While the debate over
whether plants can "feel pain" often veers from science into
philosophy,[8] there is no question[9] that plants feel stress. Stress
is a part of life, as environmental conditions change and living
things are forced to adapt or respond.

Stress in plants is not necessarily a bad thing, but we
often think of it, in human terms, as a "painful" experience.
In some cases, stress allows a plant to "learn" more about its
environment so it can better prepare for the future. In other
cases, stress helps species develop new ways to **persist**. This
isn't all that different from the human experience with difficult
situations—for some people, there is no better motivator to
overcome a challenge than a solid dose[10] of stress!

---

[8] **veers from science into philosophy** raises questions that can't be answered by science alone
[9] **no question** no doubt
[10] **solid dose** large amount

Close Read

Work with a partner.

1. Determine the meanings of your underlined words and phrases.
2. Discuss the question: **What kinds of stressors affect plants?**

Understand and Analyze

Respond to the questions. Support your responses with evidence from the text.

1. **Explain** Reread the article's introduction. Why do plants respond to stress differently from how humans do?
2. **Interpret** Reread lines 38–40. Why is death "not always a terrible option" for plants?
3. **Deduce** Reread lines 44–49. Think about everything you have read in the article. How might growing bigger or smaller leaves help a plant?
4. **Generalize** Reread lines 54–62. What is the purpose of hormones for both humans and plants?
5. **Restate** Reread lines 75–78. What does the author mean by "defensive substance and an airborne warning system"?
6. **Correlate** Reread lines 90–97. When people talk about stress and plants, why would they avoid using a term such as "painful"?

Apply the Skill: Evaluate an Argument

What is the main claim the author makes in "Do Plants Feel Stress?" Write it in the chart, along with the reasons and evidence that support it.

Claim	Reasons	Evidence

Share Your Perspective

Discuss these questions in a small group.

1. Think about the plants in your community. Does reading this article make you see them differently now? Why or why not?
2. Based on what you've learned in the article, do you think plants can feel pain? Why or why not?

Discussion Frames

At first, I thought …

But now, I think …

In relation to plants, …

What convinced you that …?

Language Convention: Understand Punctuation for Pauses and Breaks L.8.2.A

Authors use punctuation to clearly express their ideas. To indicate a break or pause, authors can use commas or dashes. When reading silently or aloud, pause when you come to this type of punctuation. Think about which type of punctuation is being used and why.

Punctuation	Purpose	Examples
comma (,)	set off a clarification	That plant is very hardy, or strong.
	separate ideas within a list	The plant's leaves are torn, missing, or broken.
	set off an introductory clause	After studying the plant, the scientist set up a camera near the plant.
	separate clauses in a sentence	The camera took pictures, but because there was so little light, the scientist couldn't see what was attacking the plant.
dash (—)	break for emphasis	The scientist finally figured out what was killing the plants—a rabbit.

Example

This first comma comes after an introductory clause.

When a plant has a difficult time, stressed by weather, predators, or disease, there are not many options—adapt or perish.

These commas show separation of ideas in a list.

This dash is used for emphasis.

PRACTICE Work with a partner. Read the sentences aloud. Use appropriate pauses. Then answer the questions.

1. "In short, you are stressed out in every possible way—physically, emotionally, and psychologically."

   In the above sentence, what is the purpose of the dash?

   a. to separate ideas in a list
   b. emphasis

2. "Plants also use jasmonic acid, a substance that works as both a defensive substance and an airborne warning system to other leaves of the plant and to nearby plants."

   In the above sentence, what is the purpose of the comma?

   a. to set off a clarification
   b. to set off an introductory clause

Read Again

Read "Do Plants Feel Stress?" again. As you read, circle details from the text that help you respond to this question:

How do plants respond to stress?

Reflect and Respond

Choose several details you circled in the text to complete the idea web.

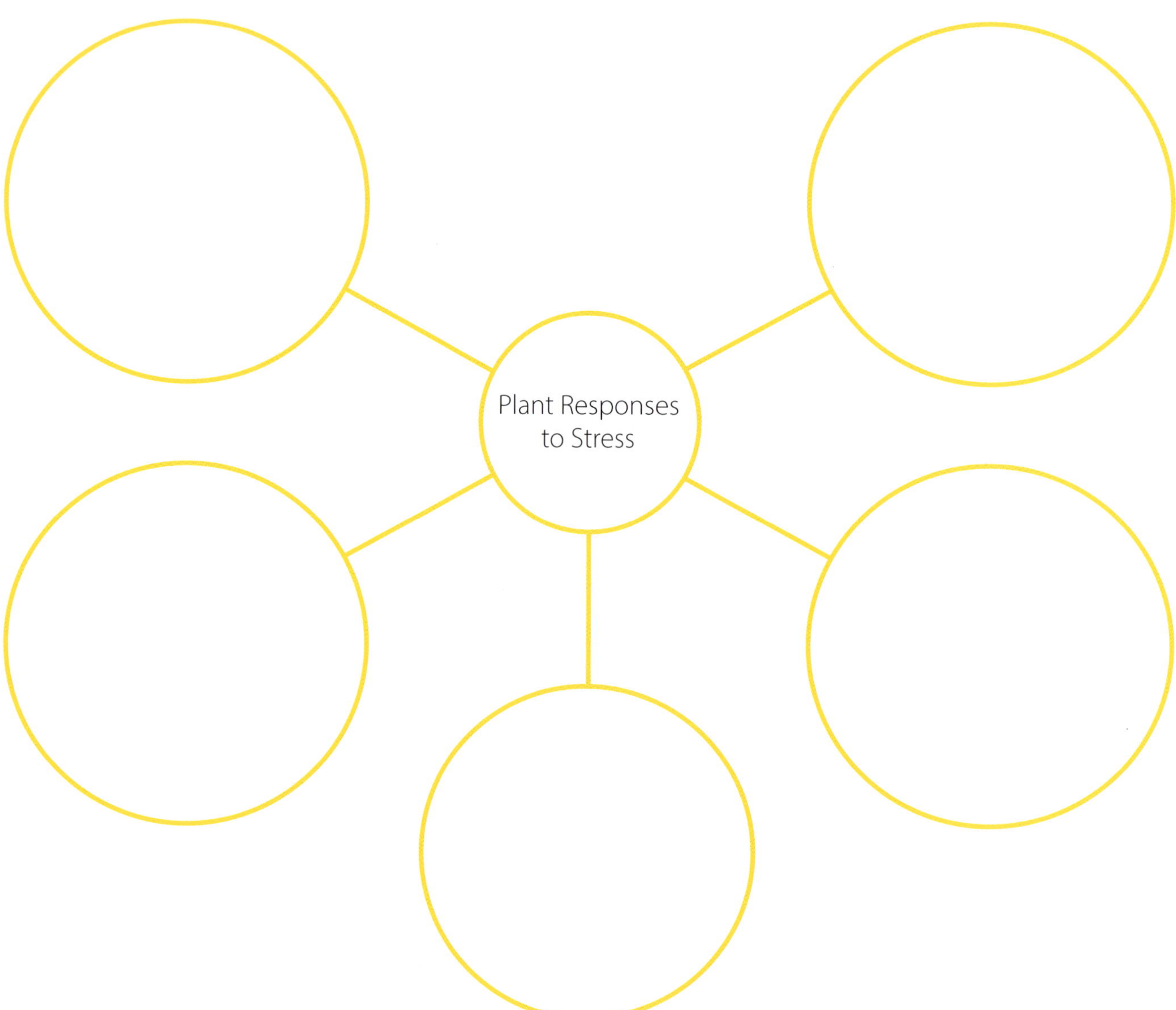

Use your idea web to respond to the question: How do plants respond to stress?

____

____

____

Discuss Your Response

Share your ideas with the class. Write one new idea you hear.

____

____

Respond to the Guiding Question

Write a response to the question:

How can stress be beneficial?

Use evidence from the text, your discussion, and your life. Use the Discussion Frames to help you. Use the rubric to check your response.

____

____

____

____

Research   SL.8.4

Choose one of these topics. Research the topic to learn more about it.

- salt stress in plants

- whether plants feel pain

Follow these steps:

1. Make notes about what you already know about the topic.

2. Write three questions you have about the topic.

3. Research the topic to find answers to your questions.

4. Write your answers to the questions.

5. Present what you learn to a small group.

How does stress affect the brain?

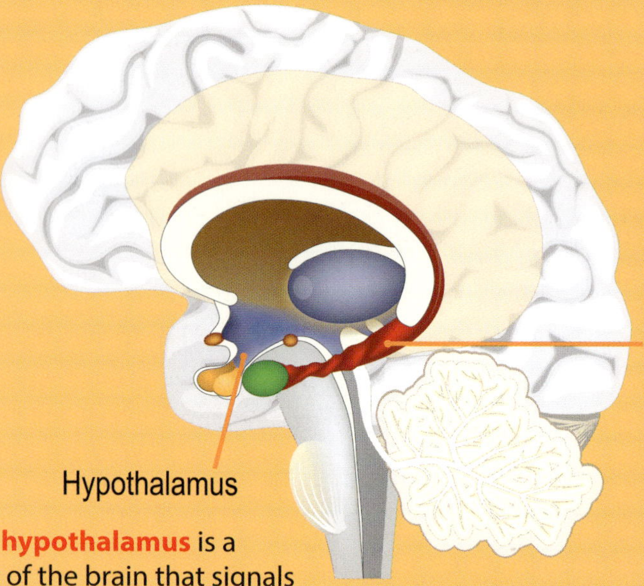

Adrenaline is a stress hormone that increases your heart rate and gives you energy.

Cortisol is a stress hormone connected to mood and fear. Too much cortisol can affect the digestive system.

Hippocampus

An excess of cortisol reduces the ability of the **hippocampus** region of the brain to form memories.

The **hypothalamus** is a part of the brain that signals the body to release cortisol and adrenaline.

Effects of long-term stress

- Heart disease
- Sleep problems
- Obesity
- Digestive problems
- Skin problems

How does exercise reduce stress?

Exercise helps your brain release endorphins, chemicals that fight pain and improve your mood.

Exercise increases the production of antibodies. These are proteins that help fight viruses and diseases.

Exercise reduces levels of the body's stress hormones, such as adrenaline and cortisol.

Exercise helps you sleep better, which can help to reduce stress.

Young women in the United Arab Emirates Cycling Girls Club gather every other Saturday morning for informal competition. Some of the club members are now also competing in triathlons.

Examine the Graphic

Use details from the graphic to respond to the questions. Discuss your responses with a partner.

1. Why do you think the author includes an image of the brain? How is this image helpful?

2. In the part of the graphic showing the effects of long-term stress on the body, what effects are listed?

3. How do the arrows help readers understand the effects of exercise on the body?

4. What does exercise increase? How does this help the body?

5. What does exercise decrease? How does this help the body?

Make Connections

Use details from "Do Plants Feel Stress?" and the graphic to discuss your responses with a partner.

1. What similarities do plants and humans share when reacting to stress?

2. Plants use stress to adapt to their surroundings. How can humans use stress to adapt to their environment?

Reflect

Reflect on your discussions. What questions do you still have about the graphic or the effects of stress? Write a list of questions and discuss them with a partner.

How can we use humor to manage stress?

First Thoughts

Imagine you're getting ready for school and realize you forgot to study for an important test. How would you respond? Rank the options from most likely (1) to least likely (4). Then compare your responses with a partner's. Which response do you think is probably the best? Why?

Response (Rank 1–4)

______ remain calm and hope for the best

______ start studying

______ stay home from school

______ explain the situation to my teacher

Key Vocabulary

PRACTICE Use context to determine the meaning of each word in bold. Then match the word to its definition.

1. Thoughtful words and actions **reinforce** social bonds.
2. You always believe I can do difficult tasks. I appreciate your **optimism**.
3. The **analytical** part of your brain thinks about and works on problems.
4. Which friend should he choose to be his partner? He has a **dilemma**.
5. Scaring people can **stimulate** fear responses such as screaming or running.
6. Being kind can **enhance** your reputation.

______ **1.** reinforce	**a.** the belief that good things will happen (n.)
______ **2.** optimism	**b.** a problem involving a difficult choice (n.)
______ **3.** analytical	**c.** to increase or improve (v.)
______ **4.** dilemma	**d.** involving logic, reasoning, or careful examination (adj.)
______ **5.** stimulate	**e.** to strengthen or support (v.)
______ **6.** enhance	**f.** to activate (v.)

Reading Strategy: Monitor Comprehension

Good readers monitor their own comprehension during and after reading. To ensure you fully understand a text, periodically pause to confirm comprehension. Read a section of text. Then pause to reflect on what you have read. Write a brief response, such as a personal reaction, a summary, or a comment about the section's content. If you are unable to write a response, ask yourself:

- Which part of the text is confusing?
- What might help me better understand the text?

Use one of these monitoring strategies:

- **Reread.** Go back and reread a sentence, a paragraph, or a whole section of the text. Rereading can help you better understand the text.
- **Read on.** Keep reading to look for answers to your questions. More information might be presented further on in the text.
- **Reflect.** Think about what you have just read. Give yourself time to think through complex ideas.

Strategy in Action

Below is an example of how one student monitored comprehension. Study the model to see if there are other things that need to be clarified.

> Studies show that laughter stimulates the immune system by increasing the number and activity of natural killer cells and other antibodies. Laughter also lowers the level of serum cortisol, a substance released by the adrenal glands during stress. In addition, laughing exercises your lungs and increases the amount of oxygen in your blood.

What I need to clarify: I don't know what "stimulates the immune system" means.

Strategy I will use: rereading

How the strategy helped: I figured out the meaning by using the context clues "natural killer cells" and "other antibodies." So laughter increases the body's anti-disease efforts.

Young women share a laugh in Kashmir, India.

Humor
HELPS

by **Carolyn J. Gard**

🎧 **4.2**

1   You flunked the world's hardest algebra test. You bang your locker door open. As you're about to stalk off[1] to your next class, your eye catches[2] a cartoon you've taped to your locker door. You laugh all the way
5   to English class.

How did a simple laugh turn your mood completely around[3]?

For years, health care professionals have known that stress and anger can lead to high
10   blood pressure, muscle tension, and sickness. They weren't sure, however, if the opposite was true. Could humor lower blood pressure and keep people well? The answer is yes. Researchers have found scientific evidence that laughter makes a
15   person feel better.

Studies show that laughter **stimulates** the immune system by increasing the number and activity of natural killer cells and other antibodies. Laughter also lowers the level of serum cortisol, a
20   substance released by the adrenal glands during stress. In addition, laughing exercises your lungs and increases the amount of oxygen in your blood.

---

[1] **stalk off** angrily walk away
[2] **your eye catches** you see
[3] **turn your mood completely around** change your emotions completely

Dr. Peter Derks found that when people listened to jokes, their brain waves spread through their entire cerebral cortex. He concluded that humor uses the whole brain—both the **analytical** and the sensory parts.

Laugh It Off

A sense of humor isn't an ability—it's an attitude.

A good sense of humor can lead to greater resilience, **optimism**, and emotional well-being. That's important because you can't always control what goes on in your life—you don't write the test questions or decide where your family lives. What you can control is how you react to these events. When you choose to laugh rather than wallow in self-pity,[4] you take control of the situation.

Suppose you're the shortest person in your entire school and you're sick and tired of being the brunt[5] of all the short-person jokes. You can get mad at the joke-tellers and storm off,[6] sure that short people have no chance of success in the world. Or you can respond with a witty remark and get on to another subject.

The first response simply makes you madder. The second response disarms your tormenters.[7] By laughing at yourself, you've become powerful. You don't let others define who you are.

Kinds of Humor

A sense of humor doesn't mean laughing at everything.

Most humor has one of three targets—yourself, a situation, or another person. When you laugh at yourself, you make those around you feel safe. If your friend is feeling bad because she gave you chicken pox, you can tell her that you wanted your face to match your polka-dot shirt.

---

[4] **wallow in self-pity** spend time feeling sad for yourself
[5] **brunt** object; target
[6] **storm off** angrily walk away
[7] **disarms your tormenters** takes away power from those teasing you

A grandson and grandmother
laugh together.

Joking about humorous situations, such as what happened when the lights went out in the middle of class, keeps the target of the joke away from others. The worst kind of humor—and the one to avoid—is humor directed at others. This includes sarcasm, put-downs,[8] and jokes that are insensitive to the feelings of others.

Healthy humor brings people together. Telling a joke about a familiar experience gives people a sense of belonging, of being part of the group.

Now, That's Funny!

While laughter seems to come more easily to some people than to others, most of us probably had a good sense of humor when we were young. One study found that the average kindergartner laughs much more frequently than the average adult. Growing up is a good thing, but you don't want to outgrow your ability to laugh.

Listen to yourself to see what you laugh at. Then collect books, magazines, comics, and videos that **reinforce** your sense of humor. When you're studying and don't think you can cram another fact into your head,[9] take a humor break. You'll come back to your project refreshed, and, just possibly, with a new killer idea.[10]

As you learn to laugh at yourself, you **enhance** your self-esteem. You relax, and you laugh more. As you laugh more, you become more fun to be with, and you'll have the wonderful **dilemma** of being too much in demand.

---

[8] **put-downs** insults
[9] **cram another fact into your head** continue to learn at that moment
[10] **killer idea** really good idea

How Does Your **Humor** Rate?

1. **It's the ultimate bad hair day. As you head for your history test, someone calls out, "Is that a new style, or did you forget to look in a mirror?" Your response?**

   a "Where'd you get your shirt––the dumpster?"
   b You storm off to class.
   c "I combed it with an egg-beater this morning. It may be ugly, but it's fast."

2. **For the second time in a week, you break a glass while you're loading the dishwasher. Your brother asks, "Juggle much?" Your answer?**

   a "You know that I hate doing this."
   b "Do it yourself and see if you can do any better."
   c "Know how many jugglers it takes to change a light bulb? One, but the juggler needs at least three light bulbs."

3. **In the pickup basketball game, you manage to get one basket while everyone else gets six. When the others laugh at you, you defend your poor showing.**

   a "You guys were cheating."
   b "I just need a little more practice."
   c With a big smile: "I didn't want to show you guys up."

4. **You're hurrying to class and fall flat, scattering books across the hall. You lie there listening to the calls of, "Enjoy your fall?" As you get up, you say,**

   a "I know one of you jerks tripped me."
   b "You might ask if I'm hurt."
   c "Yeah. It's a great way to get attention."

IF YOU CHOSE:

Mostly a's

You tend to get hostile when things go against you. Lighten up.

Mostly b's

You're resigned to your fate. You need some humor in your life.

Mostly c's

You've got a good sense of humor and have confidence in yourself. Keep smiling!

Close Read

Work with a partner.

1. Determine the meanings of your underlined words and phrases.
2. Discuss the question:

   How does humor help people physically and mentally?

Understand and Analyze

Respond to the questions. Support your responses with evidence from the text.

1. **Cite** Reread lines 8–10. What physical problems can stress cause for people?
2. **Interpret** Reread the section "Laugh It Off." How is a sense of humor "an attitude"?
3. **Categorize** Reread the section "Kinds of Humor." What are some kinds of "healthy humor"?
4. **Infer** Reread lines 67–69. Why do you think kindergartners are able to laugh so much more frequently than average adults?
5. **Correlate** Reread lines 71–75. How can listening "to yourself to see what you laugh at" help you with homework?
6. **Explain** Reread the last paragraph of the article. What does the author mean by "the wonderful dilemma of being too much in demand"?

Apply the Strategy: Monitor Comprehension

Discuss your monitoring strategies with a partner. Which strategy worked best to help you fully understand the text? Explain how you monitored your own comprehension while reading.

Share Your Perspective

Discuss these questions in a small group.

1. Which response to being teased do you think is better: getting angry or laughing at yourself? Why?
2. Name someone you know who has a good sense of humor. How do you think that sense of humor helps the person in everyday life?

Discussion Frames

In my opinion, the better response is … because …

Someone with a good sense of humor is …

His/Her sense of humor is beneficial because …

Can you explain more about …?

Vocabulary: Use a Dictionary L.8.4.C

Print and online dictionaries are excellent reference materials to use while you're reading. You can use a dictionary to figure out how to pronounce a word or to learn its definition. You can also:

- identify a word's part of speech
- clarify the exact meaning or usage of a multiple-meaning word
- see how a word is used in example phrases or sentences

Example

Here is the part of speech.

The word has multiple meanings.

Dictionary entry:
familiar [fuh-MILL-yer]
adjective
1. commonly seen: *a familiar sight*
2. close; intimate: *a familiar friend*

The entry gives examples showing how the word is used.

Apply the Strategy

Look at "Humor Helps" again. Find at least three words that you don't know well. Use a dictionary to look up the words. Complete the chart, and then share with a partner what you learn about each word. For example, share information about a word's pronunciation, part of speech, definition, and usage.

Unknown Word	What I Learned from the Dictionary

Read Again

Read "Humor Helps" again. As you read, circle details from the text that help you respond to this question:

How can people use humor to improve their lives?

Reflect and Respond

Choose several details you circled in the text to complete the idea web.

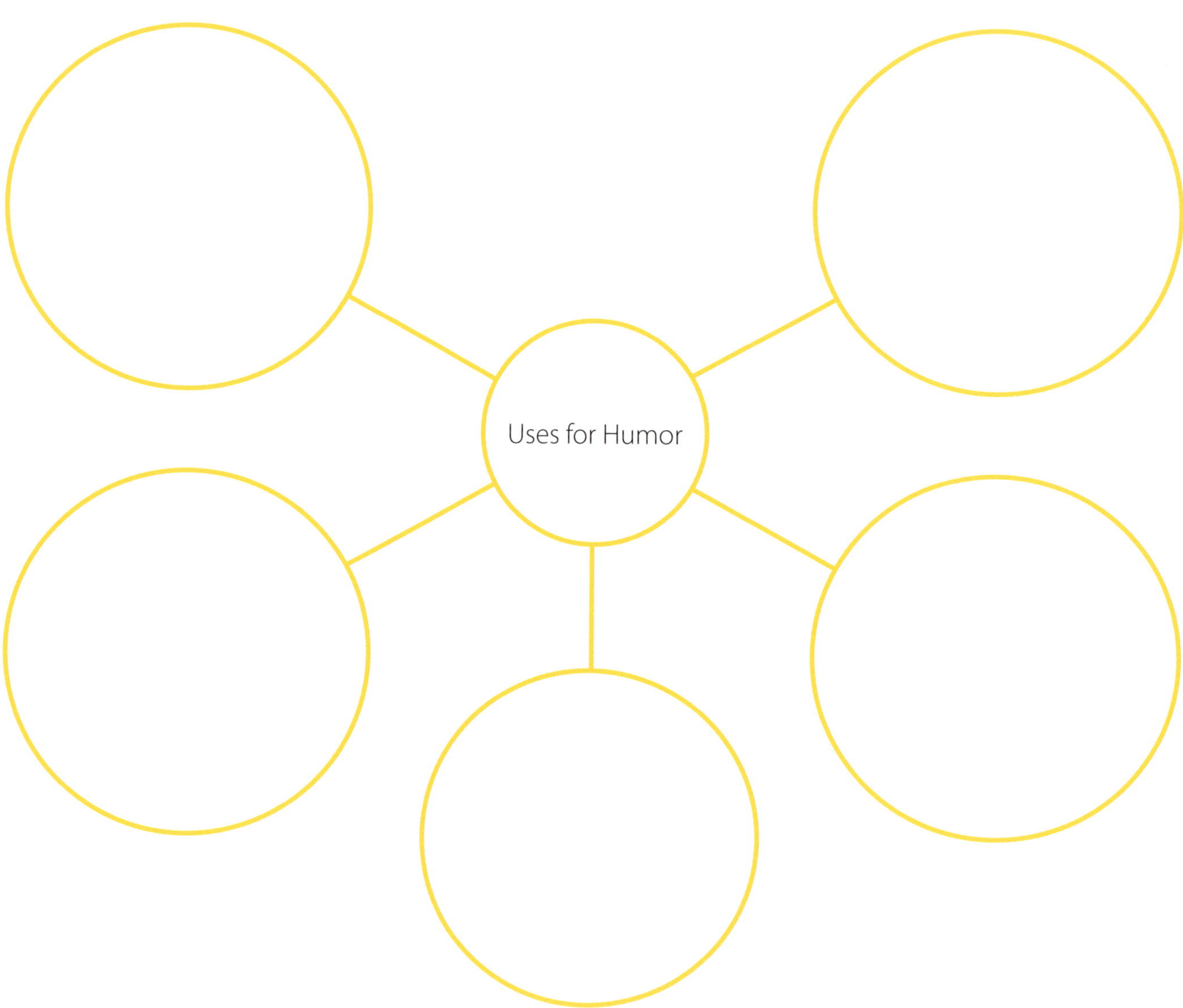

Use your idea web to respond to the question: How can people use humor to improve their lives?

____

____

____

Discuss Your Response

Share your ideas with the class. Write one new idea you hear.

____

____

____

Respond to the Guiding Question

Write a response to the question:

How can we use humor to manage stress?

Use evidence from the text, your discussion, and your life. Use the Discussion Frames to help you. Use the rubric to check your response.

____

____

____

____

Create and Present: Humor

Think about what you learned about stress and humor in "Humor Helps." Then do one of these activities:

OPTION 1: Draw a Cartoon

Draw a humorous cartoon. Include speech balloons or a caption, if needed. Share your cartoon with the class.

OPTION 2: Write Jokes

Work with a partner. Together, write two jokes that use appropriate, positive humor. Practice telling the jokes a few times. Then present or act out your jokes for the class.

How can stress affect people's actions?

Golfer Bronte Law reacts after missing a shot during the final round of the Curtis Cup Match in Nairn, Scotland.

First Thoughts

Think about a time you were performing a task while someone watched you closely. How did being watched affect your ability to do the task? Share your responses with a small group and compare reactions.

Viewing Skill: Prioritize Information

When you're watching a video, it's easy to become distracted by illustrations, animations, and sound effects, such as music. To help you stay focused, prioritize which information you should pay the most attention to. Keep track of the most important main ideas and key details.

Apply the Skill

▶ 4.1 Watch the TED-Ed animation "How to Stay Calm Under Pressure." As you watch, take notes in the chart about the main idea and key details.

Main Idea 1: Many people "choke" or have performance anxiety during important times in their lives.	
Theories About Why People "Choke"	**Details About Theories**
1.	
2.	

Understand and Analyze

▶ 4.1 Watch again. Answer the questions. Support your responses with evidence from the video.

1. **Review** What is working memory?
2. **Explain** Why do some people have trouble accessing their working memory when they're doing a complex task under pressure?
3. **Examine** How can trying to figure out the steps for a familiar action alter a person's focus?
4. **Distinguish** Which option do researchers believe is a better strategy for avoiding "choking": focusing on the mechanics of a task or focusing on the overall goal?

Share Your Perspective

1. Do you think a pre-performance routine would help you avoid "choking"? Why or why not?
2. What are some ways you have found to handle stress when you are under pressure?

How can acknowledging stress make us stronger?

First Thoughts

When you are stressed, how does talking about your feelings with others affect you? How does keeping your feelings to yourself affect you? In the chart, make notes about the two experiences. Discuss your responses with a small group.

Sharing My Feelings	Keeping Feelings to Myself

Key Vocabulary

PRACTICE Use context to determine the meaning of each word in bold. Then match the word to its definition.

1. He didn't know why he was being mean because his anger was **unconscious**.
2. She was not nervous, so she walked onto the stage with no **hesitation**.
3. I want decorations that **reflect** my personality, so they should all be very bright and cheerful.
4. The weather is **peculiar**. It's strangely cold and wet for this time of year.
5. The manager cares about his employees. He is a very kind and **conscientious** leader.

_____ **1.** unconscious   **a.** the act of pausing before moving or speaking (n.)

_____ **2.** hesitation   **b.** odd or unusual (adj.)

_____ **3.** reflect   **c.** hidden or unknown to oneself (adj.)

_____ **4.** peculiar   **d.** careful about doing something correctly (adj.)

_____ **5.** conscientious   **e.** to show or express (v.)

A **summary** is a short retelling of the most important concepts from a story. **Summarize** by focusing on key elements, such as the characters, setting, and plot. When you summarize, you tell what happens in a story in your own words. Summaries do not include the reader's opinions about the story. To summarize:

1. Pause to think about the most important characters, events, ideas, and details. Ask yourself *who, what, when, where,* and *why* questions. For example: *Why were the characters lost?*

2. Use your answers to summarize the story in your own words.

3. Review your summary to make sure it is objective. Confirm that it provides only facts and not your opinions.

Skill in Action

Read the model summary of the story "All Summer in a Day" from Unit 1. Does this summary help you understand the key elements of the story? Why or why not? Discuss your answers with a partner.

The summary gives information about *when* the events occur (on the day when the sun appears after 7 years).

The summary gives information about *where* the story takes place (Venus, in a classroom).

"All Summer in a Day" takes place on Venus in a classroom of nine-year-olds. In the story, it's always raining on Venus. The sun only comes out for a few hours once every seven years. No children in the classroom can remember ever seeing the sun—except Margot. This is because Margot is from Earth, unlike the other children who were born and raised on Venus. Margot is very different from her classmates. She misses the sun and dislikes the constant rain, so she's quiet, unhappy, and often picked on.

The summary gives important information about *who* the story is about (Margot, a girl who is different and picked on).

The summary tells *what* happened (Margot gets locked in a closet by her classmates).

On the day of the story, the rain is about to stop, allowing the sun to appear. Margot gets very upset when her classmates lock her in a closet. The classmates go outside and enjoy the rare experience when the rain stops and the sun shines. When it's raining again and they're back inside, the children suddenly remember what they've done to Margot. They feel bad and guilty. The story ends when the children let Margot out of the closet.

The summary tells *why* the events are important (Margot misses the sun, and the children feel guilty about their actions).

Bearing Up

by **Matt Hughes**

🎧 **4.3**

1   He would kick and yell his way out of dreams where the bear was after him, his chest cold and sweat-slick. When he was little, the noise brought Mom or Dad to check on him, tuck him back in, kiss the bad stuff away.

   At 13, he didn't want his parents coming to his rescue—well, maybe
5   a little, but it would have bent his self-image.[1] So it was enough if Mom called out, "Are you OK, Mike?" from across the hall, and he would call back, "Yeah, I'm OK."

   Sometimes he would hear them mumbling about him, but in the morning, nobody made a big deal about it.

10   He'd had the bear dream for as long as he could recall. The settings varied but never the sequence of events. He'd be doing something ordinary—getting off a bus, walking up his front steps—when he'd catch a flicker of movement from the corner of his eye.[2] He'd turn, and there'd be a glimpse of something dark sliding around a corner. The glimpse
15   always shot through him with a bolt of white terror. He would back up, turn around, edge off[3] in another direction. If he fled the house, the bear would lurk in the yard. Get on the bus, and it would come snuffling at the door. Try to outrun it, and he would feel its breath on the back of his neck.

   At the end of the dream, he'd be trapped,
20   the bear stalking closer and closer. Then when
it was about to touch him, there'd come
a high-pitched whine, loud enough to
make his teeth buzz, and he'd burst out
of the dream,[4] sweating and gasping.

25   Mike once asked the school
counselor, Mrs. Skinner, if she knew
anything about dreams.

---

[1] **bent his self-image** felt embarrassing
[2] **from the corner of his eye** off to the side
[3] **edge off** move
[4] **burst out of the dream** quickly wake up

"Well, dreams can be about what's going on in our lives," said Mrs. Skinner, interrupting her perpetual search for order in the jumble of her desk.

"How do I put this[5]?" she asked. "Sometimes our dreams show us situations that are, in some ways, like our real-life situations. They might **reflect** something you are looking forward to, or something stressful."

"What about scary dreams, like where something's chasing you?"

"Hmm." She picked up a yellow form and frowned at it.

"A monster in a dream might stand for[6] something that worries you, some fear that your **unconscious** mind wants you to deal with, maybe. But you don't want to, so you run from it, and you can't get away."

"So what do I do?" Mike asked.

"Stop running. Anything you meet in a dream is part of you, so what's to be afraid of?" She peered at him. "Something you want to talk about?"

He had a feeling that if he started talking about the bear, he'd wander into parts of the forest[7] he wasn't ready to deal with. Things

---

[5] **put this** say this in a way that makes sense
[6] **stand for** represent
[7] **wander into parts of the forest** have to talk about things

would come up.[8] Things like moving here from Ottawa, like leaving all his friends, like being lonely, like not fitting in. Like being stressed and scared but not knowing why.

Here was the tiny town of Comox, at the end of a little stub of land that hung off the east coast of Vancouver Island. It was home to a few thousand people. Mike's father was a Search and Rescue Technician—a specialist, he liked to say, "in getting people out of situations where, if they had any sense, they wouldn't have got themselves into in the first place.[9]"

SAR Techs went out in the slow-flying De Havilland Buffalo or in the lumbering, two-rotor Labrador helicopters. If a fisherman abandoned a burning boat, the Lab would hover in the air so that Dad could jump into the cold sea, put a harness around the man before hypothermia killed him, and wait in the water while the victim was winched to safety.

It was dangerous work. Once, a Lab was picking stranded rock climbers off a mountain. The shivering climbers had been lifted aboard, and the last rescuer was coming up the cable when an engine suddenly shuddered and died. One rotor couldn't hold the helicopter in the air. It fell, crushing the life from the SAR Tech dangling beneath it.

Mike's father said there was no point thinking about it. Somebody had to go when people needed help; if it was risky, then it was risky.

"It's not being a hero," Dad said. "It's just a job that's got to be done."

"You didn't have to be a SAR Tech though," Mike said. "You volunteered. You used to be a cook."

Dad shrugged. "Don't worry. Nothing's going to happen."

"But don't you get stressed?"

"You don't let that get in the way.[10]" His father hunted around in his mind for a moment; he wasn't good with words. "You have to walk through that part.[11] 'Cause on the other side of it is this place where everything opens up,[12] you feel really great, and … you're just there."

Mike didn't tell his dad about the bear. After dinner that night, Mike was scrubbing a skillet, not thinking about

---

75 anything much when he asked, "Mom, do you get stressed when Dad
goes on a mission?"

His mother put three plates on the counter and looked into the living
room, where Dad was watching sports.

"I used to," she admitted. "But your father's very good at what he
80 does." Then she sighed. "Besides, there's no point worrying. He loves it.
He's not going to stop doing it. It's a big part of who he is."

"Pretty dangerous though."

"It's what he does. What you and I have to do is live with it.[13]" She
put a hand on Mike's arm. "Are you afraid he might get hurt?"

85 "Nah," Mike said. "I was just wondering how you felt."

On a late September afternoon, a wind blew up—not a big wind, but
big enough to whittle white points[14] on the gray-green chop of the water
in Georgia Strait. That was too big for the comfort of[15] four couples who
had crowded into an undersized skiff to go hand-trolling[16] for salmon a few
90 miles out from the shore.

---

[13] **live with it** accept that his job is dangerous
[14] **whittle white points** cause big waves
[15] **big for the comfort of** scary for
[16] **skiff to go hand-trolling** boat to go fishing

The boat owner, a welder who worked at the sawmill, decided it would be wise to head for shore. But when he tried to start the engine, it sputtered and died. He did all the things he knew to do: checked the spark plug, checked the fuel line, checked the gas tank—and found it empty. He'd forgotten to fill up before leaving the shore.

By the time he had identified the problem, the wind was causing the overloaded skiff to wallow[17] in steepening waves. He looked at the three men and four women who had come with him, without life jackets or even warm clothing, and said, "We're going to row in. Break out[18] the oars."

The oars were pulled out, and the two strongest men tried to row the boat shoreward. But the wind was offshore and strengthening as each long minute passed. Even with two men to an oar, the skiff barely made headway.[19]

"We're in trouble," said the welder, watching the light fade behind thickening clouds. He reached for the radio. Fortunately, he was more **conscientious** about the radio's batteries than the gas tank. When he tuned to the emergency channel and said, "Mayday, mayday," CFB Comox answered right back.

"I won't be home for supper," Dad said over the phone. "Some boaters are in trouble." A few minutes later, they heard the Labrador heading out to sea.

An hour crawled by. Mike and his mom sat in the darkening kitchen, drinking tea and trying not to look out the window. The clouds were low, eight shades of gray raggedly streaming on the wind that bent the tops of the fir trees. Cold rain tittered on the glass.

They turned on the lights and drank more tea, talking about nothing. Mom started dinner and Mike set the table; then they realized that neither was hungry, so they brewed more tea.

At 8 p.m., they heard the helicopter coming back and started dinner again. But a few minutes later, the Labrador passed overhead again and headed back out.

At 9 p.m., with the sky black and the wind whispering around the eaves, Mom called the headquarters. Mike saw her knuckles whiten, watched her face go quiet.[20] She hung up.

---

[17] **wallow** roll around
[18] **Break out** Get
[19] **made headway** moved forward
[20] **go quiet** become serious

"There were eight of them in a little boat, out of gas," she said. "The
Lab couldn't carry them all. Your father volunteered to stay behind in the
boat. When they came back for him, no boat. Probably swamped by a
wave and sunk. They're looking."

At 11 p.m., Comox's missing SAR Tech was the second story on the
late news. The TV showed footage of Labradors taking off and a map of
the search. Mike watched the images and heard the reporter's voice-over.
"Georgia Strait fills a deep and narrow trench between Vancouver Island
and the rest of North America. Strong tidal currents sweep the bone-
chilling water southeast, past the Gulf Islands and into the Strait of Juan
de Fuca, then around the southern tip of the big island.
"Anything floating on the surface gets flushed into the Pacific.
Unprotected from the cold, in seas tossed by stiff winds, a person in the
water can die in hours. Add a survival suit and expert knowledge, and life
expectancy—and hope—increases. The search continues."
Mike switched off the TV.
"They'll find him," Mom said. Her friends had come over to help
them wait. They talked cheerfully, in low voices. Mike nodded and said
"yeah sure" a lot.

By midnight the sky was clearing, stars making holes in the clouds.
Mike couldn't stay inside anymore. He put on his jacket and slipped out
the back door.
They lived on two acres that backed up against a stand[21] of second-
growth timber. The yard was unfenced, the lawn ending in a thicket of
blackberry bushes that grew between their property and the woods.
Mike sat on the back steps. The wind was dying, making a stillness
under the trees, and he got up and crossed the lawn where he could cut
through a gap in the bushes. A few steps into the woods lay a waist-high,
half-buried boulder forgotten by some careless glacier.
Mike walked around the rock, then leaned his forearms on the old granite
so that he was looking back toward the house. The stone was cold, and the
wetness left by the rain seeped into his jacket sleeves. He listened: Far to the
east, a search plane's engines murmured at the edge of his hearing.

---

[21] **backed up against a stand** were right next to an area

The last clouds tattered and moved off, letting the full moon silver the floor of the woods. The kitchen light shone yellow between the stark bars of the trunks. Then the plane's engines faded into the distance, and the only sound was a drop of rainwater working its way down through the branches.

In the perfect quiet, Mike caught a flicker of movement from the corner of his eye. He turned to look, but all he could see was a darkness in the gap between the blackberry bushes.

And then the darkness shifted.

Mike froze. He heard a heavy body rustling among the thorny bushes, wet smacking noises,[22] and a whuffling exhalation of breath.

People had said that bears came into town to gorge on blackberries. Naturally, he'd imagined meeting one. But his imagination had always supplied daylight.

Back slowly away, they'd said. But the moment he moved to ease his weight off the boulder, the berry-eating noises stopped. He distinctly

---

[22] **wet smacking noises** the sound of an animal eating something

heard the animal sniff twice, followed by a deep-throated huff. Then it came toward him.

Now it was like the dream, a black mass growing larger, looming
175 between Mike and the house. And, as in the dream, he couldn't move.

The bear eased forward, slowly but without **hesitation**, until only the width of the boulder separated them. It rose up and leaned its forelegs against the stone; Mike heard the scrape of claws on granite. Then the bear stopped and stood still, as if posing for a picture of two
180 friends leaning toward each other over a small table.

Mike's neck hairs prickled his collar.[23] He was so filled by fear, it felt as if thunderless sheet lightning played across the muscles of his back and thighs.[24]

Then the lightning died, and all he could sense was the
185 unavoidable reality of the bear: the sight of its head silhouetted against the house lights; the oily-musty smell of its fur; the snuffle of its breathing; the wet warmth of its breath on his face.

It's so real, he thought. *But it feels like a dream.*

He knew it was silly, but he also knew he had to speak to the
190 bear. He whispered, "Do you want to … tell me something?"

The bear cocked its head and eased back a bit, as if deciding how to answer this unusual question.

But Mike already had the answer. As if a tap[25] had been opened, all of the fear suddenly drained out of him, and he was filled instead
195 with a **peculiar** sensation of lightness.

It could have been seconds or it could have been forever that he and the bear faced each other across the boulder. Then the back door opened and his mom called, "Mike! They found him! He's OK!"

Then the bear was gone. He heard it scuttling through the trees.
200 Mike laughed, because the feeling of lightness did not disappear with the bear.

The feeling stayed with him, even after his father came home, enfolded Mike and Mom in a hug, then ate a big stack of buttermilk pancakes and slept for 16 hours straight.

205 And the bear never came back—not to the woods, not to Mike's dreams.

---

[23] **Mike's neck hairs prickled his collar.** Mike was so terrified he had goose bumps.
[24] **as if thunderless sheet lightning played across the muscles of his back and thighs** as if electrical impulses were going off in his body
[25] **tap** water faucet

**About the Author:
Matt Hughes
(b. 1949)**

Matt Hughes is an award-winning Canadian author of numerous novels and short stories. Most of his work is in the genre of fantasy and science fiction. He was recently inducted into the Canadian Science Fiction and Fantasy Association Hall of Fame.

Close Read

Work with a partner.

1. Determine the meanings of your underlined words and phrases.
2. Discuss the question:

   What do bears represent in the story?

Understand and Analyze

Respond to the questions. Support your responses with evidence from the text.

1. **Interpret** Reread lines 10–18. How do bears appear and act in Mike's dreams?
2. **Paraphrase** Reread lines 35–37. How does Mrs. Skinner explain dreams that contain a monster or something scary?
3. **Summarize** Reread lines 51–60. Why is Mike's dad's job dangerous?
4. **Conclude** Reread lines 79–81. What does Mom mean when she says that Dad's job is "a big part of who he is"?
5. **Infer** Reread lines 121–123. How does Mom feel when she is talking to someone at headquarters? How do you know?
6. **Infer** Reread lines 189–192. Is the bear able to understand Mike in some way? Explain why or why not.

Apply the Skill: Summarize a Story

Summarize the story "Bearing Up." Then read your summary to a partner. Compare how your summaries are alike and different.

____

____

____

____

____

Share Your Perspective

Discuss these questions in a small group.

1. What animal might represent stress to you in a dream? Why?
2. Do you think standing still and confronting the bear was a better idea than running away? Why or why not?

Discussion Frames

… would represent stress for me because …

I think Mike's decision was …

I feel this way because …

Why do you think that …?

Vocabulary: Use a Thesaurus L.8.4.C

Like a dictionary, a **thesaurus** is used to look up words. A thesaurus lists synonyms—words and phrases with similar meanings. Writers and speakers often use a thesaurus to:

- find a word with a specific meaning
- find a synonym in order to vary word choice
- find a more vivid word choice

A thesaurus also may include other information, such as the word's part of speech.

Example

I am trying to think of a word that is similar to *lurk* but suggests more movement, to describe a bear that is hunting.

Thesaurus entry:
lurk: *verb*
hide, prowl, creep, skulk, slink, sneak, stalk, wait, lie in wait, move stealthily

Stalk is the word I want: it indicates that the bear isn't just hanging around but is moving with purpose.

Apply the Strategy

Look at "Bearing Up" again. Find at least three words to replace with a synonym. Look up each word in a print or online thesaurus. Rewrite the original sentence, using a synonym. Then explain how the meaning of the sentence changes. Discuss the changes with a partner.

Original Sentence	New Sentence	Change in Meaning
She <u>peered</u> at him.	*She <u>stared</u> at him.*	*"Stared" makes it sound less as if she's trying to figure out something about him.*

Read Again

Read "Bearing Up" again. As you read, circle details from the story that help
you respond to these questions:

What causes Mike stress in the story? What relieves his stress?

Reflect and Respond

Choose several details you circled in the story to complete the chart.

Causes Mike Stress	Relieves Mike's Stress

Use your chart to respond to the questions: What causes Mike stress?
What relieves his stress?

____

____

____

Discuss Your Response

Share your ideas with the class. Write one new idea you hear.

____

____

Respond to the Guiding Question

Write a response to the question:

How can acknowledging stress make us stronger?

Use evidence from the text, your discussion, and your life. Use the Discussion Frames to help you. Use the rubric to check your response.

____

____

____

____

____

CONNECT ACROSS TEXTS

Discuss the Essential Question: What are the positive and negative effects of stress?

Look at your answer to the Essential Question in the Unit Launch and your notes about stress in the Reflect and Respond sections. Discuss: How have your ideas about the Essential Question changed? What changed your ideas?

Then write one new idea you heard in the discussion. How did it affect your opinion?

____

____

Respond to the Essential Question

Write your new response to the Essential Question. Include Academic Vocabulary.

____

____

____

Assignment: Write a One-Act Play W.8.3

A play is a fiction text that is performed onstage for an audience. A play usually includes:

- dialogue: words the characters speak
- speaker identifications, indicating who speaks the dialogue
- stage directions that explain how actors should speak or move

For this assignment, you will reimagine an event from "Bearing Up" and write it as a dramatic scene. Your one-act play should begin immediately after Mike asks if the bear wants to tell him something. The scene should center on a conversation between the two characters and should relate to the topic of stress.

Your one-act play should include:

- believable dialogue between Mike and the bear
- speaker identifications for sections of dialogue
- at least three stage directions

Explore the Model

The model is a one-act play reimagining part of "Bearing Up." Read the play. Underline one new thing you learn about the bear.

Title

Bearing Up Under Pressure: A One-Act Play

Speaker identification

BEAR: Yes, I've been waiting to tell you something very important.

MIKE: [*shocked*] What is it?

BEAR: [*calmly and kindly*] I want you to know that you aren't alone. I'm your friend.

MIKE: [*stepping backward and looking confused*] But you're always chasing me in my dreams.

BEAR: I'm just trying to catch up to you—to tell you that I'm here for you.

Stage directions tell the actors how to speak or move. These directions are not read aloud.

[MIKE *turns around and speaks to himself.*]

MIKE: Can this really be happening? Is this bear really talking to me?

BEAR: I can hear you, you know. And I understand English perfectly fine.

MIKE: [*angrily*] Then why don't you understand that you *scare* me in my dreams?!

BEAR: [*shrugging*] I do. But you always run away before I can tell you to wait. I always want to explain that you don't need to be afraid of me.

MIKE: [*walking closer to* BEAR] So … you want to be my *friend*?

BEAR: Yes! The next time you see me in a dream, don't be afraid. Talk to me. Tell me what's on your mind. If you're stressed about something, we can work through it together.

Plays use believable dialogue that sounds the way people talk in real life.

MIKE: Really?

BEAR: Yes. I'll always be here for you, buddy.

[MIKE *and* BEAR *put their arms around each other's shoulders and walk away.*]

Plan Your Play

Brainstorm ideas about what happens in "Bearing Up" before the events in your play. Then think about how Mike and Bear might interact. Do they get along or disagree? What happens? How does the dialogue relate to stress? After you brainstorm, use the planning chart to organize your ideas and plan your play.

PLANNING CHART

One-Act Play for "Bearing Up"		
Bear's Thoughts/Actions	**Mike's Thoughts/Actions**	**Additional Ideas/Notes**

Write and Revise

Write Use your planning chart to write a first draft of your play. A good play uses believable dialogue and has its characters make gestures or move around the stage to emphasize how they're feeling. To help your audience connect with your play:

- Make sure your dialogue sounds like something Mike would say, based on what happens in the story "Bearing Up."
- Use imaginative details to bring Bear to life as a fictional character.
- Include descriptive details about how Mike or Bear should speak, move, or behave.

Revise Exchange plays with a partner. Use the checklist to review your partner's work and give feedback. Refer to your partner's feedback as you revise your draft.

☐ Does the play begin immediately after Mike whispers, "Do you want to … tell me something?" in the story?

☐ Does the play contain believable dialogue for Mike?

☐ Does the play contain believable dialogue for Bear?

☐ Does the play include speaker identifications for each section of dialogue?

☐ Does the play include at least three stage directions?

☐ Does the play relate to stress in some way?

Feedback Frames

What I like most about your play is …

I suggest you add more …

Can you indicate more feelings by …?

Proofread Check the grammar, spelling, punctuation, and capitalization in your play. Make sure your formatting matches the formatting of the model. Make edits to correct any errors.

Publish

Share your play according to your teacher's instructions. Read at least two of your classmates' plays.

TIP

Plays use all capital letters for character references in stage directions. Proofread to make sure your characters' names are formatted correctly.

Assignment: Perform a Play SL.8.6

You and a partner will act out a one-act play that one of you has written. Read both of your plays and decide which one you want to perform for the class. Then work together to make the play come to life.

- Remember that you are performing your play for an audience of your classmates. Perform appropriately for the classroom.
- You do not need costumes, props, or stage sets—just your imagination. Show what's happening in the play with facial expressions, body language, and words.

Plan Your Performance

To prepare, first read the play aloud several times with your partner. Then act out the play several times. Be open to suggestions from your partner about how the play should work or ways you could improve. Use the following checklist, adding items to it as needed.

Performance Plan Checklist
We will read the one-act play written by ________________________________.

Things to Practice

- ☐ Speaking clearly so the audience can hear you

- ☐ Speaking at an appropriate pace—not too fast and not too slow

- ☐ Skipping reading the stage directions aloud (Perform stage directions, but don't read them for the audience.)

- ☐ Using expression to show feelings or emphasize mood

- ☐ Acting out the scene instead of just reading it (Use gestures, body language, or movements.)

- ☐ ____

- ☐ ____

- ☐ ____

Practice Your Performance

Read the checklist below. Perform your play for another set of partners. Then watch the performance of their play. The other set of partners should complete the checklist for you and use it to give you feedback before you perform for the class.

☐ Did the actors speak loudly enough for the audience to hear?

☐ Did the actors speak at an appropriate pace?

☐ Did the actors use appropriate expression?

☐ Did the actors skip reading aloud the stage directions?

☐ Did the actors use gestures, body language, or movement?

Perform Your Play

Act out the play for your class. Then listen and watch attentively as your classmates perform their plays. Be sure to clap when each set of partners is finished.

Reflect

Discuss the questions with a small group.

1. Was writing the play easy or difficult? Why?
2. What was the most challenging part of acting out the play? Why?
3. How did feedback help you with acting?
4. Which play did you enjoy the most? Why?

Tan Le uses an EEG headset to record her own brain waves.

Helping Others Understand and Fight Stress  4.4

EXPLORER IN ACTION

Tan Le is an entrepreneur and inventor.

How can we best study our minds and their role in our lives? Researchers have been using electroencephalography machines, or EEG machines, to study the brain for decades. Historically, only experts or people who work directly in the medical field have been able to access and use EEG equipment and technology.

National Geographic Explorer Tan Le wanted to make this technology more accessible for everyday people. When speaking about "the old way" that we've researched brain waves in the past, she asks, "Why does it have to be [that] way?"

Le co-founded a company, EMOTIV, to create new kinds of EEG technology. Users can wear EMOTIV EEG headsets to measure their own brain waves. EMOTIV applies artificial intelligence (AI), machine learning, and behavioral science to see how they are responding to different scenarios.

Le says that people can use the combined technology to figure out what's causing their stress and what works to relieve it. As Le points out, stress and tension can be debilitating. She believes that finding new ways to recognize and address our own stress will help us to live better, fuller lives.

▶ **4.2** Watch the video to learn more.

1. What problem did Le want to solve? How did she want to solve it?
2. Do you think Le's company will be successful? Why or why not?

How Will You Take Action?

Choose one or more of these actions to do.

Personal

Give yourself a break from the stressors of life with a breathing exercise.

1. Close your eyes. Inhale deeply through your nose, and exhale slowly through your mouth. Do this five times in a row. Open your eyes. You should feel more relaxed.
2. Whenever you start to feel too stressed out, do the exercise.

School

Brighten someone's day by helping the person relieve stress.

1. Make five cards. Write an encouraging message on each, such as *You can achieve your goals!*
2. Hand out the cards to people at your school who might be feeling stressed.

Local

Help people in your local community relieve stress in quick, easy ways.

1. Search online for tips on how to relieve stress. Make a list. For example, *Visualize a gently flowing river.*
2. Type your **Stress Relief Quick Tips** list and print out multiple copies. Add your list to public message boards in your community.

Global

Reduce the stress of people around the world.

1. Think of an action that would help people around the world reduce their stress.
2. The World Health Organization (WHO) has a mental health program that works to help people reduce stress and stay psychologically healthy. Write a letter to the program to suggest your idea.

Reflect

1. Reflect on your Take Action project(s). What was successful? What do you wish you had done differently? Why?
2. Reread your response to the Essential Question **What are the positive and negative effects of stress?** in Connect Across Texts. How did your Take Action projects change or add to your response?
3. What will you do differently in your life because of what you learned in this unit?

5
Good Decisions

Do you agree with the quote? Why or why not?

Look at the photo and caption. Discuss the questions.

1. How might the girls make good decisions about what to buy at the market?

2. How can you know if you've made a good decision?

◄ **Girls visit an outdoor market during the Naadam Festival in Xilinhot, Inner Mongolia, China.**

221

ESSENTIAL QUESTION

How can making good decisions affect our lives?

Explore the Essential Question

Think Write your ideas about the Essential Question in the Unit Concept Map.

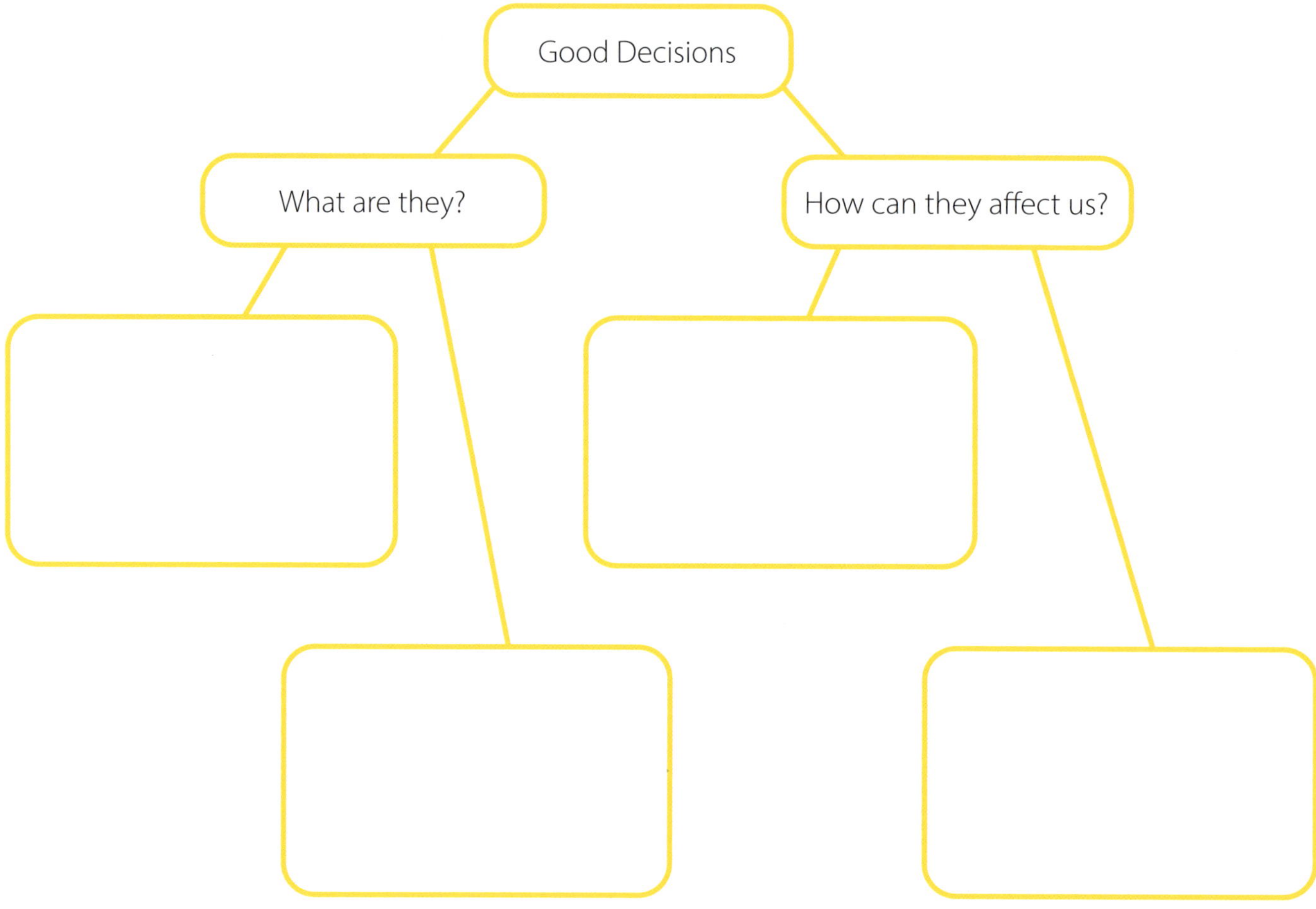

Respond Write one or two sentences to respond to the Essential Question.

Discuss Your Ideas Use your Unit Concept Map and your response to share your ideas with the class.

Discussion Frames

In my experience, a good decision ….

Consequently, …

A good decision can be defined as …

This is important because …

Academic Vocabulary

Use these words to express your ideas throughout the unit.

PRACTICE 1 Use context to determine the meaning of each word in blue. Then match the word to its definition.

When making a decision, it's a good idea to consider what outside **principles** might be influencing you. You can also have a friend **advise** you. Choose a friend who shares your values and beliefs. Then ask your friend for thoughts about your decision. Do not **restrict** yourself from telling your friend how you really feel. Find someone who can **motivate** you to be **consistent** with your actions so that you keep moving toward your goals. A good friend will help you **implement** strategies that improve your life in many ways.

Word	Definition
principles	natural laws, rules, or beliefs that influence actions and thoughts
	to stop or limit
	to encourage in a positive way
	unchanging; remaining the same over time
	to give an opinion about what someone should do
	to put a decision or plan into effect

PRACTICE 2 Work with a partner. Write each Academic Vocabulary word on a small piece of paper. Fold the papers and put them in a pile. Take turns choosing a piece of paper. Read the word aloud, and use it in a new sentence. Have your partner confirm you used the word correctly.

Example

Student 1: Restrict: I can <u>restrict</u> your movement by standing in your way.
Student 2: You used <u>restrict</u> correctly.

How can our decisions help us or harm us?

First Thoughts

Think about a good decision you have made and a bad decision you have made. How do you know they were good or bad? Complete the chart. Then discuss your decisions with a small group.

Good Decision / How I Know	Bad Decision / How I Know

Discussion Frames

The decision I recall is …

From my point of view, …

I feel this way because …

Why did you …?

Key Vocabulary

PRACTICE Use context to determine the meaning of each word in bold. Then match the word to its definition.

1. The dance team members all make **uniform** movements at the same time.
2. The river **diverged** at the bottom of the hill into three different streams.
3. The farmer **scanned** the sky to see if any rain clouds were in the area.
4. The **deserted** village is covered in weeds. No one lives there now.
5. When the sun went below the **horizon**, the sky became very dark.

______ **1.** uniform   **a.** to quickly look at or across something (v.)

______ **2.** diverge   **b.** the area in the distance where sky meets land or water (n.)

______ **3.** scan   **c.** the same; not varying (adj.)

______ **4.** deserted   **d.** to split into two or more new directions (v.)

______ **5.** horizon   **e.** abandoned; empty of people (adj.)

Reading Skill: Compare and Contrast Text Structure RL.8.5

The **structure** of a poem can include **form, rhyme, rhythm**, and **repetition**. These structural elements affect the poem's meaning and style. When you compare two poems on a similar topic, first analyze each poem's structure. Follow these steps:

1. Look at the form of each poem. Study the line breaks and stanza arrangement. Do all the stanzas have the same number of lines? Do the line or stanza breaks have a clear purpose?

2. Read the poem multiple times to determine how it uses sound and rhythm. Reading the poem aloud while clapping or snapping can help you discover its rhythm.

3. Look for repetition of sounds and words. Rhymes often appear at the ends of lines and follow a pattern. Poets may also repeat words and lines they want the reader to notice.

4. After you have analyzed the poems, compare their structures to help you better understand the content, meaning, style, or purpose of each poem.

Skill in Action

Read the poems "Sidewalking" and "The Track." Study how the reader has analyzed the poems. How does comparing and contrasting the poems help you better understand their meanings and styles?

The line breaks in the poem create a clear rhythm. The poem also has a rhyming pattern: AABA.

Both poems are one stanza long and are about a similar topic— walking paths.

This poem does not use rhyme, but it does repeat the *ov* sound in "oval" and "over."

Sidewalking

The city sidewalk,
covered in chalk,
shares happy messages
on my walk.

The Track

The sports track is a long oval.
I walk in circles, over and over—
never getting anywhere.

"Sidewalking" has more structure and uses rhyme to create a snappy, happy rhythm. "The Track" is less structured and has no rhyme. The looseness of the poem echoes the poem's meaning.

THE ROAD NOT TAKEN

by **Robert Frost**

⌒ 5.1

1 Two roads **diverged** in a yellow wood,
And sorry I could not travel both
And be one traveler,[1] long I stood
And looked down one as far as I could
5 To where it bent in the undergrowth;

Then took the other, as just as fair,
And having perhaps the better claim,
Because it was grassy and wanted wear[2]
Though as for that the passing there
10 Had worn them really about the same,

And both that morning equally lay
In leaves no step had trodden black.
Oh, I kept the first for another day!
Yet knowing how way leads on to way,
15 I doubted if I should ever come back.

I shall be telling this with a sigh
Somewhere ages and ages hence[3]:
Two roads diverged in a wood, and I—
I took the one less traveled by,
20 And that has made all the difference.

[1] **travel both / And be one traveler** be in two places at the same time
[2] **wanted wear** did not look like it had been used recently
[3] **hence** in the future

**About the Poet:
Robert Frost
(1874–1963)**

Robert Frost was a well-known and beloved American poet and playwright. He won the Pulitzer Prize for Poetry four times, along with many other awards and honors. He often wrote about nature and the outdoors.

Old Story

by **Vinicius de Moraes**

1 After crossing many paths
A man came to a clear and long road
Full of calm and light.
The man walked down the road
5 Listening to the birds' voice and receiving the strong sunlight
With his chest full of songs and his mouth full of laughter.
The man walked days and days on the long road
That was lost in the **uniform** plain.
He walked days and days …
10 The only birds flew
Only the sun stayed
The strong sun that burned his pale forehead.
After a long time he remembered to look for a fountain.
But the sun had dried up all the fountains.
15 He **scanned** the **horizon**
and saw that the road went beyond, far beyond everything.
He scanned the sky
and saw no clouds.

And the man remembered the other ways.
20 They were difficult, but the water sang in all the fountains
They were steep, but the flowers embalmed[1] the fresh air
The feet bled on the stone, but the friendly tree watched
    over the sleep.
There was a storm and there was calm
25 There was shade and there was light.

The man looked for a moment at the clear and **deserted**
    road. He looked at himself[2] for a long time and returned.

---

[1] **embalmed** gave a pleasant scent to
[2] **looked at himself** thought carefully about himself

About the Poet:
Vinicius de Moraes (1913–1980)

Vinicius de Moraes was a Brazilian poet, playwright, essayist, and songwriter. His lyrics were recorded on many albums during his lifetime.

Close Read

Work with a partner.

1. Determine the meanings of your underlined words and phrases.
2. Discuss the question: **How are the paths in the poems alike and different?**

Understand and Analyze

Respond to the questions. Support your responses with evidence from the text.

1. **Explain** Reread the first stanza of "The Road Not Taken." What is the speaker "sorry" about?
2. **Conclude** Reread the second stanza of "The Road Not Taken." Why does the speaker choose the less traveled path?
3. **Infer** Reread the last stanza of "The Road Not Taken." What does the speaker mean by "that has made all the difference"?
4. **Describe** Reread lines 1–8 from "Old Story." What is the man's road like?
5. **Summarize** Reread the second stanza of "Old Story." What are "the other ways" like?
6. **Infer** In the last line of "Old Story," the poem says the man "returned." What do you think this means? Explain.

Apply the Skill: Compare and Contrast Text Structure

In the chart below, analyze the structural elements of the poems. Then compare how each poem's structure affects its style or meaning.

Poem	Form	Rhythm	Rhyme
"The Road Not Taken"			
"Old Story"			

Share Your Perspective

Discuss these questions in a small group.

1. How might thinking about these poems affect the way you make decisions in the future?
2. Do you think the man in "Old Story" makes a good decision at the end of the poem? Why or why not?

Discussion Frames

Based on … , I think …

This indicates …

Can you support your opinion that …?

Vocabulary: Verify Meaning **L.8.4.D**

When you read an unknown word or phrase in a text, you can pause and **verify** its meaning before you continue to read. Decide what you think the unknown word or phrase means. Then confirm that you are correct. To verify the meaning of a word or phrase:

1. Search before and after the unknown word or phrase for context clues that hint at its meaning.

2. If the word has any affixes, use them to help you determine meaning.

3. To verify the word's meaning, look it up in a dictionary. Most words have multiple definitions, so be sure to read each definition listed. Choose the part of speech and definition that make the most sense, based on how the word is used in the text.

Example

I'm unsure of the word "undergrowth." The context clues "yellow wood," "looked down one as far as I could," and "bent" suggest that the speaker is in a forest and looking down.

Two roads diverged in a yellow wood,
And sorry I could not travel both
And be one traveler, long I stood
And looked down one as far as I could
To where it bent in the <u>undergrowth</u>;

The prefix *under* before *growth* suggests that the word means something— maybe smaller plants—growing under something else, such as trees.

The dictionary verifies the meaning. The definition is "grasses, saplings, weeds, and other growth on a forest floor."

Apply the Strategy

Look at the poems again. Use context clues and a dictionary to determine and verify the meanings of the words listed in the chart.

Poem	Word	Meaning/How You Confirmed Meaning
"The Road Not Taken"	Line 6: *fair*	
"The Road Not Taken"	Line 12: *trodden*	
"Old Story"	Line 21: *steep*	

Read Again

Read "The Road Not Taken" and "Old Story" again. As you read, circle details from the poems that help you respond to these questions:

How does each path affect the speaker of "The Road Not Taken" and the man in "Old Story"?

How does each poem portray a decision?

Reflect and Respond

Choose several details you circled in the poems to complete the chart.

Poem	How Path Affects Speaker or Man	Decision
"The Road Not Taken"		
"Old Story"		

Use your chart to respond to the questions: How does each path affect the speaker of "The Road Not Taken" and the man in "Old Story"? How does each poem portray a decision?

____

____

____

____

Discuss Your Response

Share your ideas with the class. Write one new idea you hear.

____

____

____

Respond to the Guiding Question

Write a response to the question:

How can our decisions help us or harm us?

Use evidence from the text, your discussion, and your life. Use the Discussion Frames to help you. Use the rubric to check your response.

____

____

____

____

____

Create and Present: Interpretive Fiction

Think about the paths that you read about in "The Road Not Taken" and "Old Story." Then do one of these activities:

OPTION 1: Create and Perform Skits

Work with a partner. Create two short skits that show what the speaker or man from each poem is doing. Use only actions or gestures— no words. Perform your skit while your partner reads the poems aloud to the class.

OPTION 2: Write a Poem

Imagine you have to choose between two paths. Write a poem that explains how you will choose your path or what your chosen path will be like. Give details about what causes you to make your decision. Read your poem to your classmates.

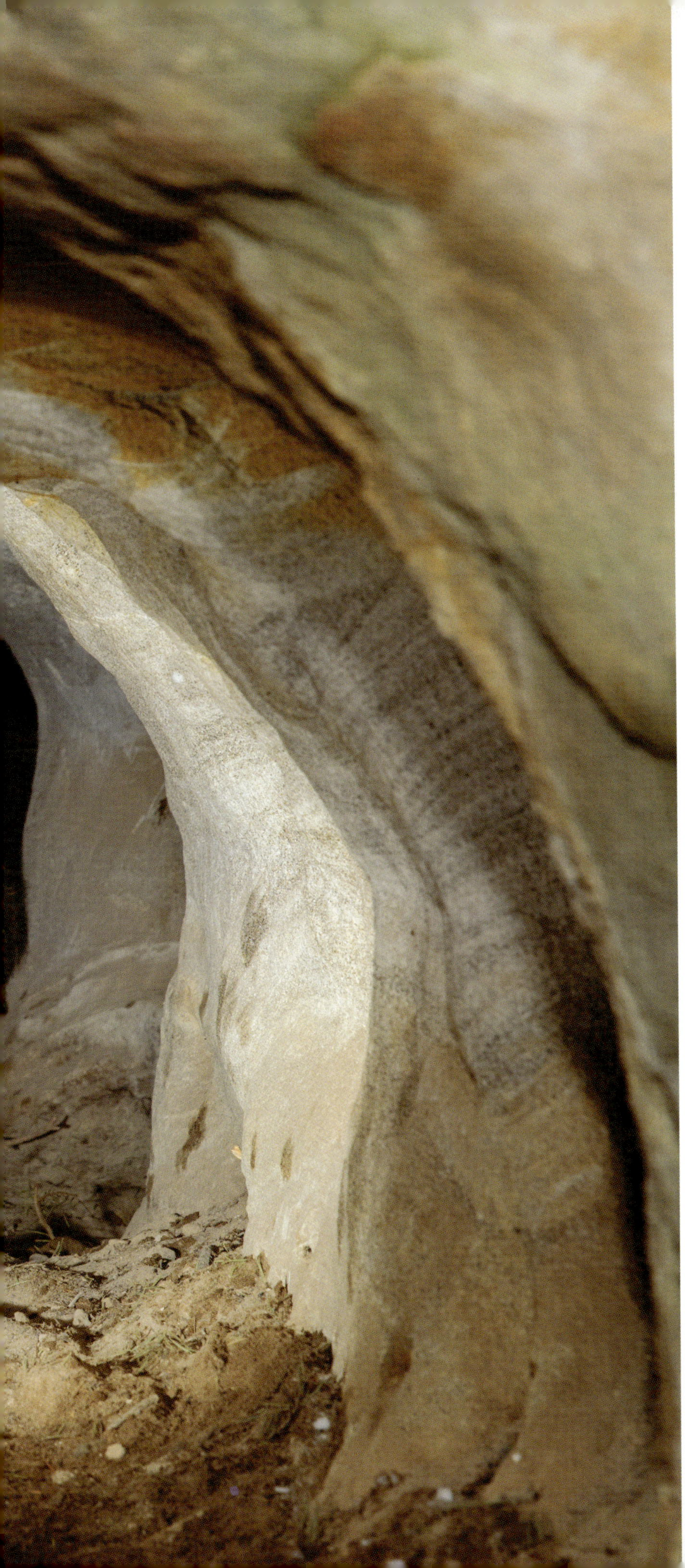

Examine the Photo

1. Look at the photo. Describe what you see.

2. How do you think the man is feeling about his decision to go into the cave?

3. Write 3–5 questions about the photo. Discuss your questions with a small group.

Find Out ▶ 5.1

Watch photographer Corey Arnold talk about his photo.

1. Did Arnold answer any of your questions? Which ones?

2. What information does Arnold share about what was happening at the moment he took the photo?

3. How do you think the people felt the next day about their decision to visit the bear? Why?

Reflect

Imagine you are the man in the photo. Write a paragraph to share how you were feeling at the moment the photo was taken about your decision to go into the cave.

Share Your Story

Take or find a photo that shows the results of a big decision. Tell your classmates the story about the photo.

ABOUT THE PHOTOGRAPHER

Corey Arnold is a National Geographic Explorer, photographer, and commercial fisherman. He enjoys photographing nature.

How can we help ourselves make good decisions?

First Thoughts

When you have to make a decision alone, how do you decide what to do? Make notes in the chart. Then share your process with a small group.

How I Make a Decision Alone
First, I …
Then I …

Key Vocabulary

PRACTICE Use context to determine the meaning of each word in bold. Then match the word to its definition.

1. When watching a movie, she has a **tendency** to fall asleep.
2. The baker feels **gratification** when he bakes a perfect cake.
3. That chair is not **suitable** for infants because they can easily fall out of it.
4. He was **tempted** to read the last page of the book to see how the story ends.
5. **Distractions** from my homework include my siblings and television.
6. She tried to fight against **procrastination** by making a weekly schedule of chores.

_____ **1.** tendency   **a.** proper; appropriate (adj.)

_____ **2.** gratification   **b.** pleasure; satisfaction (n.)

_____ **3.** suitable   **c.** something that causes a loss in focus or attention (n.)

_____ **4.** tempt   **d.** a quality that makes something likely to happen (n.)

_____ **5.** distraction   **e.** the act of delaying or postponing something (n.)

_____ **6.** procrastination **f.** to persuade someone to do something that is unwise (v.)

In writing, **structure** can refer to the order in which information is given. In informational texts, paragraphs often have a structure that helps readers understand the content. For instance, a paragraph may have a **problem-solution structure**. A paragraph with a problem-solution structure usually includes:

- a topic sentence about a problem
- supporting sentences that provide details about the problem
- one or more sentences that describe a solution

Skill in Action

Study the model. How does the structure of the paragraph help readers understand the events being described? Discuss your thoughts with a partner.

This is the topic sentence. It presents a problem.

These sentences explain Hugo's solution.

In the summer of 1830, Victor Hugo was facing an impossible deadline. Twelve months earlier, the French author had promised his publisher a new book. But instead of writing, he spent that year pursuing other projects, entertaining guests, and delaying his work. Frustrated, Hugo's publisher responded by setting a deadline less than six months away. The book had to be finished by February 1831.

This sentence explains what caused the problem.

Hugo concocted a strange plan to beat his procrastination. He collected all of his clothes and locked them away in a large chest. He was left with nothing to wear except a large shawl. Lacking any suitable clothing to go outdoors, he remained in his study and wrote furiously during the fall and winter of 1830. *The Hunchback of Notre Dame* was finished two weeks early, on January 14, 1831.

A young man procrastinates by playing
with a model motorcycle.

Read and answer the questions: **What is** *akrasia*? **Why is** *akrasia* **such a big problem?** As you read, underline any parts of the text you have questions about or find confusing.

The
Akrasia Effect:
Why We Don't Follow Through on What We Set Out to Do and What to Do About It

by **James Clear**
from **Atomic Habits**

⌒ 5.3

1   In the summer of 1830, Victor Hugo was facing an impossible deadline. Twelve months earlier, the French author had promised his publisher a new book. But instead of writing,
5   he spent that year pursuing other projects, entertaining guests, and delaying his work. Frustrated, Hugo's publisher responded by setting a deadline less than six months away. The book had to be finished by February 1831.

10   Hugo concocted a strange plan to beat his **procrastination**. He collected all of his clothes and locked them away in a large chest. He was left with nothing to wear except a large shawl. Lacking any **suitable** clothing to go outdoors,
15   he remained in his study and wrote furiously[1] during the fall and winter of 1830. *The Hunchback of Notre Dame* was finished two weeks early, on January 14, 1831.

---

[1] **furiously** quickly and with intense focus

The Ancient Problem of Akrasia

20   Human beings have been procrastinating for centuries. Even prolific artists like Victor Hugo are not immune to[2] the **distractions** of daily life. The problem is so timeless, in fact, that ancient Greek philosophers like Socrates and Aristotle coined[3] a word to describe this type of behavior: *akrasia*.

25   *Akrasia* is the state of acting against your better judgment. It is when you do one thing even though you know you should do something else. Loosely translated, you could say that *akrasia* is procrastination or a lack of self-control. *Akrasia* is what prevents you from following through on what you set out[4] to do.

30   Why would Victor Hugo commit to writing a book and then put it off for over a year? Why do we make plans, set deadlines, and commit to goals, but then fail to follow through on them[5]?

Why We Make Plans, But Don't Take Action

One explanation for why *akrasia* rules our lives and
35   procrastination pulls us in[6] has to do with a behavioral economics term called "time inconsistency." Time inconsistency refers to the **tendency** of the human brain to value immediate rewards more highly than future rewards.

When you make plans for yourself—like setting a goal to
40   lose weight or write a book or learn a language—you are actually making plans for your future self. You are envisioning what you want your life to be like in the future, and when you think about the future it is easy for your brain to see the value in taking actions with long-term benefits.

45   When the time comes to make a decision, however, you are no longer making a choice for your future self. Now you are in the moment and your brain is thinking about the present self. And researchers have discovered that the present self really likes instant **gratification**, not long-term payoff. This is one reason
50   why you might go to bed feeling motivated to make a change in your life, but when you wake up you find yourself falling into old patterns. Your brain values long-term benefits when they are in

---

[2] **are not immune to** can have problems with
[3] **coined** created
[4] **set out** plan
[5] **follow through on them** take action
[6] **pulls us in** affects us so much

the future, but it values immediate gratification when it comes to the present moment.

This is one reason why the ability to delay gratification is such a great predictor of success in life. Understanding how to resist the pull of instant gratification—at least occasionally, if not consistently—can help you bridge the gap between where you are and where you want to be.[7]

Ways People Beat Procrastination

Here are three ways people overcome *akrasia*, beat procrastination, and follow through on what they set out to do.

Strategy 1: Design future actions.

When Victor Hugo locked his clothes away so he could focus on writing, he was creating what psychologists refer to as a "commitment device." A commitment device is a choice you make in the present that controls your actions in the future. It is a way to lock in[8] future behavior, bind you to good habits, and restrict you from bad ones.

There are many ways to create a commitment device. You can improve your food habits by preparing healthful foods and having them handy so that you aren't **tempted** to buy unhealthful snacks. I've even heard of athletes who have to "make weight"[9] for a competition choosing to leave their wallets at home during the week before weigh-in so they won't be tempted to buy fast food.

In short, automating behavior beforehand is better than relying on willpower in the moment. Be the architect of your future actions, not the victim of them.

Strategy 2: Reduce the friction of starting.

The guilt and frustration of procrastinating is usually worse than the pain of doing the work. In the words of Eliezer Yudkowsky, "On a moment-to-moment basis, being in the middle of doing the work is usually less painful than being in the middle of procrastinating."

So why do we still procrastinate? Because it's not being *in* the work that is hard, it's *starting* the work. The friction that prevents

---

[7] **bridge the gap between where you are and where you want to be** reach your goals
[8] **lock in** commit to
[9] **"make weight"** be a certain weight for a competition or athletic event

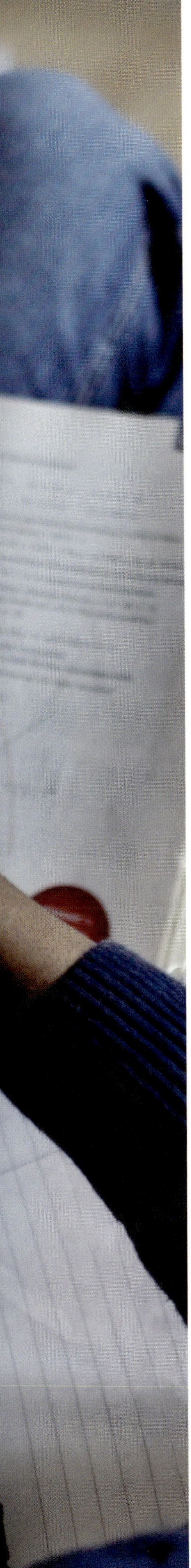

us from taking action is usually centered around starting the behavior. Once we begin, it's often less painful to do the work. This is why it is often more important to build the habit of getting started when we're beginning a new behavior than it is to worry about whether we're succeeding at the new habit.

Many people find it helpful to reduce the size of habits, by breaking them into steps. They focus on building a ritual—one with an easy first step. They are mastering the art of "showing up."[10]

Strategy 3: Utilize implementation intentions.

An implementation intention is stating an intention to implement a particular behavior at a specific time in the future. For example, "I will exercise for at least 30 minutes on [DATE] in [PLACE] at [TIME]."

There are hundreds of successful studies showing how implementation intentions positively impact everything from exercise habits to flu shots.[11] In the flu shot study, researchers looked at a group of 3,272 employees at a Midwestern company and found that employees who wrote down the specific date and time they planned to get their flu shot were significantly more likely to follow through[12] weeks later. In fact, implementation intentions can make people two to three times more likely to perform an action in the future.

Fighting *Akrasia*

Our brains prefer instant rewards to long-term payoffs. It's simply a consequence of how our minds work. Given this tendency, we often have to resort to[13] crazy strategies to get things done—like Victor Hugo locking up all of his clothes so he could write a book. I believe it is worth it to spend time building commitment devices that support goals.

Aristotle may have coined the term *enkrateia* as the antonym of *akrasia*. While *akrasia* refers to our tendency to fall victim to procrastination, *enkrateia* means to be "in power over oneself." Designing your future actions, reducing the friction of starting good behaviors, and using implementation intentions are simple steps that you can take to make it easier to live a life of *enkrateia* rather than one of *akrasia*.

---

[10] **"showing up"** starting a task or habit
[11] **flu shots** flu, or influenza, vaccinations
[12] **follow through** act on their plans
[13] **resort to** settle for

Close Read

Work with a partner.

1. Determine the meanings of your underlined words and phrases.
2. Discuss the questions:

    What is *akrasia*?

    Why is *akrasia* such a big problem?

Understand and Analyze

Respond to the questions. Support your responses with evidence from the text.

1. **Explain** Reread lines 1–18. How did Victor Hugo win the fight against procrastination?
2. **Explain** Reread lines 55–59. According to the article, what can help you be more successful in life?
3. **Conclude** Reread lines 76–78. What does the author mean by "Be the architect of your future actions, not the victim of them"?
4. **Explain** Reread lines 80–84. How can procrastination hurt you?
5. **Illustrate** Reread lines 96–106. How could using an "implementation intention" help a student who is procrastinating studying for a test? Explain how the process would work.
6. **Compare** Reread lines 113–119. What is the difference between *akrasia* and *enkrateia*?

Apply the Skill: Analyze a Problem-Solution Paragraph

Look at "The Akrasia Effect" again. Analyze the first paragraph in the section "Fighting *Akrasia*." Which sentence presents a problem? Which sentences explain more about the problem? And which offers a solution?

Problem: Sentence(s) # _____

Explanation of the problem: Sentence(s) # _____

Solution: Sentence(s) # _____

Share Your Perspective

Discuss these questions in a small group.

1. Do you think Victor Hugo's actions were wise? Why or why not?
2. Which strategy for fighting *akrasia* would work best for you? Why?

Discussion Frames

In my opinion, …

The strategy I prefer is …

I like this strategy because …

Why do you feel that …?

Vocabulary: Use Greek and Latin Suffixes L.8.4.B

A **suffix** is one or more letters added to the end of a base word or root to create a different meaning. Many common suffixes are from Greek or Latin. A suffix may have more than one meaning. Understanding suffixes can help you figure out the meaning of unfamiliar words. To use suffixes to determine meaning:

1. Read the word and try to identify the base word or root. If there is a letter or group of letters after the root, that is most likely a suffix.

2. Think about the meaning of the suffix together with the meaning of the rest of the word to figure out the meaning of the word.

3. Confirm the meaning of the word by looking it up in a dictionary.

Example

The root is *judg*. It means "to decide" or "to form an opinion."

The suffix is *-ment*. Possible meanings include "act of" and "product of."

If I put "product of" and "decide" together, I can figure out that the word means "decision" or "opinion."

Apply the Strategy

Look at the chart. Use the meanings of the roots and suffixes to figure out the meaning of each word.

Word	Root/Meaning	Suffix/Meaning	Word's Meaning
1. credible	cred / "believe"	-ible / "able to be"	
2. heedful	heed / "pay attention to"	-ful / "full of; characterized by"	
3. strictly	strict / "rigid; stern"	-ly / "in the manner of"	
4. timeless	time / "period of existence; moment"	-less / "without"	

Read Again

Read "The Akrasia Effect" again. As you read, circle details from the text that help you respond to this question:

How can we overcome *akrasia*?

Reflect and Respond

Choose several details you circled in the text to complete the idea web.

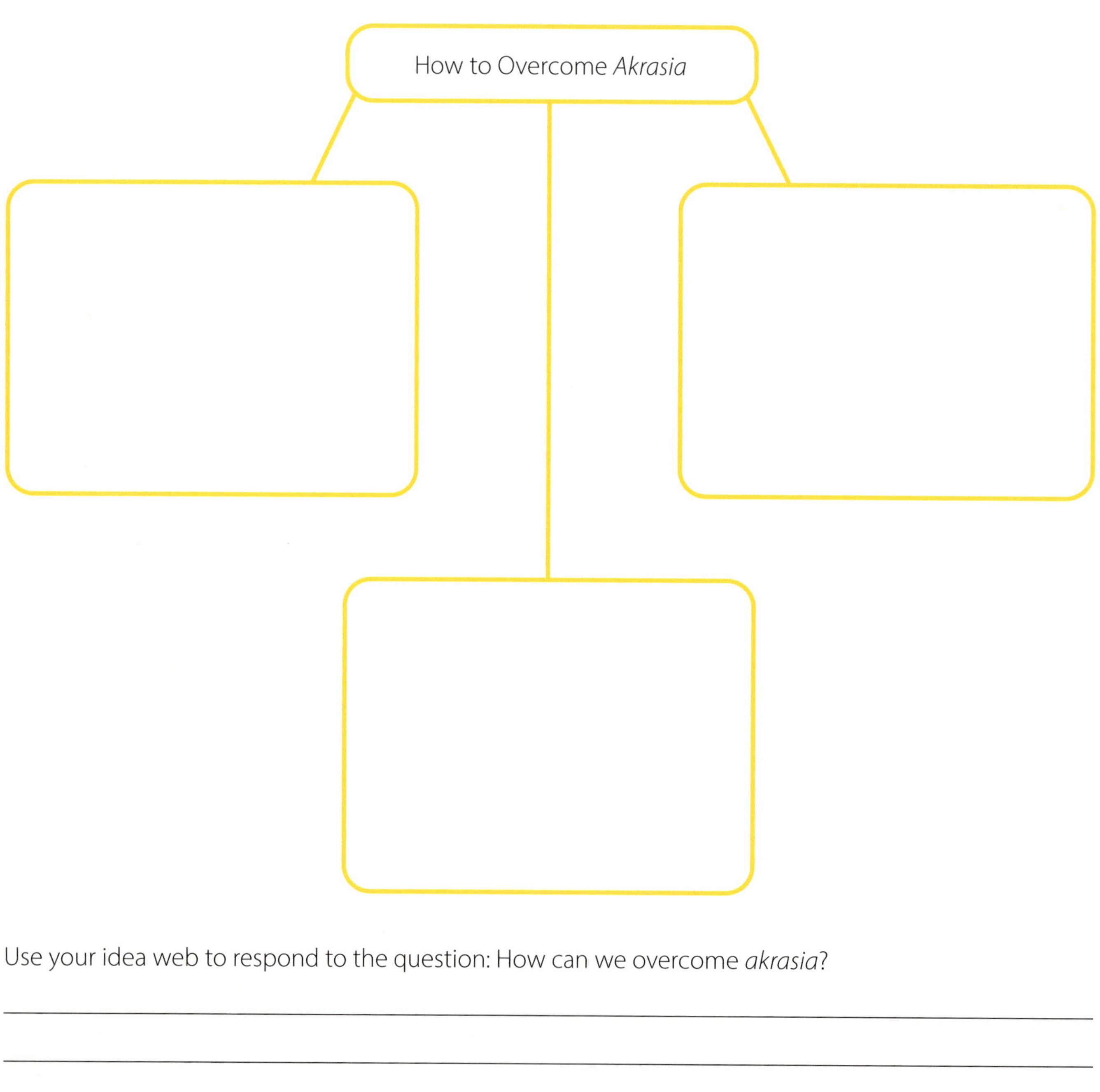

Use your idea web to respond to the question: How can we overcome *akrasia*?

____

____

____

Discuss Your Response

Share your ideas with the class. Write one new idea you hear.

Respond to the Guiding Question

Write a response to the question:

How can we help ourselves make good decisions?

Use evidence from the text, your discussion, and your life. Use the Discussion Frames to help you. Use the rubric to check your response.

Research RI.8.2

Choose one of these topics. Research the topic to learn more about it.

- bullet journaling

- vision boards

Follow these steps:

1. Make notes about what you already know about the topic.
2. Write three questions you have about the topic.
3. Research the topic to find answers to your questions.
4. Write your answers to the questions.
5. Present what you learned to a small group.

VIDEO CONNECTION
What can happen when others make decisions for us?
Oncoming car
Bicycler
Self-driving MODE
25
Battery level 85%
MENU   MUSIC   PHONE
Self-driving MODE
Activated:
LEFT REARWARD VEHICLE CAMERA
MEDIUM RANGE VEHICLE CAMERA
RIGHT REARWARD VEHICLE CAMERA
FRONT VEHICLE LIDAR
BACK VEHICLE LIDAR

First Thoughts

Make a "pros and cons" list about letting other people make decisions for you. Write at least two advantages (pros) and two disadvantages (cons). Discuss your lists with a small group. How are your lists alike or different?

Viewing Skill: Preview

Before you watch a video, you can preview the content to prepare to learn. Prior to viewing, read the title of the video and any additional information that is given. Predict what the video will be about. Write any questions you have.

Apply the Skill

▶ **5.2** Preview the TED-Ed animation "The Ethical Dilemma of Self-Driving Cars." Complete the chart.

Provided Information:
My Prediction:
My Questions:

Understand and Analyze

▶ **5.2** Watch again. Answer the questions. Support your responses with evidence from the video.

1. **Review** What do we call our behavior when we have a car accident? What would we call the same thing for a self-driving car?
2. **Explain** Who would be making all the decisions for self-driving cars instead of drivers?
3. **Contrast** How are the two motorcyclists in the video different? Why does their difference matter?
4. **Examine** What do people need to take into consideration the most when making choices about self-driving cars in the future? Why?

Share Your Perspective

1. Do you think self-driving cars are a good idea? Why or why not?
2. Should people let others, such as programmers, make decisions for them? Why or why not?

Discussion Frames

According to the video, …

My perspective is …

Why should/shouldn't people …?

How do other people influence our decisions?

First Thoughts

When has someone else stopped you from doing something you would have regretted? Write what happened in the chart. Then explain the situation to a small group.

What I Was Going to Do	Why I Stopped

Key Vocabulary

PRACTICE Use context to determine the meaning of each word in bold. Then match the word to its definition.

1. She shows **flexibility** at her job when she is able to switch her focus easily.
2. The group made a **collective** choice to watch the action movie.
3. It's fine to make **mediocre** paintings when you are learning to paint. You'll get better!
4. I don't know his last name because his handwriting is not easy to **decipher**.
5. There is an **immense** number of books in the library.
6. His **decaying** passion for soccer was apparent. He missed several games.

_____ **1.** flexibility   **a.** shared or done together by a group (adj.)

_____ **2.** collective   **b.** the ability to easily change or try new things (n.)

_____ **3.** mediocre   **c.** very great in size or amount (adj.)

_____ **4.** decipher   **d.** decreasing in health, strength, or power (adj.)

_____ **5.** immense   **e.** not very good; of moderate quality (adj.)

_____ **6.** decaying   **f.** to figure out or understand (v.)

Reading Strategy: Visualize

Good readers **visualize** as they read to better understand a text. Visualizing means making pictures in your mind, based on the author's words. Creating mental images can help you figure out what an author means, what an author is describing, or how something works. Visualizing can also help you better remember what you've just learned. To visualize, follow these steps:

1. As you read, look for descriptive details that tell how something looks, sounds, feels, smells, or tastes. Use these sensory details to create a mental picture.

2. Use your own words to describe what you see. What details did you add to your visualization, and how did this affect what you understood?

3. Explain how your visualization helps you better understand the text.

Strategy in Action

Study the model. How does the reader use visualization to better understand the text?

> The author includes many details that help me see and hear the bees in my mind.

Seeley … came back day after day to stare at the hives. He would look into the boxes and see bees coming in with loads of pollen on their legs. Other bees fanned their wings to keep the hives cool. Other bees acted as guards, pacing back and forth at the opening.

"If you lie in the grass in front of a hive, you see this immense traffic of bees zooming out of the hive and circling up and then shooting off in whatever direction they want to go," said Seeley. "It's like looking at a meteor shower."

> Visualizing the busy bee hive helps me better understand what the scene would look and sound like.

> I can feel and smell the fresh grass. I hear bees buzzing. I can see bees flying in circles and zooming away into the sky. I can also picture a meteor shower that I saw once at night.

HIVE MIND:

The World's Leading Expert on Bee Behavior Discovers the Secrets of Decision-Making in a Swarm

by Carl Zimmer
from **Smithsonian**

🎧 5.4

On the front porch of an old Coast Guard station on Appledore Island, seven miles off the southern coast of Maine, Thomas Seeley and I sat next to 6,000 quietly buzzing bees. Seeley wore a giant pair of silver headphones over a beige baseball cap, a wild fringe of hair blowing out the back; next to him was a video camera mounted on a tripod. In his right hand, Seeley held a branch with a lapel microphone taped to the end. He was recording the honeybee swarm huddling inches away on a board nailed to the top of a post.

Seeley, a biologist, had cut a notch out of the center of the board and inserted a tiny screened box called a queen cage. It housed a single honeybee queen, along with a few attendants. Her royal scent acted like a magnet on the swarm.

If I had come across this swarm spread across my back door, I would have panicked. But here, sitting next to Seeley, I felt a strange calm. The insects thrummed[1] with their own business. They flew past our faces. They got caught in our hair, pulled themselves free, and kept

---

[1] **thrummed** buzzed busily

flying. They didn't even mind[2] when Seeley gently swept away the top layer of bees to inspect the ones underneath.

A walkie-talkie[3] on the porch rail chirped.

"Pink bee headed your way,[4]" said the voice of Kirk Visscher, an entomologist.

A few minutes later, a honeybee scout flew onto the porch and alighted on the swarm. She (all scouts are female) wore a pink dot on her back.

"Ah, here she is. Pink has landed," Seeley said.

Pink was exploring the island in search of a place where the honeybees could build a new hive. In the spring, if a honeybee colony has grown large enough, swarms of thousands of bees with a new queen will split off to look for a new nest. It takes a swarm anywhere from a few hours to a few days to inspect its surroundings before it finally flies to its newly chosen home.

When Pink had left Seeley's swarm earlier in the morning, she was not yet pink. Then she flew to a rocky cove on the northeast side of the island, where she discovered a wooden box and went inside. Visscher was sitting in front of it under a beach umbrella, with a paintbrush hanging from his lips. When the bee emerged from the box, Visscher flicked his wrist and caught her in a net the size of a ping-pong paddle. He laid the net on his thigh and dabbed a dot of pink paint on her back. With another flick, he let her go.

As the day passed, more scouts returned to the porch. Some were marked with pink dots. Others were blue, painted by Thomas Schlegel of the University of Bristol at a second box nearby. Some of the returning scouts started to dance. They climbed up toward the top of the swarm and wheeled around, waggling their rears. The angle at which they waggled and the time they spent dancing told the fellow bees where to find the two boxes. Some of the scouts that witnessed the dance flew away to investigate for themselves.

Then a blue bee did something strange. It began to make a tiny beeping sound, over and over again, and started head-butting pink bees.[5]

---

[2] **didn't even mind** were not even bothered
[3] **walkie talkie** two-way radio device
[4] **headed your way** is coming toward you
[5] **head-butting pink bees** using its own head to hit the heads of pink bees

Honeybees feed their queen bee as they are watched by researchers.

Seeley had first heard such beeps in the summer of 2009.
He and his colleagues have since discovered that the
beeps come from the head-butting scouts.

When you consider a swarm like this one bee at a
time, it starts to look like a heap of chaos.[6] Each insect
wanders around, using its tiny brain to perceive nothing
more than its immediate surroundings. Yet, somehow,
thousands of honeybees can pool their knowledge and
make a **collective** decision about where they will make a
new home, even if that home may be miles away.

The decision-making power of honeybees is a prime
example of what scientists call swarm intelligence.
Clouds of locusts, schools of fish, flocks of birds, and
colonies of termites display it as well. And in the field
of swarm intelligence, Seeley is a towering figure.[7] For
40 years he has come up with experiments that have
allowed him to **decipher** the rules honeybees use for
their collective decision-making.

Growing up, Seeley would bicycle around the farms
near his house; one day he discovered a pair of white
boxes. They each contained a hive. Seeley was seduced.
He came back day after day to stare at the hives. He
would look into the boxes and see bees coming in with
loads of pollen on their legs. Other bees fanned their
wings to keep the hives cool. Other bees acted as guards,
pacing back and forth at the opening.

"If you lie in the grass in front of a hive, you see this
immense traffic of bees zooming out of the hive and
circling up and then shooting off in whatever direction
they want to go," said Seeley. "It's like looking at a
meteor shower."

For his PhD, Seeley took up[8] a longstanding
entomological question: How do honeybees choose their
homes? He climbed into trees to inspect hives. He sawed
down trees and measured honeybee cavities.[9] Seeley

---

[6] **like a heap of chaos** completely unorganized
[7] **towering figure** well-known and respected person
[8] **For his PhD, Seeley took up** To get his doctorate degree, Seeley researched
[9] **honeybee cavities** the spaces inside trees where honeybees live

Honeybees work busily
around their hive.

found that bee hive hollows were very much alike. They were at least ten gallons in volume, sat at least 15 feet off the ground, and had a narrow opening.

Seeley built 252 wooden boxes of different shapes and sizes and scattered them in forests and fields to test how particular bees were about these qualities. Swarms only moved into boxes that had the same features that Seeley had found in their tree cavities.

The architectural tastes of honeybees are not mere whims.[10] If honeybees live in an undersized cavity, they won't be able to store enough honey to survive the winter. If the opening is too wide, the bees won't be able to fight off invaders.

He took his research to Appledore Island because no native honeybees live here, and it has no big trees where the insects could make their homes. Seeley and his colleagues would bring their own honeybees and nest boxes. "This is our laboratory," Seeley said.

In one experiment, Seeley set up five boxes of different sizes. Four of the boxes were **mediocre**, by honeybee standards,[11] while one was a dream home. In 80 percent of the trials, the swarms chose the dream home.

Through years of study, Seeley and his colleagues have uncovered a few principles honeybees use to make these smart decisions. The first is enthusiasm. A scout coming back from an ideal cavity will dance with passion, making 200 circuits or more and waggling violently all the way. But if she inspects a mediocre cavity, she will dance fewer circuits.

Enthusiasm translates into attention. An enthusiastic scout will inspire more bees to go check out her site. And when the second-wave scouts return, they persuade more scouts to investigate the better site.

The second principle is **flexibility**. Once a scout finds a site, she travels back and forth from site to hive. Each time she returns, she dances to win over other scouts. But the number of

---

[10] **The architectural tastes of honeybees are not mere whims.** Honeybees choose their homes very carefully.

[11] **by honeybee standards** based on what honeybees prefer

125 dance repetitions declines until she stops dancing altogether. Seeley and his colleagues found that honeybees that visit good sites keep dancing for more trips than honeybees from mediocre ones.

This **decaying** dance allows a swarm to avoid getting stuck
130 in a bad decision. Even when a mediocre site has attracted a lot of scouts, a single scout returning from a better one can cause the hive to change its collective mind.

"It's beautiful when you see how well it works," Seeley said. "Things don't bog down[12] when individuals get too stubborn. In
135 fact, they're all pretty modest. They say, 'Well, I found something, and I think it's interesting. I don't know if it's the best, but I'll report what I found and let the best site win.'"

During the time I visited Seeley, he was in the midst of discovering a new principle. Scouts, he found, purposefully ram
140 one another head-on while deciding on a new nest location. They head-butt scouts coming from other locations—pink scouts bumping into blue scouts and vice versa[13]—causing the rammed bee to stop dancing. As more scouts dance for a popular site, they also, by head-butting, drive down[14] the number of dancers for
145 other sites.

And once the scouts reach a quorum of 15 bees all dancing for the same location, they start to head-butt one another, silencing their own side[15] so that the swarm can prepare to fly.

One of the strengths of honeybees is that they share the same
150 goal: finding a new home. People who come together to make a decision, however, may have competing interests. Seeley advises that people should be made to feel that they are part of the decision-making group so that their debates don't become about destroying the enemy, but about finding a solution for everyone.
155 "That sense of belonging can be nurtured," Seeley said. The more we fashion our decision-making after honeybees, Seeley argues, the better off we'll be.

---

[12] **bog down** slow down or get stuck
[13] **vice versa** the other way around
[14] **drive down** lower
[15] **side** dancers

Close Read

Work with a partner.

1. Determine the meanings of your underlined words and phrases.
2. Discuss the question:

   How did Thomas Seeley figure out the way bees make decisions?

Understand and Analyze

Respond to the questions. Support your responses with evidence from the text.

1. **Summarize** Reread lines 24–44. What was Pink, or the pink bee, doing?
2. **Explain** Reread lines 45–53. What is the purpose of the waggle dance?
3. **Infer** Reread lines 66–73. What can you infer about the decision-making of locusts, fish, birds, and termites?
4. **Deduce** Reread lines 103–107. Why would it be important to study honeybees at a place where no other honeybees live?
5. **Paraphrase** Reread lines 122–128. How do honeybees display flexibility with their decisions?
6. **Characterize** Reread lines 149–157. What decision-making characteristics do honeybees have?

Apply the Strategy: Visualize

Reread lines 45–58. Use sensory details from the text to visualize what is happening. Make notes about your visualization. Then explain how visualizing helped you better understand the text.

____

____

____

____

____

Share Your Perspective

Discuss these questions in a small group.

1. What is the most interesting fact you learned about the way honeybees make decisions? Why?
2. What do you think is the best lesson that humans could learn about decision-making from studying honeybees? Why?

Discussion Frames

It is interesting to note … because …

One thing humans could learn is …

Could you explain why …?

Language Convention: Use Ellipses for Omission L.8.2.B

When you quote a text, you don't need to include all the words from the original quotation. Instead, include the part of the text that is most important or proves a point you want to make. You can **omit**, or leave out, some words as long as the quotation still makes sense. To make sure readers understand that some words are missing, insert an **ellipsis** in their place. To use ellipses for omission, follow these steps:

1. If part of a quotation is unnecessary, decide which words to omit.

2. Write the quotation, using an ellipsis to show that words have been omitted.

3. Keep any capital letters that indicate the beginning of a new sentence, as well as periods that indicate the end of a sentence.

4. Reread what you have written to make sure it is grammatically correct and makes sense.

Examples

Reread lines 139–145 from "Hive Mind." Compare the quotations below to the original text.

> "Scouts, he found, purposefully ram one another head-on while deciding on a new nest location…. As more scouts dance for a popular site, they also, by head-butting, drive down the number of dancers for other sites."

The ellipsis replaces text at the end of a sentence, so a period is used with the ellipsis.

> "As more scouts dance for a popular site, they also … drive down the number of dancers for other sites."

This ellipsis replaces text in the middle of a sentence, so no period is added.

PRACTICE Look at "Hive Mind" again. Choose two quotations from the first part of the article. Write each, including only the most important ideas and omitting unnecessary words. Insert ellipses to show where words have been omitted. Make sure your quotations still make sense.

Quotation 1: ____

____

Quotation 2: ____

____

Read Again

Read "Hive Mind" again. As you read, circle details from the text that help you respond to this question:

What strategies do bees use to help each other choose the right home?

Reflect and Respond

Choose several details you circled in the text to complete the idea web.

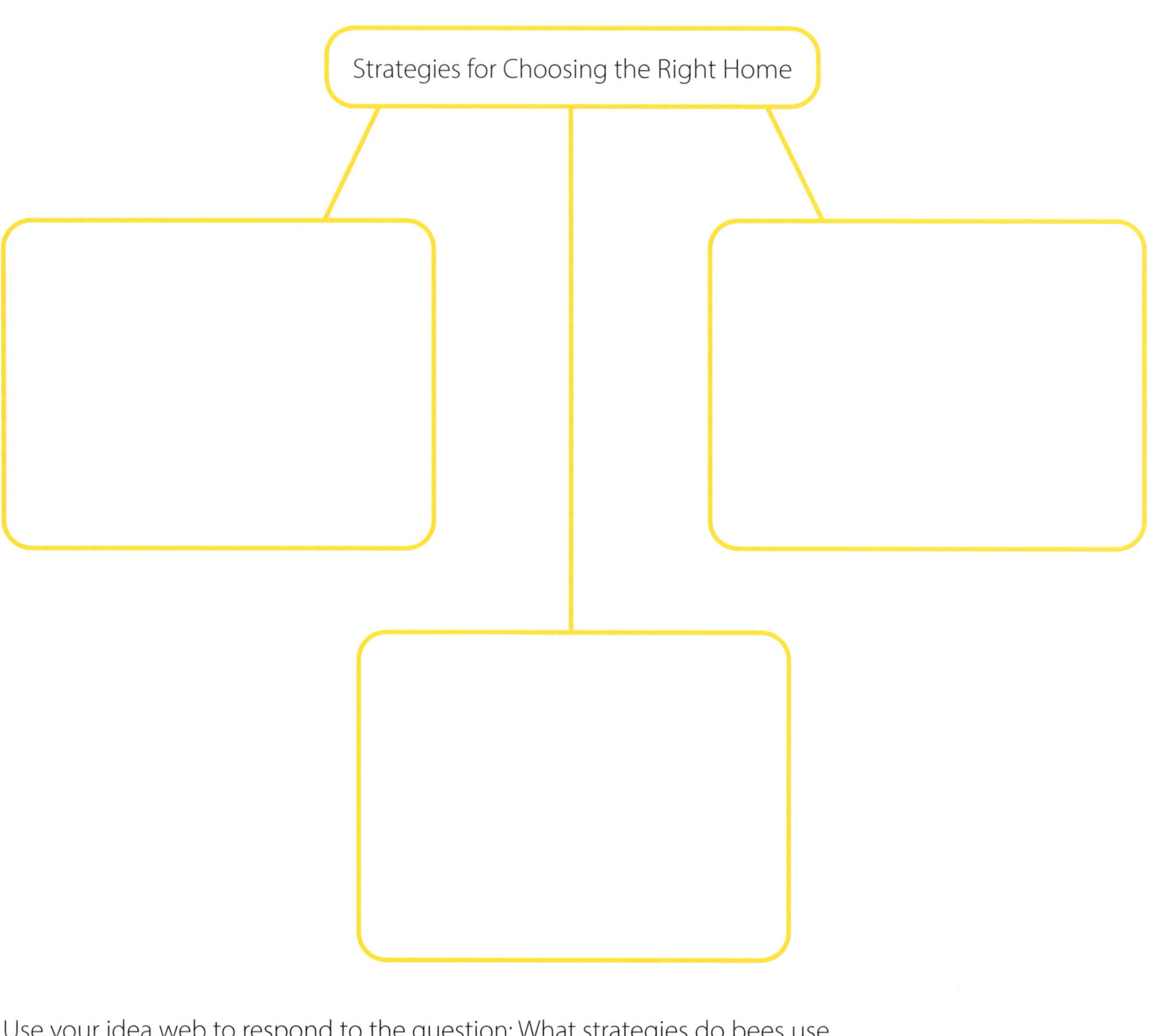

Use your idea web to respond to the question: What strategies do bees use to help each other choose the right home?

____

____

____

Discuss Your Response

Share your ideas with the class. Write one new idea you hear.

____

____

Respond to the Guiding Question

Write a response to the question:

How do other people influence our decisions?

Use evidence from the text, your discussion, and your life. Use the Discussion Frames to help you. Use the rubric to check your response.

____

____

____

____

CONNECT ACROSS TEXTS

Discuss the Essential Question: How can making good decisions affect our lives?

Look at your answer to the Essential Question in the Unit Launch and your notes about making decisions in the Reflect and Respond sections. Discuss: How have your ideas about the Essential Question changed? What changed your ideas?

Then write one new idea you heard in the discussion. How did it affect your opinion?

____

____

Respond to the Essential Question

Write your new response to the Essential Question. Include Academic Vocabulary.

____

____

____

____

Academic Vocabulary

advise (v.)

consistent (adj.)

implement (v.)

motivate (v.)

principle (n.)

restrict (v.)

Assignment: Write a Problem-Solution Essay W.8.2

For this assignment, you will write a problem-solution essay to give information about a global problem and suggest up to three solutions.

Your essay should be five paragraphs long and should be organized in a logical order. It should include:

- an introductory paragraph with a topic sentence that introduces the problem
- at least three paragraphs that present facts, examples, or quotations that support your ideas about the problem and possible solutions
- a final paragraph that restates the problem and makes a conclusion about the solutions you have suggested

Explore the Model

The model discusses the problem of single-use plastics. Read the model. Underline the problem and possible solutions. Circle facts, examples, and quotations that support the solutions.

The Problem of Single-Use Plastics

In today's busy world, many people get meals "on the go." Restaurants often include single-use plastics along with the food. While these items are convenient for customers, they are a big problem for the environment. According to the Plastic Waste Makers Index, "Single-use plastics . . . are some of the hardest items to recycle," and "end up creating global waste mountains." However, there are a couple of simple things restaurants and customers can do to be part of the solution.

Single-use plastics include items like forks, knives, spoons, drinking straws, cups, bags, and condiment packages. Consumers use these items with a meal and then throw them away. However, the trash does not always end up in a landfill. Some single-use plastics get into rivers or oceans. Other plastics wind up on land or in wildlife areas. Birds and animals can eat the plastics and get sick. Plastics also take a long time to break down.

One solution to the single-use problem is to use biodegradable or reusable items. For example, restaurants can provide wooden spoons and paper drinking straws. They can also provide items that can be washed and reused at the restaurant.

Customers can be part of the solution, too. We can decide to reduce our use of single-use plastics. For example, we can bring reusable cups and utensils from home. We can also cook more meals at home or eat only at restaurants that are doing their part to reduce plastic waste.

If restaurants and consumers work together, they can help end the single-use plastic problem. People can still eat meals to go, but they can be more responsible and do their part to make the world a cleaner place for future generations.

Plan Your Problem-Solution Essay

Choose a problem that is global—or one that affects a lot of people—to write about in your essay. What are some actions you and others can take to help solve the problem? Research your topic. Make notes about key details you can include in your essay. Organize your ideas in the outline below.

OUTLINE

Introduction

Topic sentence about problem:

Body

Details about problem:

Solution:

Solution:

Solution:

Conclusion

Concluding statement:

Write and Revise

Write Use your outline to write a first draft of your essay. A good problem-solution essay explains how a problem affects many people and provides realistic solutions. As you write, remember to:

- define your problem and state up to three possible solutions
- use appropriate signal words and phrases, such as *problem, solution, because, as a result, however,* or *as an option*
- include key details related to the problem and solution(s)

Revise Exchange essays with a partner. Use the checklist to review your partner's work and give feedback. Refer to your partner's feedback as you revise your draft.

- [ ] Does the introductory paragraph introduce the problem?
- [ ] Is the problem clearly stated and explained?
- [ ] Does the essay propose 1–3 realistic solutions?
- [ ] Are relevant facts and examples included?
- [ ] Does the final paragraph restate the problem and possible solution(s) and express a conclusion about them?

Proofread Check the grammar, spelling, punctuation, and capitalization in your essay. Make edits to correct any errors.

Publish

Share your essay according to your teacher's instructions. Read at least two of your classmates' essays.

TIP It can be difficult to see your own errors. Give yourself time between writing and proofreading. Change your focus to another task for at least 10–20 minutes. Then return to your essay to look for errors and make corrections.

Assignment: Give a Multimedia Presentation to a Group SL.8.4, SL.8.5

For this assignment, you will present your problem-solution essay to your classmates. Your presentation will include a multimedia display that emphasizes the importance of the problem you chose and explains up to three possible solutions.

Plan Your Presentation

To prepare, reread your essay several times. Think about how to best present the problem and solutions to your audience. Brainstorm multimedia that can support your ideas, such as a chart, a poster, an illustration, an infographic, some music, or a video clip.

Presentation Plan	
Information from My Essay	**Multimedia Ideas**

Practice Your Presentation

Prepare the multimedia you will need for your presentation. Create any charts, images, or posters. If you plan to use music or a video, practice starting and stopping the media as needed. Read the checklist below. Then practice giving your presentation to a partner. Your partner should complete the checklist for you and use it to give you feedback before you present your essay.

<table>
<tr><td>☐</td><td>Did the speaker stay focused?</td></tr>
<tr><td>☐</td><td>Did the speaker present a problem and 1–3 possible solutions?</td></tr>
<tr><td>☐</td><td>Did the speaker make eye contact?</td></tr>
<tr><td>☐</td><td>Did the speaker talk clearly and with appropriate volume?</td></tr>
<tr><td>☐</td><td>Did the multimedia clearly support the given information?</td></tr>
</table>

Feedback Frames

You could improve the presentation by . . .

I liked how you made eye contact to emphasize . . .

The multimedia is effective/ineffective because . . .

Deliver Your Presentation

Present your problem and possible solutions to a group. Then listen carefully and attentively as your group members present their problems and solutions.

Reflect

Discuss the questions with a small group.

1. Are you satisfied with how you presented your problem and solutions? Why or why not?

2. What problems and solutions did your group share? Will they change any of your actions in the future? If so, how?

3. How did your partner's feedback help you?

Mangroves in Boca de Camichín, Nayarit, Mexico

Making Good Decisions for Future Generations 🎧 5.5

EXPLORER IN ACTION
Octavio Aburto
is a photographer,
marine biologist,
and conservationist.

It can be overwhelming to think about making good decisions for our entire planet. One way to get started is to contribute to solutions in your local area. National Geographic Explorer Octavio Aburto decided to help his community by studying mangroves.

Mangroves are an important part of life in La Paz City, Mexico. They help filter drinking water and protect the area from erosion and hurricanes. The roots of these magnificent trees provide safe habitats for many species of fish. The fish grow up to become food for the community through the local fishing industry.

In the last 50 years, Earth has lost half its mangroves to pollution, coastal development, and agriculture. Octavio took action to preserve the mangroves around La Paz City by counting individual fish and using drones to map the forests. Octavio says, "Mangroves represent a very, very tiny area in this planet, but they provide a huge amount of services for humans, so we need to protect them for the future generations." Thanks to Octavio's hard work, La Paz City has been able to set new conservation priorities that will protect the mangroves well into the future.

▶ **5.3** Watch the video to learn more.

1. How will Octavio's work improve La Paz City for future generations?
2. Why are people like Octavio important to our planet?

How Will You Take Action?

Choose one or more of these actions to do.

Personal

Choose the less traveled path for yourself.

1. Think of a routine activity from your life. How can you change it to challenge yourself? For example, you could try a new food, sport, or hobby.
2. After trying something new, talk with a friend or family member about your experience. Encourage that person to try something new, too.

School

Help other students stop procrastinating.

1. Create a study group to help other students with their assignments. Commit to leading the group.
2. Schedule a time for the group to meet each week. Invite your classmates to join you.
3. Have each group member add the meeting to their calendar or create a reminder.

Local

Encourage people in your community to make good decisions.

1. Create a list titled **Questions to Ask Yourself When Making Decisions**. Add questions for people to consider.
   ### Examples
   How might this decision affect others?
   Why do I feel this action is important?
2. Make copies of your list, and post them on community message boards.

Global

Help to share solutions to a global environmental problem.

1. Search online to identify global environmental issues, such as the worldwide loss of mangrove habitats.
2. Choose one issue, and research an organization that is working to address it.
3. Explore their website to find out how you can help share their message. Then take action!

Reflect

1. Reflect on your Take Action project(s). What was successful? What do you wish you had done differently? Why?
2. Reread your response to the Essential Question **How can making good decisions affect our lives?** in Connect Across Texts. How did your Take Action project(s) change or add to your response?
3. What will you do differently in your life because of what you learned in this unit?

6
Helping Others

Do you agree with the quote? Why or why not?

Look at the photo and caption. Discuss the questions.

1. Describe what you see in the picture. How will the rescuers help free the whale?

2. Would you want to be one of the rescuers? Why or why not?

◀ Rescuers work together to help a stranded whale in Mar del Plata, Argentina.

273

ESSENTIAL QUESTION

What responsibility do people have to help others?

Explore the Essential Question

Think Write your ideas about the Essential Question in the Unit Concept Map.

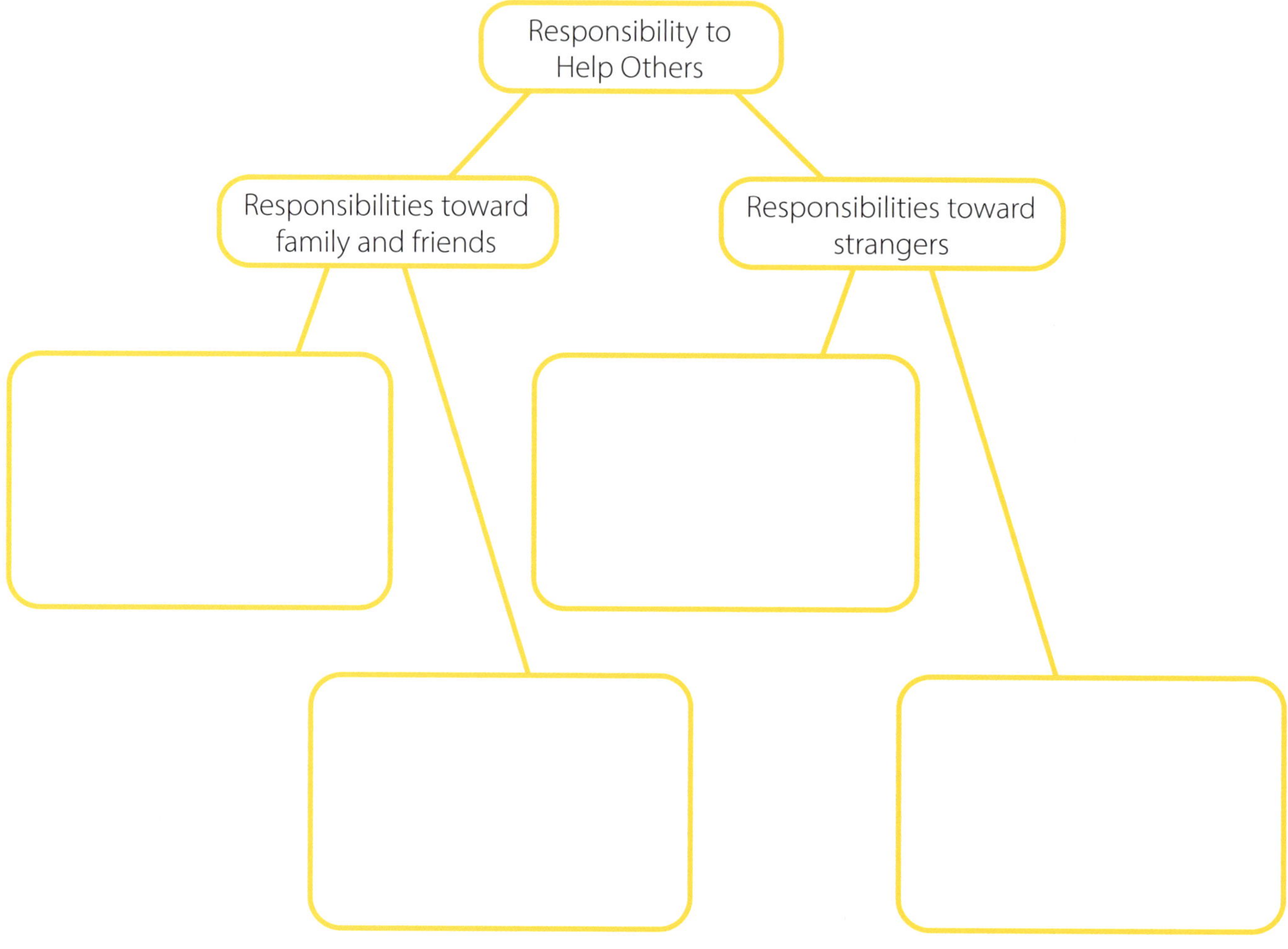

Respond Write one or two sentences to respond to the Essential Question.

Discuss Your Ideas Use your Unit Concept Map and your response to share your ideas with the class.

Discussion Frames

I think …

In my opinion, …

It seems to me that …

Academic Vocabulary

Use these words to express your ideas throughout the unit.

PRACTICE 1 Use context to determine the meaning of each word in blue. Then match the word to its definition in the chart below.

People help others in many ways. When there is an emergency in a public location, many people **assemble**, but only some offer to help. Some **volunteers** have **expertise** in fields like medicine, but others with no specialized skills help, too. Every day, victims of emergencies **survive** because of helpers. People also help others in non-emergency situations. For example, they may **devote** time to help sick family members. Although most children receive their parents' help, **eventually** most of them grow up to give back by helping others. This is because people are social beings, and helping others is part of what makes us human.

Word	Definition
survive	to remain alive
	a person who willingly works without pay
	to gather together
	specialized skills and mastery
	finally; ultimately
	to give all or a lot of one's time or resources

PRACTICE 2 Work with a partner. Take turns making statements about ways people help others. Use one of the Academic Vocabulary words in each statement. Keep making statements until you and your partner have each used all of the words.

Example

Student 1: Some firefighters are <u>volunteers</u> rather than paid employees.

Student 2: Many parents <u>devote</u> their lives to helping their children have good lives.

Why do emergencies inspire us to help others?

First Thoughts

What emergency from the past do you remember hearing about? Who did it involve? Who helped and how? Complete the chart, and then share your ideas with a small group.

Emergency	Who Was Involved	Who Helped? How?

Key Vocabulary

PRACTICE Use context to determine the meaning of each word in bold. Then match the word to its definition.

1. The **monsoon** brought heavy rains to the area every afternoon.
2. Improving teamwork was **pivotal** to their championship win.
3. People from countries all around the **globe** participate in the Olympics.
4. We took a less popular **route** to the beach because we wanted to avoid traffic.
5. She's looked everywhere for her keys but still hasn't found them. Her chances of getting to the airport on time look **grim**.
6. The flight home was a **harrowing** experience, with long delays and canceled flights.

_____ **1.** grim   **a.** difficult and upsetting (adj.)

_____ **2.** monsoon   **b.** extremely important (adj.)

_____ **3.** globe   **c.** world (n.)

_____ **4.** pivotal   **d.** not hopeful or encouraging (adj.)

_____ **5.** harrowing   **e.** way; path (n.)

_____ **6.** route   **f.** rainy season (n.)

Reading Strategy: Ask Questions

Asking yourself questions about a text as you are reading it can help you fully understand and analyze it.

There are several kinds of questions you can ask and various strategies for finding answers.

- To answer **comprehension questions**, such as *What is happening?*, carefully reread the text to be sure you understand it, or continue reading to find the answer.
- To answer **research questions**, such as *What does that word mean?* or *Where is this place located?*, you may need to consult an outside source such as a dictionary or a map.
- To answer **inference questions**, which often start with *Why* or *How*, you need to "read between the lines"—that is, use clues in the text to make inferences about what you read.

Sometimes you can use more than one strategy to answer a question. For example, you might make an inference to answer a question early in the text and then find that the answer is given directly later in that text.

Strategy in Action

Study the model. Work with a partner to identify the kinds of questions the reader is asking.

Why are these people being called? When I continue reading, I see that later sentences answer this, saying "they were among the best cave divers in the world."

from The Daring Cave Divers Who Saved the Thai Soccer Team

Racing against rising waters, an elite group assembled from across the globe pulled off a harrowing rescue of 12 boys and their coach a mile and a half underground.

Last summer, a few days after a boys' soccer team went missing in Thailand's fourth-longest cave system, cell phones began lighting up around the world like modern-day Bat Signals. One belonged to a former fireman from Coventry, England. Another to an IT consultant 80 miles away in Bristol.

How did a whole team go missing? I infer from the title and the opening paragraph that the team was in a flooded cave.

What is a "Bat Signal"? I haven't heard this term before. I will do an online search to find out what it means.

Rescuers assess the situation inside the Tham Luang Nang Non cave system in Chiang Rai, Thailand, as they search for the missing soccer team.

The Daring Cave Divers
Who Saved the Thai Soccer Team

by **Joel K. Bourne, Jr.**
from **Nationalgeographic.com, March 14, 2019**

Racing against rising waters, an elite group assembled from across the **globe** pulled off a **harrowing** rescue of 12 boys and their coach a mile and a half underground.

🎧 **6.1**

1   Last summer, a few days after a boys' soccer team went missing in Thailand's fourth-longest cave system, cell phones began lighting up around the world like modern-day Bat Signals.[1] One belonged to a former fireman from
5   Coventry, England. Another to an IT consultant 80 miles away in Bristol. There was a retired veterinarian from Perth, Australia, and an anesthesiologist from Adelaide. They had one unique skill set in common—they were among the best cave divers in the world.

10   The phone calls were short and to the point, no time for long debriefings. The Tham Luang cave was flooding fast. Soon the **monsoon** would begin, sealing the 12 boys, aged 11 to 17, and their coach in a watery tomb. The cave divers dropped everything and flew to the Chiang Rai
15   province in northern Thailand to help. There they joined an international team of technical divers from Thailand, military and rescue divers from the U.S., Australia, and China, and the formidable Thai Navy Seals, who were in charge of the search in the midst of a glaring global media spotlight.

---

[1] **Bat Signals**   emergency calls for help, made by shining a light in the sky

20   "There are probably a few hundred cave divers in the world,
but only a very few at that level," says Richard Harris, the
anesthesiologist who played a **pivotal** role in the rescue. "They are
the first guys you call."

       The situation at Tham Luang, however, was **grim**. The Thai
25 Navy Seals, along with a group of European expat technical
divers, were struggling to push past a large cavern about a half-
mile inside the cave. One of the boys had mentioned a popular
cavern called Pattaya Beach before he disappeared, but that was
another half-mile deeper inside. The divers were thwarted[2] by
30 a torrent[3] of muddy water pouring in from that direction. Ben
Reymenants, a Belgian expat diver from Phuket, was an early
volunteer. He told a reporter it was like "dropping to the bottom
of the Colorado River and hand over hand fighting your way
upstream."

35   Because of the extreme lethality of the sport, cave diving
rescuers tend to be the undertakers[4] of the caving community,
more accustomed to retrieving the deceased than to rescuing the
living. British diver John Volanthen, the IT consultant, believed
Tham Luang would be no different. He and his diving partner,
40 ex-fireman Richard Stanton, arrived the Wednesday after the boys
went missing on Saturday. They slowly, steadily began pulling
themselves upstream, fixing heavy climbing rope along the **route**
for others to follow. For the next four days, the international divers
and the Seals worked 12 to 14 hours in the cave. They inched their
45 way forward a meter at a time in total darkness, surfacing in each
cavern to check for the boys.

       Ten days later, the children had still not been found. Some
of the rescuers calculated their chance of survival at 10 percent
at best. Volanthen and Stanton were determined to go as far as
50 they could that day, using their air supply sparingly. They reached
Pattaya Beach. No boys. They kept going, digging into their reserve
air supply, and shutting off their tanks when they surfaced to make
it last as long as possible. Finally, in the ninth cavern, more than
one and a half miles from the entrance, they removed their masks
55 and were assaulted by a foul odor.

---

[2] **thwarted** blocked
[3] **torrent** flood
[4] **undertakers** people who prepare deceased people for funerals

Rescue workers carry a drain hose into the cave system.

Their flickering flashlights revealed the boys' gaunt but smiling faces—immortalized in a helmet-cam video that soon went viral. You can hear Stanton counting in the background and Volanthen's calm voice saying, "How many are you? 13? Brilliant!"

60   Seven Thai Navy Seals, including a doctor, struggled to reach the kids the next day with food and medical supplies. They began trying to strengthen the boys for what came next. The doctor and three Seals had run out of air on the way in and would stay with the boys until the end. But what came next

65   was the dilemma. The boys would have to pass through at least a half-mile of passages that were completely flooded. One plan was to stock the boys with food to last for six months until the water subsided. That was ruled out when divers found that oxygen levels in the cave air had already fallen from

Members of the Royal Thai Navy and international volunteers prepare to begin the rescue of the boys and their coach. ▼

70 21 to 15 percent. They wouldn't survive a month. One plan
involved drilling a tunnel into the cavern. But it was deemed
too complicated and too dangerous. Teams of volunteer rock
climbers, even famed bird-nest collectors of Libong Island, had
scoured the mountain's exterior looking for an alternative route
75 to the boys. They found nothing.

The only path left was to dive the boys and their coach out.
But none of them had diving experience. Even the Thai Navy Seals
who managed to make it back from the boys' cavern felt it would
be impossible to dive them out of the tunnel, with all its twists and
80 turns, vertical passages, and snags. The water was more than 50
feet deep in places. The narrowest pinch point was less than two
feet wide. Tragically demonstrating the danger, a former Thai Navy
Seal named Saman Gunan died while moving air tanks into the
cave. It put the risk to the half-starved boys in stark relief. In the
85 end, the British team decided there was only one option: sedate
the boys, put them in sealed full-face masks, and then bind their
arms behind them with zip ties, so if they did wake up and panic
they wouldn't disrupt the rescue. The divers built special harnesses
for the boys with handles on their backs so they could swim them
90 out like human duffle bags. "We were faced with an impossible
decision," says Volanthen. "Stay where they were and they are all
going to die. If we brought them out, there was a chance some
might survive."

Harris was called in for both his cave-diving expertise and
95 his medical skills. He was one of only two known cave-diving
anesthesiologists in the world. At first he was totally opposed to
the plan. "I didn't think it would work at all," Harris says. "I put
their odds of survival at zero." And yet, it did work. Slowly and
methodically, one by one, each boy donned[5] a wetsuit, was given
100 anti-anxiety medication, then injected with a heavy sedative that
has the added benefit of scrambling memories. The boys were
surprisingly okay with it. And who could blame them? They were
cold, hungry, and ready to see their families again. And they were
incredibly brave. The boys were in the ninth cavern. Only the
105 experienced cave divers—all volunteers—would transport the
boys between caverns nine and three. Skilled technical dive

---

[5]**donned** put on

instructors would help them along at each cavern. At cavern
three, the boys would be given a medical check by the U.S.
military team and passed along to a hundred or so rescuers from
110   a half-dozen nations, who gently passed them along on a rescue
sled. One by one out they came, and were quickly evacuated to
a hospital in Chiang Rai. There they were found to be in good
health. None remembered the terrifying trip.

The three-day rescue had difficulties. John Volanthen swam
115   three kids out, and the last one got tangled in telephone wires that
had been laid down before the cave flooded. He had to cut the
unconscious boy loose before they could proceed. Danish expat
Ivan Karadzic, one of the support divers, lost the guide line when
his borrowed caving helmet began to choke him and he couldn't
120   unlatch the strap. Luckily he found the guide line in the total
blackness and was able to move on. Chris Jewell, one of the British
divers, wasn't so lucky. He dropped the guide line while shifting
his human package from one hand to the other and couldn't find
it. He ended up feeling a cable at the bottom and following it back
125   into the cavern he'd just come from. Harris was following him out
and saw him there, the blood drained from his face. He took the
child the rest of the way out.

When it was all over, and the media trucks were gone, many
of the divers were given medals for valor. But they were quick to
130   deny any heroism and heaped praise on the boys and the entire
volunteer army that turned out to save them. Karadzic, the former
Danish insurance salesman turned technical dive instructor in Koh
Tao, says he'd heard there were more than 7,000 volunteers on the
mountain. Some cooked the 20,000 meals a day provided free to
135   the rescue teams. Some ran the pumps or diverted streams at the
top of the cave to keep the water at bay, buying the boys precious
time. Engineers, hydrologists, and drilling teams pumped out
groundwater, flooding the rice fields of hundreds of poor Thai rice
farmers who lost their crop and asked for no compensation. Taxi
140   drivers drove volunteers to and from the airport for free. Others
did laundry for the rescue teams. It was a truly international and
community effort. "I've received thousands of messages from
around the globe, thanking us for not just saving the kids, but for
getting the world together and setting an example for mankind,"
145   says Karadzic. "Even if you've never been in a cave before, it was

something everyone in the world could relate to. Who hasn't been a kid once, scared to death of the dark?"

For many, just reading about cave diving is scary. Why anyone would choose to do it for fun remains a bit baffling. "It's a very
150 cerebral[6] sport," says Dr. Richard Harris. "There's no adrenaline rush.[7] It's very much a meditative state of mind. The whole idea is to be very relaxed, calm, and smooth in the water. A lot of cave divers are fairly introverted, often quiet. But you couldn't find a more competent, pragmatic, and courageous group of guys."
155 After receiving one of Australia's highest awards for civilian bravery, Harris's fellow rescuer Craig Challen might have been speaking for all cave divers when he told reporters, "We're just a couple of ordinary blokes[8] with an unusual hobby."

____

[6] **cerebral** intellectual
[7] **adrenaline rush** a physical feeling of intense excitement caused by a sudden release of hormones
[8] **blokes** guys

The boys enjoy supplies delivered by the divers as they wait to be rescued from the cave. ▼

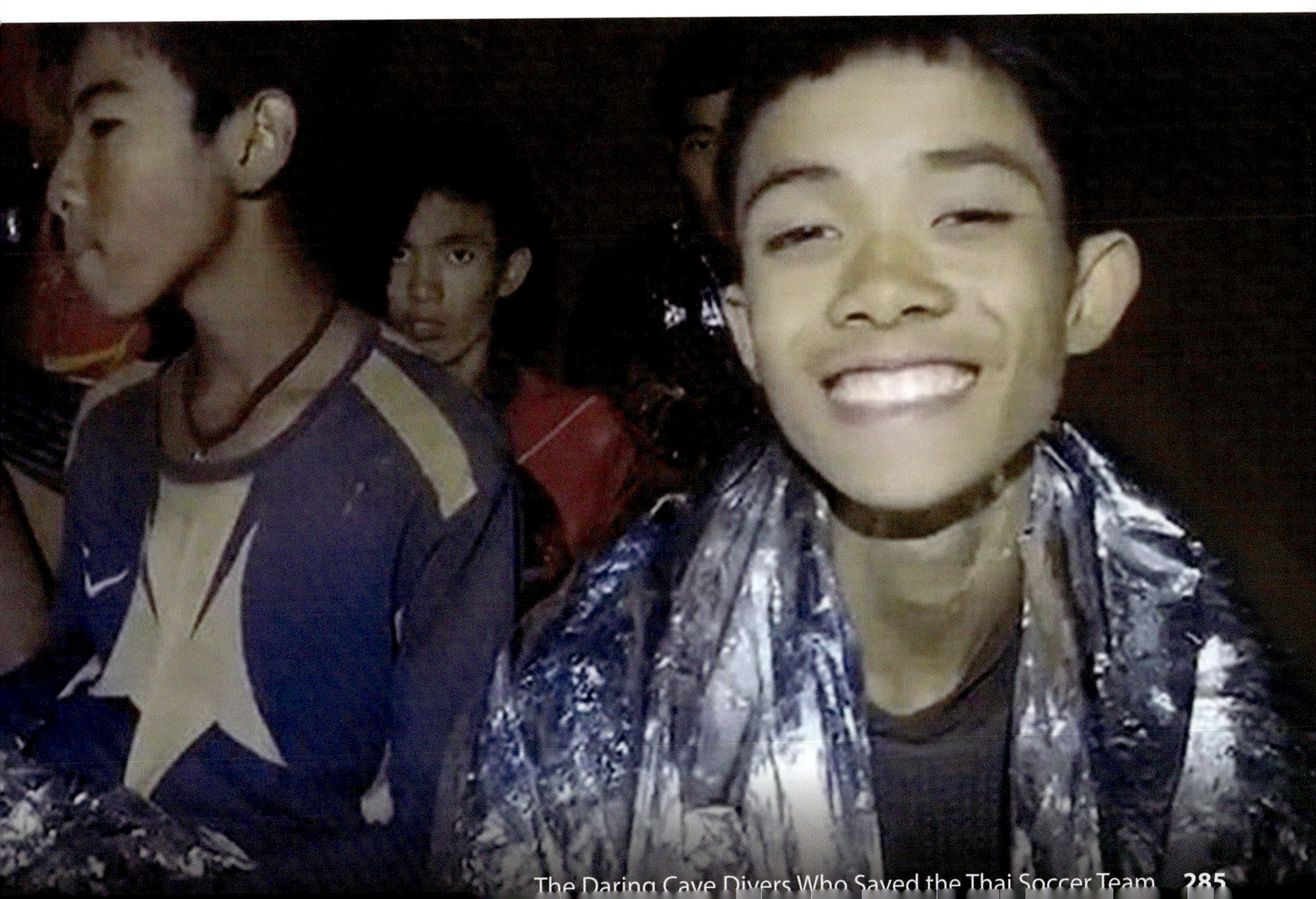

Close Read

Work with a partner.

1. Determine the meanings of your underlined words and phrases.

2. Discuss the questions: **Who were the helpers? What did they do to help?**

Understand and Analyze

Respond to the questions. Support your responses with evidence from the text.

1. **Explain** Reread lines 35–39. What did John Volanthen expect to find? Why?

2. **Understand** Reread lines 47–59. What was the first clue that they had found the boys?

3. **Interpret** Reread lines 76–84. Why was Saman Gunan's death such a bad sign for the rescue mission?

4. **Analyze** Why were so many people needed to help with the rescue?

5. **Interpret** Why did people say that the rescuers had set an example for humankind?

Apply the Strategy: Ask Questions

Complete the chart with questions you asked yourself while reading "The Daring Cave Divers Who Saved the Thai Soccer Team." Then note the answers and the strategies you used to find them.

Questions I Asked	Answers	Strategy I Used
How did the boys feel while they were in the cave?	*I think they felt scared, tired, and hungry. They probably wished they hadn't gone on the outing.*	*made an inference based on the text*

Share Your Perspective

Discuss these questions in a small group.

1. Do you agree with Karadzic that people wanted to help because they have all been a kid scared of the dark? What other reasons might make people want to help?

2. If you lived near Tham Luang, would you have wanted to help with the rescue? Why or why not? If you did help, what would you have done?

Discussion Frames

I agree/disagree with Karadzic because …

Do you have other ideas about …?

Language Convention: Understand Verb Mood L.8.1.C

Mood is the form a verb takes to express the speaker's attitude. There are three types of verb moods:

The **indicative mood** is used to state facts and opinions.

> **Examples:** The cave **was flooding** fast.
> Cave divers **are** fairly introverted.

The **interrogative mood** is used to ask questions.

> **Examples:** How many **are** you?
> **Did** they **have** food with them?

The **imperative mood** is used to give commands.

> **Examples:** **Wear** this wetsuit.
> Don't **worry**.

PRACTICE 1 Read each sentence. Write the verb's mood: *indicative, interrogative,* or *imperative.*

	Mood
1. The best option was still a difficult one.	*indicative*
2. Hold on to me.	
3. The phone calls were short and to the point.	
4. Did you find them?	
5. Help me!	
6. How long can they stay alive?	

PRACTICE 2 Write six sentences about the cave rescue: two in indicative mood, two in interrogative mood, and two in imperative mood.

____

____

____

____

____

____

____

Read Again

Read "The Daring Cave Divers Who Saved the Thai Soccer Team" again. As you read, circle details from the text that help you respond to this question:

Why did people decide to help rescue the boys?

Reflect and Respond

Use some of the details you circled to complete the idea web.

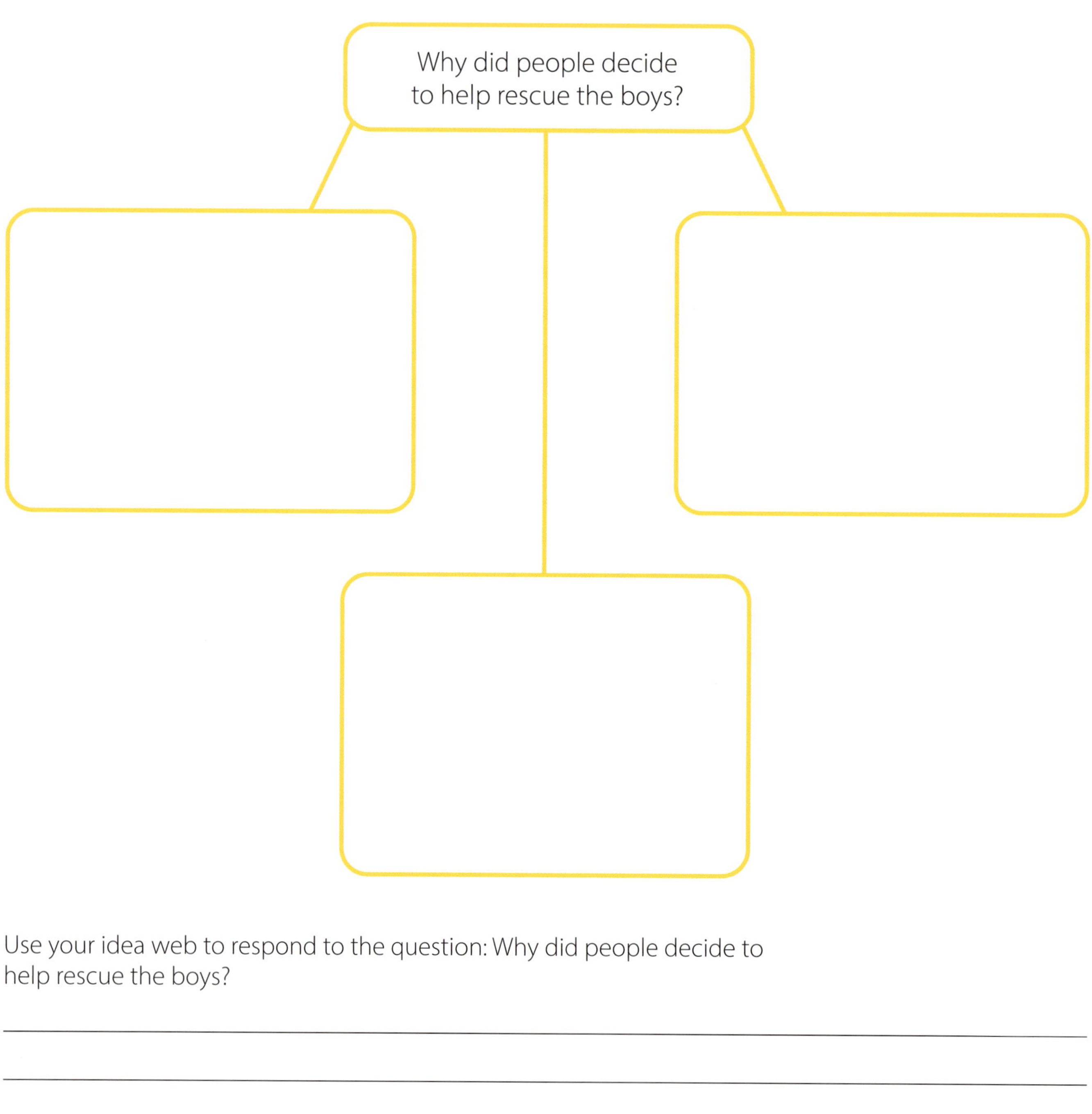

Use your idea web to respond to the question: Why did people decide to help rescue the boys?

____

____

____

Discuss Your Response

Share your ideas with the class. Then write one new idea you hear.

____

____

Respond to the Guiding Question

Write a response to the question:

Why do emergencies inspire us to help others?

Use evidence from the text, your discussion, and your life. Use the Discussion Frames to help you. Use the rubric to check your response.

____

____

____

____

Create and Present: The Experience of Being Rescued

Imagine you are one of the boys on the soccer team. Then do one of these activities.

OPTION 1: Write a Thank-You Letter

Write a thank-you letter to someone who helped (in any way) with the rescue mission. Then read it to your classmates.

OPTION 2: Write and Perform a Skit

Work in a small group. Write a short skit about the conversation that might have taken place between the boys, their coach, and the rescuers (Stanton and Volanthen) when they first found the team.

Here's an example of the first few lines of a skit:

VOLANTHEN: How many are you? 13? Brilliant!
COACH: Yes, we are all here. We were out exploring, and the
                  water rose so high we couldn't get back out safely.
                  I don't know how long we have been here.
BOY: Please help us.
STANTON: Don't worry …

Practice your skit, and then perform it for the class.

Boys from the soccer team attend a public event in Bangkok, Thailand.

Examine the Photo

1. Look at the photo. Describe what you see.

2. Do you think the people in the photo are helping others? Why or why not?

3. Write 3–5 questions about the photo. Discuss your questions with a small group.

Find Out ▶ 6.1

Watch photographer Cristina Mittermeier talk about her photo.

1. Does she answer any of your questions? Which ones?

2. According to Mittermeier, do the Coral Gardeners help others? Give details to support your answer.

3. What important ideas does she share about how everyone on the planet needs to help each other?

4. What do these ideas help you understand about the people in the photo?

Reflect

Imagine you are one of the people in the photo. Write a story about how and why you started working for the Coral Gardeners.

Share Your Story

Take or find a photo that shows your idea of helping others. Tell your classmates the story behind the photo.

ABOUT THE PHOTOGRAPHER

Cristina Mittermeier is a Mexican photographer, marine biologist, and ocean conservationist.

In emergency situations, what separates onlookers from action-takers?

First Thoughts

When there's an emergency situation in public, most people observe what is happening rather than helping. This is called the "bystander effect." However, some people do try to help. You are going to read an article about why these people act differently. Predict the reasons you will read about.

Key Vocabulary

PRACTICE Use context to determine the meaning of each word in bold. Then match the word to its definition.

Dr. Lawrence Kohlberg was a **psychologist** best known for his theory on **moral** development. He studied how children develop beliefs about ethical or good behavior. In the first stage of moral development, *preconventional*, children's moral beliefs are based on rules from parents and teachers. In the second stage, *conventional*, a child's beliefs about what is right are related to society. Children in this phase are likely to be **bystanders** in an emergency for fear of being different if they act rather than observe. While the **implications** of moral development do not necessarily extend to consequences such as **altruism**, they can. An act of extreme generosity is a **phenomenon** that is most likely to align with *postconventional*, Kohlberg's final stage of moral development.

______ **1.** altruism   **a.** ethical and right (adj.)

______ **2.** bystander   **b.** an observable event (n.)

______ **3.** implication   **c.** an expert in the science of the human mind (n.)

______ **4.** moral   **d.** one who does not participate (n.)

______ **5.** phenomenon   **e.** generous beliefs and acts (n.)

______ **6.** psychologist   **f.** a consequence or effect (n.)

Reading Skill: Analyze an Author's Purpose RI.8.6

An **author's purpose** is the reason for writing. An author might write to inform, entertain, persuade, or teach a moral lesson. Usually, authors do not state their purpose for writing. You have to infer the purpose by using clues from the text and making connections to what you know. To determine an author's purpose:

1. Before reading, consider the context in which the text was written. If possible, identify when and where it was written, the type of publication in which it appeared, and the author's background.

2. Read the title and introduction. What do the word choices and text structure tell you about the author's purpose? For example, an author might begin with an intriguing "hook," suggesting that the purpose is at least partly to entertain.

3. Pay attention to language. Persuasive texts include opinions, while informational texts are often written like a textbook or news story and include facts, numbers, and quotations. Authors who want to entertain might tell a story or use descriptive details.

4. How does the author conclude the text? Does the text restate an opinion or main idea, or does it end with an anecdote? The answers to these questions can help you determine the author's purpose.

Skill in Action

Look again at "The Daring Cave Divers Who Saved the Thai Soccer Team." What do the elements of the text indicate about the author's purpose for writing? Do you think the purpose of the article is more to inform or more to entertain? Read the possible answers in the chart below, and discuss your ideas with a partner.

Context	The article was written for Nationalgeographic.com. The purpose of most articles in *National Geographic* is to inform or entertain.
Title and Introduction	The title and the first paragraph show that the author is going to tell a story.
Language Choices	The article is written like a news story and includes many quotations and numbers. It also uses exciting details and descriptive language, like "lighting up around the world like modern-day Bat Signals," "watery tomb," and "thwarted by a torrent of muddy water."
Conclusion	The conclusion includes several quotations and more numbers. It also discusses cave diving and how it is an unusual hobby. This supports the idea that the author's purpose is to both inform and entertain.

Imagine that you are walking along a crowded, busy street, and you see a woman on the other side of the street trip and fall. She does not get up immediately. You think she may be hurt. Would you cross the street to check on her and offer to help her up? Many of us think that of course we would stop and help. But what if no one else stops to help? What if others glance at her and continue walking? Would it make a difference if a police officer or crossing guard were standing near her? Would you assume that that person would help—so you don't need to? Read on to learn about the reasons some people do or don't stop to help others.

What Is the "Bystander Effect" and How Do People Overcome It?

In emergency situations, what separates onlookers from action-takers?

by Catherine A. Sanderson
from *Discover* magazine and adapted from Catherine Sanderson's book *The Bystander Effect*

🎧 6.2

1   Numerous studies have shown that we are less likely to intervene when other people are present. We assume that others will do something, and we don't have to. **Psychologists** call this **phenomenon** the **bystander** effect.

Competitors in the Boston Marathon help a struggling runner toward the finish line.

A pedestrian checks on a cyclist who was blown over by strong storm winds in London, United Kingdom.

However, this is not a hard-and-fast[1] rule; sometimes people in groups are able to break out of the bystander role. But who are these people, and what makes them different from the rest of us?

Psychologists use the term "courageous bystanders" to describe those who display **moral** courage and choose to do something rather than watch in silence. These people stand up against the status quo when they feel inaction will compromise their values, even in the face of potentially negative social consequences. The traits that these people have in common range from their individual skill sets to their personalities—and might even be reflected at a neurological level.

Specialized Skills

If you act, will it matter? Asking this question might be the difference between standing up or standing by. It also helps explain why people with specialized training are more likely to spring into action in an emergency. Doctors, nurses, soldiers, or volunteer firefighters may feel more responsible to act in some scenarios—and research shows they usually do.

In one study, researchers recruited students from both a nursing program and a general education program to take what they were told was a simple questionnaire. Half of the students were placed in a room alone to work on their questionnaire; the others were in a room with another student (who was actually the researchers' accomplice[2]). As they were working, they heard a man fall from a ladder outside the room and scream out in pain.

General education students who were alone were much more likely to help than those who were with another person. But the percentage of nursing students who helped was the same whether they were alone or not. This doesn't mean that nursing students are nicer people—it reflects the fact that they knew what to do and therefore felt a greater responsibility to act.

Research has also shown that people feel more responsibility if they are in a position of authority. In some instances, the person with the specialized knowledge isn't the person with authority. Even so, they may take charge.

---

[1] **hard-and-fast** strict

[2] **accomplice** secret partner or assistant

40   During my senior year of college, I was sitting in a classroom on the fourth floor of a building when the room suddenly started swaying back and forth as a result of an earthquake. The students all turned to the authority—the professor—to figure out what to do.

45   Her response was not what we had expected: She grabbed the edge of the table and yelled, "I'm from New York!"—a city without many earthquakes. Her statement clearly indicated that she had no idea what to do.

    Another student then yelled, "I'm from California"—where
50 earthquakes are common—thus establishing his credibility in this emergency. Then he said, "Get under the table."

Confidence Is Key

    Besides wielding[3] expertise in certain situations, courageous bystanders tend to have high self-esteem and feel
55 confident about their own judgment, values, and ability. But courageous bystanders don't just feel confident that they are right—they believe their actions will make a difference.

    To better understand the specific personality traits that underpin moral courage, Tammy Sonnentag and Mark
60 Barnett studied the characteristics of over 200 seventh and eighth graders. They first asked the students to rate their own willingness to stand up to others and say or do the right thing in the face of social pressure to stay silent and go along with the crowd.

65   Next, they asked all students in each grade, and one teacher, to rate the tendency of each student to adhere to his or her moral beliefs and values in the face of pressures not to do so. That way, researchers could assess whether students who self-identified as courageous actually did behave in
70 ways that were visible to others and weren't just imagining themselves to be courageous.

    The researchers found a high level of agreement between students themselves, their peers, and their teacher about who was courageous. Those who fit the bill[4] also tended to possess
75 particular personality traits: They generally felt good about

---

[3] **wielding** having
[4] **fit the bill** matched the description

Delaney Reynolds is the founder of Sink or Swim, a group that fights climate change and sea level rise. She refuses to just "stand by," choosing instead to act.

themselves, rating themselves highly on statements such as "I feel
I have a number of good qualities" and "I am able to do things as
well as most other people." They were also confident about their
ability to accomplish their goals and to stand up to social pressure,
agreeing with statements like "I will be able to successfully
overcome many challenges" and "I follow my own ideas even
when pressured by a group to change them."

But these students didn't just feel confident and good about
themselves. They also believed they had a social responsibility to
share their beliefs. They agreed with statements like "I feel a social
obligation to voice my opinion" and "If everyone saw things the
way that I do, the world would be a better place." This belief in
the correctness of their views helped them speak up when other
students tended to stay quiet.

And, perhaps most important, these students were reportedly
less concerned about fitting in with the crowd. That means when
they have to choose between fitting in and doing the right thing,
they will probably choose to do what's right.

One drawback with studies such as this one is that they rely
on self-reporting about intentions. What we really want to know
is whether certain personality variables actually predict helping
behavior in the real world. After all, many of us, maybe even most
of us, imagine that we'd step up in an emergency, but we often
don't live up to our good intentions.

Bigger, Better Brains?

The morally courageous certainly have a tendency toward
certain traits, but are their brains anatomically different from the
rest of the population?

A scientific study examined differences in patterns of brain
activity in 19 people who had engaged in a quite extraordinary act
of generosity: donating a kidney to a total stranger. The donors'
amygdala—a part of the brain that processes emotions—was
found to be 8 percent larger than it is in most people, and it also
showed greater activity.

But we need to be cautious about interpreting this finding.
It's possible that these kidney donors were born with a larger and
more active amygdala, which caused them to care more about
other people. It's also possible, though, that engaging in this type

of extreme **altruism** could actively rewire the brain. Regardless of
the causal connection, it does appear that extraordinary altruists
show distinct patterns of neural activity that are associated with
a greater responsiveness to emotion. People who demonstrate
this type of selfless giving may experience the costs of helping
differently from the rest of us. Not helping may actually make
them feel worse.

There is also evidence that people who engage in extraordinary
acts of altruism show distinct patterns of neurological responses
to two types of painful experiences: experiencing pain themselves
and watching someone else experience pain.

In one study, researchers measured empathy in nearly
60 people, half of whom had donated a kidney to a stranger
and half of whom had not. Each participant was then paired
with a stranger to complete a series of trials. In one set of trials,
participants watched their partner receive painful pressure
to the right thumbnail while researchers used fMRI imaging
to record their brain activity. In another set, the participants
themselves received the thumbnail pressure, again while their
brain activity was assessed. Researchers then compared the two
sets of brain activity.

For most of us, experiencing pain ourselves feels far worse
than watching a stranger experience pain. But the brains of
those who had demonstrated extraordinary altruism responded
in almost the same way to their own pain as to that of others,
suggesting that they were experiencing someone else's pain as
though it were their own. For people who feel others' pain so
deeply, the choice to donate a kidney to a stranger may therefore
make sense: If they feel pain themselves from knowing that
someone else is in pain, helping that person would make them
feel better.

Donating a kidney to a stranger may be an extreme example.
Few people will think less of you for not choosing to do so, and it
does have physical risks. But the discoveries of these studies have
much broader **implications**, since the ability to feel empathy is
an important characteristic of those who are willing to face social
consequences for doing the right thing.

Close Read

Work with a partner.

1. Determine the meanings of your underlined words and phrases.

2. Discuss the question: **What traits do "courageous bystanders" have?**

Understand and Analyze

Respond to the questions. Support your responses with evidence from the text.

1. **Explain** Reread paragraphs 1–3. In your own words, explain what the author means by "courageous bystander." Why are they different from most people?

2. **Compare** Reread lines 17–18. What is the difference in the meanings of "standing up" and "standing by"? Write an example sentence for each word.

3. **Understand** Reread lines 23–35. Why does the author say that the nursing students felt a greater responsibility to act?

4. **Understand** Reread lines 72–93. Why is it important for courageous bystanders to have confidence?

5. **Interpret** Reread lines 94–99. What is self-reporting in research? Why does the author say it is a drawback to rely on it?

6. **Analyze** Why does the author say these studies have broader implications?

Apply the Skill: Analyze Author's Purpose RI.8.6

Complete the chart below with clues from "What Is the 'Bystander Effect' and How Do People Overcome It?" to help you analyze the author's purpose for writing the article.

Context	The article was written for *Discover* magazine. Most of the articles in *Discover* magazine are written to inform.
Title	
Main Ideas and Details	
Conclusion	
Author's Purpose:	

Share Your Perspective

Discuss these questions in a small group.

1. Do you think people can be taught to be morally courageous? Why or why not?

2. If you were in a public setting and witnessed an emergency, do you think you would stand up and help or stay silent and go along with the crowd? Why?

Language Convention: Understand Conditionals L.8.1.C

Conditional is another mood that verbs express. In sentences with conditional verbs, something causes something else to happen. There are three kinds of conditional mood—*first conditional* for real situations in the present or future, *second conditional* for unreal situations in the present, and *third conditional* for unreal situations in the past.

There are two clauses in conditional sentences—the *if* clause and the result clause.

	If Clause	Result Clause	
First Conditional	simple present	*will* + base verb	If you **call** me, I <u>will answer</u>. If they **have** time, they <u>will come</u>.
Second Conditional	simple past	*would* + base verb	If I **had** medical training, I <u>would help</u>. If he **were*** a doctor, he <u>would help</u>.
Third Conditional	past perfect	*would have* + past participle	If I **had been** there, I <u>would have called</u> for help. If we **had known** you were sick, we <u>would have visited</u> you.

* For the *if* clause in second conditional, use *was* or *were* with the subjects *I, he, she,* and *it. Were* is more formal.

PRACTICE 1 Identify the mood in each sentence. Write *FC* for first conditional, *SC* for second conditional, or *TC* for third conditional.

_____ **1.** If I had realized you were lost, I would have looked for you.

_____ **2.** If I had more confidence, I would stand up for what's right.

_____ **3.** If it rains, we won't go to the caves.

_____ **4.** If they hadn't had the accident, they wouldn't have missed the dinner.

_____ **5.** If she were the donor, she would have told us.

PRACTICE 2 Complete the sentences with the form of the verbs given in parentheses.

1. third conditional *(know/help)*: If I _____________ , I _____________ .

2. second conditional *(be/go)*: If it _____________ a nice day, I _____________ on a hike.

3. third conditional *(be/hear)*: If they _____________ home, they _____________ you.

4. second conditional *(have/care)*: If she _____________ a kinder heart, she _____________ more.

5. first conditional *(be/get)*: If there _____________ an earthquake, we _____________ under our desks.

What Is the "Bystander Effect" and How Do People Overcome It?   **303**

Read Again

Read "What Is the 'Bystander Effect' and How Do People Overcome It?" again. As you read, circle details from the text that help you respond to this question:

What makes "courageous bystanders" take action?

Reflect and Respond

Use three of the details you circled in the article to complete the idea web.

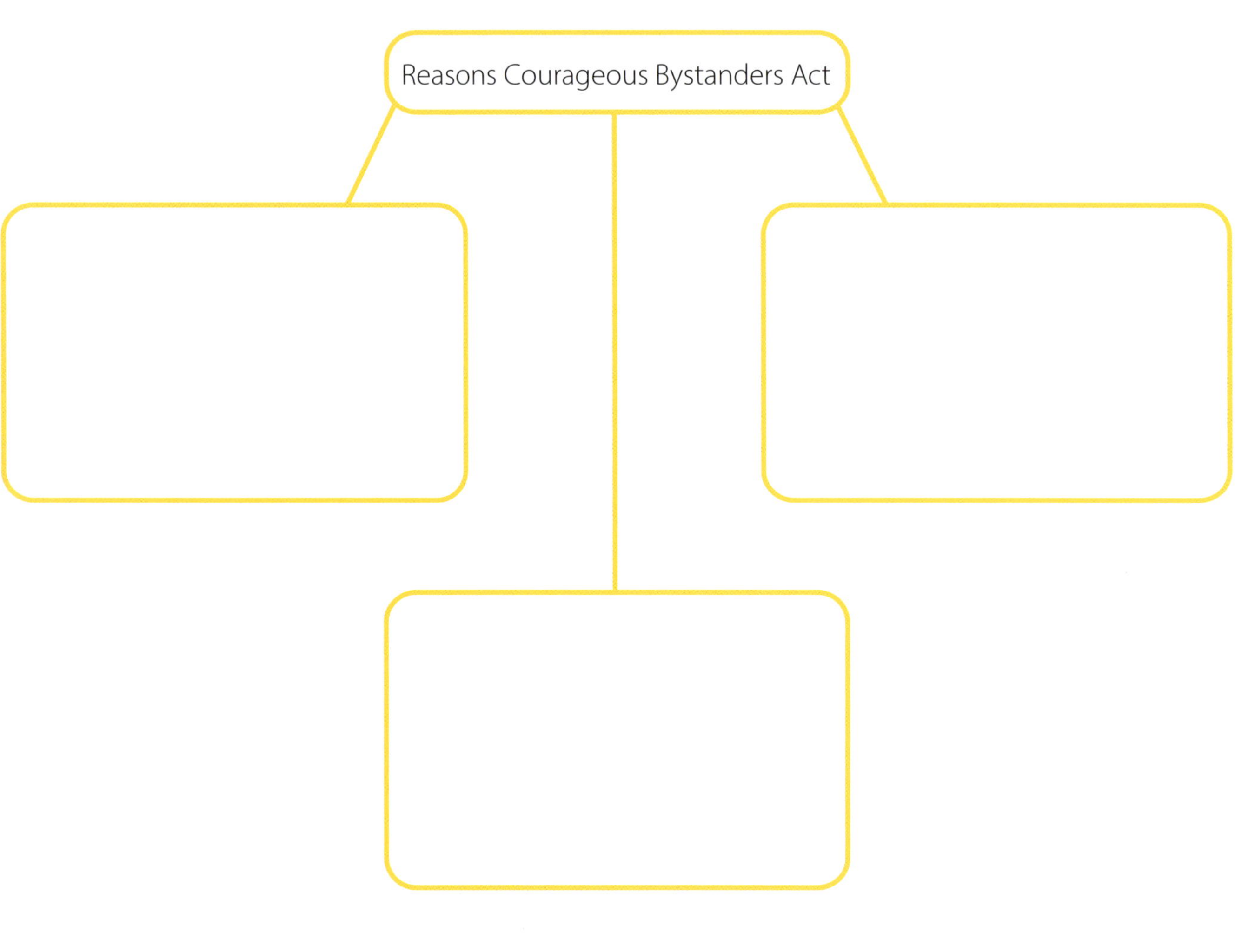

Use your idea web to respond to the question: What makes "courageous bystanders" take action?

____

____

____

____

Discuss Your Response

Share your ideas with the class. Then write one new idea you hear.

____

____

____

Respond to the Guiding Question

Write a response to the question:

In emergency situations, what separates onlookers from action-takers?

Use evidence from the text, your discussion, and your life. Use the Discussion Frames to help you. Use the rubric to check your response.

____

____

____

____

____

Research W.8.7

Choose one of these topics. Research the topic to learn more about it.

- the bystander effect
- the amygdala (part of the brain)

Follow these steps:

1. Make notes about what you already know about the topic.
2. Write three questions you have about the topic.
3. Research the topic to find answers to your questions.
4. Write your answers to the questions.
5. Present what you learn to a small group.

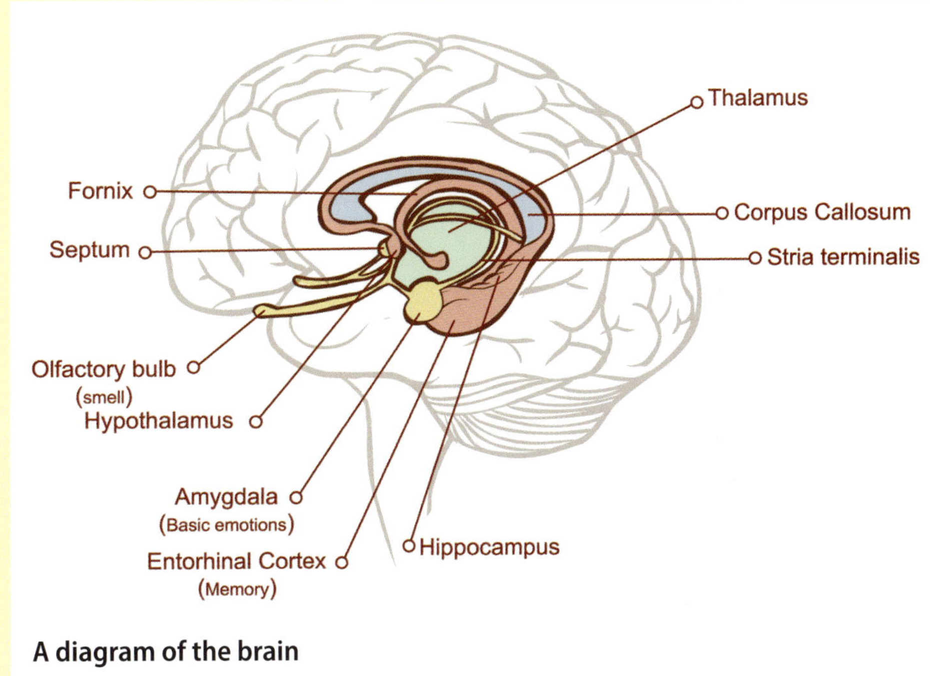

A diagram of the brain

VIDEO CONNECTION

How does
helping the
planet help
people?

First Thoughts

Make a list of the plastic products you use during a typical day. Write *S* next to single-use plastics, or items you use once before throwing them away or recycling them. Work in a small group to compare your lists.

Viewing Skill: Identify Mood

The word **mood** can describe the atmosphere or feeling created by a text or a video. Videos combine several features to help create mood. The images, their brightness or darkness, the music and background sounds, and the speakers' tone of voice all contribute to mood. When you watch a video, pay attention to these features. How do they make you feel?

Apply the Skill

▶ **6.2** Watch the video "Plastics 101." Pay attention to the different features of the video. Take notes in the chart. Then describe the overall mood.

	Images	Music	Tone of Voice
0:00–0:15	several bright pictures	upbeat music that sounds curious	bright and questioning
0:16–3:37			
3:38–5:28			
Overall mood:			

Understand and Analyze

▶ **6.2** Watch again. Answer the questions. Support your responses with evidence from the video.

1. **Compare** What is the difference between the plastic used 3,500 years ago and the plastic used today?
2. **Understand** Why is plastic such a huge problem today?
3. **Explain** What makes single-use plastics particularly bad?
4. **Infer** Since plastic is so bad for the planet, why don't people just stop making and using plastic? What is a better approach?

Share Your Perspective

1. How does reducing our use of plastic help other people?
2. How can you reduce your use of single-use plastics?

Why is "tough love" sometimes the best way to help someone?

First Thoughts

"Tough love" is an expression that describes the harsh treatment given to someone in order to help the person change a harmful behavior. Here is an example:

> Juan often forgets to bring his homework to school. He calls his mother and asks her to bring it to school for him. One day, she decides to use tough love and doesn't drop off his forgotten homework. Juan gets a zero on his homework that day. The next day, Juan puts his homework in his backpack right after he finishes it, so he remembers to take it to school.

What are some other examples of tough love? Describe them.

Key Vocabulary

PRACTICE Use context to determine the meaning of each word in bold. Then match the word to its definition.

1. The actress's performance as Helen Keller was **convincing**. I believed she was blind and deaf.
2. My aunt is a **scholar**. She has a doctoral degree in biology and studies the skeletons of birds.
3. He needed to write his report, but he **procrastinated** and kept doing other things instead.
4. The **appointed** time for my interview was 3:00 p.m., but I arrived a few minutes early.
5. Although he is rich and famous now, he comes from a **humble** background.
6. Many students want to go to well-known universities for the **prestige**. They believe they will get better jobs later because people respect the university.

_____	**1.** humble	**a.**	highly educated person (n.)
_____	**2.** procrastinate	**b.**	high regard (n.)
_____	**3.** convincing	**c.**	believable (adj.)
_____	**4.** appointed	**d.**	simple; of low rank (adj.)
_____	**5.** scholar	**e.**	to put off (v.)
_____	**6.** prestige	**f.**	assigned (adj.)

A literary text usually expresses a **theme**—the main idea or message of the work. The theme is usually introduced early in the story, through the characters and setting, and develops alongside the characters and plot. To determine and analyze the theme:

1. Read the title for clues about the theme.

2. Identify the setting and characters. In what ways do the characters change in the story? How do they help establish the theme?

3. Determine the key events in the plot. Do they help convey a message about life?

4. Identify the message expressed by the title, setting, characters, and plot.

Skill in Action

Read the story and analysis below. With a partner, discuss how details about the characters and plot help develop the story's theme.

The Boy Who Cried Wolf

The boy is given a responsibility.

Once upon a time, a shepherd sent his son to guard their flock of sheep. "Be sure to tell the villagers if you see a wolf," he warned. Days passed, yet no wolf came. Growing bored, the boy decided to play a trick on the villagers.

He does not take it seriously. He starts telling lies for fun.

"Wolf!" yelled the boy. The villagers ran to help but found only the boy, laughing at his prank. A few days later, the boy played his trick again. The villagers came running, but there was no wolf. They became angry with the boy.

The next day, the boy saw a wolf. "Wolf!" cried the boy. Tired of his tricks, the villagers ignored the boy, and the hungry wolf devoured the sheep.

People no longer believe the boy, so they don't help him when he really needs help.

I think the story's theme is that lying and playing tricks on others can have harsh consequences.

A Friend's Gift

adapted from a Vietnamese tale

🎧 **6.3**

1   Duong Le[1] and Luu Binh[2] had been friends since they were children. They studied together and played together at the village school. And they had the same goal: each wanted to become a mandarin—a highly respected government official. Mandarins led very comfortable lives.

5   However, anyone wishing to be a mandarin had to take a civil service examination. This was a very difficult test—not just anyone could become a mandarin. Candidates had to devote all their time to prepare for it, so they could not be employed. This was not a problem for Luu Binh, who had inherited a small fortune and did not have to work for a living.

10 Duong Le, however, came from a family that didn't have much money. His parents could not afford to let him live at home without paying for room and board. Duong Le would have to work for a living, so he couldn't spend whole days studying for the exam.

    One afternoon Duong Le said to Luu Binh, "You and I must part

15 ways. You will pass the examination and become a mandarin, while I will not."

    Luu Binh answered, "No, my friend, I can't allow that to happen. You must come live in my house. The next examination is two years away. With plenty of time to study, we'll both pass. Then

20 you'll never have to worry about money." When Duong Le protested,[3] Luu Binh said warmly, "In the name of true friendship, you must let me do this."

    So Duong Le moved into Luu Binh's house, and they began their studies.

25 As schoolchildren, they had already memorized several books of classic Chinese literature;

---

[1] **Duong Le** pronounced "dwong lay"
[2] **Luu Binh** pronounced "loo bihn"
[3] **protested** said no

now they studied other books and practiced writing skills. They would
spend hours discussing a difficult question or debating current issues.

At first both worked steadily from morning until night, but soon Luu
Binh got tired of working so hard. One day, in the middle of studying,
he sat back in his chair. "We shouldn't have to kill ourselves to pass this
exam," he said to Duong Le. "In fact, we'll probably do better if we rest
every now and then. Come on, let's go get something to eat."

"You go ahead," Duong Le answered. "I have to finish memorizing
this poem."

"It isn't necessary for you to work so hard," argued Luu Binh.

"To me, it is. I have to pass the examination the first time I take it. If I fail,
there'll be no second chance for me, and I'll have to get a menial job or go
hungry. I certainly can't continue living on your charity.[4]"

"You worry too much. We'll both pass easily, you'll see."

This conversation ended with Duong Le staying in his room and Luu
Binh going out to find entertainment. For the rest of the two years, Duong Le
studied constantly, and Luu Binh studied when he felt like it.

On the **appointed** day, the two friends reported to the government
building for the examination, along with hundreds of other candidates.
Guards searched the candidates for hidden notes and then locked them in

---

[4] **charity** aid

small cells. The building was very quiet except for an occasional cough and rustling of paper. Anyone who attempted to communicate with a neighbor immediately failed the test.

Afterward, everyone nervously awaited the results. "How did it go?" asked Duong Le.

"There were many things I didn't know, so I found it difficult," answered Luu Binh.

"Now comes the hardest part—waiting for the results. I'm sure you did fine, Luu Binh."

When the examinations were graded and the scores were announced, Duong Le's name was on the short list of those who had passed. He would receive his degree and, eventually, a mandarin's post in another province. Luu Binh's name, however, was not on the list—he had failed.

Luu Binh was humiliated. "Never mind," Duong Le said. "You don't need a degree anyway, since you have enough money to live comfortably. If you want a degree just for the **prestige** it brings, you can take the examination again."

After Duong Le left to take up his new post, Luu Binh felt lonely. Of course he had other friends, but they liked him only because he knew how to have a good time. Duong Le had appreciated Luu Binh's more serious talents.

Luu Binh decided to follow his friend's suggestion and take the examination again. However, he still lacked discipline. The examination was another three years away, so he told himself that two years of studying would be plenty and that he could afford to relax and enjoy life for a year.

After the twelve months had passed, Luu Binh began studying, but as before, he found it impossible to make himself work steadily. He **procrastinated** often, and he took time off for dining with his friends, going to the theater, and playing games. As the months passed, he spent less and less time studying and more and more time amusing himself.

When only three months remained, Luu Binh finally faced reality. He found that he had spent his entire fortune and was in debt. This time, he knew, he had to pass. So he closed himself in his room and forced himself to study.

However, his efforts were too little, too late, and he failed the test a second time.

He felt very sorry for himself for a time, but finally he accepted his situation. He sold his house and everything in it, including his books, and then paid off his debts. He rented a cheap room that was dark and cramped[5] and found a clerk's job in the village magistrate's office. The work was boring and paid poorly.

Luu Binh's life sank into a dull, unsatisfying routine. As he worked, his mind often wandered to the happier days of the past. He wondered how Duong Le was doing and what Duong Le would think if he knew what had happened to his old friend.

Then one day Luu Binh had an idea. "I'll go to Duong Le and ask him for a job. Even if it is a lowly clerical position, at least I'd be working for Duong Le, who'll treat me as an old friend. We'll spend hours discussing literature and grand ideas. It will be like old times!"

Luu Binh was so sure that Duong Le would welcome him that he resigned from his position at the magistrate's. He packed his few belongings and left for the city where Duong Le served as mandarin.

When he arrived in the city, Luu Binh took a room at an inn and found out where Duong Le lived. When Luu Binh knocked at the door of Duong Le's beautiful house the next morning, a guard answered. Luu Binh explained that he was an old friend of the mandarin. "You'll have to speak to His Lordship's secretary," the guard said gruffly.

Inside, Luu Binh greeted the secretary politely and introduced himself. The secretary could tell by Luu Binh's clothing that he had no official rank and said coldly, "His Lordship is very busy. Please state your business."

"Please give him my name and tell him that I need a job and have experience as a clerk," said Luu Binh. It was embarrassing to tell the secretary that he came in search of such a lowly position. "I would be grateful to have any position, no matter how **humble**."

"Wait here," the secretary said curtly.

When he came back, the secretary said, "His Lordship doesn't know any Luu Binh."

"What?" said Luu Binh. "There must be some mistake. We were schoolchildren together. We studied for the civil service examination together!"

"You are mistaken. His Lordship says he has never heard of you."

"Let me talk to him," demanded Luu Binh.

The secretary took Luu Binh's arm and tried to steer[6] him toward the door. But Luu Binh shook him off. "If Duong Le saw me, I know he would remember me!"

---

[5] **cramped** crowded and small
[6] **steer** direct

The guard heard the commotion, rushed into the room, and helped
the secretary drag Luu Binh into the street. There the two gave Luu Binh a
shove that sent him sprawling in the dust.

Luu Binh trembled with shock and indignation[7] as he struggled to his
feet and brushed himself off. How could Duong Le insult his old friend in
such an outrageous manner? It was beyond belief.

Luu Binh slowly walked back to the inn, muttering[8] bitterly to himself
all the way. "So that's how he treats his oldest and best friend! If it weren't
for me, he wouldn't be where he is today." Kicking a stone down the street,
he grew more upset as he thought about it. "That's gratitude for you!
Educated man, ha! Duong Le knows the Book of Classic Poetry by heart,
but he can't remember his friend's name! A learned man is supposed to be
honorable, just, humble, and kind. Duong Le, the learned man—ha!"

Luu Binh knew he must get home and try to get his old job back
before they hired somebody else, so he quickly made arrangements to
leave the inn.

As he was gathering his belongings, a refined young woman came to
his door and asked to speak with him. "I am Chau[9] Long, the landlady of
this inn," she said.

"I am Luu Binh, your humble guest."

"I understand you are a **scholar**," said Chau Long.

Luu Binh gave a short laugh. "A failed scholar," he answered.
"I have taken and failed the civil service examination twice."

"Would you like to try again?" she asked.

"Yes, but I must work for a living, so I have no time to study."

"If I let you stay here, free, you could then devote your time to
studying."

"But why should you do such a thing?"

Chau Long bowed her head and seemed to wipe a tear from her eye.
"My young son was studying to become a scholar, but he died. I want
to honor his memory by helping another scholar succeed and become a
mandarin."

"That's most generous. I don't know what to say."

"Say nothing—save your energy for studying. You will have a place to
sleep and food to eat, and if you need a book, let me know and I'll bring it
from my son's library."

---

[7] **indignation** anger
[8] **muttering** talking in a low, angry voice
[9] **Chau** pronounced "chow"

160   "How can I ever repay you?" said Luu Binh, with tears in his eyes.

"You never need to repay me. Just pass the test."

There was only a year and a half to prepare for the examination. But Luu Binh resolved not to waste a minute. Every morning he got up early and worked until dark, stopping only to eat—and sometimes he even
165   forgot to do that.

From time to time, Chau Long would check on him. She usually insisted that he rest. "You are working too hard," she would say. "There's no sense in killing yourself."

Luu Binh would laugh at this. One day he replied, "That's just what
170   I used to say to a former friend of mine, but luckily for him, he was too smart to listen to me."

At last the day of the examination arrived. Luu Binh answered all the questions easily. Even before the results were announced, he felt sure he

had passed. When the list of successful candidates was published, Luu
Binh's name was at the very top!

Eager to share his triumph with the person who had made it possible,
Luu Binh rushed to the inn. He asked for Chau Long, but nobody had
seen her for several days. Then he asked when she would return. Finally,
one of the kitchen staff answered, "You've been her guest for so long that
you know more about her comings and goings than we do."

The puzzling reply discouraged Luu Binh from asking any more
questions, but each day he checked at the front desk for Chau Long.

One day, there was a letter for him, but not from Chau Long. Still,
delight showed on Luu Binh's face as he read the letter and discovered that
he had been appointed to an important position in the capital.

He put off leaving the inn, hoping that Chau Long would appear, but
she never did. So he wrote a letter expressing his deep appreciation and left
it for her. Then he set out for the capital to begin his new life as a mandarin.

Years went by. One day, while traveling on official business, Luu Binh
happened to be close to the home of Duong Le. Although he no longer
considered the man his friend, he was curious to see how Duong Le
would receive him, so he decided to pay him a call.

The same guard and secretary were there. However, this time both treated Luu Binh with the utmost respect. When Luu Binh's name was announced, Duong Le hurried out to greet him and led him into a private sitting room. Both were acting as if the earlier visit hadn't happened. They were sipping tea and reminiscing[10] about the old days at the village school when a woman brought in some refreshments. Luu Binh stared at her in amazement.

"You're the missing mistress of the inn!" exclaimed Luu Binh.

"This is my wife, Chau Long," said Duong Le, chuckling.

"Your wife?" stammered Luu Binh. "But I thought … that is, I'm sure she said …"

Duong Le laughed. "Chau Long, would you explain everything?"

"You see," Chau Long said, "when you came to see Duong Le six years ago, he wanted to help you. But he knew it wouldn't really be helping if you were given the clerical job you were seeking. That would have left you in an inferior position for the rest of your life. Duong Le wanted you to pass the examination and become a mandarin, so he insulted you and turned you away."

"I was very hurt by that," said Luu Binh.

"It was painful for you both. But then Duong Le gave you a chance at a much better life by paying your room and board at the inn and lending his books to you. The rest was up to you, and you succeeded brilliantly."

"Then, that story about your son and his books …?"

"I made that up," said Chau Long with a smile.

Luu Binh smiled back at her and said, "You gave a most **convincing** performance." He turned to Duong Le. "I must ask you the question I asked Chau Long six years ago: How can I ever thank you?"

"You don't have to thank me," answered Duong Le. "Remember all those years ago when you gave me room, board, and books? You made it possible for me to study for the examination. I only did for you what you had already done for me."

There was silence in the room for a few moments. Then Luu Binh said, "You have given me another gift today."

"What is that?" asked Duong Le.

"You have given me back the friend I thought I'd lost. To know that we're still friends and will always be friends makes me very happy."

"I understand," said Duong Le. "It makes me very happy, too."

---

[10] **reminiscing** remembering

Close Read

Work with a partner.

1. Determine the meanings of your underlined words and phrases.
2. Discuss the questions:

   What gift does each friend give?
   How are the gifts the same, and how are they different?

Understand and Analyze

Respond to the questions. Support your responses with evidence from the text.

1. **Understand** Reread the first two paragraphs. What is a mandarin? Why do Luu Binh and Duong Le want to be mandarins, and what do they have to do to become one?
2. **Infer** Reread lines 45–50. Why do the guards search Luu Binh and Duong Le?
3. **Explain** Reread lines 94–97. Why is Luu Binh so confident that Duong Le will help him?
4. **Infer** Reread lines 114–126 and 193–196. Why do the guard and secretary treat Luu Binh so differently the two times he visits Duong Le?
5. **Deduce** Why doesn't Duong Le just tell Luu Binh he will pay for his expenses while he studies?
6. **Contrast** How does Luu Binh change during the story? Contrast the younger Luu Binh with the character as he is at the end of the story.

Apply the Skill: Analyze Theme RL.8.2

Identify the theme of "A Friend's Gift." Then note details from the story that show how the theme is developed.

Theme:
How the theme develops:

Share Your Perspective

Discuss these questions in a small group.

1. Do you think it would have been better if Duong Le had met with Luu Binh the first time Luu Binh came to Duong Le's house? Should Duong Le have told Luu Binh he would pay for Luu Binh to study? Explain.
2. What are the benefits and drawbacks of using tough love?

Discussion Frames

I think … because …

The benefits of tough love are …

The drawbacks are …

Can you explain …?

Vocabulary: Identify Word Relationships   **L.8.5.B**

Identifying relationships between words in a text can help you figure out the meaning of unfamiliar words. Some common **word relationships** are synonyms (words with the same meaning), antonyms (words with opposite meanings), part/whole, and category/item.

Transition words and phrases can help you identify word relationships.

Relationship	Transition Words and Phrases	Example
synonyms	in fact, like, similarly, too	Luu Binh found studying **tiresome**. In fact, he found it so **dull** that he often avoided it for days. *Tiresome* and *dull* are synonyms.
antonyms	in contrast, on the contrary, unlike	Duong Le was not **idle**. On the contrary, he was quite **diligent**. *Idle* and *diligent* are antonyms.
part/whole	also, even more, included in that, part of	Duong Le offered **support**: money, books, and also a **place** to study. A place to study is part of Duong Le's support.
category/item	for example, one of	He read several **stories**. One of them was an old **tale**. A tale is a type of story.

Apply the Strategy

Look at "A Friend's Gift" again. Then answer the questions.

1. Read this sentence: *Although Luu Binh had several years to study, he spent only part of the time—three months—preparing for the exam.*

    What relationship does *months* have to *years*?

    a. part/whole   **b.** category/item

2. Read this sentence: *Luu Binh wants a prestigious position, in contrast to his menial job as a clerk.*

    The words *prestigious* and *menial* are

    a. synonyms   **b.** antonyms

3. Read this sentence: *Chau Long shared many books. For example, she brought Luu Binh volumes of poetry.*

    What relationship does *books* have to *volumes of poetry*?

    a. part/whole   **b.** category/item

Read Again

Read "A Friend's Gift" again. As you read, circle details from the text that help you respond to this question:

Why are Duong Le's actions a gift to Luu Binh?

Reflect and Respond

Use some of the details you circled to complete the idea web.

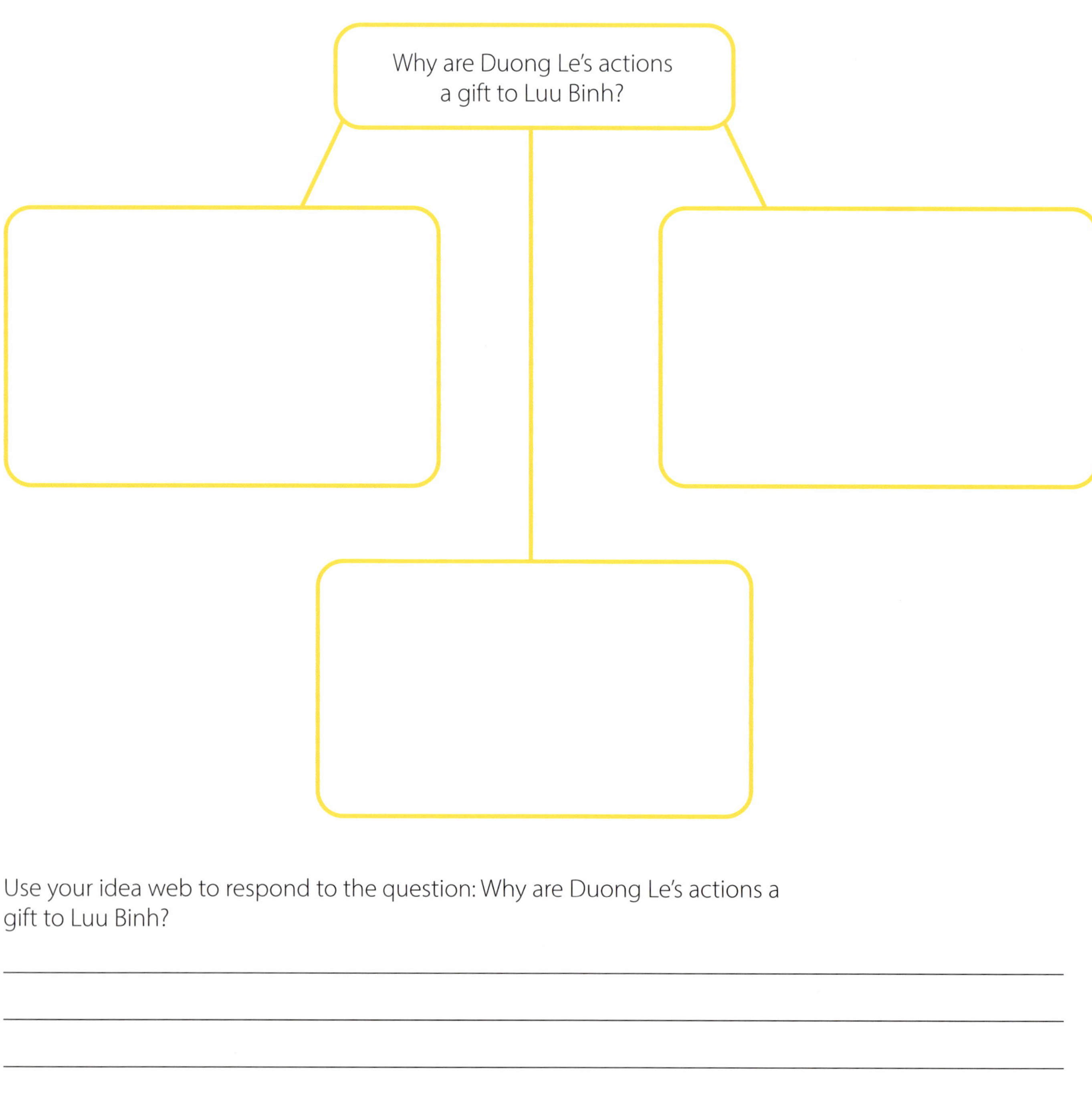

Use your idea web to respond to the question: Why are Duong Le's actions a gift to Luu Binh?

____

____

____

____

Discuss Your Response

Share your ideas with the class. Then write one new idea you hear.

____

____

____

Respond to the Guiding Question

Write a response to the question:

Why is "tough love" sometimes the best way to help someone?

Use evidence from the text, your discussion, and your life. Use the Discussion Frames to help you. Use the rubric to check your response.

____

____

____

____

____

CONNECT ACROSS TEXTS

Discuss the Essential Question: What responsibility do people have to help others?

Look at your answer to the Essential Question in the Unit Launch and your notes about helping others in the Reflect and Respond sections. Discuss: How have your ideas about the Essential Question changed? What changed your ideas?

Then write one new idea you heard in the discussion. How did it affect your opinion?

____

____

Respond to the Essential Question

Write your new response to the Essential Question. Include Academic Vocabulary.

____

____

____

Assignment: Write a Personal Narrative W.8.3

A personal narrative is a story about an experience or event from your life. The story is written from a first-person perspective and explains what you learned from the event. For this assignment, you will write a personal narrative about a time you helped someone or someone helped you.

Your personal narrative should include:

- a topic sentence that introduces the experience
- a sequence of events that has a beginning, middle, and end
- descriptive details and sensory language that describe actions and emotions
- dialogue or quotations
- a reflective conclusion that states what you learned or how the event changed you

Explore the Model

Read the model personal narrative about a time the writer and some friends helped someone. Underline the descriptive details and sensory language. Circle the dialogue or quotations.

A panda keeper, dressed in a panda outfit, does a quick check of a cub at Wolong National Nature Reserve in Sichuan province, China.

The Tiniest Meow

On the coldest day of the year, the tiniest meow brought the neighborhood kids together for a rescue mission. It was the biggest snowfall our town had seen in years. The morning after the snow stopped, I got a frantic text from my friend Pamela. It said, "Lilo is missing!!! Please come help!" Lilo, Pamela's kitten, was small, gray, fuzzy, and adorable. He was also full of energy and sometimes escaped through their dog door.

I bundled up and walked over. The snow was cold and heavy and stuck to my boots and snow pants. It felt like ice crystals were forming in my nose every time I breathed in. I got to Pamela's and saw two other friends, Tomas and Penelope, also there to help. The three kneeled around the porch.

"We found him!" Pamela exclaimed.

"But he's trapped under the porch," added Tomas. I kneeled in the snow, next to my friends, and together, we listened. Soon we heard the tiniest meow coming from under the porch.

"Poor little Lilo!" I said.

Pamela's mom brought out gardening tools. Little by little, we scooped out the cold, wet snow until we heard a clank. The shovel had hit an icy barrier.

Pamela cried, "We'll never get to him!" I had a bad feeling she was right, but then Penelope yelled, "Hot water!" We tried it—and it worked! We melted and chipped our way through the ice until we had cleared a small tunnel under the porch. Pamela put food at the entrance and called Lilo's name. The tiny meows grew louder until, at long last, out walked Lilo—scared, cold, and hungry—but okay. Pamela scooped him up, and we all cheered!

When I got back home, I thought back on the morning. It didn't matter that it was cold out or that we hadn't eaten. Saving Lilo had kept us warm because we were working together for a good cause.

Plan Your Personal Narrative

Choose an event to write about. Complete the chart to plan your personal narrative.

Personal Narrative Planning Chart

Topic Sentence:		
Events (beginning / middle / end)	Descriptive / Sensory Details	Dialogue
Reflective Conclusion:		

Write and Revise

Write Use your planning chart to write a first draft of your personal narrative. A good personal narrative includes transition words and phrases that indicate chronology, or the sequence of events. To connect the events in your personal narrative, use transition phrases, such as these:

- At the outset,
- All of a sudden,
- In that moment,
- Little by little,
- Before long,
- Next,
- Soon after,
- At long last,
- In the end,

Revise Exchange personal narratives with a partner. Use the checklist to review your partner's work and give feedback. Refer to your partner's feedback as you revise your draft.

- ☐ Is the personal narrative about a specific event or experience in the writer's life?
- ☐ Is the narrative written from a first-person perspective?
- ☐ Does the narrative follow a sequence of events that has a beginning, middle, and end?
- ☐ Does the narrative use descriptive details and sensory language?
- ☐ Does the narrative include dialogue or quotations?
- ☐ Does the narrative include a reflective conclusion about what the writer learned?

Proofread Check the grammar, spelling, punctuation, and capitalization in your narrative. Make edits to correct any errors.

Publish

Share your narrative according to your teacher's instructions. Read at least two of your classmates' narratives.

TIP Check your punctuation in dialogue and quotations. There should be quotation marks around the words a person says and a comma that sets off the quotation from the rest of the sentence.

Assignment: Conduct an Interview SL.8.1

An **interview** is a type of a one-on-one discussion. The purpose of an interview is to find out more about a person's experiences and feelings about a specific topic or event. Imagine you are on a talk show. Work with a partner to take turns interviewing each other about the topic of your personal narratives. One of you is the talk-show host, and the other is the person who had the experience of helping others or being helped.

In a good interview:

- The interviewer is prepared with questions to find out relevant information and keep the discussion going.
- The interview questions are open ended and start with *who, what, where, when, why,* and *how*.
- The interviewer asks relevant follow-up questions that build on the answers of the interviewee, getting more details or clarifying information.
- The interviewee answers the questions with appropriate and clear ideas and details.
- The interviewee stays on topic and speaks openly and freely.

Plan Your Interview

Use the interview guide to plan the questions and possible follow-up questions to ask your partner.

<table>
<tr><td align="center">Interview Guide</td></tr>
<tr><td>

• **Question:**

   • Possible follow-up question:

   • Possible follow-up question:

• **Question:**

   • Possible follow-up question:

   • Possible follow-up question:

• **Question:**

   • Possible follow-up question:

   • Possible follow-up question:

</td></tr>
</table>

Practice Your Interview

Read the checklist below. Then practice your interview with a partner. You and your partner should complete the checklist for each other and use it to give feedback before you conduct the interview for the class.

☐ Did the interviewer come to the interview prepared?

☐ Did the interviewer ask open-ended questions?

☐ Did the interviewer ask relevant follow-up questions that built on the interviewee's answers?

☐ Did the interviewee answer the questions with appropriate details?

☐ Did the interviewee speak openly and freely but still stay on topic?

Conduct Your Interview

Conduct your interview in front of the class, keeping in mind the feedback from your practice interview.

Reflect

Discuss the questions with a small group.

1. What surprised you about writing your personal narrative or participating in the interview?
2. What was easy about writing the personal narrative? What was difficult?
3. What was easy about interviewing or being interviewed? What was difficult?
4. How was the feedback on your writing and interviewing helpful?
5. What is something you learned from one of your classmates' interviews?

Starting a Food Waste Movement 🎧 6.4

EXPLORER IN ACTION

Tristram Stuart is an activist, author, and conservationist.

Every year, about a billion people suffer from hunger. At the same time, one-third of the world's food is wasted, simply because of how it looks. National Geographic Explorer Tristram Stuart has taken action to stop this waste of food. How? By starting a food waste movement that encourages people to eat ugly food.

Stuart points out that "ridiculously strict cosmetic standards" set by supermarkets worldwide are leading to a global food waste scandal. Food is thrown away at every point along the way, from the field to the plate. Stuart first recognized the issue of food waste as a teenager raising livestock. "Most of the food that I was giving my animals was actually perfectly fit for human consumption. It was coming from supermarket dumpsters." Stuart started the organization Feedback, which attempts to get people to limit their own food waste and, ultimately, end world hunger. Feedback hosts events such as massive free feasts, huge public meals that serve food that would have been wasted.

Will Stuart's food waste movement end world hunger? Maybe not on its own, but it has certainly made an impact. Since he began his campaign over 20 years ago, food waste has gone from "a neglected issue that no one knew about to one that is now treated as a global priority."

▶ **6.3** Watch the video to learn more.

1. What problem is Stuart trying to solve? How can it help solve another problem? What action has he taken?

2. Do you think eliminating food waste could solve the world's hunger problem? Why or why not? What challenges do you see?

How Will You Take Action?

Choose one or more of these actions to do.

Personal

Help another person by doing three "random acts of kindness."

1. Throughout the day, pay extra attention to other people.
2. Do at least three random acts of kindness. For example, hold the door open for someone, help someone pick up something they dropped, or help make dinner.
3. Reflect. How does helping others make you feel?

School

Participate in a class activity about your willingness to help others.

1. Reread the section "Confidence Is Key" in the article about the bystander effect.
2. Work in small groups to role-play being a courageous bystander. Create a scenario in which a bystander needs to intervene, and take turns role-playing the intervention.
3. Have a discussion about what you learned from the activity.

Local

Volunteer at a local charity.

1. Research the different charities in your community. Choose one, and contact them to ask about volunteering.
2. Volunteer.
3. Reflect. What did you learn by volunteering at the charity? How did it make you feel?

Global

Find out more about the goals and work of a global organization such as Feedback.

1. Go to the website for the global charity organization of your choosing. Read about their mission and work.
2. Get more information about joining the charity, or other ways to help.
3. Make an action plan for one way to help, and implement it.

Reflect

1. Reflect on your Take Action project(s). What was successful? What do you wish you had done differently? Why?
2. Reread your response to the Essential Question **What responsibility do people have to help others?** in Connect Across Texts. How did your Take Action project(s) change or add to your response?
3. What will you do differently in your life because of what you learned in this unit?

7
Competition

Do you agree with the quote? Why or why not?

Look at the photo and caption. Discuss the questions.

1. Describe the rugby players in the photo. How do you think they are feeling?

2. How do you think the photo would look if the team hadn't won?

◀ **Rugby teammates celebrate after winning the UC Championship Final in Christchurch, New Zealand.**

How does competition affect us?

Explore the Essential Question

Think Write your ideas about the Essential Question in the Unit Concept Map.

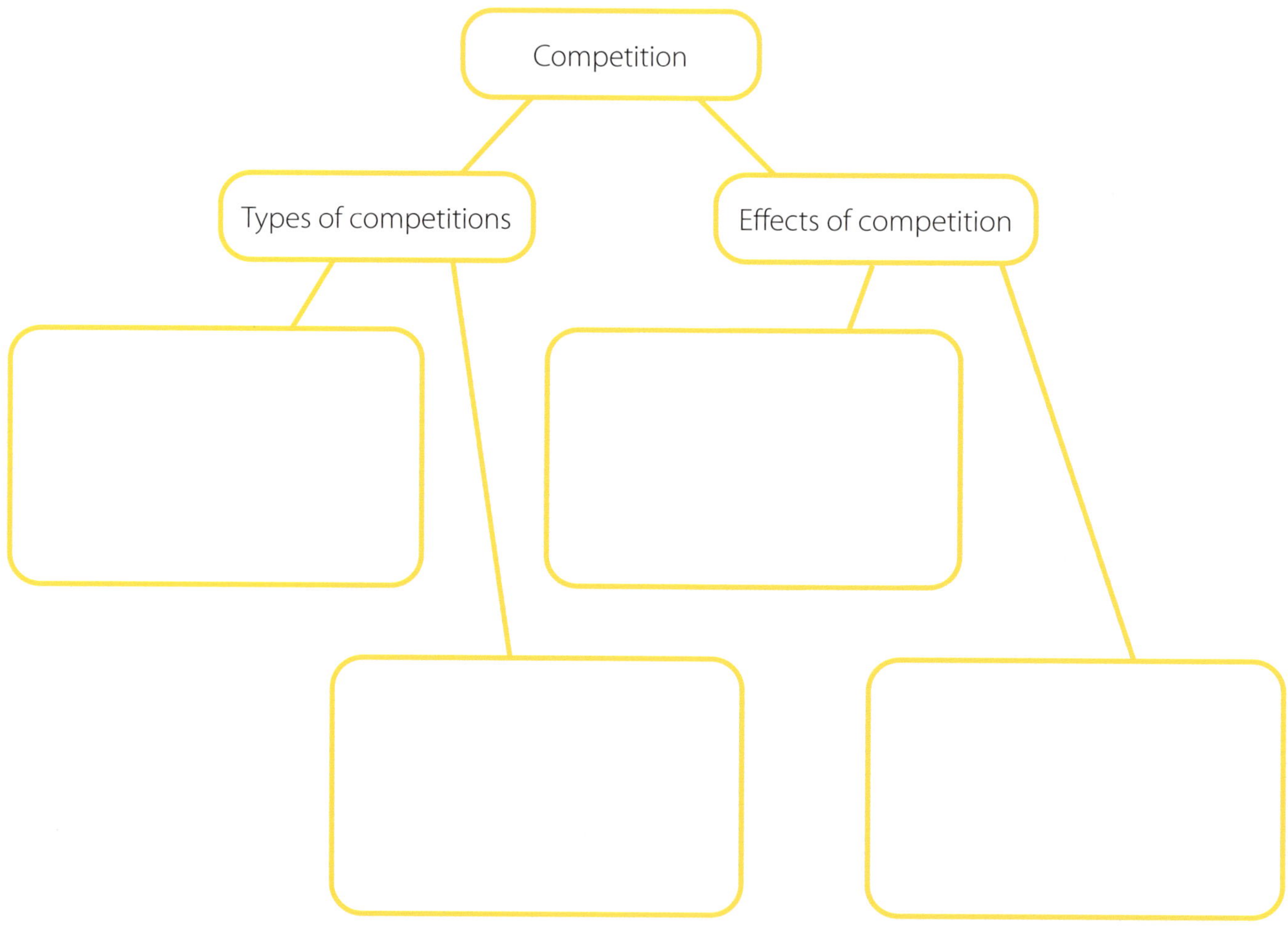

Respond Write one or two sentences to respond to the Essential Question.

____

____

____

Discuss Your Ideas Use your Unit Concept Map and your response to share your ideas with the class.

Discussion Frames

I think …

In my opinion, …

It seems to me that …

Academic Vocabulary

Use these words to express your ideas throughout the unit.

PRACTICE 1 Use context to determine the meaning of each word in blue. Then match the word to its definition in the chart below.

Close your eyes and **visualize** a competition. What do you see? Many people will picture a formal sports competition. But competitions can be **mental** as well as physical, informal as well as formal. Competitions also vary greatly in terms of *who* is competing. A competition can be between **teams** or **individuals**, or it can even be a competition with a single person competing against himself or herself to **achieve** a personal best. No matter the circumstances, most competitors agree that they perform best when they can **concentrate** on the task without distractions.

Word	Definition
team	a group of players on one side of a competition
	to imagine; to form an image in one's mind
	to successfully reach; to accomplish
	to focus one's attention on a particular activity
	relating to the mind or brain
	one person

PRACTICE 2 Work with a partner. Take turns being the reader and the listener.

Reader: Choose a vocabulary word from the chart. Read its definition aloud.

Listener: Listen to your partner read a definition. Say the vocabulary word your partner defines.

Example

Reader: *This word means "to successfully reach" or "to accomplish."*
Listener: *Is it* achieve?
Reader: *Yes!*

What are the benefits and drawbacks of youth competition?

First Thoughts

Think about a competition you or a friend participated in. What was positive about participating in the competition? What was negative? Why? Complete the chart. Then share your experience and ideas in a small group.

Positive Parts of the Experience	Negative Parts of the Experience

Key Vocabulary

PRACTICE Use context to determine the meaning of each word in bold. Then match the word to its definition.

1. Professional athletes' **perseverance** helps them to keep going even when times are tough.

2. I'm not **inclined** to read that novel because I don't like scary books.

3. Her win was a **victory** for female chefs all over the world.

4. We play our **rivals** tonight. They are difficult opponents to beat.

5. He has many **accomplishments** in chess, including winning several tournaments.

6. Exercising **promotes** a good mood because the body releases chemicals that lower stress.

_____ **1.** perseverance   **a.** something that has been achieved successfully (n.)

_____ **2.** inclined   **b.** a win (n.)

_____ **3.** victory   **c.** a person or team you compete against (n.)

_____ **4.** rival   **d.** likely to do something (adj.)

_____ **5.** accomplishment   **e.** to support or actively encourage (v.)

_____ **6.** promote   **f.** persistence through difficulties or delayed success (n.)

Reading Skill: Determine the Author's Viewpoint RI.8.6

The author's **viewpoint** refers to the author's opinions and beliefs about the topic. Authors often include other viewpoints in their writing in order to provide full coverage of a topic. Identifying the author's viewpoint can help you understand a text better. To determine the author's viewpoint:

1. Examine the title and introduction. If the author's purpose is to persuade readers, the author might clearly state the viewpoint. In most cases, though, you will have to infer the viewpoint from clues in the text.

2. Look for clues to the author's viewpoint in the body of the text.

3. Read the conclusion. It may include a summary of the text that states or restates the author's viewpoint.

Skill in Action

Reread the text from "What Is the 'Bystander Effect' and How Do People Overcome It?" from Unit 6. Then look at the chart below. Which part of the text gives you the best clues to the author's viewpoint?

Clues in title and introduction	The title tells me the author's point of view is that the bystander effect is a bad thing because it's something that people need to overcome. The introduction describes people who are not affected by the bystander effect and calls them "courageous."
Clues in the body of the text	The main ideas and details throughout the article suggest that the author thinks it is good to be willing to do things differently from other people.
Clues in conclusion	The conclusion says that helping others is "doing the right thing."

Author's Viewpoint: Everyone should try to help in an emergency even if no one else is helping.

The Pros and Cons of Teen Competition

by **Kathryn Rogers**

🎧 **7.1**

1   Is competition good for teens? Is it harmful? Does it encourage teens to develop positive habits and characteristics, or does it undermine[1] their self-esteem and make the world less friendly? Ask teens, their
5   families, teachers, coaches, and mental health specialists, and you'll get a wide variety of responses. Let's look at the pros and cons of competition in teens.

Pros

You and a friend are walking along, when your
10 friend suddenly yells, "I'll race you to the corner!" You run, right? And most likely you run faster than if you were running by yourself. That's because competition encourages us to try hard and give our best. Some people have the energy and will to always try their
15 hardest just for their own satisfaction. But many others find that the challenge of a game, race, or contest lights an inner spark.[2] Beyond the joy of **victory**, the rewards of competition—such as praise, applause, prizes, and awards—teach young people that society rewards effort.
20 Competition also **promotes** other traits and habits that make us better citizens and better people. Through sports, games, and other skill-based contests, teens can learn to follow rules, take turns, set goals, and assess and take risks. Those competing on teams learn what it

---

[1] **undermine** weaken
[2] **inner spark** feeling of interest

Students and parents take part in a chess competition at a school in Shenyang, Liaoning province, China.

Players from Team Japan and Team Sweden shake hands following the ice hockey gold medal game of the Winter Youth Olympics.

means to work for the good of the group instead of just oneself. Good sportsmanship—being a team player and winning or losing graciously—serves both the individual and society as a whole.

Similarly, to be a serious competitor, teens have to learn the value of commitment. That might mean getting up early to run drills[3] even when it's cold and raining, or missing a fun event because of an out-of-town academic tournament. It might mean working hard when you'd rather just goof around.[4] True competitors learn to give up short-term satisfaction for the thrill[5] of true **accomplishment**.

Talent and intelligence are terrific advantages in life, but **perseverance** can be even better. And competition teaches perseverance. You might be on the losing end now, but often the future promises a next game, next performance, next tryout, next shot at the goal. Those who double down[6] can make progress and learn to keep going.

And losing itself is valuable. Competition teaches us how to take failure in stride. Sometimes you drop the ball, sometimes you hit the wrong notes, sometimes you slog[7] through a losing streak,[8] but life goes on. Experiences like these teach resilience and perspective; they can help you navigate life when you encounter inevitable setbacks. Getting through tough times teaches us that we *can* get through tough times.

Cons

So what about the downsides of competition for teens?

One problem with competition is that it increases pressure and stress at an already stressful time of life. Teens are dealing with a lot of change personally, socially, and academically. Added pressure can create anxiety and other ills, especially if parents, coaches, or peers overemphasize winning. Also, if a person consistently loses, their self-esteem may suffer, and they may begin to doubt themselves in other areas of life. Teens who have not developed resilience and perspective may brood on and magnify their failings to a harmful degree.

---

[3] **run drills** do repetitive exercises
[4] **goof around** play and have fun
[5] **thrill** excitement
[6] **double down** work hard
[7] **slog** move with great effort
[8] **losing streak** many losses in a row

Competition can also create division by fostering an us-versus-them mentality. We have all seen or heard of sports fans being ugly to the other side—chanting taunts[9] or calling names. Sometimes brawls break out between teams or their fans. It's a shame that people would behave in this way over a game, but it sometimes happens.

When competition turns nasty, no one benefits. And nasty competition can promote cheating: people who think the other team members are "the bad guys" may cheat to defeat them. Plus, when people see others cheating, they are more **inclined** to cheat, too. When cyclist Lance Armstrong was determined to win the Tour de France, he decided that cheating was justified because so many other cyclists were cheating.

---

[9] **chanting taunts** shouting mean things

Competition can also lead teens to view others as enemies to be defeated rather than peers to collaborate with. Friendships and other trusting relationships are undermined when we view others mainly as **rivals**.

Healthy Competition

So is competition helpful or harmful for teens? It's both—or it can be. But there are things we all can do to promote healthy competition at any age.

You may have heard the saying "It's not whether you win or lose; it's how you play the game." Emphasizing sportsmanship and effort rather than winning or losing can help create a positive experience. Embrace teamwork, shared goals, and effort, whether or not they lead to victory.

View failure as a learning opportunity. Mistakes may sting,[10] but they can be our best teachers if we learn from them. As the author Samuel Beckett once wrote, "Ever tried. Ever failed. No matter. Try again. Fail again. Fail better." Failing "better" is the road to success. That's why novice chess players might enter a tournament—not to win but to get better by playing against more advanced players and learning their techniques. Focusing on opportunities to learn can change the way we think about competition.

Another way to make competition healthy is to create personal goals other than just winning. For instance, many people enter large road races with no intention of winning. The Mexico City Marathon might have 35,000 runners from all over the world, and the vast majority[11] of them cannot possibly win. But they can try for a "personal best" and run their own fastest marathon, joining with thousands of others, all competing with just themselves.

Conclusion

In short, competition has both benefits and drawbacks for teens. It is up to us, when we compete, to embrace the positives and use competition to become better people. And it is also up to us to be aware of the negatives—and there will be negatives—and find healthy ways to cope with[12] them. Healthy competition can help us examine our own attitudes about winning and losing and lead us to value the riches that even our failures have to offer.

---

[10] **sting** hurt
[11] **the vast majority** most
[12] **cope with** manage

Close Read

Work with a partner.

1. Determine the meanings of your underlined words and phrases.

2. Discuss the question: **How can we encourage healthy competition?**

Understand and Analyze

Respond to the questions. Support your responses with evidence from the text.

1. **Give Examples** Reread lines 17–19. What examples does the author give of how society rewards effort?

2. **Understand** Reread the third paragraph. What are three ways that competition can make us better people?

3. **Interpret** Reread lines 41–47. What does the author mean by "take failure in stride"? How do you know?

4. **Interpret** Reread lines 86–88. Explain Beckett's quotation in your own words.

5. **Analyze** What is the author's overall belief about competition for teens?

Apply the Skill: Determine the Author's Viewpoint

Complete the chart to determine the author's viewpoint in "The Pros and Cons of Teen Competition."

Clues in title and introduction	*The title tells me the author's viewpoint is that there are both pros and cons to teen competition. The introduction says there are different opinions about it.*
Clues in body of the text	
Clues in conclusion	
Author's Viewpoint:	

Share Your Perspective

Discuss these questions in a small group.

1. Do you agree with Beckett that failing is a good way to learn? Explain.

2. If you could participate in one type of competition, what would it be? Why would you choose it? Who would you compete against?

Discussion Frames

I agree/disagree with Beckett because …

I would participate in… because …

Why do you agree/disagree that …?

Language Convention: Use the Passive Voice   L.8.1.B, L.8.3.A

In English, verbs can be in **active voice** or **passive voice**. In active voice, the focus is on the person or thing that *does* the action of the verb (*She catches the ball*). In passive voice, the focus is on the person or thing that *receives* the action of the verb (*The ball is caught*). We usually use active voice, but there are times when passive voice is more appropriate. Use passive voice:

1. When the doer of the action is unknown, unimportant, or obvious:

   Our house **was built** in 1929. [*We don't know exactly who built it.*]

   A new stadium **is being built** south of the city. [*It's not important who is building it.*]

   The mail **was delivered** this morning. [*It's obvious that the mail carrier delivered it.*]

2. To help connect ideas across sentences:

   The team of judges created a series of <u>tasks</u>. <u>The tasks</u> **were completed** by multiple contestants from all over the world.
   [*By using the passive voice in the second sentence, the writer is able to place the object of the first sentence,* tasks, *at the beginning of the second sentence. This helps connect the ideas in the two sentences.*]

PRACTICE 1   Underline the passive voice in each sentence. Then check (✓) the most likely reason the writer uses the passive voice.

	Doer of the action is unknown / unimportant / obvious	Connects ideas
1. These trophies were manufactured in China.		
2. The tournament had over 100 players. The players were hosted by enthusiastic residents of the city.		
3. The game was canceled due to bad weather.		
4. Our gear is tested so it holds up even in an intense game.		

PRACTICE 2   Write two sentences about competition, using the passive voice. For each sentence, explain why you used the passive voice.

____

____

____

Read Again

Read "The Pros and Cons of Teen Competition" again. As you read, circle details from the text that help you respond to this question:

What examples does the article give to show how competition is both good and bad for teens?

Reflect and Respond

Use some of the details you circled to complete the idea web.

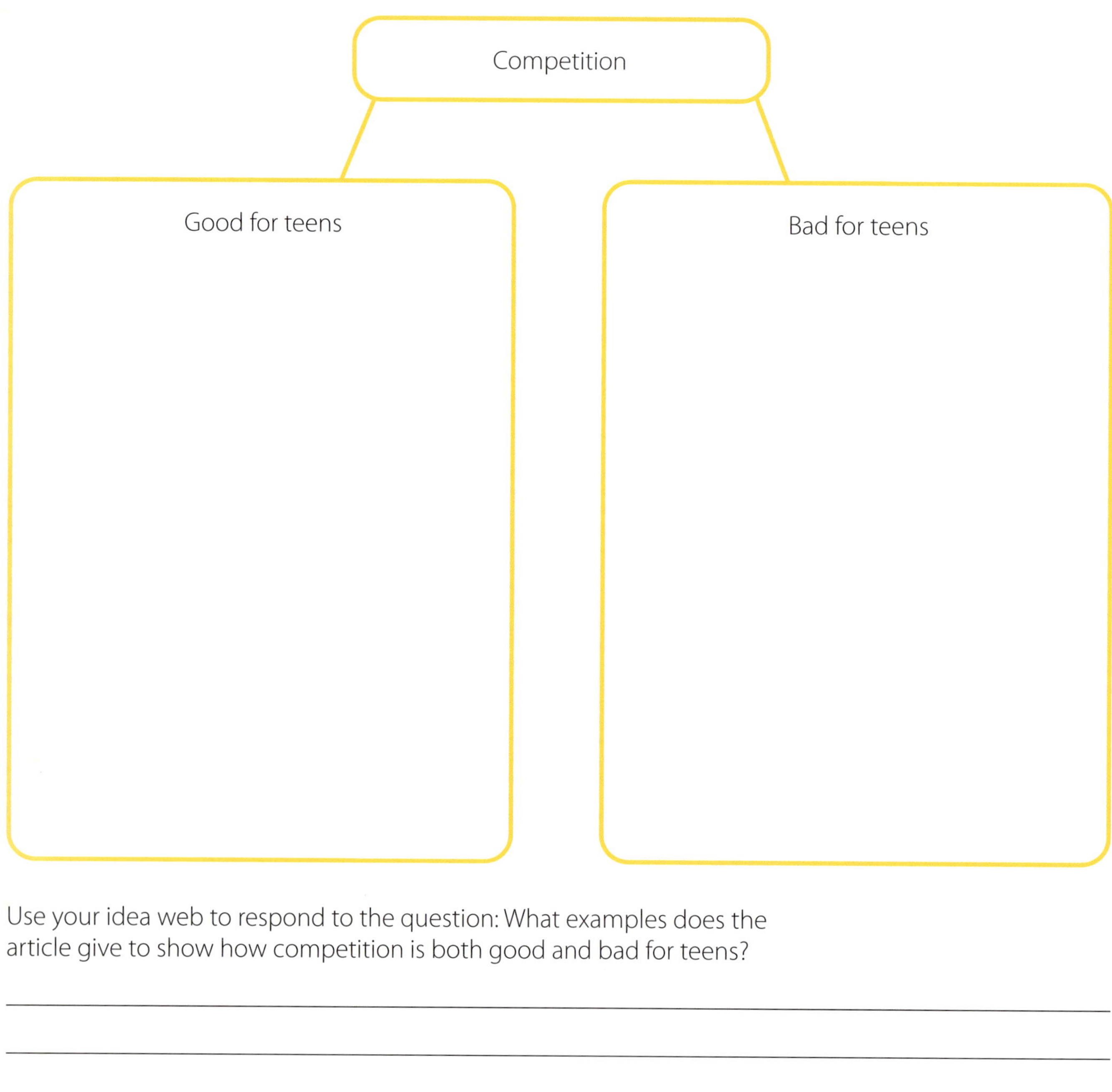

Use your idea web to respond to the question: What examples does the article give to show how competition is both good and bad for teens?

____

____

____

Discuss Your Response

Share your ideas with the class. Write one new idea you hear.

____

____

____

Respond to the Guiding Question

Write a response to the question:
What are the benefits and drawbacks of youth competition?

Use evidence from the text, your discussion, and your life. Use the Discussion Frames to help you. Use the rubric to check your response.

____

____

____

____

Research W.8.7

Choose one of these topics. Research the topic to learn more about it.

- chess tournaments around the world
- the Mexico City Marathon

Follow these steps:

1. Make notes about what you already know about the topic.
2. Write three questions you have about the topic.
3. Research the topic to find answers to your questions.
4. Write your answers to the questions.
5. Present what you learn to a small group.

Competitors play ping pong in Bryant Park in New York City.

First Thoughts

Think of a competition or event near where you live. Who participates in the event? Who watches and supports the competitors? What effect does the competition have on the community? Discuss with a small group.

Viewing Skill: Identify Cause and Effect

Identifying **cause-and-effect relationships** while watching a video can help you understand the video's most important ideas. Pay attention to what happens (the effect) and why it happens (the cause). Sometimes, there is a series of cause-and-effect events, in which one event causes another event, which then causes other events. As you watch, take notes about causes and effects.

Apply the Skill

▶ **7.1** Watch the video "United by Ping Pong." Match each cause to its effect.

Causes	Effects
_____ **1.** The park provides ping pong.	**a.** The ball shatters against the net.
_____ **2.** Someone wins a game.	**b.** People come to play.
_____ **3.** It's below 32 degrees.	**c.** They form a community.
_____ **4.** People play ping pong together.	**d.** He or she gets to play the next game.

Understand and Analyze

▶ **7.1** Watch again. Answer the questions. Support your responses with evidence from the video.

1. **Understand** Where is Bryant Park? What makes it unique?
2. **Explain** How does the playing differ in the morning and evening?
3. **Infer** What makes playing in bad weather desirable for the players?
4. **Analyze** How can the ping-pong community provide opportunities beyond the park?

Share Your Perspective

1. Sometimes competition divides people, and sometimes it brings them together and builds friendships. What do you think makes the difference?
2. Would you enjoy playing ping pong at Bryant Park? Why or why not?

> **Discussion Frames**
>
> I think … because …
>
> In my opinion, …
>
> The way I see it, …
>
> What are your thoughts about …?

How can competition make us feel?

First Thoughts

People compete for different reasons. In your opinion, what is the most important reason to compete? Rank the reasons from 1 (most important) to 5 (least important). Then discuss your answers with a partner.

Reasons to Compete	to win	to have fun	to achieve a "personal best"	to learn the value of hard work	to be involved and active
Rank (1–5)					

Key Vocabulary

PRACTICE Use context to determine the meaning of each word in bold. Then match the word to its definition.

1. After the storm, the water was **churned up**. It was difficult to sail the boat in the rough waves.

2. Amelie is a **well-rounded** person. She's a good student, an excellent singer, a great friend, and even captain of the soccer team.

3. Teenagers today experience **pressure** to do well in school and other activities so that they can get into college or find a job.

4. Sunny days are the **norm** in the desert. Cloudy skies are rare.

5. Sometimes Vince can be too **pushy**. It's hard to work with him when he gets involved in everything and takes over.

6. Maria is a **pro** at baking and has even won a baking tournament. Everything she makes is delicious and looks like it came out of a magazine!

_____ **1.** pro   **a.** unpleasantly assertive and overly ambitious (adj.)
_____ **2.** pushy   **b.** something that is usual; standard (n.)
_____ **3.** churned up   **c.** expert; professional (n.)
_____ **4.** norm   **d.** agitated and wavy (adj.)
_____ **5.** pressure   **e.** balanced in activities and experiences (adj.)
_____ **6.** well-rounded   **f.** stress (n.)

Reading Skill: Analyze Dialogue and Inner Monologue **RL.8.3**

Dialogue is a written conversational exchange between two or more characters in literature. **Inner monologue** is similar to dialogue, but the "conversation" is in the character's mind. Authors use dialogue and monologue to move the events in a story forward and guide the reader's understanding. To analyze dialogue and inner monologue, ask yourself:

- What does the dialogue or inner monologue tell about the character's feelings, motives, personality, or actions?
- What does it tell about the events of the story?
- How does it shape the reader's expectations about how the plot will develop?

Skill in Action

Study the model. How does the reader analyze the inner monologue?

from **Goldfish**

I'm one of the fastest swimmers in my county. That's why I'm here—trying out for a High Performance Training Camp that will set me on my way to Team Great Britain. I've wanted this for as long as I can remember. So … you know, no pressure, not a big deal, whev.

I think I'm sweating inside my ears.

This is inner monologue because these are thoughts in the character's mind.

I think the speaker means that this IS a big deal.

Since the inside of our ears doesn't usually sweat, it emphasizes how nervous she is. It also makes me think the character likes to make jokes.

from
Goldfish
by **Nat Luurtsema**

🎧 **7.2**

1   I'm one of the fastest swimmers in my county. That's why I'm here—trying out for a High Performance Training Camp that will set me on my way to Team Great Britain. I've wanted this for 5   as long as I can remember. So … you know, no **pressure**, not a big deal, whev.[1]

I think I'm sweating inside my ears.

I pad along the side of the pool, watching the heat[2] before mine. Older swimmers power up and 10   down; they look so strong—they're not so much swimming as punching their way through water.

We're all in a vast glass room. I want to use the word *palace*. It's a palace made of glass, filled with four Olympic-sized swimming pools! It's basically 15   my dream home. The sounds of splashing and shouting bounce off the concrete walls. Ninety percent of the people in this room are having the most important day of their lives.

I look around for my best friend, Hannah, and 20   spot her by the changing room. I give her a quick smile. I think she feels a bit queasy, because she does an elaborate mime of puking[3] into the pool. An official eyes[4] her disapprovingly.

I know how she feels. I tuck a stray hair into my 25   swimming cap with a shaking hand.

Hannah rotates her shoulders backward and then forward. She swims butterfly, which gives you

---

[1] **whev** whatever
[2] **heat** one set of races in a larger competition
[3] **does an elaborate mime of puking** pretends to vomit
[4] **eyes** looks at

really big shoulders, but she's not self-conscious about it; she just
wears men's T-shirts. People love Hannah. She's fun. She has huge
blond curly hair and big blue eyes and she never stops talking,
organizing, and planning. She's been my best friend since we were
six, and now, looking at how nervous she is, I find myself feeling
protective even though I'm in the same position.

Well, not exactly the same; her parents are really **pushy**. She
ignores it or it would drive her crazy. Mine think swimming is
less important than either schoolwork or being a **well-rounded**
human being—we agree to disagree.

Hannah's standing next to me now. She smiles and pulls at the
front of my swimming cap. I fold my arms and pretend to ignore her.
She pulls the elastic six inches away from my forehand and I brace[5]
for her to snap it, but instead she nudges her face next to mine and
starts trying to pull my swimming cap over her head as well as mine.
Ridiculous human being. This is why I bring spare caps.

I can't keep a straight face. I start giggling and help her pull the
thick elastic further over her head. It hurts—her nose is digging
hard into my cheekbone, but I'm determined to get it. *Beep*!
Hannah's eyes widen at the sound of the whistle. This is her race!

She hurriedly pulls her head away, making her swimming cap
ping off and nearly land in the pool. I can see a couple of officials
looking very unimpressed at us. Sor-ree.[6] Just trying to lighten a
very heavy mood here. I dive to retrieve Hannah's cap while she
fights her frizzy mop[7] of hair into a bun.

We hug quickly and she hurries to the nearest pool, where
the butterfly swimmers are waiting by the diving blocks. Some
impressive shoulders in that group.

Now I'm alone and back to feeling sick and scared about my
own race. I tuck my ears into my swimming cap, and everything
becomes a smooth roaring noise.

An official comes to check my name against a list she has on
her clipboard. I can't help but notice that she has a very fluffy top
lip. She catches me staring at it and I quickly look down.

"Louise?" she asks.

---

[5] **brace** get ready
[6] **Sor-ree** Sorry
[7] **frizzy mop** curly head

"Brown," I say, to her shoe, and she ticks my name off.

She must be one of only ten people in the place who aren't
feeling hysterical. If the fire alarm went off, I think we'd all run in
circles, screaming and slapping our faces.

My race is called and I join a line of girls who look just like
me. Tall girls are the **norm** here. I'm going to fit in so well in the
Training Camp! Finally, someone to borrow clothes from.

I look around for Debs, who coaches me and Hannah. She's
standing by the pool where I'll be doing my race, arms folded,
staring intently at me. She gives me a nod. She's not the most
affectionate person. That nod means "Go on, Lou, I know you can
do it! Supportive things, etc.!"

Up on the blocks[8] I scuff my feet and stare dead[9] ahead. You
swim no one's race but your own.

---

[8] **blocks** diving platforms
[9] **dead** straight

The official nods and I bend into my dive, wrapping my
fingertips over the edge of the block and swaying gently to loosen
my hips. There's a pause that feels never-ending, and I focus on
the spot in the water where I want my dive to take me.

The starting pistol bangs. There's an explosion of power from
my legs, and I dive hard. I can hear the block rattle as I push away
from it with all my strength. A cold, hard slap against my thighs,
and I spring into butterfly stroke. Hannah's faster at this, but I'm
pretty good too. I whip my arms up and over my head, my fingers
then cutting into the water in front of my face. As my arms pull
down, my hips tilt, and my legs kick together like a mermaid tail.
This is the closest I ever get to elegant.

Backstroke now, my second-fastest stroke, and I hold my
head steady as I stare up at the ceiling. I practiced this last night
when everyone else had finished training. I count signposts
on the ceiling so I don't ram my head into the side of the pool

and slow myself down. Debs says this is the mindset of a consummate[10] **pro**.

I had to Google *consummate*. It's either a compliment or a French soup.

I feel so happy when I swim, strong and graceful and like everything is right with the world. This is my Thing.

The individual medley is a strange race—most people are slowest on the breaststroke, fastest on the crawl. I'm the other way around, so I always pull ahead on laps[11] five and six, hopefully opening up enough of a lead that some freakish[12] monkey-armed girl with a fast crawl time can't catch me on seven and eight.

And here's seven and eight, harder in a pool where everyone's so powerful. The water is **churned up** and throwing me about. So much for feeling graceful—this is like fighting water. But I can't sense anyone on the left or right of me, so I must've pulled ahead. Excellent, it's all going according to plan.

---

[10] **consummate** excellent
[11] **laps** pool lengths
[12] **freakish** weird

Now it's about hanging on to this lead. I carve my right hand back past my face to make a groove in the water just long enough to turn my face and grab a huge, ragged breath. In this choppy water it's difficult, so each time I'm just praying I find air. I can't afford to choke.

Final lap and I'm completely in my rhythm. I know the end is approaching, but I have to keep swimming my hardest so no one catches me. I don't care if I smash my head into the edge of the pool— anything to maintain this speed to the end. My wrist hits something hard with a crack that I feel down to my hip, and I've done it.

I've done it! I won.

I fling my head out of the water, rip off my swimming cap and goggles, squeeze the water from my eyes, and look behind me. That's my first thought—how far behind are they?

But there's no one there.

They're all next to me. Everyone. There is *no one* behind me, no one still swimming.

The girl on my left looks bored; the one on the right is casually cleaning her goggles with spit. Oh my … *one of them is already out of the pool?!* I did that once, against a team in Swindon that was so slow I got out before the last girl finished. Debs yelled at me for that. Unsportspersonlike,[13] she said.

*Deb*s! Where is she, where's my coach? Maybe I swam extra lengths by mistake? That must be it. Hilarious, of course that's what happened. Dumb but understandable on a high-pressure day. This is *not* a Big Deal. Should I talk to someone, an official? Where is everyone going? Coach! Debs! Hello! No one is looking me in the eye. Did I *die* in that pool? Am I a ghost?

I might as well have. I came in last. For the first time since I started competing at ten years old, I was the slowest swimmer. I'm weak and cold. My legs are heavy as the adrenaline drops out of me. I don't know what to do … where to go….

I have to find Hannah, and I look around frantically for her. There she is! She's throwing back her hair, laughing and shaking hands with an official who's handing her a slip of paper. She must have won her race. She catches my eye and her smile fades.

My best friend and I want to kill her.

---

[13] **unsportspersonlike** impolite

About the Author: Nat Luurtsema

Nat Luurtsema is a British screenwriter, author, stand-up comedian, and actor. Her young adult novel *Girl Out of Water* has been translated into several languages.

Close Read

Work with a partner.

1. Determine the meanings of your underlined words and phrases.
2. Discuss the questions:

    What is Louise's reason to compete in this race? How does she do?

Understand and Analyze

Respond to the questions. Support your responses with evidence from the text.

1. **Explain** Read the first two paragraphs. How does Louise feel going into the race? How do you know?
2. **Compare** Reread lines 34–37. Compare Louise's attitude with her parents' attitude about swimming.
3. **Understand** Reread lines 67–69. How confident is Louise as she begins the race?
4. **Analyze** Why does Louise think she swam extra lengths?
5. **Infer** After the race, why isn't anyone looking Louise in the eye?

Apply the Skill: Analyze Dialogue and Inner Monologue

Analyze Louise's inner monologue during and after the race. How do Louise's thoughts guide your understanding of what is happening and your expectations about what will happen next?

Louise's Thoughts During and After the Race	My Understanding and Expectations
Excellent, it's all going according to plan.	*This makes me think she is winning the race.*
I've done it! I won.	
But there's no one there.	
Oh my . . . *one of them is already out of the pool?!*	
This is *not* a Big Deal. Should I talk to someone, an official? Where is everyone going?	
My best friend and I want to kill her.	

Share Your Perspective

Discuss these questions in a small group.

1. Do you agree with Louise's parents that swimming is less important than schoolwork? Why or why not?
2. If you were Louise, how would you feel about Hannah after the race? Explain your answer.

Discussion Frames

I agree/disagree with Louise's parents because …

If I were Louise, I would feel …

Could you say more about …?

Vocabulary: Interpret Verbal Irony L.8.5.A

Verbal irony is when the literal meaning of the words someone says is different from (and often the opposite of) what the person actually means. Three common types of verbal irony are **overstatement**, **understatement**, and **sarcasm**.

Overstatement	The speaker exaggerates a situation.	*After we finished the first mile of the 10-mile hike, my dad smiled and said, "Almost done!"*
Understatement	The speaker implies or says that something is less important than it really is.	*I've wanted this as long as I can remember. So … not a big deal.*
Sarcasm	The speaker makes an ironic statement with the intention of insulting or making fun of someone (including oneself) or something.	*Her coat was old and tattered, with a large stain on the front. With a smirk, Joe yelled, "Nice coat, Debbie!"*

Apply the Strategy

Read the following sentences. Look closely at the words and context to identify the type of verbal irony.

1. Eduardo fell and scraped the whole front of his leg. Later, he is wearing a large bandage. He says, "It's just a little scratch."

   a. overstatement
   b. understatement
   c. sarcasm

2. I just found out I failed my math test. "Way to go, Einstein," I say to myself.

   a. overstatement
   b. understatement
   c. sarcasm

3. My brother found a dollar and held it up, saying "We're rich!"

   a. overstatement
   b. understatement
   c. sarcasm

4. Aunt Maria looked out at the flooded street and said, "We got a little rain, I see."

   a. overstatement
   b. understatement
   c. sarcasm

Read Again

Read "Goldfish" again. As you read, circle details from the text that help you respond to this question:

How does Louise feel at different times during the competition?

Reflect and Respond

Use some of the details you circled in the story to complete the idea web.

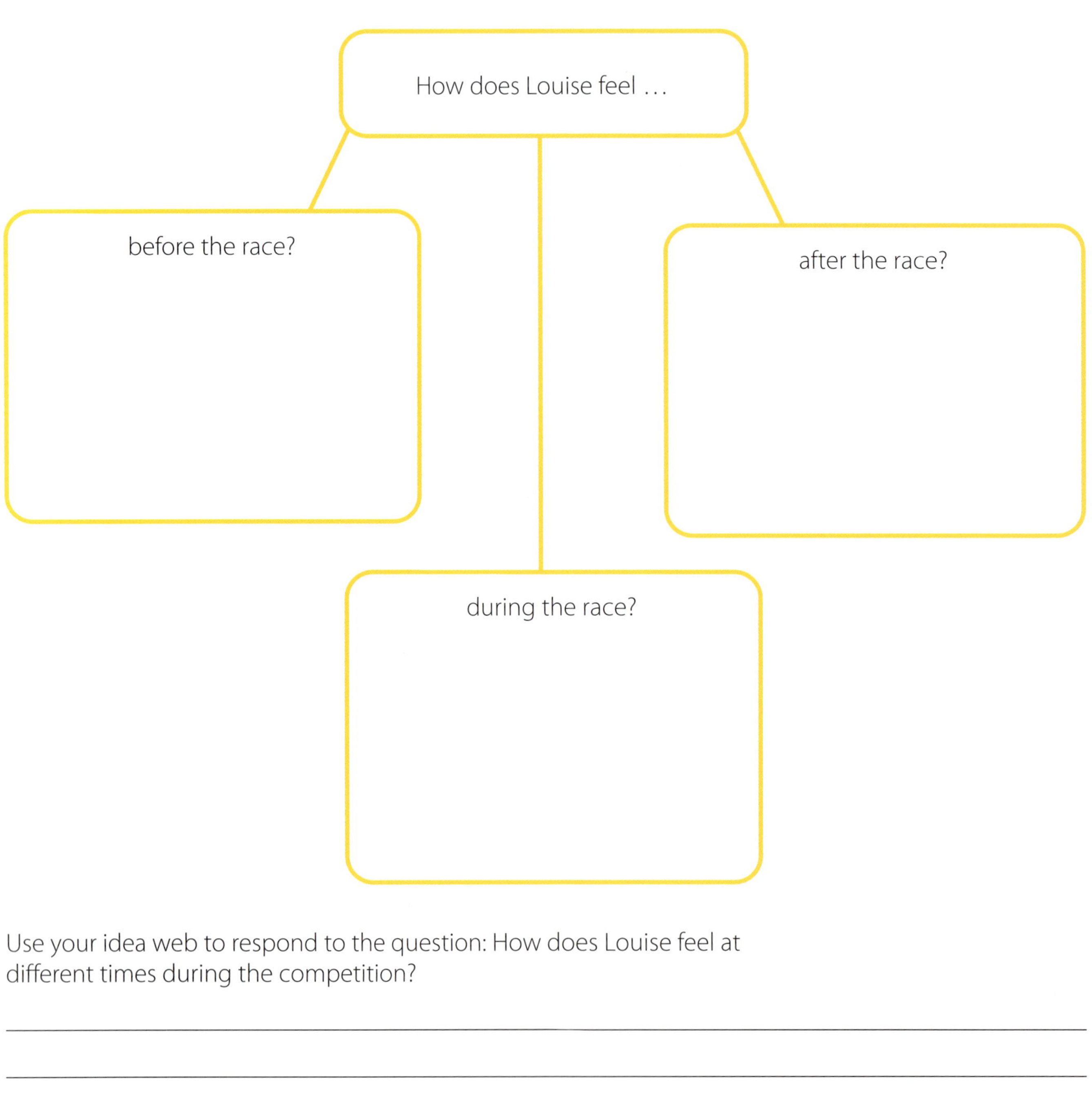

Use your idea web to respond to the question: How does Louise feel at different times during the competition?

____

____

____

Discuss Your Response

Share your ideas with the class. Write one new idea you hear.

____

____

____

Respond to the Guiding Question

Write a response to the question:
How can competition make us feel?

Use evidence from the text, your discussion, and your life. Use the Discussion Frames to help you. Use the rubric to check your response.

____

____

____

____

Create and Present: After the Race

Imagine what happens next in "Goldfish." Then do one of these activities:

OPTION 1: Write a Letter

Imagine you are Louise. Write a letter to the officials at the training camp, explaining why they should still let you attend. Then read it to your classmates.

OPTION 2: Write and Perform a Skit

Work in a small group. The race has ended. Write a short skit of a conversation between Louise and her parents, her coach, or Hannah.

Here's an example of the first few lines of a skit:

LOUISE'S FATHER: There's our swimmer! We're so proud …

LOUISE: Please, Dad, just don't. … I did terribly! Now I'll never get into the training camp. My whole life is ruined!

LOUISE'S MOTHER: Honey, I know you love swimming and you must feel disappointed that you didn't win today, but there's more to life than winning …

Practice your skit, and then perform it for the class.

THE STADIUM OF TOMORROW

INTERACTIVE FAN EXPERIENCE

Opening and closing ceremonies at the Olympics currently provide LED lights for the crowd to wave at key moments. In the stadium of the future, fans share their emotions through LED clothing or even experience what the players are feeling.

AUTOMATED AMENITIES

Customers avoid the long lines at refreshment stands by ordering food and drinks to be delivered by drone to their seats. Fans in mobile hospitality pods have their food and drinks served by robots; trashbots take their garbage away.

Augmented reality

A large hologram with the score and stats hovers over the field, while small screens are at each seat.

An electric audience

Fans in LED jerseys might feel the heartbeats of a favorite player or light up in colors to reflect the mood of the game.

Hospitality pods

Electromagnetic pods move along rails within the stadium, allowing fans a view from any location they choose.

Drone delivery

Loaded by robots, drones deliver peanuts, hot dogs, and other snacks to your seat.

RETHINKING THE PLAYING FIELD

The surface of the field changes materials for different sports—from artificial turf for football to grass for soccer to wood for basketball. The lines marking the area of play are projected onto the field, allowing the field to vary in size and shape.

Transparent field

A see-through field over an underground viewing area allows fans to watch the game from below.

Examine the Graphic

Use details from the graphic to respond to the questions. Discuss your responses with a partner.

1. What is something the graphic makes you wonder?

2. What is something you find surprising?

3. How are the Stadium of Tomorrow and the stadiums of today alike? How are they different?

4. What changes would you make to the Stadium of Tomorrow? Why?

Make Connections

Use details from "Goldfish" and the graphic to discuss your responses with a partner.

1. How does the Stadium of Tomorrow compare to the one where Louise swims?

2. What do you think Louise would think about the Stadium of Tomorrow?

Reflect

Use ideas from the graphic and your discussions to answer this question: Would you rather attend events in today's stadiums or the Stadium of Tomorrow? Why? Explain your answer.

How can competition help make us stronger?

First Thoughts

Make some notes about these questions. Then discuss your ideas with a partner.

1. Why do you think some people are more competitive than others?

2. Is competitiveness something people are born with, or do we learn to be competitive?

3. Are you competitive? If so, what do you think made you that way?

Key Vocabulary

PRACTICE Use context to determine the meaning of each word in bold. Then match the word to its definition.

> I will never forget the first time I rode my bike without training wheels. At first, my mom ran alongside the bike, **gripping** the back of my seat tightly so I wouldn't fall. Eventually she let go, and I was balancing! I could feel my heart beat faster as **adrenaline** rushed through my body from fear and excitement. I was riding along just fine when my tire hit a rock. I went **hurtling** through the air and **collapsed** on the ground. I hit my knee hard. It was **throbbing** from the pain, but I was still so excited from the **exhilaration** of riding. So I quickly put on a bandage, and within minutes I was back on my bike.

_____ **1.** grip	**a.**	to pound with pain (v.)
_____ **2.** adrenaline	**b.**	to fall down suddenly and dramatically (v.)
_____ **3.** hurtle	**c.**	a chemical released by the body in times of stress, anger, or fear (n.)
_____ **4.** collapse	**d.**	excitement (n.)
_____ **5.** throb	**e.**	to move quickly and uncontrollably (v.)
_____ **6.** exhilaration	**f.**	to hold tightly onto (v.)

Discussion Frames

My feeling is . . .

I think that . . .

This is because . . .

Are you . . . ?

Do you feel that . . . ?

Reading Strategy: Make Text-to-Self Connections

Successful readers make connections as they read in order to better understand a text. Connecting what you read to your own experiences can help you understand and relate to what the author is saying. To make text-to-self connections:

1. As you're reading, notice parts of the text that remind you of your own life or things you have learned about.

2. Explore your connection: Have you had experiences like the author's? Have you read about or learned about something similar?

3. Use details from your experiences and knowledge to help you connect with the text. Do you share the author's viewpoint? Do you have a different viewpoint?

Strategy in Action

Study the model from "The Grand Slam," and notice the text-to-self connections one reader makes. Then consider what text-to-self connections you might make to this passage.

I also press snooze on my alarm clock, usually to get a few more minutes of sleep. She must be excited, because she presses snooze but doesn't go back to sleep.

from **The Grand Slam**

Vrring! Vrring! The alarm clock rattles off. It's 4:20 a.m. I hit the snooze button and grab my phone to check the weather. It's near freezing outside, but the November skies are clear.

"Great! I won't have to worry about icy or wet roads today," I think to myself as I pull the blankets up around me and enjoy a few more minutes in bed, contemplating the day ahead.

It's race day—the 2014 New York City Marathon—the last major marathon of the year.

I don't even like walking on icy or slippery roads. I bet they make a race much harder!

I learned that a marathon is a race that is 26.2 miles long. People train for a long time, so they must feel excited and nervous on race day. The New York City Marathon is famous. Cheering spectators line the streets.

Runners cross the Verrazzano-Narrows Bridge near the start of the New York City Marathon.

The Grand Slam

by **Tatyana McFadden**

🎧 **7.3**

1   Vrring! Vrring! The alarm clock rattles off.[1] It's 4:20 a.m. I hit the snooze button[2] and grab my phone to check the weather. It's near freezing outside, but the November skies are clear.

5   "Great! I won't have to worry about icy or wet roads today," I think to myself as I pull the blankets up around me and enjoy a few more minutes in bed, contemplating the day ahead.

It's race day—the 2014 New York City Marathon—the 10 last major marathon of the year. If I win the marathon today, I win the Grand Slam, which is when one person wins the four biggest marathons in the world—Boston, Chicago, London, and New York—all in the same year. I won the Grand Slam last year, so if I win today's race, I 15 will have achieved it two years in a row! No one—with or without a disability—has ever done this before.

"No pressure here!" I tell myself as my thoughts run to all the things that can go wrong. I've trained hard, and I have the course mapped out in my head. I remind 20 myself to stay focused and have fun!

I pull myself out of bed and dress. I'm too anxious to eat much before a race, so I have only a little oatmeal and peanut butter. I check my racing chair and make sure I have everything I need.

25   By 6:00 a.m., I'm on the bus that takes me and some of the other racers to the start of the marathon at the base of

---

[1] **rattles off** rings
[2] **snooze button** button that resets an alarm so it goes off again in a few minutes

the Verrazano Bridge. It's still dark when we arrive, and an almost-
full moon hangs over the city. The early morning air is chilly, and
there is a light wind. All the racers are stretching, trying to warm
30   up. I start my own routine, getting my muscles ready.

I greet a few fellow racers and wish everyone luck. When 7:30
rolls around, it's time to take our places at the starting line. I can
feel the tension in the air.

Because there are so many competitors, there are different
35   starting times for different groups. The professional wheelchair
racers—about 50 of us—are at the front of the pack. We are followed
by other professional athletes with disabilities, amateur racers with
disabilities, other professional athletes, and finally by the amateur

Racers in the wheelchair division compete in the New York City Marathon.

runners. Trying to navigate through 50,000 other racers, especially
in racing chairs, is not easy, so I'm glad to be at the front.

Gripping my wheels, I try to focus on the racecourse and
visualize each stretch of road, each turn, each hill. In a few
minutes I will race in one of the most grueling marathons of the
year—26.2 miles across roadways, bridges, and hills, the whole
way being watched by thousands of people lined up along the
course, and many more watching on television!

The crowd grows quiet as the seconds on the clock tick down.
I stare straight ahead, trying not to look at the other racers, or at
the crowds nearby.

"Just relax and breathe!" I say to myself. My mind counts
down the seconds, "... five ... four ... three ... two ... one ...."

"Runners on your mark!"

"CRACK!" A blast from the starting gun, and the men are off.
I feel a jolt[3] of **adrenaline** even though it's not my turn to start.
Then two minutes later, "CRACK!" The gun goes off a second
time, and the women blast out from the starting line. I'm off!

I push to get ahead of the other racers. My eyes are focused
on the crest[4] of the bridge—I have to get over that first rise. To
the left of me, the pale purple-blue outline of the skyscrapers of
Manhattan peeks through the haze of morning light.

Now I'm over the crest and picking up speed as I head down
the other side of the bridge. I'm going too fast.

"Slow down! Slow down!" I think as I brake. On the
Brooklyn side, the spectators are cheering. My heart pounds with
excitement.

"Just keep calm!" I caution myself.

At the bottom of the hill, the course turns at almost a ninety-
degree angle. This isn't a big deal for runners, but for those of us
in racing chairs, going too fast around a sharp corner can send us
hurtling. At the turn is a huge wall of hay bales, stacked high to
catch racers who don't make the turn. Even so, hay isn't the softest
cushion. If I hit the wall of hay too fast, I could crack the frame or
a wheel, or worse, injure myself and be unable to continue.

I make the turn safely, veering close to the cheering spectators
and onto the streets of Brooklyn. I race along Fourth Avenue

---

[3] **jolt** burst
[4] **crest** top

through neighborhoods of tiny shops, factories, and low-rise brick row houses. There are no big hills to climb in Brooklyn and Queens, only a few sharp turns to navigate, so I settle into my pace and concentrate on the motion of my arms propelling[5] me along.

People line the streets, waving and shouting, and I hear, somewhere in the distance, a band playing. It's like a big street party, but I speed by the crowd, alone in my own little world. I'm in my "zone," concentrating on the road, barely aware of what's going on around me. I feel each breath, each push of my arms, each turn of my wheels.

"Pace yourself!" I think. If I push too fast here, I'll be too tired for the second half of the race.

An hour into the race I've reached Mile 15. The Queensboro Bridge and the towers of Manhattan rise in front of me. I speed up as I come onto the incline over the East River. The cold wind off the water hits me. I race across the bridge, descending into midtown Manhattan and onto First Avenue.

"Go! Go! Go!" The cheering behind the barricades on First Avenue hits me with a wall of sound. It's exciting and invigorating to know that all these people have gathered on this cold morning to watch us race—to watch me race! My heart pumps even faster.

First Avenue is one very long, slow-rising hill. I need to reset my pace again. All I can think about is that I have another ten miles to go. The climb is exhausting. My arms are feeling stiff and sore.

I head up and into the Bronx and then turn back across a small rusted metal bridge and into Manhattan again for the last big stretch down Fifth Avenue and into Central Park.

I am ahead of the other racers, but I'm not sure by how much. If I look back now, it might cost me valuable seconds. And if I don't watch in front of me, I could hit a rock or pothole in the road that could send me tumbling.

"Keep going!" I repeat over and over.

Racing down Fifth Avenue, I turn into Central Park. I know the hills of the park well. I had trained there earlier in the week and memorized all the dips and turns. Most of the way is slightly downhill, which scares me a little. Because I'm lighter than many of the racers, maintaining control going down a hill has caused me trouble before. Luckily, this hill isn't that steep.

---

[5] **propelling** pushing

"GO, TATYANA, GO!" I hear my name. I wonder if it's my
family or friends. I steal a quick glance, but the crowd is a sea
of colored parkas. My arms are **throbbing** now as I pour on the
speed for the final blast to the finish line. All I can think about is
the pain. My arms are cramping, my stomach's in knots, and my
eyes are blurring from the icy wind.

"Less than one mile to go!" I reassure myself. I push harder
and faster.

On either side of me, spectators cheer me on as I fly by. Ahead
of me, I see the fountain at 59th Street. From there it's a simple
quick four blocks to the finish line! I am almost there! My mind
fills with a dozen thoughts—

"Grand Slam!"

Tatyana McFadden (USA) holds hands with her competitor Manuela Schar (Switzerland) after finishing the New York City Marathon.

"Focus!"

"Watch the road!"

"FOCUS!"

130 "Is there anyone behind me?"

"FOCUS!"

"GO, GO, GO!" the crowd chants. The frenzied cheers fill my head and give me a last burst of energy.

I come out from under the trees and turn onto 59th Street. My
135 chair starts to wobble. I try to slow down and steady myself, but it's too late. I cut the turn too tightly! My head hits the pavement

Tatyana McFadden crosses
the finish line of the
New York City Marathon.

hard. My racing chair topples[6] over me. People are running to help.
The police try to help me up. I'm shaking.

"Don't touch me!" I shout.

If someone tries to help me get up and going again, there is a
chance I could be disqualified. My head is swirling. I'm breathless.
My body is vibrating.

"Stay calm! Stay calm!" I repeat over and over.

"I am so close! Is the chair all right? Did anyone pass me?" My
mind is dizzy with thoughts of what to do.

Pushing my chair and myself back upright, I pray that the
wheels didn't crack or the tires haven't blown out. The crowd is
silent, holding its breath. I push off.

"Don't look back. Don't look back!" I tell myself. Stopping
to see where the other racers are would cost me valuable time.
I know a race is often won by a lead of less than the length of a
nose—a few tenths of a second. I just need to power through to
the finish line. I only have a few more meters to go and can see the
blue ribbon at the finish line. It isn't far.

"*Ya sama, ya sama!*—I can do it! I can do it!"

I push harder and harder, not knowing how close anyone is
behind me. The finish line is just ahead. Almost there! I feel the
slight resistance of the finish line ribbon against my chest. I did it!
I've won it again! The Grand Slam!

I **collapse** back into my chair, my arms pulsing, my shoulder
bruised, and try to catch my breath. My body hurts from the race and
from the fall, but I am filled with the **exhilaration** of finishing the
marathon, coming in first place, and winning a second Grand Slam.
It took every ounce of physical and mental energy I had, but I did it!

I am now an eleven-time gold, silver, and bronze-medal
Paralympic athlete, fifteen-time World Champion—and now,
with this race—winner of twelve major world marathons and two
Grand Slams.

I am humbled. When I fell down in the race, I could have
admitted defeat. I had messed up, but then I reminded myself
of something I had once heard: Failure is not falling down, but
refusing to get up. Much of my life I have fallen down. It sort of
comes with the territory of having a disability, but rarely, if ever,
have I refused to get up and keep going.

---

[6] **topples** falls

**About the Author:
Tatyana McFadden
(b. 1989)**

Tatyana McFadden is
a Russian American
professional
wheelchair racer
and marathoner. She
has won seventeen
Paralympic medals
and multiple World
Major Marathons,
including four
consecutive Grand
Slams.

Close Read

Work with a partner.

1. Determine the meanings of your underlined words and phrases.
2. Discuss the question: **What does Tatyana McFadden think about during the race?**

Understand and Analyze

Respond to the questions. Support your responses with evidence from the text.

1. **Explain** Reread the third paragraph. What does "Grand Slam" mean in the world of marathons? What makes McFadden's Grand Slam unique?
2. **Understand** Reread lines 34–36. Which racing group is McFadden in? What characteristic do people in her group have in common?
3. **Explain** Reread lines 80–85. What does McFadden mean when she says she's in her "zone"?
4. **Deduce** Why doesn't she want anyone to touch her when she falls?
5. **Analyze** Reread the last paragraph. How is McFadden's fall a metaphor for her life?

Apply the Strategy: Make Text-to-Self Connections

Complete the chart to make connections with "The Grand Slam." Copy sentences from the text, and relate them to yourself or what you know.

Text	Connections

Share Your Perspective

Discuss the questions in a small group.

1. Would you—or do you—enjoy watching competitors in a long race such as a marathon? Why or why not?
2. Do you think it was smart for Tatyana to refuse help after she fell? Explain.

Discussion Frames

I think …

I agree / don't agree that …

This is because …

Can you say why …?

Language Convention: Use Mood Consistently L.8.1.D

When writing sentences with more than one clause, it's important to use mood consistently so you don't confuse the reader. One common error in mood choice is using a compound sentence with one imperative clause (giving a command) and one indicative clause (making a statement).

Imperative-Indicative Shift

Incorrect: Just relax [imperative], and you should breathe [indicative]!

Correct: Just relax and breathe! [all imperative]

Correct: You should relax and breathe! [all indicative]

Another common error in mood choice is using mixed conditionals in a single sentence.

Conditional Shift

Incorrect: If I push too fast [first conditional], I would be too tired for the second half of the race [second conditional].

Correct: If I push too fast, I'll be too tired for the second half of the race. [all first conditional]

Incorrect: If I push too fast [first conditional], I would have been too tired for the second half of the race [third conditional].

Correct: If I had pushed too fast, I would have been too tired for the second half of the race. [all third conditional]

PRACTICE 1 Read the sentences. Write *IIS* for imperative-indicative shift, *CS* for conditional shift, or *C* if the sentence is correct.

_____ **1.** If he went to practice every day, he will get a better score.

_____ **2.** Go home, and you should get a good night of sleep before the competition.

_____ **3.** Watch the road, and don't take the turn too fast.

_____ **4.** Do the warmup exercises, and you should run five laps.

_____ **5.** If I win the marathon today, I will win the Grand Slam.

_____ **6.** If she had looked back, it will cost her valuable seconds.

PRACTICE 2 Rewrite each of the incorrect sentences from PRACTICE 1 in two correct ways.

Read Again

Read "The Grand Slam" again. As you read, circle details from the text that help you respond to this question:

What keeps Tatyana McFadden going during the difficult race?

Reflect and Respond

Use some of the details you circled to complete the idea web.

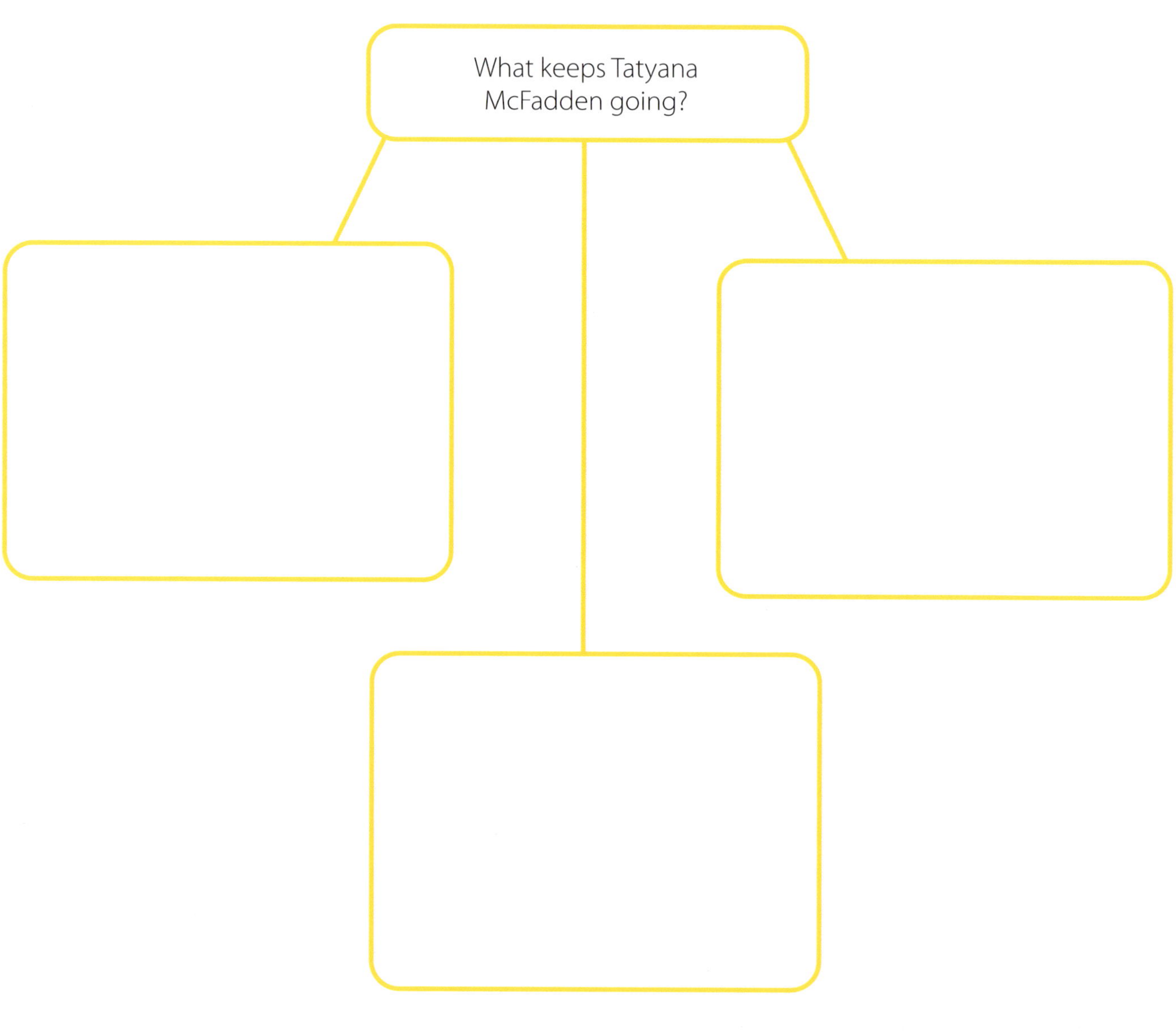

Use your idea web to respond to the question: What keeps Tatyana McFadden going during the difficult race?

____

____

____

Discuss Your Response

Share your ideas with the class. Write one new idea you hear.

____

____

____

Respond to the Guiding Question

Write a response to the question:

How can competition help make us stronger?

Use evidence from the text, your discussion, and your life. Use the Discussion Frames to help you. Use the rubric to check your response.

____

____

____

____

CONNECT ACROSS TEXTS

Discuss the Essential Question: How does competition affect us?

Look at your answer to the Essential Question in the Unit Launch and your notes about competition in the Reflect and Respond sections. Discuss: How have your ideas about the Essential Question changed? What changed your ideas?

Then write down one new idea you heard in the discussion. How did it affect your opinion?

____

____

Respond to the Essential Question

Write your new response to the Essential Question. Include Academic Vocabulary.

____

____

____

____

____

Assignment: Include a Counterargument in an Argumentative Essay W.8.1

An argumentative essay makes a claim and supports it with reasons and evidence. One way to strengthen an argumentative essay is to include a **counterargument** paragraph. A counterargument is the opinion of people who disagree with your claim. For this assignment, you will write an argumentative essay about whether you think a particular type of competition is good or bad for a specific age group. Your essay should include a counterargument paragraph that:

- identifies a common counterargument to the claim
- clearly states that the counterargument is weak, incomplete, or not up-to-date
- discusses the problem(s) with the counterargument, using evidence or examples

Explore the Model

Read the argumentative essay about why the writer thinks competition is bad for young musicians. Underline the main claim and the three supporting reasons. Circle the counterargument.

The Bard Youth Chinese Orchestra performs, using traditional Chinese instruments.

Competitions in Music Education Should Be Reconsidered

Learning to play a musical instrument is common in middle and high school. Part of students' education includes participation in music competitions in which musicians individually perform a prepared piece for an audience and judges. The judges rate each musician's performance and declare a winner. Although an accepted part of music education, competitions have many downsides and should be reconsidered.

Music competitions emphasize winning over learning. Musicians spend time "overlearning" one song at the expense of general learning and creativity. A survey showed that students who participated in competitions spent over 80 percent of their practice time working on their competition song in the month leading up to the competition.

Competition in music education contributes to anxiety in an already stressful time of life. According to "The Pros and Cons of Teen Competition" by Kathryn Rogers, the teen years already involve a lot of pressure and change. Adding competition to music can magnify that pressure and ultimately damage self-esteem for those who don't win.

Competitions only have one winner, so the majority of contestants lose. My sister was an excellent cellist and participated in three music competitions as a teenager. She performed beautifully, but others won. She was devastated. Her takeaway from the experience was not that other contestants won; it was that *she lost*. After her third loss, she lost interest in the cello and eventually quit.

People in favor of music competitions believe competitions motivate young musicians to practice and build related skills. While true, this claim fails to consider other activities, such as performances and cooperative activities, that could offer the same benefits without all of the downsides.

In conclusion, competition has many negatives for young musicians. It emphasizes winning over learning, it contributes to teen anxiety, and the majority of participants end up losing. It's time to reconsider including competition as part of music education.

Plan Your Essay

Choose an age group and an activity type as your topic. Decide whether
you think competition is good or bad for that age group and activity type.
Complete the outline to plan your argumentative essay.

OUTLINE

Topic

Claim:

Supporting Reason 1:	Supporting Reason 2:	Supporting Reason 3:
Evidence:	Evidence:	Evidence:

Counterargument

Problem with Counterargument:

Conclusion—Restated Claim

Summary of Reasons:

Write and Revise

Write Use your outline to write a first draft of your argumentative essay. To connect sentences and paragraphs in your essay, use transition phrases that introduce an opposing opinion, such as:

- On the contrary,
- Nevertheless,
- Even though …
- While it's true that …
- In contrast,
- On the other hand,

Revise Exchange argumentative essays with a partner. Use the checklist to review your partner's work and give feedback. Refer to your partner's feedback as you revise your draft.

- [ ] Does the essay include an introductory paragraph that gives the topic and states the claim?
- [ ] Does each body paragraph provide a different reason supporting the claim and evidence to back it up?
- [ ] Is there a paragraph that presents a typical counterargument?
- [ ] Does the counterargument paragraph clearly explain the problem(s) with the counterargument?
- [ ] Does the concluding paragraph restate the claim and summarize the supporting reasons?

Proofread Check the grammar, spelling, punctuation, and capitalization in your essay. Make edits to correct any errors.

Publish

Share your essay according to your teacher's instructions. Read at least two of your classmates' essays.

Assignment: Participate in a Debate SL.8.1

A debate is a structured argument between two teams who take turns speaking *for* or *against* an assigned claim. Because the claim is assigned, debate participants sometimes have to argue in favor of an opinion that they do not agree with. Work in teams of three to debate the claim **Competition is good for teenagers**.

Both teams will prepare for the debate by doing research, developing arguments, and anticipating the other team's counterarguments. Follow this structure for the debate:

1. The affirmative team presents its argument in support of the claim. (2–5 minutes)
2. The opposing team presents its argument against the claim. (2–5 minutes)
3. Teams prepare their rebuttal (a response to the other team's argument) and closing statement. (3–5 minutes)
4. The opposing team presents its rebuttal. (1–3 minutes)
5. The affirmative team presents its rebuttal. (1–3 minutes)
6. The opposing team presents its closing statement. (1–2 minutes)
7. The affirmative team presents its closing statement. (1–2 minutes)
8. The audience votes on which side made a stronger argument.

Plan for the Debate

With your team, complete the outline to prepare for the debate.

Overall Argument:		
Reason 1: Evidence:	Reason 2: Evidence:	Reason 3: Evidence:
Expected Counterargument:		
Rebuttal (Response to Counterargument):		
Closing Statement:		

Practice the Debate

Use your outline to prepare for the debate. Decide who will speak during different parts of the debate—the argument, the rebuttal, and the closing statement. Be sure that each team member gets approximately the same amount of speaking time.

Read the checklist below. Then practice your debate with your team. Team members should complete the checklist and use it to give each other feedback.

- ☐ Did the speaker cover the key points from the outline for that part of the debate?

- ☐ Was the speaker's argument thorough and persuasive?

- ☐ Did the speaker use a voice that was easy to hear and understand?

- ☐ Did the speaker make eye contact with the audience and members of the other team?

- ☐ Did the speaker speak at an appropriate pace and speak for the time allotted?

Feedback Frames

I enjoyed . . . about your argument.

I suggest you add . . .

You could improve your argument by . . .

Have the Debate

Participate in the debate, keeping in mind the feedback from your team members.

1. Have a formal debate with another team. Your teacher will help you follow the outline structure and timeline.

2. During other teams' debates, watch closely and take notes so you can provide feedback after their debates.

3. After each debate, vote for the team you felt made the most persuasive argument.

4. Give feedback to each team by using the checklist above.

Reflect

Discuss the questions with a small group.

1. What surprised you about participating in the debate?

2. What was your biggest challenge in writing the counterargument paragraph?

3. In what ways was working on a team for the debate helpful? In what ways was it challenging?

4. How was the feedback on your writing and debate helpful?

Helping Big Cats and People Coexist ∩ 7.4

EXPLORER IN ACTION
Shivani Bhalla is a conservationist and "lion protector."

Large cats have always lived in Kenya, but in recent years mounting pressures have made it harder for them to peacefully exist alongside humans. National Geographic Explorer Shivani Bhalla has been working with local communities to prevent human-lion conflict.

Due to habitat loss, the amount of food available for lions has been decreasing. As a result, lions have been attacking livestock. Local people respond with anger and resentment. They retaliate by killing lions which has led to a significant decrease in the lion population. Bhalla's lion conservation project, Ewaso Lions, works with local warriors, women, children, and community elders to reduce human-carnivore conflict. Bhalla and her team also work with livestock owners to reduce ecological problems.

Will Bhalla's efforts be enough to preserve Kenya's lion population? Her organization's unique approach to encouraging locals to find ways to coexist with lions has already made an impact. This is positive for both the people and the lions because, as Bhalla asserts, "Kenya is not Kenya without lions."

▶ **7.3** Watch the video to learn more.

1. Why is Bhalla's approach of working with the local warriors so effective?
2. Do you think conserving lions in their natural habitat is important for Kenya? Why or why not?

How Will You Take Action?

Choose one or more of these actions to do.

Personal

Compete with yourself for a "personal best."

1. Choose an activity that you enjoy, are good at, or would like to get better at.
2. Set a goal to do your personal best in that activity. Set a timeline, and make a plan for meeting the goal.
3. Ask yourself, "How does it feel to compete against myself?"

School

Participate in a class competition to solve a problem at your school.

1. Make a list of problems that exist at your school. As a class, choose one to try to solve.
2. Work in groups to brainstorm solutions. Then have a class competition to choose the best solution.
3. Work with teachers and administrators to implement the solution.

Local

Suggest ways for a local competition to become more inclusive.

1. Research a competition in your area. What accommodations do they make to include people with disabilities, either as competitors or spectators?
2. Contact the organizers to propose ways to make it more inclusive of people with disabilities.

Global

Research an international competition.

1. Choose a large international competition for any activity or sport.
2. Research it. How global is the participation?
3. Write a letter to the organizers petitioning them to include more populations and cultures.

Reflect

1. Reflect on your Take Action project(s). What was successful? What do you wish you had done differently? Why?
2. Reread your response to the Essential Question **How does competition affect us?** in Connect Across Texts. How did your Take Action project(s) change or add to your response?
3. What will you do differently in your life because of what you learned in this unit?

8 In the Future

Do you agree with the quote? Why or why not?

Look at the photo and caption. Discuss the questions.

1. Looking at the stars often makes people think of the past or the future. Why do you think that is?

2. Imagine a new photo will be taken in 100 years. Do you think the night sky then will look the same or different? Why?

◀ **Stars fill the night sky over the Atacama Desert, Chile.**

How will life be different in the future?

Explore the Essential Question

Think Write your ideas about the Essential Question in the Unit Concept Map.

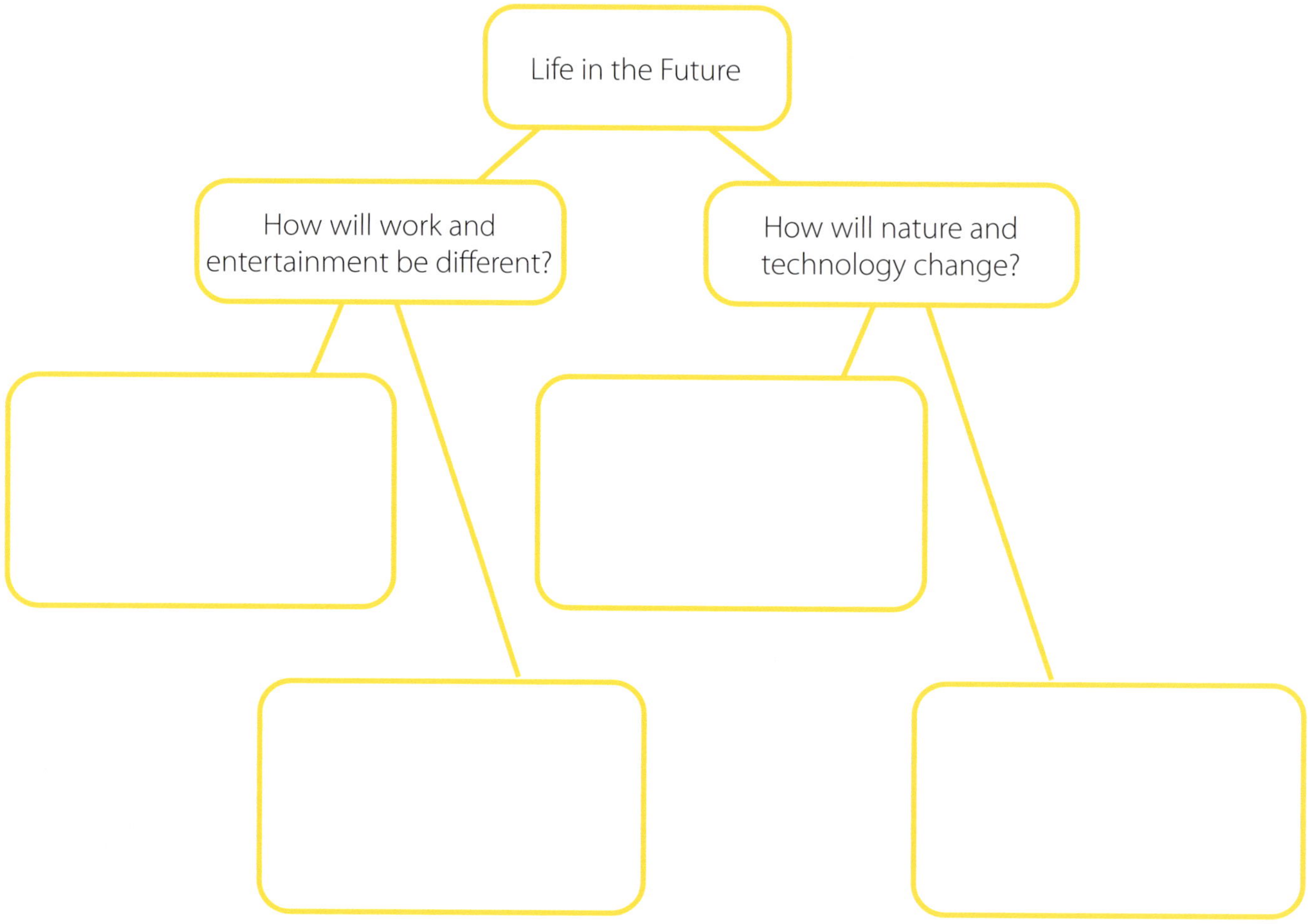

Respond Write one or two sentences to respond to the Essential Question.

Discuss Your Ideas Use your Unit Concept Map and your response to share your ideas with the class.

Discussion Frames

I predict …
People will …
In the future, …

Academic Vocabulary

Use these words to express your ideas throughout the unit.

PRACTICE 1 Use context to determine the meaning of each word in blue. Then match the word to its definition.

Can you make a **prediction** about what life will be like in 50 or 100 years? Think about your **role** in society. What kind of person will you be? What kind of work will you **pursue**? It's easy to make predictions about our own **specific** lives. But what **global** changes will occur? It takes much more creativity to imagine what life will be like for everyone on the planet. Technology, art, language, and work could change in ways that aren't **conceivable** right now. For example, what if we live in floating houses?

Word	Definition
conceivable	imaginable; possible
	individual; particular
	the part that someone or something has in a situation
	a statement about what might happen in the future
	relating to the whole world
	to seek; to perform

PRACTICE 2 Work with a partner. Take turns making predictions about what life will be like in 50 or 100 years. Use one of the Academic Vocabulary words in each prediction. Keep making predictions until you and your partner have each used all the words.

Example

Student 1: People will <u>pursue</u> new kinds of work that we haven't even thought of yet.

Student 2: It is <u>conceivable</u> that computers will drive all cars in 50 years.

Academic Vocabulary

conceivable (adj.)
global (adj.)
prediction (n.)
pursue (v.)
role (n.)
specific (adj.)

How might people and nature change in the future?

First Thoughts

Think about people who will be living a hundred years from now. How will their lives be different from ours? What kinds of things will they do? Discuss your ideas with a partner. Then complete the chart.

Spending Time with Friends	Working at Jobs	Interacting with Nature

Key Vocabulary

PRACTICE Use context to determine the meaning of each word in bold. Then match the word to its definition.

1. He packed a **sufficient** amount of food for the small picnic.
2. Many people learn about fashion **trends** through social media.
3. She would really like the process of cleaning her room to be **automated**.
4. When automobiles became popular, they caused **disruption** for railroad companies.
5. The **urban sprawl** around the edges of Chicago is increasing each year.
6. During the huge storm, the **infrastructure** on the island was destroyed.

_____ **1.** infrastructure   **a.** the spreading of people and buildings outside a city (n.)

_____ **2.** trend   **b.** enough to meet basic needs; adequate (adj.)

_____ **3.** automate   **c.** something that is becoming more common or popular (n.)

_____ **4.** urban sprawl   **d.** something causing interruption or disorder (n.)

_____ **5.** sufficient   **e.** the basic resources needed for a community (n.)

_____ **6.** disruption   **f.** to use technology or a machine for labor (v.)

Reading Strategy: Use Cohesive Devices to Connect Ideas

Good writers support their ideas with helpful information. A writer can share an idea and then give an example of that idea, or explain causes and effects related to that idea. To signal that they are giving more information, writers use **cohesive devices**, or transition words or phrases. Readers can use these devices to figure out how ideas in a text relate to each other.

Transition Words/Phrases	Purpose
for example, for instance, such as	to give examples
likewise, similarly, in contrast, however, on the other hand, instead, although	to make comparisons and contrasts
first, before, after, next, then, to begin with, in the past/future, last, by that day	to show time order or steps in a process
as a result, because, since, for that reason, therefore	to show causes and effects

To analyze how cohesive devices connect ideas:

1. Look for a transition word or phrase in a paragraph.

2. Identify the purpose of the transition.

3. Use the purpose of the transition to connect the ideas that come before and after the transition.

Strategy in Action

Study the model. With a partner, discuss how the author uses cohesive devices to clarify the main idea.

This is the main idea.

On the other hand signals a contrast. The author tells how Student B's opinion contrasts with Student A's.

<u>Most people have their own ideas about the future.</u> For example, Student A might believe the future will be very positive. On the other hand, Student B might believe the future will be very negative.

The transition *For example* connects the sentence to the one before it. The author gives an example of an idea about the future.

Read and answer the question: **How will the world be different in 200 years?** As you read, underline any parts of the text you have questions about or find confusing.

Future Timeline

FutureTimeline.net imagines what our lives will be like in 2200–2210.

🎧 8.1

1 **2200: Traditional employment is becoming obsolete**

The average citizen today is likely to spend the vast majority of their time in a virtual reality of some kind. Physical society and culture still exist—but most people
5 skip them, in favor of the superhuman abilities they can experience online. It is very rare to meet a friend or colleague in person[1] now. You are far more likely to encounter a form of artificial intelligence today than you are a living, breathing human. Urban centers have
10 become eerily deserted, with most people to be found in their homes—or in digital libraries and entertainment venues—engaged in complex simulations that offer perfect re-creations of the real world. To observers from earlier centuries, these virtual environments would appear truly
15 dazzling in their speed and complexity, with an almost unimaginable level of detail, creativity and ingenuity.

A **trend** which began during the Industrial Revolution has now reached its ultimate conclusion.[2] Working hours had gradually declined over the centuries, thanks to a
20 combination of technology, automation, improvements in working conditions and employee rights, changing labor demands, and a shift in the cultural mood. By 2050, the average person in a developed country was employed for

---

[1] **in person** physically in the same place
[2] **reached its ultimate conclusion** ended

A man experiences
virtual reality.

under 30 hours per week, and this fell to 20 hours by 2100. Working hours
25   continued to fall in the 22nd century as machines—including lifelike
androids—took on ever more complex and sophisticated roles.

As humans began to enhance their cognitive abilities, the nature of work
itself was changing. More and more people were moving from "drudge" jobs
into their own personal, creative, and intellectual pursuits. The line between
30   work and play was beginning to blur. At the same time, average spending on
various household items and utilities was steadily declining.

By 2200, this trend is complete. In most countries, basic items such
as food, energy, and clothing are now essentially free, with little or no
need for the average person to work in order to acquire them. Recent
35   advances in replicator technology provide an abundance of resources—
eliminating famine, disease, and the need for war. Literally everything has
been **automated**, digitized, and made easier. Take[3] emergency services, for
example. Hospital visits are rarely required now, as practically all medical
treatments are available at home or within a person's own body. Most
40   police officers are robots, although physical crimes have been largely
eradicated. Human firefighters are no longer needed, since they are
robotic too, while building regulations and nanotechnology materials can
prevent most fires from occurring in the first place.[4]

This process of falling employment was, of course, by no means a
45   smooth transition. It caused profound economic and political **disruption**
throughout the 21st and 22nd centuries. By 2200, however, the world

---

[3] **Take** Think about
[4] **occurring in the first place** happening

has fully adapted to these changes and is entering a period of artistic
and cultural splendor. Whether as explorers in space, or designers of
entire new worlds in cyberspace, humans are free to pursue their greatest
dreams and personal aspirations—unshackled from the confines of[5]
traditional economic and monetary systems.

2210: A global rewilding effort is underway

Human activity in the 19th through 22nd centuries led to catastrophic
damage of the natural world. Of the approximately 30 million known
species of flora and fauna, more than half were lost as a result of
pollution, climate change, deforestation, mining, agriculture, **urban
sprawl**, overfishing, and hunting. Extinctions on this scale had occurred
only five times previously in Earth's history.

Various wars, industrial accidents, and nanotechnology experiments
also played a role in making large tracts of the world essentially lifeless.
Permanent damage was done to countless habitats. The Amazon rainforest,
perhaps the most egregious example, shrank to become mostly desert by
2100. Meanwhile, ocean acidification caused by rising CO_2 levels resulted
in the decimation of coral reefs. The Arctic became devoid of ice during
summer months, while melting in Greenland, Iceland, West Antarctica, and
elsewhere led to sea level rises of nearly two meters by the 22nd century.

All of this occurred despite an in-depth scientific knowledge of the
processes underway. Long-term sustainability and sensible management
of resources were sacrificed in favor of short-term profits, political
influence, and personal gain. By the time most governments began to
enact serious measures, it was already too late.

---

[5] **unshackled from the confines of** freed from the limits of

Biodiversity fell away to such an extent[6] that, for those born in the late 20th century, the planet became unrecognizable. Younger generations growing up in this new world found themselves bitterly resentful at what their predecessors had allowed to happen. Many in Asia, Africa, and South America would never get to experience a real forest, or come face to face with animals larger than a dog, or witness the range of colorful and exotic species that were commonplace before—except in zoos or through virtual reality.

By the 23rd century, however, technology was advancing to a whole new magnitude of power and possibilities. Super-intelligent entities were now dominating business and government, formulating policies to benefit everybody rather than the few. Meanwhile, a new and gigantic system of orbital **infrastructure** was being planned, allowing people to directly control the Earth's climate. Consumer devices were also becoming available that could reproduce food and other items without needing to plunder natural resources.

An idea began to emerge that quickly gained momentum. It would require an international, concerted effort over a number of generations, but it had support from across the political spectrum.

In essence, it would involve the re-creation of extinct animals and plants, brought back to life by a combination of fossil records, DNA samples, computer models, and molecular engineering. Once grown or reproduced in **sufficient** numbers, these would be distributed back to their original native environments: as close as possible to how they lived prior to human industry. They would then be managed in such a way that people could cause them no harm—and vice versa.[7]

This rewilding effort became the single largest environmental project in history. Entire deserts were transformed back into lush landscapes, fed by artificial rain and other forms of weather control. Vast areas of abandoned wasteland became rich ecosystems teeming with life, even ancient animals such as mammoths. Toxic lakes and rivers were made clean. The oceans were de-acidified, cooled, and made habitable once again to countless fish, mollusks, crustaceans, and other aquatic invertebrates. Urban sprawl in cities was dramatically reversed and scaled back, with a focus instead on highly compact vertical structures.

Slowly, Earth recovered. Humanity had reached an equilibrium with its surroundings. Though it would take another few decades, the final elements were falling into place[8] to ensure the future preservation of biodiversity.

---

[6] **fell away to such an extent**   lessened so much

[7] **vice versa**   animals and plants could not harm people

[8] **falling into place**   beginning to happen

Close Read

Work with a partner.

1. Determine the meanings of your underlined words and phrases.
2. Discuss the question:

   How will the world be different in 200 years?

Understand and Analyze

Respond to the questions. Support your responses with evidence from the text.

1. **Cite** Reread the first paragraph. According to the text, how will people mostly interact in the future?
2. **Review** Reread the second paragraph. What will cause people to work fewer hours in the future?
3. **Explain** Reread lines 32–43. What does the author mean by "Literally everything has been automated, digitized, and made easier"?
4. **Cite** Reread the first two paragraphs of "2210: A global rewilding effort is underway." Which factors will have the greatest negative effect on wildlife and the environment?
5. **Examine** Are the author's predictions for the future realistic? Why or why not?
6. **Compare** How are the sections for 2200 and 2210 alike and different?

Apply the Strategy: Use Cohesive Devices to Connect Ideas

Work with a partner. Reread the fourth and fifth paragraphs of the article. Identify cohesive devices. Discuss how the transitions link the author's ideas.

Share Your Perspective

Discuss these questions in a small group.

1. Which of the author's predictions do you like best? Why?
2. Would you want to live in the year 2200? Why or why not?

Discussion Frames

The prediction I like best is … because …

In my opinion, …

What do you think will …?

How would you feel if …?

Language Convention: Identify Participles L.8.1.A

A **participle** is a form of a verb. Two types of participles are **present participles** and **past participles**. Both types can be used as adjectives to describe nouns. A present participle is a verb form that ends with *-ing*. A past participle is a verb form that usually ends with *-ed*.

Verb	Form	Used as an Adjective
fly	present participle (*-ing*)	There might be <u>flying</u> cars in the future.
fade	past participle (*-ed*)	That kind of technology is now a <u>faded</u> memory.

PRACTICE 1 Read each sentence. Circle the participle. What type of participle is it? Check (✓) *Present* or *Past*.

	Present	Past
1. To imagine the future can be an overwhelming activity.		
2. A good starting point is to think about life today.		
3. Some people do not enjoy their assigned classes.		
4. The provided opportunities could greatly change due to technology.		
5. Many plants and animals face challenging experiences.		
6. Protected water, parks, and wild spaces are very important to help make a better future.		

PRACTICE 2 Work with a partner. Reread the first paragraph of the section "2200: Traditional employment is becoming obsolete." Identify five participles that are used as adjectives.

Read Again

Read "Future Timeline" again. As you read, circle details from the text that help you respond to this question:

According to the article, what will happen to people and wildlife in the future?

Reflect and Respond

Choose several details you circled in the article to complete the chart.

People	Wildlife

Use your chart to respond to the question: According to the article, what will happen to people and wildlife in the future?

____

____

____

____

Discuss Your Response

Share your ideas with the class. Write one new idea you hear.

____

____

____

Respond to the Guiding Question

Write a response to the question:

How might people and nature change in the future?

Use evidence from the text, your discussion, and your life. Use the Discussion Frames to help you. Use the rubric to check your response.

____

____

____

____

____

Research RI.8.2

Choose one of these topics. Research the topic to learn more about it.

- how virtual reality is being used in education

- using DNA to help bring back extinct animals

Follow these steps:

1. Make notes about what you already know about the topic.
2. Write three questions you have about the topic.
3. Research the topic to find answers to your questions.
4. Write your answers to the questions.
5. Present what you learned to a small group.

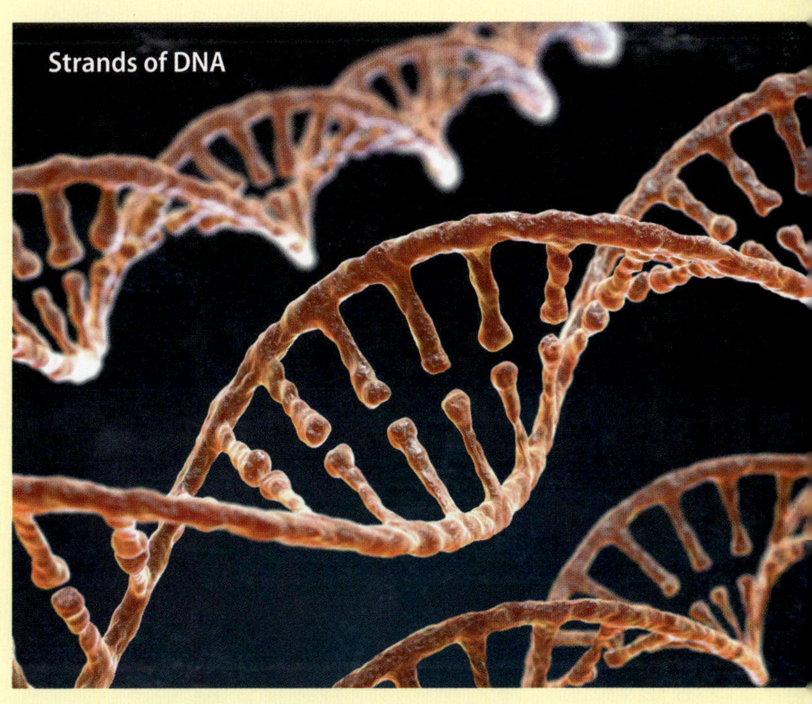

How can we meet future energy needs?

Panels reflect sunlight to a solar tower at a concentrated solar power plant in Spain. The concentrated light creates heat, which is used to generate electricity.

First Thoughts

What things in your school use power? Think of the appliances, tools, or systems that the school uses. Make a list. Compare lists in a small group.

Viewing Skill: Use Visual Cues to Learn New Words

When you watch a video, you can use visual cues to figure out the meanings of unknown words or phrases. Often, visuals reinforce or extend the meaning of the audio. If you do not know a word used in the audio, observe visual cues to see if they help you understand it.

Apply the Skill

▶ **8.1** Watch the TED-Ed animation "Can 100% Renewable Energy Power the World?" In the chart, write any words or phrases that you don't understand. Use visual cues to help you figure out their meanings.

Unknown Word	Visual Cue	Word's Meaning

Understand and Analyze

▶ **8.1** Watch again. Answer the questions. Support your responses with evidence from the video.

1. **Review** When do experts predict we will run out of fossil fuels?
2. **Contrast** The video shows images of a fossil fuel–powered world and a renewables-powered world. How are the images different?
3. **Explain** What are some of the challenges of relying only on lithium ion batteries?
4. **Infer** Why might distance be such a big problem for a solar power plant located in a desert?

Share Your Perspective

1. Do you think world governments would agree to make the "connected energy network"? Why or why not?
2. Will we be able to use only renewable resources for power in the future? Why or why not?

> **Discussion Frames**
>
> I predict that …
>
> I speculate that …
>
> What is your reason for …?

How can the past shape the future?

First Thoughts

Imagine yourself two years ago. What advice would you give your past self?
Imagine yourself two years in the future. What do you want to tell your
future self? Complete the chart. Then share your ideas with a partner.

Advice to My Past Self	Message to My Future Self

Key Vocabulary

PRACTICE Use context to determine the meaning of each word in bold.
Then match the word to its definition.

1. I can see the **variation** in this group of goats. They are all different colors.

2. Will you **assure** me that you will be home at 4 p.m.?

3. She has pictures of her **ancestors** in the family photo album.

4. I need more time to **contemplate** where I want to go to college.

5. The cat is **capable** of knocking over that lamp.

6. You are **fundamentally** kind at heart. You are almost always good to others.

_____ **1.** ancestor   **a.** at a very basic level (adv.)

_____ **2.** assure   **b.** family member from the past (n.)

_____ **3.** contemplate   **c.** to promise in a positive way (v.)

_____ **4.** fundamentally   **d.** differences among members of a species or group (n.)

_____ **5.** capable   **e.** having the potential for (adj.)

_____ **6.** variation   **f.** to think seriously and carefully about something (v.)

Reading Skill: Cite Text Evidence to Support Inferences   RL.8.1; RL.8.4

You make an **inference** when you figure out an idea that is not directly stated in a text. Information from the text that supports your thinking is called **text evidence**. It's important to support your inferences with specific details from the text to show that your new ideas relate to the content. To support your inferences with evidence:

1. Read what the text states directly. Then think about what the text is stating indirectly.
   Ask yourself: *What is being implied, or suggested?*

2. Make an inference by combining clues from the text with your personal experience or knowledge.
   Ask yourself: *What do I already know about this topic or these details?*

3. Cite the text evidence that supports your inference.
   Ask yourself: *How does the text support my inference?*

Skill in Action

Study the model. Do the inferences make sense? Why or why not?

**from Letter to Someone Living
Fifty Years from Now**

Most likely, you think we hated the elephant, the golden toad, the thylacine and all variations of whale harpooned or hacked into extinction.

I know that harpooning and hacking are actions that involve blades. These are human actions.

I know that elephants and some whales are currently endangered. I looked online and found out that golden toads and thylacines are already extinct.

Inferences	Text Evidence That Supports the Inferences
In fifty years, the animals listed in the poem will all be gone.	• The poet uses the past tense to describe the animals. • The poet uses the word *extinction*.
In fifty years, humans will have killed all the whales.	• The poet uses *harpooned* and *hacked* to describe how "all variations of whale" became extinct.

A House Called *Tomorrow*

by Alberto Ríos

8.2

1   You are not fifteen, or twelve, or seventeen—
    You are a hundred wild centuries

    And fifteen, bringing with you
    In every breath and in every step

5   Everyone who has come before you,
    All the yous that you have been,

    The mothers of your mother,
    The fathers of your father.

    If someone in your family tree was trouble,
10 A hundred were not:

    The bad do not win—not finally,
    No matter how loud they are.

    We simply would not be here
    If that were so.

15 You are made, **fundamentally**, from the good.
    With this knowledge, you never march alone.

You are the breaking news of the century.
You are the good who has come forward

Through it all, even if so many days
20 Feel otherwise. But think:

When you as a child learned to speak,
It's not that you didn't know words—

It's that, from the centuries, you knew so many,
And it's hard to choose the words that will be your own.

25 From those centuries we human beings bring with us
The simple solutions and songs,

The river bridges and star charts and song harmonies
All in service to a simple idea:

That we can make a house called tomorrow.
30 What we bring, finally, into the new day, every day,

Is ourselves. And that's all we need
To start. That's everything we require to keep going.

Look back only for as long as you must,
Then go forward into the history you will make.

35 Be good, then better. Write books. Cure disease.
Make us proud. Make yourself proud.

And those who came before you? When you
   hear thunder,
Hear it as their applause.

**About the Poet:
Alberto Ríos**
(b. 1952) Alberto Ríos has written many award-winning books of poetry and prose. His work has been included in multiple anthologies, and he served as Arizona's first state poet laureate.

Letter to Someone Living
FIFTY YEARS
from Now

by **Matthew Olzmann**

🎧 8.3

1   Most likely, you think we hated the elephant,
     the golden toad, the thylacine and all **variations**
     of whale harpooned or hacked into extinction.

     It must seem like we sought to leave you nothing
5   but benzene, mercury,[1] the stomachs
     of seagulls rippled with jet fuel and plastic.

     You probably doubt that we were **capable** of joy,
     but I **assure** you we were.

     We still had the night sky[2] back then,
10   and like our **ancestors**, we admired
     its illuminated doodles
     of scorpion outlines and upside-down ladles.

     Absolutely, there were some forests left!
     Absolutely, we still had some lakes!

15   I'm saying, it wasn't all lead paint[3] and sulfur dioxide.[4]
     There were bees back then, and they pollinated
     a euphoria[5] of flowers so we might
     contemplate the great mysteries and finally ask,
     "Hey guys, what's transcendence[6]?"

20   And then all the bees were dead.

---

[1] **benzene, mercury** toxic chemicals
[2] **still had the night sky** could see the stars clearly
[3] **lead paint** dangerous, toxic paint
[4] **sulfur dioxide** air pollution
[5] **euphoria** feeling of intense happiness (figurative)
[6] **transcendence** the state of rising above the ordinary

**About the Poet:
Matthew Olzmann**

Matthew Olzmann's work includes essays, stories, and poems. His work has received many awards and has been included in numerous literary magazines.

Close Read

Work with a partner.

1. Determine the meanings of your underlined words and phrases.
2. Discuss the question: **How can our actions affect people in the future?**

Understand and Analyze

Respond to the questions. Support your responses with evidence from the text.

1. **Paraphrase** Reread lines 1–8 of "A House Called Tomorrow." What message is Ríos trying to send?
2. **Interpret** Reread lines 25–29 of "A House Called Tomorrow." Explain what "we human beings bring with us" into the future. Why do we bring these things?
3. **Explain** Reread lines 13–15 of "Letter to Someone Living Fifty Years from Now." What does Olzmann mean by "it wasn't all lead paint and sulfur dioxide"?
4. **Examine** Olzmann ends "Letter to Someone Living Fifty Years from Now" in a shocking way. Why do you think he ends it this way?
5. **Compare** How are the two poems alike? How are they different?

Apply the Skill: Cite Text Evidence to Support Inferences

Make inferences about the speaker's view of the current generation in each poem. Cite text evidence to support your inferences.

Poem	Inferences	Text Evidence
"A House Called Tomorrow"		
"Letter to Someone Living Fifty Years from Now"		

Share Your Perspective

Discuss these questions in a small group.

1. Which poem more affected the way you think about the future? Why?
2. How do the poems relate to things that are happening in the world today?

Discussion Frames

The poem that affected me more was …

It made me feel …

Currently, …

This relates to the poem by … because …

Why were you affected by …?

Vocabulary: Analyze Figurative Language L.8.5

Figurative language is nonliteral language, or language that goes beyond the dictionary meaning of words and phrases. Good writers use figurative language to make their writing more interesting. Two kinds of figurative language are **similes** and **metaphors**. A simile uses *like* or *as* to make a comparison. A metaphor makes a comparison without using *like* or *as*. Instead, metaphors make comparisons directly. Metaphors often use *be* verbs, such as *is, are, was,* or *were*. To analyze similes and metaphors:

1. Look in the text for a comparison that uses nonliteral language.

2. Think about and visualize the comparison the author is making.

3. Use your own words to restate the simile or metaphor in a literal way.

Example

You are not fifteen, or twelve, or seventeen—
You are a hundred wild centuries

The first line is literal language. The author is telling me that I am not one of these actual ages.

The author is making a direct comparison in the second line. The language is nonliteral because I can't literally be centuries old. This is a metaphor. I think the author means "You are older and wiser than you think you are."

Apply the Strategy

Look at the poems again. Read each metaphor. Think about what is being compared. Write what you think the author means.

Metaphor	Meaning
"You are the breaking news of the century."	
"We still had the night sky back then, and like our ancestors, we admired its illuminated doodles of scorpion outlines and upside-down ladles."	

Read Again

Read "A House Called Tomorrow" and "Letter to Someone Living Fifty Years from Now" again. As you read, circle details from the poems that help you respond to this question:

What do the poems suggest we do now to make a better future?

Reflect and Respond

Complete this chart with several details you circled in the poems.

"A House Called Tomorrow"	"Letter to Someone Living Fifty Years from Now"

Use your chart to respond to the question: What do the poems suggest we do now to make a better future?

____

____

____

Discuss Your Response

Share your ideas with the class. Write one new idea you hear.

____

____

Respond to the Guiding Question

Write a response to the question:

How can the past shape the future?

Use evidence from the text, your discussion, and your life. Use the Discussion Frames to help you. Use the rubric to check your response.

____

____

____

____

____

____

Create and Present: Your Own Poetry

Consider your reactions to the poems you read. Then do one of these activities.

OPTION 1: Write a Response Poem

Work with a partner. Choose one of the poems you read. Write a response poem, addressed to the poet, to share how you feel about the poet's ideas. Title your poem "Letter to Alberto Ríos" or "Letter to Matthew Olzmann." Read your poem to the class.

OPTION 2: Write a Poem to Your Future Self

Write a poem to yourself fifty years from now. You might include reminders of what you are like now, hopes for what the future will bring, or advice for your future self.

UNCOVER THE STORY

CITIES OF THE FUTURE
URBAN HUBS

In a densely developed hub, sustainable land use within and outside its borders helps people thrive by providing water, food, and recreation. High-capacity transit reduces emissions and speeds commute times.

Mixed densities
A mix of housing types within each district provides diverse workforce housing and eases crowding.

Contamination cleanup
Instead of being covered or buried, hazardous sites and contaminated soil near cities are cleaned.

SPONGE CITY
All parks and infrastructure allow water to percolate through soil to recharge the water table. Such "sponge city" measures are already being tested in Shanghai.

Green roofs
Solar panels and roof gardens are common on top of buildings, encouraging sustainable energy and small-scale farming.

Automated recycling
Waste collection and recycling centers are fully automated for faster and more comprehensive reuse of waste.

PRINCIPLES OF
CITY DESIGN

ECOLOGY
The future city is designed around natural features and forces, protecting wildlife habitat and natural resources. Based on a unified vision for the region, the city is compact and dense to limit impacts on the ecosystem.

Examine the Graphic

Use details from the graphic and the poems to respond to the questions. Discuss your responses with a partner.

1. Why is the urban hub in the graphic called a "sponge city"?

2. Would you want to live in this urban hub? Why or why not?

3. What challenges might people living in the urban hub face?

4. What information does the graphic give about future schools?

Make Connections

Use details from "A House Called Tomorrow," "Letter to Someone Living Fifty Years from Now," and the graphic to discuss your responses with a partner.

1. How does the graphic's city of the future address problems expressed in "Letter to Someone Living Fifty Years from Now"?

2. "A House Called Tomorrow" tells readers to "go forward into the history you will make" and make positive changes. How does the city of the future do these things?

Reflect

Reflect on your discussions. What questions do you still have about the graphic or cities in the future? Write a list of questions and discuss them with a partner.

How accurately can we predict the future?

First Thoughts

Think of an invention that could make the world a safer or better place for people in the future. Make notes about how it will help others and how it works. Then tell a partner about the invention.

How It Will Help	How It Works

Key Vocabulary

PRACTICE   Use context to determine the meaning of each word in bold. Then match the word to its definition.

1. I think there will be **colonies** on the moon someday. I want to go live there.
2. The user can call friends, read books, or search the internet on a cellular **device**.
3. Whether the future will be better or worse is a matter of **speculation**.
4. The curling iron was an **innovation** that made styling hair easier.
5. Eating vegetables every day is a **practical** way to stay healthy.
6. You will reach your **destination** on the other side of the hill.

______ **1.** innovation   **a.** a tool that people use to do tasks (n.)

______ **2.** destination   **b.** a home or society established in a new place (n.)

______ **3.** speculation   **c.** a new way of doing something or a new idea (n.)

______ **4.** colony   **d.** a prediction or guess about something (n.)

______ **5.** practical   **e.** a location where someone or something is going (n.)

______ **6.** device   **f.** likely to be useful or successful (adj.)

Reading Skill: Analyze Connections in a Text RI.8.3

Nonfiction texts often give information about ideas, people, or events. Comparing, contrasting, or categorizing the information can help you better understand how the ideas, people, or events are connected. These connections help you understand the text as a whole. To analyze connections in a text:

1. Identify two or more ideas, people, or events in the text.

2. Think about how the text connects the ideas, people, or events. Are they connected through similarities, differences, or categories?

3. Summarize the connection.

Skill in Action

Study the model. How are the ideas in the text connected? How is figuring out the connection helpful?

> One thought that occurs to me is that men will continue to withdraw from nature in order to create an environment that will suit them better. By 2014, electroluminescent panels will be in common use. Ceilings and walls will glow softly, and in a variety of colors that will change at the touch of a push button.
>
> Windows need be no more than an archaic touch, and even when present will be polarized to block out the harsh sunlight. The degree of opacity of the glass may even be made to alter automatically in accordance with the intensity of the light falling upon it.

This paragraph shares ideas about light from ceiling and wall panels.

This paragraph shares ideas about light from windows.

These ideas are connected because they are about light. I can categorize the ideas as "Ideas About Light in the Future." Figuring out the connection helps me understand that people will want "soft," comfortable, controlled light in the future, rather than natural light. That is part of people continuing to "withdraw from nature."

This futuristic landscape was set up at the World's Fair in New York, USA, in 1964.

Read and answer the question: **How did Asimov think technology would affect the future?** As you read, underline any parts of the text you have questions about or find confusing.

Visit to the World's Fair of 2014

A World's Fair is a large gathering where organizations and companies from many different countries share new inventions and technologies. This type of international event is sometimes called a World's Expo or a Specialized Expo. Each gathering has its own unique theme. In 1964, the theme of "Peace Through Understanding" was important because the threat of nuclear war was very serious at that time.

by **Isaac Asimov**
from **The New York Times, August 16, 1964**

🎧 **8.4**

1   The New York World's Fair of 1964 is dedicated to "Peace Through Understanding." Its glimpses of the world of tomorrow rule out thermonuclear warfare. And why not? If a thermonuclear war takes place, the future will not be worth discussing. So let the
5   missiles slumber eternally on their pads and let us observe what may come in the nonatomized[1] world of the future.

    What is to come, through the fair's eyes at least, is wonderful. The direction in which man is traveling is viewed with buoyant hope, nowhere more so than at the General Electric pavilion.
10   There the audience whirls through four scenes, each populated by cheerful, lifelike dummies[2] that move and talk with a facility that, inside of a minute and a half, convinces you they are alive.

---

[1] **nonatomized** non-nuclear
[2] **dummies** mannequins or machines

The scenes, set in or about 1900, 1920, 1940, and 1960, show
the advances of electrical appliances and the changes they are
bringing to living. I enjoyed it hugely and only regretted that they
had not carried the scenes into the future. What will life be like,
say, in 2014 A.D., 50 years from now? What will the World's Fair of
2014 be like?

I don't know, but I can guess.

One thought that occurs to me is that men will continue to
withdraw from nature in order to create an environment that will
suit them better. By 2014, electroluminescent panels will be in
common use. Ceilings and walls will glow softly, and in a variety of
colors that will change at the touch of a push button.

Windows need be no more than an archaic touch,[3] and even
when present will be polarized to block out the harsh sunlight.
The degree of opacity[4] of the glass may even be made to alter
automatically in accordance with the intensity of the light falling
upon it.

There is an underground house at the fair which is a sign of
the future. If its windows are not polarized, they can nevertheless
alter the "scenery" by changes in lighting. Suburban houses
underground, with easily controlled temperature, free from the
vicissitudes[5] of weather, with air cleaned and light controlled,
should be fairly common. At the New York World's Fair of
2014, General Motors' "Futurama" may well display vistas of
underground cities complete with light-forced vegetable gardens.
The surface, G.M. will argue, will be given over to large-scale
agriculture, grazing, and parklands, with less space wasted on
actual human occupancy.

Gadgetry[6] will continue to relieve mankind of tedious jobs.
Kitchen units will be devised that will prepare "automeals,"
heating water and converting it to coffee; toasting bread; frying,
poaching, or scrambling eggs, and so on. Breakfasts will be
"ordered" the night before to be ready by a specified hour the
next morning. Complete lunches and dinners, with the food semi-
prepared, will be stored in the freezer until ready for processing.

---

[3] **archaic touch** old-fashioned decoration
[4] **degree of opacity** level of clearness
[5] **vicissitudes** changing conditions
[6] **Gadgetry** Electronic tools

The 1964 World's Fair included this exhibit imagining buildings of the future.

I suspect, though, that even in 2014 it will still be advisable to have
a small corner in the kitchen unit where the more individual meals
can be prepared by hand, especially when company is coming.
    Robots will neither be common nor very good in 2014, but
they will be in existence. The I.B.M. exhibit at the present fair has
no robots but it is dedicated to computers, which are shown in all
their amazing complexity, notably in the task of translating Russian
into English. If machines are that smart today, what may not be

A robot vacuum cleans the floor of the "Miracle Kitchen of the Future" exhibit in 1959.

in the works 50 years hence[7]? It will be such computers, much miniaturized, that will serve as the "brains" of robots. In fact, the I.B.M. building at the 2014 World's Fair may have, as one of its prime exhibits, a robot housemaid—large, clumsy, slow-moving but capable of general picking-up, arranging, cleaning, and manipulation of various appliances. It will undoubtedly amuse the fairgoers to scatter debris over the floor in order to see the robot lumberingly remove it and classify it into "throw away" and "set aside." (Robots for gardening work will also have made their appearance.)

General Electric at the 2014 World's Fair will be showing 3-D movies of its "Robot of the Future," neat and streamlined, its cleaning appliances built in and performing all tasks briskly. (There will be a three-hour wait in line to see the film, for some things never change.)

The appliances of 2014 will have no electric cords, of course, for they will be powered by long-lived batteries running on radioisotopes. The isotopes will not be expensive for they will be by-products of the fission-power plants[8] which, by 2014, will be supplying well over half the power needs of humanity. But once the isotype batteries are used up, they will be disposed of only through authorized agents of the manufacturer.

An experimental fusion-power plant or two will already exist in 2014. (Even today, a small but genuine fusion explosion is demonstrated at frequent intervals in the G.E. exhibit at the 1964 fair.) Large solar-power stations will also be in operation in a number of desert and semi-desert areas—Arizona, the Negev, Kazakhstan. In the more crowded, but cloudy and smoggy areas, solar power will be less **practical**. An exhibit at the 2014 fair will show models of power stations in space, collecting sunlight by means of huge parabolic[9] focusing **devices** and radiating the energy thus collected down to earth.

Jets of compressed air[10] will lift land vehicles off the highways, which, among other things, will minimize paving problems. Smooth earth or level lawns will do[11] as well as pavements.

---

[7] **in the works 50 years hence** in development 50 years from now

[8] **by-products of the fission-power plants** things that happen to be made in the process of creating nuclear power

[9] **parabolic** curved

[10] **Jets of compressed air** Controlled bursts of air

[11] **do** function

90   Bridges will also be of less importance, since cars will be capable
of crossing water on their jets, though local ordinances[12] will
discourage the practice.

Much effort will be put into the designing of vehicles
with "Robot-brains"—vehicles that can be set for particular
95   **destinations** and that will then proceed there without interference
by the slow reflexes of a human driver. I suspect one of the major
attractions of the 2014 fair will be rides on small roboticized cars
which will maneuver in[13] crowds at the two-foot level, neatly and
automatically avoiding each other.

100   For short-range travel, moving sidewalks (with benches on
either side, standing room in the center) will be making their
appearance[14] in downtown sections. Compressed air tubes will
carry goods and materials over local stretches, and the switching
devices that will place specific shipments in specific destinations
105   will be one of the city's marvels.

Communications will become sight-sound, and you will see as
well as hear the person you telephone. The screen can be used not
only to see the people you call, but also for studying documents
and photographs and reading passages from books. Synchronous
110   satellites, hovering in space, will make it possible for you to direct-
dial any spot on earth, including the weather stations in Antarctica.

For that matter, you will be able to reach someone at the moon
colonies.

Conversations with the moon will be a trifle uncomfortable, in
115   that 2.5 seconds must elapse between statement and answer (it takes
light that long to make the round trip). Similar conversations with
Mars will experience a 3.5-minute delay even when Mars is at its
closest. However, by 2014, only unmanned ships[15] will have landed on
Mars, though a manned expedition will be in the works and the 2014
120   Futurama will show a model of an elaborate Martian colony.

As for television, wall screens will have replaced the ordinary
set; but transparent cubes will be making their appearance in
which three-dimensional viewing will be possible. In fact, one

---

[12] **ordinances** laws or rules
[13] **maneuver in** move through
[14] **making their appearance** starting to be used
[15] **unmanned ships** ships without people aboard

The two-wheeled concept car Ford Gyron is displayed at the Detroit Motor Show in 1961.

popular exhibit at the 2014 World's Fair will be such a 3-D TV, built
life-size, in which ballet performances will be seen. The cube will
slowly revolve for viewing from all angles.

One can go on indefinitely in this happy extrapolation,[16] but all
is not rosy.

As I stood in line waiting to get into the General Electric
exhibit at the 1964 fair, I found myself staring at the grim sign
blinking out the population of the United States, with the number
(over 191,000,000) increasing by 1 every 11 seconds. During the
interval which I spent inside the G.E. pavilion, the American
population had increased by nearly 300 and the world's population
by 6,000.

---

[16] **extrapolation** prediction

In 2014, there is every likelihood that the world population will
be 6,500,000,000 and the population of the United States will be
350,000,000. Boston-to-Washington, the most crowded area of its
size on the earth, will have become a single city with a population
140   of over 40,000,000.

Population pressure will force increasing penetration of[17]
desert and polar areas. Most surprising and, in some ways,
heartening,[18] 2014 will see a good beginning made in the
colonization of the continental shelves. Underwater housing
145   will have its attractions to those who like water sports, and will
undoubtedly encourage the more efficient exploitation of ocean
resources, both food and mineral. The 2014 World's Fair will have
exhibits showing cities in the deep sea with bathyscaphe liners[19]
carrying men and supplies across and into the abyss.

150   Ordinary agriculture will keep up with great difficulty
and there will be "farms" turning to the more efficient micro-
organisms. Processed yeast and algae products will be available in
a variety of flavors. The 2014 fair will feature an Algae Bar at which
"mock-turkey" and "pseudo-steak" will be served. It won't be bad
155   at all (if you can dig up those premium prices[20]), but there will be
considerable psychological resistance to such an **innovation**.

Although technology will still keep up with population through
2014, it will be only through a supreme effort and with but partial
success. Not all the world's population will enjoy the gadgety world
160   of the future to the full. A larger portion than today will be deprived
and although they may be better off, materially, than today, they will
be further behind when compared with the advanced portions of
the world. They will have moved backward, relatively.

Nor can technology continue to match population growth if
165   that remains unchecked. Consider Manhattan of 1964, which has
a population density of 80,000 per square mile at night and of
over 100,000 per square mile during the working day. If the whole
earth, including the Sahara, the Himalayan Mountain peaks,
Greenland, Antarctica, and every square mile of the ocean bottom,
170   to the deepest abyss, were as packed as Manhattan at noon, surely

---

[17] **penetration of** movement into
[18] **heartening** encouraging
[19] **bathyscaphe liners** submarines or other underwater vehicles
[20] **dig up those premium prices** afford to pay for it

you would agree that no way to support such a population (let
alone make it comfortable) was conceivable. In fact, support would
fail long before the World-Manhattan was reached.

Well, the earth's population is now about 3,000,000,000 and is
doubling every 40 years. If this rate of doubling goes unchecked,[21]
then a World-Manhattan is coming in just 500 years. All earth
will be a single choked Manhattan[22] by A.D. 2450 and society will
collapse *long before that!*

The situation will have been made the more serious by the
advances of automation. The world of A.D. 2014 will have few routine
jobs that cannot be done better by some machine than by any human
being. Mankind will therefore have become largely a race of machine
tenders.[23] Schools will have to be oriented in this direction. Part of
the General Electric exhibit today consists of a school of the future
in which such present realities as closed-circuit TV and programmed
tapes aid the teaching process. It is not only the techniques of
teaching that will advance, however, but also the subject matter
that will change. All the high-school students will be taught the
fundamentals of computer technology, will become proficient in
binary arithmetic, and will be trained to perfection in the use of the
computer languages that will have developed out of those like the
contemporary "Fortran"[24] (from "formula translation").

Even so, mankind will suffer badly from the disease of boredom,
a disease spreading more widely each year and growing in
intensity. This will have serious mental, emotional, and sociological
consequences, and I dare say that psychiatry[25] will be far and away
the most important medical specialty in 2014. The lucky few who
can be involved in creative work of any sort will be the true elite[26] of
mankind, for they alone will do more than serve a machine.

Indeed, the most somber[27] **speculation** I can make about
A.D. 2014 is that in a society of enforced Leisure,[28] the most glorious
single word in the vocabulary will have become *work*!

---

[21] **goes unchecked** does not slow down or stop

[22] **choked Manhattan** giant, packed city

[23] **machine tenders** people who take care of or fix machines

[24] **the contemporary "Fortran"** a computer programming language written in 1957

[25] **psychiatry** the study of mental health

[26] **elite** special, superior class

[27] **somber** sad, dark, and serious

[28] **of enforced Leisure** with no work for people to do

About the Author:
Isaac Asimov
(1920–1992)

Isaac Asimov was
a scientist and an
award-winning
author of nonfiction
and science fiction.
He often wrote works
speculating on the
role of technology in
the future.

Close Read

Work with a partner.

1. Determine the meanings of your underlined words and phrases.
2. Discuss the question:

   How did Asimov think technology would affect the future?

Understand and Analyze

Respond to the questions. Support your responses with evidence from the text.

1. **Explain** Reread lines 30–40. Explain how people in the future will "withdraw from nature" but will still use and depend on nature.
2. **Give Examples** Reread lines 77–86. Give examples of three ways people will get power for homes and businesses in the future.
3. **Summarize** Reread lines 157–163. Summarize how technology will help the population only in a partially successful way.
4. **Cite Evidence** Why will people "suffer badly from the disease of boredom"?
5. **Focus** What is the focus of the first paragraph? What does this tell you about life in 1964?
6. **Conclude** How would Asimov have felt about life today? Why?

Apply the Skill: Analyze Connections in a Text

List at least five ideas that Asimov presents about the future. Show how the ideas are connected by sorting them into categories.

Category: _______________	Category: _______________	Category: _______________

Share Your Perspective

Discuss these questions in a small group.

1. Which part of the text do you find most interesting? Why?
2. Which prediction do you think was the most accurate? Explain.

Discussion Frames

The most interesting detail was … because …

The most accurate prediction was …

For example, …

Can you give details about …?

Vocabulary: Analyze Connotations L.8.5.C

Words can have multiple layers of meaning. A **denotation** is the specific dictionary definition of a word. A **connotation** is a feeling or association connected to a word. Connotations can be classified as neutral, negative, or positive. When you read, pause to consider the connotations of specific or important words. This can help you better understand an author's intent.

Word	Denotation	Similar Words
unique	unlike others (adj.)	individual (neutral connotation) weird (negative connotation) special (positive connotation)
job	work that needs to be completed (n.)	assignment (neutral connotation) chore (negative connotation) endeavor (positive connotation)

To analyze connotations:

1. Identify a word in a text.
   Ask: *How does this word make me feel? What ideas or emotions are associated with this word?*

2. Think about whether the word's connotation is neutral, negative, or positive. Use a dictionary or a thesaurus if needed.

3. Try replacing the word with a word that has a similar meaning but a different connotation. See how the word changes the meaning of the text.

Apply the Strategy

Read each sentence. Discuss the connotations of the bold words with a partner. Circle the option that has the most neutral connotation.

1. I predict big **changes/advances** in health care.

2. We will **use/exploit** all of the resources.

3. That technology will be **old/outdated**.

4. The jobs will be **repetitive/tedious**.

5. There will be vast **improvements/differences** in how we communicate.

Read Again

Read "Visit to the World's Fair of 2014" again. As you read, circle details from the text that help you respond to these questions:

Which of Asimov's predictions were the most accurate? Which were the least?

Reflect and Respond

Use some of the details you circled to complete this chart.

Most Accurate Predictions	Least Accurate Predictions

Use your chart to respond to the questions: Which of Asimov's predictions were the most accurate? Which were the least?

____

____

____

Discuss Your Response

Share your ideas with the class. Write one new idea you hear.

____

____

____

Respond to the Guiding Question

Write a response to the question:

How accurately can we predict the future?

Use evidence from the text, your discussion, and your life. Use the Discussion Frames to help you. Use the rubric to check your response.

____

____

____

____

CONNECT ACROSS TEXTS

Discuss the Essential Question: How will life be different in the future?

Look at your answer to the Essential Question in the Unit Launch and your notes about life in the future in the Reflect and Respond sections. Discuss: How have your ideas about the Essential Question changed? What changed your ideas?

Then write one new idea you heard in the discussion. How did it affect your opinion?

____

____

Respond to the Essential Question

Write your new response to the Essential Question. Include Academic Vocabulary.

____

____

Assignment: Write a Poem W.8.3.D

A poem is a form of creative writing that may use rhyme, rhythm, and figurative language to express ideas. Poets use line breaks to emphasize particular words, phrases, or ideas. Stanzas, or groups of lines that are separated by spaces, often group related lines.

Poets can use unusual, extra, or incorrect punctuation—or no punctuation at all. They may play around with grammar, fonts, or syllables, or even use their lines to make shapes on the page. Writing poetry is about expressing ideas in an interesting and creative way.

For this assignment, you will write a poem to express your ideas about life in 50 years. Your poem should be at least three stanzas long, and it should:

- focus on one of these topics: home, robots, technology, nature, jobs, or space
- include at least three details about that topic
- use rhyme, rhythm, or figurative language

Explore the Model

Read the poem and identify the topic. Then circle three details about the topic, and underline at least two examples of figurative language.

The International Space Station orbits Earth.

Floating Above

The sky tonight is a blanket of diamonds.
Planets and stars wink at me.
White, blue, red, purple—so many colors.

In 50 years, I will be the one in the sky
winking at everything down below.
My city will float above the earth.

The buildings will be held up
miles and miles above the ground.
How? With lasers, I suppose—
or by some new technology.

I'll zip to work or the grocery store
in speedy, sleek vehicles.
Each trip will be a giant blur.
Zoom! I'm there! Bam! I'm home!

And everything on earth will be
the blanket I see when I look down.
But instead of a rainbow of diamonds,
there will only be dirt.

Plan Your Poem

Choose a topic related to life in 50 years. Complete the chart below with as
many details, descriptive words, and thoughts about figurative language as
you can. Create similes and metaphors that you can include in your poem.
Later, you can choose the best details to include in your writing. For now,
focus on gathering as many ideas as you can.

Poem Planning Chart
Subject: (Your Topic) ________________________________ in 50 Years Poem Title:
Details:
Descriptive Words:
Figurative Language:

Write and Revise

Write Use your chart to help you write your poem. You may need to write more than one draft. Good poets experiment with the order of ideas, types of language, and positions of line breaks until they are happy with how the poem looks and sounds.

Don't forget to give your poem a title. Often, the title of a poem is the most important part because it gives readers a clue about the poem's subject or the poet's feelings.

Experiment with words and ideas. For example:

- Describe a literal detail using a metaphor, simile, or some other type of figurative language.
- Use a thesaurus to find interesting word choices.
- Change the stanzas to group related ideas or create emphasis.

Revise Exchange poems with a partner. Use the checklist to review your partner's work and give feedback. Refer to your partner's feedback as you revise your draft.

☐ Does the poem have a title?

☐ Is the poem about the future?

☐ Does the poem include at least three details about the topic?

☐ Does the poem have an example of figurative language, such as a simile or metaphor?

☐ Does the poem include at least three stanzas?

☐ Are rhymes, rhythm, or figurative language used?

Proofread Check the poem for accidental spelling or punctuation errors. Make edits to correct any errors.

Publish

Share your poem according to your teacher's instructions. Read at least two of your classmates' poems.

TIP

When proofreading poetry, pay attention to capitalization. Do you want every line to be capitalized, lowercase, or a mix of both? Go back through the beginnings of your lines to ensure your personal style is consistent.

Assignment: Present a Poem with Multimedia SL.8.5

For this assignment, you will use your poem in a multimedia presentation for your class. Reread your poem. Think of one or two types of multimedia that you could present as you recite the poem. Multimedia includes:

- video clips
- audio/sound clips
- images of photographs/paintings
- additional text

Plan Your Presentation

Think about the language or imagery in your poem. Brainstorm multiple ways to support your text with an image, a sound, or a prop. Use the chart to plan your presentation.

Multimedia Presentation Plan		
What?	When?	How?
color photograph of the night sky showing the Milky Way	*very beginning through first stanza*	*computer projection*

Prepare Your Presentation

Use your chart to make a checklist of the multimedia you need for your presentation. Search for options. For example, look for more than one photograph of a certain scene. Choose the best match for your words. Things to keep in mind:

- You will need to turn images on and off, start and stop the music, or otherwise present the multimedia as you read your poem.
- It may be helpful to instead create a video that includes all your multimedia to play in the background as you recite your poem.

Practice Your Presentation

Read the checklist below. Then practice your presentation with a partner. Your partner should complete the checklist for you and use it to give you feedback before you deliver your presentation.

☐	Did the poet read the title?
☐	Did the poet speak clearly and loudly?
☐	Did the poet's tone and expression match the poem?
☐	Did the multimedia relate to or support the text in the poem?

Feedback Frames

You could have spoken more clearly in …

Your expression was effective in …

The multimedia supported / did not support …

Present Your Poem with Multimedia

Share your multimedia presentation. Invite your classmates to provide feedback.

Reflect

Discuss the questions with a small group.

1. Which part of your own poem do you like the most? Why?
2. How did you decide what to use in your multimedia presentation?
3. How did your partner's feedback affect your ideas?
4. Which of your classmates' poems are similar? How?

Xiaolin Zheng holds a solar sticker.

Powering the Present and the Future ⌒ 8.5

EXPLORER IN ACTION

Xiaolin Zheng is a nanoscientist, professor, and research team leader.

People need energy to power their devices, homes, and cars. Right now, much of the world is powered by coal and oil. These fossil fuels create pollution and are nonrenewable. How can we get the energy we need while also protecting Earth? National Geographic Explorer Xiaolin Zheng is working toward a solar solution.

Zheng points out that traditional solar panels are expensive to produce, purchase, and install. Her research team has figured out a way to make solar cells into thin, flexible stickers. These solar stickers are just as powerful as traditional solar panels, are far less expensive, and could potentially be used to power just about anything—anywhere. For example, Zheng says a solar sticker could be put on the back of a cell phone to be used as a battery charger.

Will people use solar stickers to power their cell phones, homes, businesses, cars, or even airplanes in the future? Zheng hopes so. She says, "People feel better if they know they're doing something good for the Earth. If you realize the electricity you are using does not generate pollutions and is renewable—I think people will be happier."

▶ **8.2** Watch the video to learn more.

1. How will Xiaolin Zheng's actions today help people in the future?
2. Would you be happier using solar power stickers instead of other power sources? Why or why not?

How Will You Take Action?

Choose one or more of these actions to do.

Personal

Ensure a better future by setting personal goals.

1. Think about what your life will be like in 50 years. What goals do you want to have achieved?
2. Write plans for making these goals happen. For example: *I want to be a veterinarian. I can achieve this goal by getting good grades and going to college.*

School

Encourage your school's future students.

1. Write letters to the students who will be attending your school in 50 years. Encourage the students to study hard, dream big, and believe in themselves.
2. Work in a small group. Make a time capsule box for the letters. Give the time capsule to your teacher.

Local

Give a gift to benefit your community in the future.

1. Work in a small group to research ways to help or improve your community. For example, you could plant a tree or suggest that an organization donate a bench for public use.
2. Find authority figures in your community who can help you make your idea a reality.

Global

Improve the world's environment for people who will live 50 years from now.

1. Track your usage of single-use plastic items every day for one week.
2. Use your research to create a graphic showing which items you used and reusable items that you could have used instead.
3. Share your graphic with the class, and urge everyone to join you in using fewer single-use plastics.

Reflect

1. Reflect on your Take Action project(s). What was successful? What do you wish you had done differently? Why?
2. Reread your response to the Essential Question **How will life be different in the future?** in Connect Across Texts. How did your Take Action project(s) change or add to your response?
3. What will you do differently in your life because of what you learned in this unit?

Academic Vocabulary words are noted in blue.

A

access *(n.)* permission or ability to use

accomplishment *(n.)* something that has been achieved successfully

achieve *(v.)* to successfully reach; to accomplish

acquaintance *(n.)* someone who is known slightly but is not a close friend

acute *(adj.)* sudden and severe

adrenaline *(n.)* a chemical released by the body in times of stress, anger, or fear

advise *(v.)* to give an opinion about what someone should do

alter *(v.)* to change

altruism *(n.)* generous beliefs and acts

analytical *(adj.)* involving logic, reasoning, or careful examination

ancestor *(n.)* family member from the past

appointed *(adj.)* assigned

assemble *(v.)* to gather together

assure *(v.)* to promise in a positive way

automate *(v.)* to use technology or a machine for labor

B

boundary *(n.)* the limit of something; border

broaden *(v.)* to extend or expand

bystander *(n.)* one who does not participate

C

capable *(adj.)* having the potential for

channel *(v.)* to direct towards

churned up *(adj.)* agitated and wavy

civilization *(n.)* an organized, functioning society

collaborative *(adj.)* involving the effort of two or more people working together

collapse *(v.)* to fall down suddenly and dramatically

colleague *(n.)* a co-worker or collaborator

collective *(adj.)* shared or done together by a group

colony *(n.)* a home or society established in a new place

conceivable *(adj.)* imaginable; possible

concentrate *(v.)* to focus one's attention on a particular activity

confident *(adj.)* sure; certain

conform *(v.)* to act in the same way as others

connectedness *(n.)* a feeling of belonging or connection with others

conscientious *(adj.)* careful about doing something correctly

consequence *(n.)* importance; significance

consistent *(adj.)* unchanging; remaining the same over time

construct *(v.)* to build

contemplate *(v.)* to think seriously and carefully about something

convincing *(adj.)* believable

crafted *(adj.)* made or created

creative *(adj.)* having imaginative or original ideas

curiosity *(n.)* a desire to know or learn something

D

debate *(n.)* a discussion that considers different views on a question

decaying *(adj.)* decreasing in health, strength, or power

decipher *(v.)* to figure out or understand

demonstrate *(v.)* to prove something through an action; to show clearly

deserted *(adj.)* abandoned; empty of people

destination *(n.)* a location where someone or something is going

device *(n.)* a tool that people use to do tasks

devote *(v.)* to give all or a lot of one's time or resources

digital *(adj.)* electronic

dilemma *(n.)* a problem involving a difficult choice

diminished *(adj.)* smaller or fewer

displaced *(adj.)* removed from something, such as a home or job

disruption *(n.)* something causing interruption or disorder

distraction *(n.)* something that causes a loss in focus or attention

diverge *(v.)* to split into two or more new directions

domain *(n.)* an area or field of knowledge

E

economic *(adj.)* related to money

encounter *(v.)* to meet or experience unexpectedly

endure *(v.)* to last; to survive

enhance *(v.)* to increase or improve

entangled *(adj.)* involved in difficulties from which it is hard to escape

eventually *(adv.)* finally; ultimately

exhilaration *(n.)* excitement

expertise *(n.)* specialized skills and mastery

external *(adj.)* existing outside something

F

flexibility *(n.)* the ability to easily change or try new things

frail *(adj.)* weak or easily hurt

function *(v.)* to act or perform

fundamentally *(adv.)* at a very basic level

G

generation *(n.)* a group of people born and living at approximately the same time

genius *(n.)* a person who is exceptionally smart or creative

global *(adj)* relating to the whole world

globe *(n.)* the world

gratification *(n.)* pleasure; satisfaction

grim *(adj.)* not hopeful or encouraging

grip *(v.)* to hold tightly onto

H

harrowing *(adj.)* difficult and upsetting

hesitation *(n.)* the act of pausing before moving or speaking

horizon *(n.)* the area in the distance where sky meets land or water

humble *(adj.)* simple; of low rank

hurtle *(v.)* to move quickly and uncontrollably

I

identity *(n.)* the set of qualities that make up an individual; a person's characteristics

immense *(adj.)* very great in size or amount

implement *(v.)* to put a decision or plan into effect

implication *(n.)* a consequence or effect

inclined *(adj.)* likely to do something

individual *(n.)* one person

individuality *(n.)* the state of being different from others; uniqueness

inequality *(n.)* a difference in amount; unevenness

influence *(v.)* to affect another's feelings or actions

infrastructure *(n.)* the basic resources needed for a community

inherent *(adj.)* inborn; belonging by nature

innovation *(n.)* a new way of doing something or a new idea

innovator *(n.)* a person who comes up with new ideas, methods, or devices

interactive *(adj.)* requiring active involvement

intervene *(v.)* to interrupt or come between

intimate *(adj.)* closely connected; familiar; close

investigation *(n.)* a research study

isolation *(n.)* the state of being alone

J

judgment *(n.)* reasoning; sense

L

lament *(v.)* to feel or express sadness or regret

literacy *(n.)* the ability to read and write

M

maintain *(v.)* to continue an existing action, feeling, or state

majority *(n.)* more than half of a group of people

media *(n.)* the internet, newspapers, magazines, television, and other means of communication that reach and influence people

mediocre *(adj.)* not very good; of moderate quality

mental *(adj.)* relating to the mind or brain

mode *(n.)* a way; a style

momentum *(n.)* the speed of movement

monsoon *(n.)* a rainy season

moral *(adj.)* ethical and right

motivate *(v.)* to encourage in a positive way

N

nervous system *(n.)* a body system that sends and receives signals about feelings and movements

network *(n.)* an interconnected system of things or people

norm *(n.)* usual; standard

normative *(adj.)* following common standards and rules

novel *(adj.)* new

O

obsolete *(adj.)* no longer used

obvious *(adj.)* easily seen or understood

optimism *(n.)* the belief that good things will happen

P

peculiar *(adj.)* odd or unusual

peer *(adj.)* relating to someone the same age or grade, or in a shared group

perceptual *(adj.)* relating to the senses

perseverance *(n.)* persistence through difficulties or delayed success

persist *(v.)* to keep existing despite hardship

phenomenon *(n.)* an observable event

physically *(adv.)* related to or involving the body

pivotal *(adj.)* extremely important

practical *(adj.)* likely to be useful or successful

precisely *(adv.)* exactly; strictly

prediction *(n.)* a statement about what might happen in the future

pressure *(n.)* stress

prestige *(n.)* high regard

principle *(n.)* a natural law, rule, or belief that influences actions and thoughts

pro *(n.)* an expert; a professional

procrastinate *(v.)* to put off

procrastination *(n.)* the act of delaying or postponing something

produce *(v.)* to make

promote *(v.)* to support or actively encourage

psychologist *(n.)* an expert in the science of the human mind

pursue *(v.)* to seek; to perform

pushy *(adj.)* unpleasantly assertive and overly ambitious

Q

quest *(n.)* a mission; an expedition

R

reflect *(v.)* to show or express

regulation *(n.)* the act of controlling something

reinforce *(v.)* to strengthen or support

renewable *(adj.)* capable of being replaced

resilient *(adj.)* able to survive or recover from difficult conditions

restrict *(v.)* to stop or limit

revise *(v.)* to correct or improve

rhetorical *(adj.)* related to speaking or writing

rival *(n.)* a person or team you compete against

role *(n.)* the part that someone or something has in a situation

route *(n.)* a way; a path

S

savor *(v.)* to enjoy or appreciate fully

scan *(v.)* to quickly look at or across something

scholar *(n.)* a highly educated person

sequence *(n.)* the order in which events happen

span *(v.)* to extend across

specific *(adj.)* individual; particular

speculation *(n.)* a prediction or guess about something

stimulate *(v.)* to activate

stressor *(n.)* a thing that causes stress

sufficient *(adj.)* enough to meet basic needs; adequate

suitable *(adj.)* proper; appropriate

survival *(n.)* the state of staying alive

survive *(v.)* to remain alive

survivor *(n.)* one who lives through a difficult time or event

T

team *(n.)* a group of players on one side of a competition

tempt *(v.)* to persuade someone to do something that is unwise

tendency *(n.)* a quality that makes something likely to happen

throb *(v.)* to pound with pain

trend *(n.)* something that is becoming more common or popular

U

unconscious *(adj.)* hidden or unknown to oneself

unexecuted *(adj.)* not performed or carried out

uniform *(adj.)* the same; not varying

urban sprawl *(n.)* the spreading of people and buildings outside a city

V

value *(n.)* belief about what is important

variation *(n.)* differences among members of a species or group

viable *(adj.)* capable of growing and living

victory *(n.)* a win

virtual *(adj.)* created or happening in a computer or an online world

vital *(adj.)* very important or necessary

visualize *(v.)* to imagine; to form an image in one's mind

visually *(adv.)* in a way that relates to seeing or sight

volunteer *(n.)* a person who willingly works without pay

W

well-rounded *(adj.)* balanced in activities and experiences

A

Account A description of facts, conditions, or events. *See also* Autobiographical account, Scientific account

Adventure story A fiction story that tells about events that are dangerous or exciting. Adventure stories are often fast-paced, have realistic details, include a plot that describes one character having a strong conflict with nature or other characters, and focus on suspense. *See also* Suspense

Allegory A story with a message. Usually, the message is not stated directly and the author uses symbols to help the reader determine the message. *See also* Symbol

Allusion Literary language that hints at something outside the text. It draws on knowledge that many people are likely to share. Allusions often come from literature, history, or popular culture.

Analogy Language that uses a comparison or familiar idea to explain a more complex or unfamiliar idea.

Anecdote A short, entertaining, true story about something that really happened. Writers use anecdotes to give more information about a person, an event, or an idea.

Argument A type of writing or speaking in which the author tries to convince readers that a particular viewpoint is correct. Arguments include a claim that is supported by reasons and evidence. *See also* Argumentative Essay; Claim; Evidence; Reason

Argumentative Essay An essay that expresses a clear opinion and gives evidence to support it. The purpose is to persuade an audience to agree with the writer's opinion. These essays are often referred to as *argument essays*. *See also* Evidence; Reason

Article A short piece of nonfiction writing that gives facts and information on a specific topic. Articles appear in newspapers and magazines. *See also* Informative article; Nonfiction; Opinion article; Science article

Autobiographical account An account of a person's life, or events from that person's life, told from the writer's point of view.

Autobiography The story of a person's life, written by that person. *See also* Autobiographical account; Personal narrative

B

Biography The story of a person's life, written by another person.

C

Caption Text that gives information about something shown visually, such as a photograph. Captions are usually just a few sentences.

Character A person, an animal, or an imaginary creature in a work of fiction. Authors develop characters by showing how the characters grow and change in response to events in the plot. *See also* Characterization; Character traits

Characterization The way a writer creates and develops a character. Writers use a variety of ways to bring a character to life: through descriptions of the character's appearance, thoughts, feelings, and actions; through the character's words; and through the words or thoughts of other characters. *See also* Character; Character traits

Character traits The special qualities of personality that writers give their characters. Character traits are revealed through a character's thoughts, words, and actions, and determine how a character responds to events in a story. *See also* Character; Characterization

Claim A statement that clearly identifies an author's ideas or opinion. This is also known as the *thesis*. *See also* Argument; Counterargument; Evidence; Reason

Climax The turning point or most important event in a plot. The climax is often the most exciting event in the story.

Conflict The main problem faced by a character in a story or play. The character may be involved in a struggle against nature, another character, or society. The struggle may also be between two elements in the character's mind. *See also* Rising Action

Connotation The implied meaning of a word or phrase, or what the word makes the readers think and feel. *See also* Denotation

Counterargument The opinion of people who disagree with a claim.

D

Debate An organized argument between two teams in which each side argues either for or against a topic or in favor of one opinion. The purpose of a debate is to persuade the audience to agree with a particular point of view.

Denotation The dictionary meaning of a word or phrase, or literal meaning. *See also* Connotation

Diagram A drawing that shows how something looks, how it works, or how it is structured.

Dialogue What characters say to each other. Writers use dialogue to develop characters, move the plot forward, and add interest. In most writing, dialogue is set off by quotation marks; in scripts, however, dialogue appears without quotation marks. *See also* Dialogue Tag

Dialogue Tag An indicator of who is being quoted in text.

Drama A kind of writing in which a plot unfolds in the words and actions of characters performed by actors. *See also* Play; Skit

E

Epilogue A section or speech at the end of a book, story, or work of drama that functions as a conclusion or comment to what has occurred.

Essay A short piece of nonfiction that discusses a single topic. Its purpose may be to inform, entertain, or persuade. *See also* Argumentative essay; Exposition essay; Informational essay; Nonfiction; Problem-Solution essay; Topic

Evidence Information that support a claim. Through facts, examples, and statements from experts. *See also* Argument; Claim; Reason

Excerpt A part taken out of a longer text.

Exposition The section of a text that introduces the main characters and the setting of the story.

Exposition essay A short piece of nonfiction in which the writer covers a topic in depth in order to teach readers about it. These essays present facts, and opinions based on facts, about an important topic. Language in an exposition essay is often formal and may include technical and scientific terms.

F

Fable A very short story that gives advice on how to live. Many fables have animals instead of humans as characters. Fables often end with a short, witty statement of their lesson. *See also* Fiction

Falling action The actions and events in a plot that happen after the climax. Usually, the major problem is solved in some way, so the remaining events lead to the conclusion of the story.

Fiction Narrative writing about imaginary people, places, things, or events. *See also* Adventure story; Historical fiction; Myth; Novel; Realistic fiction; Short story

Figurative language The use of language to express an idea in a way that is different from its common or literal meaning. *See also* Hyperbole; Idiom; Imagery; Literature; Metaphor; Personification; Poetry; Simile; Symbol

First-person point of view A point of view in which one of the characters tells the story. The narrator doesn't know the thoughts and feelings of the other characters. *See also* Narrator; Point of view; Third-person point of view

Flashback The part of a story that takes place in an earlier time than the rest of the story.

Form The physical structure of a poem, such as the length of the lines and the rhymes, the rhythms, and the repetitions within. *See also* Poem

Free verse Poetry that does not use regular rhyme or rhythm. *See also* Poetry; Rhyme; Rhythm

G

Genre A type or class of literary works grouped according to form, style, and/or topic. Major genres include fictional narrative prose (such as short stories and most novels), nonfiction narrative prose (such as autobiographies, accounts, and biographies), drama, poetry, and the essay. *See also* Essay; Fiction; Literature; Nonfiction; Poetry

Graphic A piece of text that show information visually. *See also* Infographic

H

Historical fiction Fiction based on events that actually happened or on people who actually lived. However, many of the characters, events, and details are created by the author. It may be written from the point of view of a "real" or an imaginary character, and it usually includes invented dialogue. *See also* Fiction

How-to article An article that explains how to do something. The article contains a list of materials and step-by-step instructions.

Hyperbole Figurative language that exaggerates, often to the point of being funny, to emphasize something. *See also* Figurative language

I

Idiom A phrase or expression that means something different from its dictionary meaning. Idioms cannot be understood literally word for word because an idiom's meaning is not the same as that of the individual words that make it up.

Imagery The use of strong, descriptive details that help readers see or imagine a scene in their minds. Imagery can help the reader imagine how people, places, and things look, sound, taste, smell, and feel. It can also make the reader think about emotions and ideas that commonly go with certain sensations. Because imagery appeals to the senses, it is sometimes called *sensory language*. *See also* Figurative language; Sensory details; Symbol

Infographic A type of graphic that presents information visually with a small amount of text in the form of labels and captions. *See also* Captions; Labels

Informative article An article that presents information in a straightforward manner, without judgment or personal opinion. The author's purpose is to inform.

Informational essay A type of essay in which a writer examines a topic. The writer selects, organizes, and analyzes information to inform the readers about the topic.

Informational report Writing that summarizes key information from an interview, a survey, or a scientific study.

Inner monologue The "conversation" that occurs in a character's mind that explains more about the feelings, motives, personality, or actions of that character.

Interview A discussion between two or more people in which questions are asked and answered so that the interviewer can get information. During an interview, someone is usually asked questions about themselves, an area of expertise, or something they are interested in.

J

Journalism The work of gathering and reporting news for newspapers, magazines, radio, television, and other media. *See also* News feature

L

Label A few words that tell readers about what something is. It often has an arrow pointing to what is being labeled.

Letter A written message that is commonly sent between family members, friends, or acquaintances or as a formal exchange with a business or government organization. Letters include a greeting and closing, or sign-off, which appears just before the letter writer's name.

Literature Works written as prose or poetry. *See also* Poetry; Prose

M

Map A picture representation of an area that shows its physical features, such as mountains, streets, and rivers.

Memoir A type of literary nonfiction in which the author writes about experiences from their own lives and often tells what these experiences meant to them. A first-person point of view is used to describe these experiences. Unlike autobiographies, memoirs do not necessarily cover all of the important events in the author's life. *See also* Autobiography, First-person point of view

Metaphor A type of figurative language that compares two unlike things by saying that one thing is the other thing. A metaphor does not use the words *like* or *as* in the comparison. Instead, metaphors often use *be* verbs, such as *is, are, was,* or *were. See also* Figurative language; Simile; Symbol

Monologue A long speech in a drama.

Mood The overall feeling or atmosphere a writer creates in a piece of writing. *See also* Tone

N

Narrative Writing that tells about real or imagined events using descriptive details. Narrative writing includes nonfiction works such as accounts, autobiographies, and biographies, as well as fictional works such as short stories, novels, and plays. *See also* Account; Autobiography; Biography; Fiction; Narrator; Nonfiction; Personal narrative; Play; Plot; Short Story; Story

Narrator Someone who gives an account of events. In fiction, the narrator is the teller of a story. Narrators differ in how much they participate in a story's events. In a first-person narrative, the narrator is the "I" telling the story. In a third-person narrative, the narrator is not directly involved in the events and refers to characters by name or as *he, she, it,* or *they*. Narrators also differ in how much they know and how much they can be trusted by the reader. *See also* Character; Point of view

News feature A nonfiction article that gives facts about real people and events. A news feature brings important current information to an audience that wants to be informed about a topic. It should begin with the basic details of the event: who, what, where, when, why, and how. The rest digs deeper with examples and details that bring that basic information to life for the audience. These features are also called *news articles. See also* Article; Journalism; Nonfiction

Nonfiction Written works that tell about real events and people and give factual Information. *See also* Autobiography; Biography; Essay; Personal narrative; Report

Novel A long, fictional narrative. Novels are the length of books and are often broken into chapters. *See also* Character; Fiction; Plot; Prose; Setting; Short story

Nuance A small distinction in meaning, opinion, or attitude in word meanings. A writer uses nuance to create a tone or mood. This is also referred to as *shades of meaning*.

O

Ode A type of poem that celebrates or expresses thoughts and feelings about people or objects. Some odes have distinct rhyming patterns, and some are even written with a specific number of syllables in each line. *See also* Poem

Onomatopoeia The use of words that name the sounds they refer to or describe.

Op-ed Op-ed, short for "opposite the editorial page," is a feature article that expresses the opinion of the author that is not necessarily connected to the newspaper or magazine in which it is printed.

Opinion article Writing in which the author argues his or her viewpoint and tries to convince the reader to think or do something.

Opinion piece Writing in which the writer states their opinion or beliefs about a specific topic and uses facts, studies, and experts' opinions to persuade readers to agree. *See also* Op-ed; Opinion article

Overstatement A type of verbal irony in which the speaker exaggerates a situation.

P

Panel discussion A discussion in which a group of experts discusses a topic. The purpose of a panel discussion is to hear multiple views on a topic to deepen understanding.

Personal narrative A true account of a certain event or set of events in a person's life, written by that person. *See also* Account; Autobiography; Memoir

Personification A type of figurative language that gives human qualities to animals, objects, and ideas. *See also* Figurative language

Pie chart A type of graph in which a circle is divided into sections that represent a portion of the whole.

Play A work of drama, especially one written to be performed on a stage for an audience. *See also* Drama

Plot The sequence of events and situations in a story or play. Plot is usually divided into five main parts: *exposition, rising action* (or *conflict*), *climax, falling action,* and *resolution. See also* Climax; Conflict; Drama; Exposition; Falling action; Fiction; Resolution; Rising action; Story

Poem A form of literary expression written in lines that can be broken (or ended) where the poet chooses to emphasize words or ideas to create rhyme or rhythm. Poems don't always strictly follow grammatical rules. Poems are written to share an experience or make the reader feel a strong emotion. *See also* Connotation; Figurative language; Rhyme; Rhythm

Poetry A form of literary expression that uses words and sounds to engage reader's senses. Poetry is writing set on short lines, often with an obvious rhythm and rhyme. *See also* Connotation; Figurative language; Poem; Rhyme; Rhythm

Point of view The perspective from which the events of a story are told, or narrated. *See also* First-person point of view; Narrator; Third-person point of view

Problem-solution essay A type of essay that explains the importance of an issue. The essay describes the problem and solution with facts, details, and examples and describes the impact of the proposed solution.

Prose A form of writing in which the rhythm is less regular than that of poetry and more like that of ordinary speech. *See also* Poetry; Rhythm

Purpose An author's reason for writing. Most authors write to share personal thoughts or experiences, entertain, explain, inform, describe, or persuade.

R

Realistic fiction Fiction that tells about events that could happen in real life. It includes realistic characters, settings, and plot events. *See also* Fiction

Reason A logical explanation that connects a piece of evidence to a writer or speaker's claim and explains the author's thinking. *See also* Argument; Claim; Evidence

Repetition The repeating of individual vowels and consonants, syllables, words, phrases, lines, or groups of lines. Repetition can be used because it sounds pleasant, to emphasize certain words, or to help tie the parts of a text into one structure. *See also* Poetry; Rhyme

Report A usually short piece of nonfiction writing on a particular topic. It differs from an essay in that it normally states only facts and does not directly express the writer's opinions. *See also* Essay; Informational report; Nonfiction; Topic

Resolution The part of a plot that provides details that show how the conflict of a story is solved.

Rhyme The repetition of ending sounds in different words. Rhymes usually come at the end of lines of poems, but they may also occur within a line. *See also* Poem; Poetry; Repetition

Rhythm The natural rise and fall, or "beat," of language. Rhythm is present in all language, but it is most obvious in poetry. *See also* Poetry; Prose

Rising action The part of a plot that presents actions or events that lead to the climax. These events develop the main character and introduce the conflict. *See also* Conflict

S

Sarcasm A type of verbal irony in which the speaker makes an ironic statement with the intention of insulting or making fun of someone (including oneself) or something.

Satire A type of writing in which writers use humor by presenting ideas in unexcepted ways. Writers use satire to comment or criticize a subject or society in a humorous way.

Scene A section of text in which there is action and sometimes dialogue. A scene has a beginning, middle, and end and changes when the settings changes, the action ends, or characters arrive or depart.

Science article An article that gives information about a topic having to do with the natural world. It often includes research results, or what scientists learn from what they study. Science articles are often printed in science journals.

Science fiction A genre of fiction writing that involves story elements that don't exist in the everyday world. It tells a made-up story that is usually set in the future and revolves around some aspect of science and technology, such as space travel, time travel, robots, or aliens invading Earth.

Scientific account Writing in which the author explains scientific ideas to readers who may not be professional scientists.

Script Written directions for dramas, including stage plays and radio plays, that include a list of characters, stage directions, dialogue, and a sequence of scenes. *See also* Dialogue; Stage directions

Sensory details Details that help readers see, feel, hear, smell, and taste what is happening in a text.

Setting The time and location in which the events of a story occur.

Short story A brief, fictional narrative. Like the novel, it organizes the action, thought, and dialogue of its characters into a plot. But it tends to focus on fewer characters and to center on a single event. *See also* Character; Fiction; Novel; Plot; Story

Sidebar A boxed text or image of a main text. Writers sometimes include a sidebar to provide additional information about something mentioned in a text. Sidebars can include text features such as bolded text, headings, and bullets.

Simile A type of figurative language that uses the words *like* or *as* to compare two things. *See also* Figurative language; Metaphor

Skit A short, informal performance that is usually performed by two or more actors. Skits educate, inform, or amuse the audience.

Speech A message on a specific topic that is spoken before an audience.

Stage directions Instructions that tell the actors in a drama how to speak and what gestures to use.

Stanza A group of lines that forms a section of a poem and has the same pattern as other sections of the same poem. In printed poems, stanzas are separated from each other by a space. *See also* Poem

Statistic Numerical data about a topic that can be used as evidence to support a claim. *See also* Claim; Evidence

Story A series of events (actual or imaginary) that can be selected and arranged in a certain order to form a narrative or dramatic plot. *See also* Drama; Narrative; Plot

Stream of consciousness A narrative point of view that follows one character's thoughts as they move from subject to subject. This style of narrative places readers inside the character's head, allowing them to follow the character's thoughts. *See also* Narrative; Point of view

Structure The physical form of a type of writing.

Style The way a writer uses language to express the feelings or thoughts they want to convey. A writer's style results from their choices of vocabulary, sentence structure and variety, imagery, figurative language, rhythm, repetition, and other resources.

Subtitle The translated words that appear in videos.

Suspense A growing sense of curiosity that readers feel about how a story will end.

Symbol A word or phrase that stands for something else, often using figurative language to communicate meaning. *See also* Figurative language

T

Theme An idea that repeats throughout the text and suggests a message the author wants to communicate. Writers sometimes state the theme directly, but usually the reader needs to infer the theme. *See also* Topic

Timeline A graphic representation of time, such as a chronological arrangement of events in the order of their occurrence or a schedule for when processes will be carried out.

Third-person point of view A point of view in which the story is told by someone who is not in the story. The narrator shares the thoughts and feelings of more than one character. *See also* First-person point of view; Narrator; Point of view

Tone A writer's or speaker's attitude toward his or her topic or subject. A writer's tone may be positive, negative, or neutral. The words the writer chooses, the sentence structure, and the overall pattern of words convey the intended tone. *See also* Connotation; Figurative language; Literature; Mood; Rhythm; Topic

Topic What or who is being discussed in a piece of writing; the subject of the piece. *See also* Theme

U

Understatement A type of verbal irony in which the speaker implies or says that something is less important than it really is.

V

Verbal irony Language in which the literal meaning of the words someone says is different from (and often the opposite of) what the person actually means. *See also* Overstatement, Understatement, Sarcasm

Viewpoint A character's perspective (what the character sees, feels, and thinks) in a work of fiction. Details that help a reader understand a character's point of view include descriptions of the characters and their feelings, and dialogue. *See also* Point of view

P notes picture. *Ptg* notes painting.

A

active voice, 343

affixes, 71

allusions, 63, 70

analogies, 63, 70

argumentative essay, 158–161. *See also* counterargument

arguments, 171, 178

ask questions, 277, 286

author's purpose, 293, 302

author's viewpoint, 334, 342

C

categorize, 145

cause-and-effect relationships, 347

characters, 37, 46

cite text evidence, 23, 30

claims, 171, 178

cohesive devices, 391, 398

collaborative discussions, 110–111

commas, 179

compare, 225, 230

comprehension, monitor, 185, 192

concluding sentence, 147, 154

conditional mood, 303, 375

conditionals, 303

connections, 417, 428. *See also* text-to-self connections, text-to-text connections

connotations, 429

context clues, 17

contrast, 225,230

counterargument, 378–381

cues, visual, 403

D

dashes, 179

debates, 382–383

denotations, 429

details, supporting, 147, 154

dialogue, 349, 358

dictionary, 193

E

ellipses, 261

essay. *See* argumentative essay, problem-solution essay

evidence, 171, 178. *See also* text evidence

F

facial expressions, interpreting, 75

figurative language, 141, 411. *See also* personification, hyperbole, metaphors, similes

figure of speech. *See* figurative language

form, 225, 230

G

gerunds, 155

Greek word parts, 103, 127, 245

H

humor, analyze, 133, 140

hyperbole, 141

I

imperative mood, 287, 375

indicative mood, 187, 375

inferences, 405

infinitives, 31

information:
  categorize, 145
  prioritize, 197

informational reports, 106–109

inner monologue, 349, 358

interrogative mood, 287

interviews, 326–327

irony, 359

L

Latin word parts, 103, 127, 245

M

metaphors, 411

monitor comprehension, 185, 190

M

monologue, 349, 358

mood, 307

mood, verb, 287. *See also* conditional mood, imperative mood, indicative mood, interrogative mood

multimedia presentations, 269–269, 436–437

N

narrative. *See* personal narrative

O

omissions, 261

overstatement, 359

P

paragraph, analyze, 147, 154

paraphrase, 119, 126

participles, 399. *See also* past participles, present participles

passive voice, 343

past participles, 399

pause to check understanding, 35

performance, 216–217

personal narrative, 322–325

personification, 141

perspectives, categorize, 145

plays, 212–217

plot, 37, 46

poems, 225, 230, 432–435

predict, 7, 16

prefixes, 71, 127

presentations, 54–55, 268–269, 436–437

present participles, 399

preview, 7, 16

prioritize information, 197

problem-solution essay, 264–267

problem-solution structure, 237, 244

punctuation, 179. *See also* commas, dashes

purpose, author's, 293, 302

P notes picture. *Ptg* notes painting.

Text Credits

UNIT 1

What's Your Group ID? by Kathiann Kowalski from Current Health 2, November 2001 issue. Copyright © 2001 by Scholastic Inc. Reprinted by permission of Scholastic Inc.

Asch Conformity Experiments. Cherry, Kendra. ©Dot Dash. Retrieved from https://www.verywellfamily.com/competition-among-kids-pros-and-cons-4177958.

All Summer In a Day by Bradbury, Ray. The Magazine of Fantasy. Reprinted by permission of Don Congdon Associates, Inc. © 1954, renewed 1982 Ray Bradbury.

UNIT 2

From A Poet's Lament by Jum'a bin 'Adil al-Rumaythí (translated into English). © Cengage Learning 2022.

The Art of Poetry No. 83, Billy Collins by The Paris Review Issue No. 159, 2001. Copyright © 2001 by The Paris Review, used by permission of The Wylie Agency LLC.

From Leonardo Da Vinci by Walter Isaacson. Copyright © 2017 by Walter Isaacson. Reprinted with the permission of SSA, a division of Simon & Schuster, Inc. All rights reserved.

How Creativity Powers Science by Jennifer Cutraro. From Science News for Students, May 24, 2012. Used with permission.

UNIT 3

What's Technology Got to Do with the Economy? by Economy Editorial Team. Economy, 18 Nov. 2018, www.ecnmy.org/engage/whats-technology-got-economy/.

Obituary: The Book chapter 222 by Katrina Onstad. Publisher: Nelson; iLit series. Reprinted with permission by Fletcher and Company.

How Not to be Alone by Jonathan Safran Foer from The New York Times. © 2013 The New York Times Company. All rights reserved. Used under license.

UNIT 4

Do Plants Feel Stress? by By John Staughton from ABC Science. https://www.scienceabc.com/nature/do-plants-feel-stress.html.

Humor Helps by Carolyn J. Gard from Current Health 2, April/May 1998 issue.

Copyright © 1998 by Scholastic Inc. Reprinted by permission of Scholastic Inc.

Bearing Up by Matt Hughes. Scholastic Scope, Scholastic Inc., scope.scholastic.com/issues/2017-18/020118/Bearing-Up.html.

UNIT 5

The Road Not Taken by Robert Frost.

Old Story by Vinicius De Moraes. Retrieved from www.viniciusdemoraes.com.br/pt-br/poesia/livros/o-caminho-para-distancia. Reprinted with permission from VM Enterprises, Inc.

Excerpt(s) From Atomic Habits: An Easy & Proven Way To Build Good Habits & Break Bad Ones by James Clear, Copyright © 2018 By James Clear. Used By Permission Of Avery, An Imprint Of Penguin Publishing Group, A Division Of Penguin Random House LLC. All rights reserved.

From Atomic Habits by James Clear, published by Random House Business. Copyright © James Clear, 2018. Reprinted by permission of The Random House Group Limited.

Hive Mind: the world's leading expert on bee behavior discovers the secrets of decision-making in a swarm by Carl Zimmer. Smithsonian, vol. 42, no. 11, Mar. 2012. Reprinted by permission of the author.

UNIT 6

The Daring Cave Divers Who Saved the Thai Soccer Team by Joel K. Bourne, Jr. from Nationalgeographic.com, March 14, 2019.

From Why We Act: Turning Bystanders Into Moral Rebels by Catherine A. Sanderson, published by Harvard University Press. Copyright © 2020 by Catherine A. Sanderson. All rights reserved.

What is the Bystander Effect by Catherine A. Sanderson. Reprinted by permission of HarperCollins Publishers Ltd. © 2020 Catherine A. Sanderson.

A Friend's Gift. In Asian myths. Lagbao, F. Y. (1997). Logan, IA: Perfection Learning.

UNIT 7

The Pros and Cons of Tenn Competition by Kathryn Rogers/Cengage Learning.

From Goldfish: A Novel by Nat Luurtsema Copyright © 2016. Reprinted By Permission Of Feiwel & Friends. All rights reserved.

From Girl Out of Water by Nat Luurtsema. Cover illustration © 2018 Agathe Sorlet Text © 2016 Nat Luurtsema. Reproduced by permission of Walker Books Ltd London SE11 5HJ www.walker.co.uk.

The Grand Slam by Tatyana McFadden and Tom Walker. Tatyana McFadden: Ya Soma! Moments from My Life. Inspired Edge Publications, 2016.

UNIT 8

Future Timeline. Retrieved from https://www.futuretimeline.net/23rdcentury/2200-2249.htm#trends-in-working-hours-2050-2100-2200-future-timeline. Reprinted by permission of www.FutureTimeline.net.

A House Called Tomorrow by Alberto Ríos. Copyright © 2018 by Alberto Ríos. Used with the permission of the author. Retrieved from https://poets.org/poem/house-called-tomorrow.

Letter to Someone Living Fifty Years from Now by Matthew Olzmann. Copyright © 2017 by Matthew Olzmann. Originally published in Poem-a-Day on April 14, 2017, by the Academy of American Poets. Retrieved from https://poets.org/poem/letter-someone-living-fifty-years-now. Reprinted with permission of the author.

Visit to the World's Fair of 2014. Copyright © 1964 Isaac Asimov. Published by The New York Times.

Illustrator Credits

UNIT 1 All Summer in a Day, Igor Morski.

UNIT 4 Bearing Up, Paulo Domeniconi.

UNIT 6 A Friend's Gift, Xuan Loc Xuan.

UNIT 7 Goldfish, Gustavo Hildebrand Ferrara.

UNIT 8 A House Called Tomorrow, Helena Perez Garcia.

Photographic Credits

Cover ©Phillip Chang/Solent News

UNIT 1

2–3 ©powerofforever/E+/Getty Images. 8–9 ©Mariana Bazo/Reuters. 11 ©Martin Parr/Magnum Photos. 12–13 ©Alstair Berg/DigitalVision/Getty Images. 14 ©Robert Harding Picture Library/National Geographic Image Collection. 19 ©Karina Mansfield/Moment/Getty Images. 20–21 ©Matt Moyer/National

Geographic Image Collection. 21 (br) ©Ami Vitale/National Geographic Image Collection. 25 ©EcoView/Adobe Stock. 29 © Klaus Vedfelt/DigitalVision/Getty Images. 33 ©SDI Productions/E+/Getty Images. 33 ©Paul Sutherland/National Geographic Image Collection. 45 ©Ulf Andersen/Hulton Archive/Getty images. 56 (t) ©Courtesy of Ingeborg Mehus, (b)©Ingi Mehus/Hamas Kashash.

UNIT 2

58–59 ©Andy Buchanan/AFP/Getty Images. 64–65 ©Matthieu Paley. 66–67 ©Karen Hollingsworth, karenhollingsworth.com. 69 (t) ©Zulkefli Sarji/EyeEm/Getty Images, (br) ©Rob Kim/Stringer/Getty Images. 73 ©SDI Productions/E+/Getty Images. 74 ©Dina Litovsky/National Geographic Image Collection. 78–79 ©Tino Soriano/National Geographic Image Collection. 80 ©RICCARDO VECCHIO/National Geographic Image Collection. 82–83 ©RMN-Grand Palais/Art Resource, NY. 85 ©Paolo Woods and Gabriele Galimberti/National Geographic Image Collection. 89 ©API/Getty Images. 90–91 ©National Geographic Image Collection. 94–95 ©Spencer Lowell. 97 ©Spencer Lowell. 100–01 © Mark Peterson/Redux. 106 ©Douglas Kirkland/Corbis Premium Historical/Getty Images. 112 (t) ©Asher Jay/National Geographic Image Collection, (cl) ©Asher Jay/National Geographic Image Collection.

UNIT 3

114–15 ©Mario Cucinella Architects. 120–21 ©Visual China Group/Getty Images. 122–23 ©Ciril Jazbec/National Geographic Image Collection. 124–25 ©Teera Konakan/Moment/Getty Images. 129 ©Zephyr_p/Shutterstock.com. 130–31 ©Johan Scherft. 131 ©Johan Scherft. 134–35 ©Steve McCurry/Magnum Photos. 136–37 ©Steve McCurry/Magnum Photos. 138 ©Pulsar Imagens/Alamy. 139 © Photograph by Joanna Haughton, https://photobyjoh.com. 143 ©praetorianphoto/E+/Getty Images. 144–45 ©MR.Cole_Photographer/Moment/Getty Images. 148–49 ©MR.Cole_Photographer/Moment/Getty Images. 151 ©Danilo Dungo. 152 ©Annie Griffiths/National Geographic Image Collection. 158 ©AleksandarNakic/E+/Getty Images. 164 (t) ©Thierry Falise/LightRocket/Getty Images, (cl) ©Kat Keene Hogue/National Geographic Image Collection.

UNIT 4

166-67 ©Lucas Foglia. 172–73 ©Thomas Marent/Minden Pictures. 174–75 ©Frans Lanting/National Geographic Image Collection. 176 ©Scenics & Science/Alamy. 181 ©www.sierralara.com/Moment/Getty Images. 182–83 ©Annie Griffiths/National Geographic Image Collection. 182 ©ttsz/iStock/Getty Images. 186–87 ©Ami Vitale/Getty Image News. 188–89 ©Olesia Bilkei/Shutterstock. 195 ©Tom Wang/Shutterstock. 196–97 ©David Cannon/David Cannon Collection/Getty Images. 207 ©Courtesy of Matt Hughes, photo by Liza Groen Trombi. 218 ©Courtesy of Tan Le.

UNIT 5

220–21 ©Xinhua News Agency/Getty Images. 226–27 ©Lars van de Goor Photography Art. 227 (br) ©Everett Collection Inc/Alamy. 228–29 ©Robert Harding Picture Library/National Geographic Image Collection. 229 (br) ©AP Images/Agencia Estado. 233 ©Jesse Kraft/Alamy. 234–35 © orey Arnold/National Geographic Image Collection, 235 (br) ©Courtesy of Corey Arnold. 238–39 © Michael Blann/Getty Images. 242–43 ©Maskot/Getty Images. 247 ©Josie Elias/Shutterstock. 248–49 ©Scharfsinn/Shutterstock. 252–53 ©Anand Varma/National Geographic Image Collection. 255 ©Anand Varma/National Geographic Image Collection. 256–67 ©William Jones-Warner/iStock/Getty Images. 264 ©Sarayut Thaneerat/EyeEm/Getty Images. 270 (t) ©Courtesy of Octavio Aburto, 270 (cl) Courtesy of Octavio Aburto.

UNIT 6

272–73 ©DIEGO IZQUIERDO/TELAM/AFP/Getty Images. 278–79 ©Linh Pham/Getty Images. 281 ©Kyodo News/Getty Images. 282 ©Tham Luang Rescue Operation Center/AP Images. 285 ©Xinhua Xinhua/eyevine/Redux. 289 ©REUTERS/Alamy. 290–91 ©290–91 ©Cristina Mittermeier. 291 (br) ©Andy Katz. 294–95 ©MediaNews Group/Boston Herald via Getty Images. 296 ©Richard Baker/In Pictures/Getty Images. 298–99 © Victoria Will/National Geographic Image Collection. 305 ©corbac40/iStock/Getty Images. 306–07 ©Jorge Gamboa. 322 ©Ami Vitale/National Geographic Image Collection. 328 ©Murdo Macleod, http://www.murdophoto.com/.

UNIT 7

330–31 ©Kai Schwoerer/Getty Images. 336–37 ©Visual China Group via Getty Images/Visual China Group via Getty Images. 338–39 ©RvS.Media/Basile Barbey/Getty Images. 340 ©Tim de Waele/Velo/Getty Images. 345 ©Arijit Sen/Hindustan Times/Getty Images. 346–47 ©Mauro Repossini/iStock Unreleased/Getty Images. 357 ©Jade Anouka. 361 ©GABRIEL BOUYS/AFP/Getty Images. 362–63 ©Haisam Hussein/National Geographic Image Collection. 366 ©David Madison/Stone/Getty Images. 368 ©Kevin Morris/Corbis Sport/Getty Images. 371©REUTERS/Alamy. 372 ©Alex Trautwig/Getty Images Sport/Getty Images. 373 ©Matthew J. Lee/Boston Globe/Getty Images. 378 ©Li Muzi Xinhua/eyevine/Redux. 384 ©Michael Nichols/National Geographic Image Collection, (tl) ©Kat Keene Hogue/National Geographic Image Collection.

UNIT 8

386–87 ©Babak Tafreshi/National Geographic Image Collection. 392–93 ©Khoa Minh/Alamy. 394–95 ©Madison Wells/EyeEm/Getty Images. 396–97 ©Colin Anderson Productions pty ltd/Digital Vision/Getty Images. 401 ©iLexx/iStock/Getty Images. 402–403 ©Photograph by Markel Redondo for Greenpeace. 407 ©Evie Carpenter/Phoenix New Times. 408 ©Babek Tafreshi/National Geographic Image Collection. 409 ©Matthew Olzmann. 413 ©lechatnoir/E+/Getty Images. 418–19 ©Associated Press/AP Images. 421 ©AP Images. 422 ©Robert Lerner, photographer, LOOK Magazine Photograph Collection, Library of Congress, Prints & Photographs Division, [Reproduction number e.g., LC-L9-60-8812, frame 8]. 425 ©Archive Photos/Getty Images. 427 ©Douglas Kirkland/Corbis/Getty Images. 432 ©Torontonian/Alamy. 438 ©Kat Keene Hogue/National Geographic Image Collection.